Peacebuilding for Adolescents

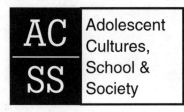

Joseph L. DeVitis and Linda Irwin-DeVitis
General Editors

Vol. 2

PETER LANG
New York • Washington, D.C./Baltimore • Boston • Bern
Frankfurt am Main • Berlin • Brussels • Vienna • Canterbury

Peacebuilding for Adolescents

Strategies for Educators
and Community Leaders

Edited by
Linda Rennie Forcey
and Ian Murray Harris

PETER LANG
New York • Washington, D.C./Baltimore • Boston • Bern
Frankfurt am Main • Berlin • Brussels • Vienna • Canterbury

Library of Congress Cataloging-in-Publication Data

Peacebuilding for adolescents: strategies for educators and community leaders /
edited by Linda Rennie Forcey and Ian Murray Harris.
p. cm. — (Adolescent cultures, school, and society; vol. 2)
Includes bibliographical references and index.
1. Peace—Study and teaching—United States. 2. Youth and peace—
United States. 3. School violence—United States—Prevention.
I. Forcey, Linda Rennie. II. Harris, Ian M. III. Series.
JZ5534.P43 327.1'72'07—dc21 98-46242
ISBN 0-8204-3745-X
ISSN 1091-1464

Die Deutsche Bibliothek-CIP-Einheitsaufnahme

Peacebuilding for adolescents: strategies for educators and community leaders /
ed. by Linda Rennie Forcey and Ian Murray Harris.
–New York; Washington, D.C./Baltimore; Boston; Bern;
Frankfurt am Main; Berlin; Brussels; Vienna; Canterbury: Lang.
(Adolescent cultures, school, and society; Vol. 2)
ISBN 0-8204-3745-X

Cover art by Michelle Stellmacher

The paper in this book meets the guidelines for permanence and durability
of the Committee on Production Guidelines for Book Longevity
of the Council of Library Resources.

© 1999 Peter Lang Publishing, Inc., New York

All rights reserved.
Reprint or reproduction, even partially, in all forms such as microfilm,
xerography, microfiche, microcard, and offset strictly prohibited.

Printed in the United States of America

Ian Murray Harris and Linda Rennie Forcey dedicate this book to their spouses, Sara Spence and Charles Forcey

And to the memory of young people whose loss of life to senseless violence has motivated all of us to do this work

Preface

This past year has seen fifty-six incidents of violence in schools in the United States that have either killed or maimed students or teachers. This is only the worst total among the many aggressive and violent incidents taking place in schools around the world. The most serious of these, like the shootings in Peducah, Kentucky, or Jonesboro, Arkansas, have produced headlines worldwide. Other violent events in schools—fights, harassments, weapons violations, and bullying incidents—never make the news, but still leave injured the participants and trouble others, who have to struggle over ways to respond to the aggravations. School authorities, frustrated and frightened, often seek quick solutions. These are more often than not get-tough measures to provide secure school environments.

The editors of this book and the authors of its articles argue for a new approach to these alarming problems that grows out of peace theory. They find school violence to be rooted in deeper cultural norms and behaviors that are exhibited in homes and communities across the United States. In other words, these violent events reflect a violent culture. If we understand how deeply violence permeates our schools, we can promote a peaceful culture. Our authors call for a holistic approach that offers no quick fixes, but rather builds in the minds of young people a commitment to the ways of peace.

Most people concerned about the problems of school violence are essentially trying to put out fires. We ask why these fires start in the first place. What can we do to keep them from breaking out? Such questions come hard to overburdened teachers and school administrators concerned about teaching from set curricula and preparing students for competitive examinations. They are, nevertheless, essential to educational enterprises. Unless school authorities address the devastating effects of violence upon youth adequately, angry, frightened and confused students will continue to drop out of school and give up on learning assignments that seem irrelevant to their violent communities. Having a peaceful world, with peaceful communities, families, and schools is essential to the healthy development of children. These essays will give powerful examples of how images of peace can be built in the minds of youth.

The editors of this book would like to thank Pete Forcey, whose insightful editing has enhanced this volume, and Kathleen R. Babbitt, a freelance copyeditor, proofreader, and indexer, whose unerring comments have made this a much better manuscript.

Table of Contents

Chapter 1	Introduction Linda Rennie Forcey and Ian Murray Harris	1
Part I	**Confronting Violence**	**15**
Chapter 2	Dr. King's Giant Triplets: Racism, Materialism, and Militarism Nathan Rousseau and Sonya Rousseau	17
Chapter 3	Countering School Violence: The Rise of Conflict Resolution Programs Molly K. Pont-Brown and John D. Krumboltz	35
Chapter 4	Redefining School Violence in Boulder Valley Colorado Matthew W. Greene	57
Part II	**Classroom Strategies for Peacebuilding**	**89**
Chapter 5	Peace and Conflict Curricula for Adolescents Linden L. Nelson, Michael R. Van Slyck, and Lucille A. Cardella	91
Chapter 6	The Speak Your Piece Project: Exploring Controversial Issues in Northern Ireland Alan McCully, Marian O'Doherty, and Paul Smyth	119
Chapter 7	How Can Caring Help? A Personalized Cross- Generational Examination of Violent Adolescent Experiences in Schools Barbara J. Thayer-Bacon	139

Chapter 8	Adventure-Based Learning in the Name of Peace *Nadja M. Alexander and Teresa B. Carlson*	161

Part III **School Strategies for Peacebuilding** **175**

Chapter 9	A Developmental Approach to the Use of Conflict Resolution Interventions with Adolescents *Michael Van Slyck and Marilyn Stern*	177
Chapter 10	Nonviolent Interventions in Secondary Schools: Administrative Perspectives *Robert C. DiGiulio*	195
Chapter 11	Integrating a Multicultural Peacebuilding Strategy into a Literacy Curriculum *Rebecca Wasson, Rebecca Anderson, and Melanie Suriani*	213
Chapter 12	Disturbing the Peace: Multicultural Education, Transgressive Teaching, and Independent School Culture *Peter Adam Nash*	227

Part IV **School and Community** **237**

Chapter 13	Stop the Violence: Conflict Management in an Inner-City Junior High School through Action Research and Community Problem Solving *Arjen E. J. Wals*	239
Chapter 14	Special Needs, Special Measures: Working with Homeless and Poor Youth *Dé Bryant, Jennifer Hanis, and Charles Stoner*	263
Chapter 15	Community-Based Service: Re-Creating the Beloved Community *Bonnie Winfield*	289
Chapter 16	A Summer Institute on Nonviolence *Ian Murray Harris*	309

Appendix A	331
Appendix B	341
Appendix C	343
List of Contributors	345
Index	353

Chapter 1

Introduction

Linda Rennie Forcey and Ian Murray Harris

Teenagers in the United States and around the world are relentlessly exposed to cultural messages that promote violence as a way to solve problems and to feel empowered. Since adolescence is the time when the child becomes an adult through a series of profound physical, sexual, and emotional changes, the consequences of these day-to-day violent messages are often traumatic and terrible. Violence permeates the homes, communities, and schools of many children. Religious and ethnic conflicts in Ireland, India, and countries of the former Soviet Union, and in Asia, Latin America, and Africa claim a disproportionate number of young people as both victims and perpetrators. As a consequence, many of these adolescents in warring cultures grow up to be frightened and angry, often seeking retribution unless somebody intervenes in their lives to teach them to value peace.

In the United States, among all persons fifteen to twenty-four years old, homicide is now the second leading cause of death; more male teens die of gunfire than of all the diseases combined; and among African-American youth homicide is the leading cause of death.[1] Many teenage males acquire a sense of power and control with a gun, all too readily available to them. There are, if averaged, four and one-half guns in every U.S. household.[2] Almost one quarter of all teenagers have access to guns at home, and 12 percent admit to having carried a weapon during a prescribed thirty-day period.[3] For many young people the question becomes not, "What will you be when you grow up?" but rather, "What will you be if you grow up?"

Research has shown that because of the threat of violence, one third of the teachers in the United States find themselves less than eager to come to school.[4] Violence and the threat of violence are having an impact on the teachers and students, even in the classroom.[5] Students worried by violence are distracted from the cognitive lessons they are supposed to master. A Harris study shows that "a substantial proportion of students witnesses violent incidents, in or around school, on a fairly regular basis. Three in ten say they witness violence sometimes and 6% very often see violence. . . . Fewer than three in five say they see violence rarely (44%) or never (15%) in or around school."[6]

These cultural messages of violence have indirect consequences too. Two thousand students in the United States drop out of school each day; 100,000 remain homeless and thousands turn to drugs and alcohol for solace. Furthermore, assaults on lesbian and gay youths are rampant and generally go unreported; sexual harassment of young women, a form of gendered violence, occurs in public and private places; and untold numbers suffer violence to their self-esteem caused by racism and other social and economic inequities.

The public in the United States and elsewhere is constantly challenged by media images that present teenagers as menacing and rebellious. Alexander Cockburn, writing in *The Nation*, calls this the "war on kids," where the violence of adults is "handed down in the form of blows, sexual predation and punishment."[7] The explosion of juvenile crime has led politicians to pass very severe laws and, at the same time, lower the age at which juveniles can be tried as adults. Adults, fearing teenagers, often threaten them with punitive actions rather than providing the love and care all adolescents need. Unfortunately, many educators and community leaders have not envisioned effective responses to increased levels of youth violence outside the criminal justice system. They have most frequently sought peace at schools by severe punishment of those charged with disruptive acts. Security guards are hired, metal detectors to screen students are installed, and new policies for the expulsion of troublemakers are devised. Most school officials rely only on such violent, reactive intervention strategies to deter the young from violence. Such methods, however, have little redemptive impact on the root causes of much of the violence in schools.

For all of this, some educators have turned to Peace Studies as a way to stem this tide. A relatively new, interdisciplinary field of study which has mostly focused on war prevention, social and economic justice, and ecological security, Peace Studies requires, usually through the contribution of a variety of disciplines, an integration of interpersonal and systems-oriented approaches to the problems of teenage violence.[8] Peace Studies offers middle and high school educators, as well as other community leaders, theories and strategies that address the violent youth culture. In contrast to traditional educational leaders, Peace Studies educators tend to view adolescent violence as part of broader social problems that involve family, school, community, and all of society. They rest their analysis on a multidisciplinary and a multicultural understanding of adolescent development. They see adolescent identities as socially constructed which precludes any child being held to be "born bad." They believe that the causes of violence are interwoven with the realities of familial or social injustice, economic inequality, and oppression. They favor alternative dispute resolution initiatives to help young people manage conflicts successfully and nonviolently both inside and outside the school setting. They teach nonviolence and positive conflict resolution techniques so that young people can learn alternative ways of behaving to the violent role models around them.

This book, relying largely on the work of peace scholars from many disciplines, presents proactive strategies for adolescent peacebuilding. The essays seek to show how teachers, guidance counselors, school administrators, and community leaders can think about, teach, and implement peacebuilding skills. As peace researchers our contributors take a broad view, ranging over three strategic levels of analysis: personal, school, and community. They discuss the strengths of a peacebuilding approach that can promote among young people an understanding of the root causes of violence in all its varieties, whether brought about by poverty, racism, sexism, economic inequality, or militarism. They argue for the promotion of a culture of nonviolence in the schools so that educators can begin to work toward the creation of what Dr. Martin Luther King Jr. called the "beloved community."

Peace Studies examines problems of violence in the schools in three different modes: *peacekeeping; peacemaking;* and *peacebuilding.*[9] In the peacekeeping mode, educators use violence prevention activities to create an orderly learning climate in schools. For peacemaking, educators use conflict resolution techniques to teach students to manage their own conflicts constructively. With peacebuilding, finally, educators try to teach how the power of nonviolence can demonstrate to the young the futility of inflicting violence on others. While all of the contributors to this volume transcend mere "peacekeeping" to focus on either "peacemaking" or "peacebuilding," the three approaches build on each other, are interconnected in subtle ways, and all three are integral and necessary components of a peaceable school environment.

At the peacekeeping level, we can suggest briefly here, educators use peace-through-strength strategies to create a safe school climate. In schools with high levels of physical violence there are often daily weapons searches, frequent detentions and expulsions, and the use of such devices as metal detectors at school entrances. Some schools have also installed extensive surveillance and warning systems to monitor students. Others have turned to such devices as school uniforms, (primarily to reduce theft of expensive clothing and jewelry), ID badges, closed-circuit television surveillance, and staff walkie-talkies.

Violence prevention programs are also part of such peacekeeping strategies to reduce levels of youth violence. Their tactics frequently have an educational component as suggested by most of their names—anger management, racism/sexism prevention, drug/alcohol education, gang discrediting, domestic violence prevention, and handgun discouragement. These programs help youths understand the consequences of violent behavior, with the hope that this will lead to the avoidance of self-destructive and cruel behavior. The expectation is that giving young people such constructive ways to address the causes of violence will reduce the incidence and intensity of violent confrontations.

Most educators engaged in peacekeeping rely on the use of adult authority to enforce rules. Such school districts, however, have faced considerable controversy over the disproportionate number of African-American and Latino/Latina students who become the subjects of the enhanced school exhortation and discipline.[10] In other respects, Peace Studies educators also argue that those who primarily focus on punitive security measures ignore crucial aspects of much adolescent violence. As Ian Harris has pointed out, deterrence policies neither provide students with an understanding of the problems of violence nor strategies to avoid it. Rather, these policies mirror a generally punitive criminal justice system.[11] Peacekeepers thus rely on a peace-through-strength approach that may deter violence, but is otherwise very limited. Peace scholars, in fact, would describe it as a "negative peace approach."

Most proponents of peacemaking strategies in schools seek to be more "positive." They use conflict resolution techniques to create a climate more conducive to learning in school that can empower young people to realize how conflicts may be resolved without force. These efforts go beyond the peacekeeping strategies mentioned above (expulsion, suspension, detention, or court intervention). They already have in some schools greatly reduced violence, vandalism, referrals for discipline, and chronic school absenteeism.[12] Educators involved in such conflict resolution programs demonstrate to students how conflict can become a peaceful yet positive force that can foster both personal growth and institutional change. Proponents of peacemaking argue that conflict resolution programs help young people, and school personnel as well, acquire a deeper understanding of themselves and others through improved communication. Generally a higher level of citizenship activity can result from young people becoming involved in creating a peaceful school climate. Students who learn about nonadversarial conflict resolution and its relationship to the legal system can acquire a heightened knowledge of peacemaking strategies at all levels of society.

This comprehensive approach to conflict resolution in schools, what we have called "peacemaking," has also been referred to as the "peaceable" school system.[13] With peacemaking, conflict resolution principles and processes are learned and utilized by every member of the school community—teachers, counselors, administrators, students, and custodial staff. Conscious planning leads to noncoercive school and classroom management practices. Staff in peaceable schools move away from merely relying upon punishment, while portraying the more positive consequences that will encourage self-discipline by students. This approach implies moving schools away from mere competition toward cooperative structures that can promote a general win-win climate. Staff at peaceable schools promote peacemaking as a normative activity that can contribute to individual, group, and institutional goals. A key component is peer mediation, a process whereby students themselves apply the techniques of mediation to resolve conflicts among their fellow students.

Educators in peaceable schools often try to involve parents, too, in building respect for the conflict resolution processes.[14] Clearly, efforts to model cooperative behavior in classrooms can be undermined by coercive parental discipline. Children within trusting and loving relationships can best develop peacemaking skills. Families are the settings for such learning and schools can contribute to their peacefulness by providing guidelines for consistent, safe, and loving approaches to self-discipline. Teachers, administrators, and social workers at peaceable schools soon find themselves involved in various community programs that work with parents to develop positive nurturing skills.

While conflict resolution strategies are becoming increasingly popular among secondary school educators, within the field of Peace Studies there are some tensions about the promise of conflict resolution programs. This is particularly so for those programs that rely solely on peer mediation processes without making them an integral part of a larger school conflict resolution effort. Some fear that peer mediation may tend to promote social control rather than social change because in the past issues of social justice have rarely been part of the field of conflict resolution. Conflict resolution programs based on peer mediation thus offer no panacea for ridding a school of all its violence.[15] In fact, Linda Lantieri and Janet Patti, affiliates of the highly successful Resolving Conflict Creatively Program (RCCP), argue that peer mediation should never be used unless accompanied by multicultural and antibias education.[16]

Finally, the term peacebuilding, as we use it in this volume, refers to the primary goal of most Peace Studies programs, that is, to create in all people a desire to learn how nonviolence can provide the basis for a just and sustainable future. It includes the goals of peacekeeping and peacemaking as defined above, but is much broader. A key assumption as well as a fundamental orientation of a peacebuilding approach is nonviolence. Nonviolence, as exemplified by its leading twentieth-century advocates, Mohandas K. Gandhi, the Mahatma, and Martin Luther King Jr., has three guiding principles: (1) to explicitly state one's intentions to conduct and resolve conflict without violence; (2) to adopt provisions to demonstrate and carry out one's intention; and (3) to avoid all killing or imposing of suffering on others while holding fast to the truths one believes.[17] For Peace Studies, nonviolence is a philosophy of life that focuses on how people treat themselves and others and a strategy for change that seeks to implement standards of justice, nonviolent social institutions, and inclusive social norms. A nonviolent approach to education teaches students that there *are* alternatives to violence.[18]

Educational reformers adopting the goals of peace education study different forms of violence, both international and domestic. At the international level, they provide insights into an interstate war system that depends on military might to resolve differences between states with force. At the national level, they teach about defense and the effects of militarism upon the welfare of citizens. Peace educators also promote concepts of ecological security based upon reverential relationships to the natural environment. At the cultural level, moreover, peace educators teach about social norms that promote violence. At an interpersonal level, they teach nonviolent skills to resolve conflicts. At the psychic level, they help students challenge violent ways of thinking and relating to others. A student of Peace Studies thus acquires innumerable theoretical concepts about the dangers of violence and the possibilities for peace, as well as skills necessary to living nonviolently.

Peace education also incorporates gendered concepts of care, compassion, and connectedness in the curriculum. These educational reform efforts include but also transcend earlier efforts to integrate women's peace movement participation into the history class.[19] The goal, therefore, is not just to stop the violence, both direct and indirect, but also to create in people's minds the conditions for positive peace. When young people watch the news they witness acts of violence, whether judicial, military, or terrorist, being committed around the world. The history they study is the history of wars and violence. But nonviolence has its own proud history, one that can provide positive images of peace.

Peace educators reach beyond the traditions of established academic fields of study with nontraditional pedagogical beliefs, many of which are borrowed from women's studies. They, like women's studies educators, engage their students in a multidisciplinary search for answers to the many problems of violence that are so rampant in the world. They favor a Socratic approach to learning, one embodying a consciousness of worldviews, a global vision, and a sensitivity to issues of gender, race, and class. They dare to think aloud with students as they unabashedly struggle to find coherence and meaning in the complex processes of social change around them.[20] This pedagogy also demands recognition of the central role personal values play as teachers and their students consider the inequities adolescents often face from factors of class, race, and gender.

Peace Studies tries to foster positive images that lead to a respect for cultural differences so that young people may learn to live peaceably in diverse communities around the world. It considers, for example, the composition of a village of 100 people representative of the world's population: 57 Asians; 25 Europeans; 14 North and South Americans; and 8 Africans. Thus, 70 of the 100 would be people of color; 70 of the 100 would be believers of faiths other than Christian; one half of the world's wealth would be in the hands of six U.S. citizens; and only one among the hundred would have a university education.[21] In the year 2020, according to *Time* magazine, nonwhite and Latino/Latina residents in the United States will have more than doubled to nearly 115 million, while the white population will have remained the same.²² Peace Studies educators take seriously these predictions of demographic change and argue, therefore, that multicultural and antibias education must play a major role in creating a peaceable classroom.

The goal of Peace Studies education thus goes beyond merely stopping violence and reducing conflict in schools. The goal, to sum it all up, is to get young people to adopt a peaceful philosophy of life and way of living. Peace education, therefore, does not just mean a quiet classroom. It means creating a learning environment in which students and teachers can act on problems constructively, try to manage their conflicts creatively, and take on the challenge of promoting a more just society. In response to rising levels of youth violence, peace education is being adopted throughout the world with many different models by administrators, community leaders, teachers, staff, and students.

This collection of essays will provide teachers, administrators, and community leaders with knowledge about some of the models that promote strategies for effective and lasting peacebuilding. We know it lays out no easy path. As Kevin Clements recently pointed out, "The creation and enhancement of cultures of peace and structures to give expression to them require considerable human ingenuity."²³ Changing the cultural values that support violent behavior requires vigilance: teachers, administrators, and community leaders must be willing to take risks to develop new ways for teaching the wisdom of nonviolence. We share Linda Lantieri and Janet Patti's new vision of education whereby all adolescents, not just the privileged few, will have the following rights:

1. To go to schools, play in playgrounds, and grow up in homes surrounded by adults who protect them and listen to them, instead of having to live in constant fear for their emotional and physical safety

2. To go to bed each night dreaming hopeful thoughts for their future instead of reliving the nightmares of their day

3. To be able to go to the corner store and have enough money to buy a treat or simply satisfy their hunger instead of witnessing the selling of drugs

4. To be raised in families where adults are ever present with their love, nurturance, clear limits, and strong values instead of coming home to empty houses

5. To attend schools where valuing nonviolence and diversity is the norm instead of being overwhelmed by feelings of isolation, rejection, and failure

6. To inherit a world free of violence and hatred, that children may truly know what peace and justice are[24]

Our book is divided into four sections: Confronting Violence; Classroom Strategies for Peacebuilding; School Strategies for Peacebuilding; and School and Community. The authors included in each section are from the United States unless otherwise noted. The first section sets the stage for the others, opening with an essay by sociologist Nathan Rousseau and reference librarian Sonya Rousseau on the peace legacy of Martin Luther King Jr. The authors describe the interrelationship of the "giant triplets of racism, materialism and militarism," as viewed by King. They point to ways in which middle and high school teachers might examine and challenge in detail these aspects of our culture; and suggest how they might help their students take "the peace offensive." In chapter 3, education specialists Molly Pont and John Krumboltz describe the pervasiveness of violence in U.S. schools, and trace the ways in which conflict resolution programs have developed to counter school violence. They question how effective these programs are. The fourth chapter by political scientist Matthew Greene invites readers to take a close look at a Boulder Valley Study in which a diverse group of separate Colorado municipalities sought to identify areas of both educator conflict and consensus about the nature of and alternatives to adolescent school violence.

We move into more specific strategies for peacebuilding, those of the classroom, in the second section. Psychologists Linden Nelson, Michael Van Slyck, and Lucille Cardella offer educational objectives for peacebuilding (the development of social problem and conflict resolution competencies, assertiveness training, peaceful attitudes and values, and efficacy and outcome expectancies) and argue for fundamental and pervasive changes in curriculum and pedagogy. The authors also review five peacebuilding curricula for adolescents and their teachers. Next, researchers Alan McCully, Marian O'Doherty, and Paul Smyth, from Northern Ireland, outline the context, philosophy, and practice of an educational initiative called "Speak Your Piece," an Irish television series designed to engage adolescents in dialogue about controversial cultural and political issues.

In chapter 7, philosopher Barbara Thayer-Bacon calls for schools to provide caring environments. Using her own experiences as an adolescent and as a teacher, as well as those of her three teenaged children, she makes the case, as a teacher, that caring is vital to lessening the violence of our schools. The final chapter in Part II is a piece about adventure-based learning (ABL) in the name of peace, written by Nadja M. Alexander and Teresa B. Carlson, two adventure-based educators from Australia. Arguing that adolescence is a crucial time during which values, attitudes, and skills are being developed, the authors show with practical strategies how ABL can help to develop effective communication, an ability to cooperate with others, an awareness of how to handle frustration or stress, a tolerance for and understanding of individual differences, as well as the acquisition of the relevant problem-solving skills.

In Part III, we turn to the broader school strategies required for peacebuilding in schools. Michael Van Slyck, founder of the Research Institute for Dispute Resolution, and Marilyn Stern, a clinical psychologist, present in chapter 9 a developmental approach to the use of conflict resolution interventions with adolescents. They show results from research on youth-oriented conflict resolution that clearly indicate positive effects that go beyond the domain of overt conflict. They include coping skills that both promote adjustment and enhance developmental outcomes. In chapter 10, Assistant Professor of Education Robert DiGiulio, formerly a high school principal, analyzes the perspectives of secondary school administrators on school violence. He argues that those who take the "crime-and-punishment" or "school-as-prison" approach have much less success than those who emphasize nonadversarial interventions and community-building education. Next, education professors Rebecca Wasson, Rebecca Anderson, and Melanie Suriani illustrate ways in which a multicultural peacebuilding strategy based on the works of Mahatma Gandhi and Paulo Freire can be integrated in a literacy curriculum to promote communities that focus on caring for others. In chapter 12, Peter Nash, a high school English teacher, shows how teaching for peacebuilding that calls for an appreciation of multiculturalism and radical pedagogy can be uncomfortable and at times risky for teachers. He offers several strategies for making multicultural reform a major component of peace education.

Peacebuilding, as all these essays in their different ways suggest, is a continuous process that requires the broadest possible representation of students, educators, parents, and community leaders. Although there can be no set formula for peacebuilding for adolescents, we hope our final section, School and Community, will stimulate the imagination and visionary powers of our readers to reach beyond current boundaries. Arjen Wals, an environmental education researcher teaching in the Netherlands, presents action research and community problem solving (AR&CPS), an approach to education that provides a bridge between school and community on the one hand, and between learning for school and learning for life on the other. Using a case study of a middle school in inner-city Detroit, Wals shows how AR&CPS can be an essential ingredient to the development of community-grounded peace with sustainability. Psychologists Dé Bryant, Jennifer Hanis, and Charles Stoner describe a Social Action Project (SOCACT) that fosters empowerment among homeless and poor adolescents in the United States and Nigeria. They focus on one of five joint community-university components—the Youth Community Theater whose purpose is to encourage multicultural explorations of heritage, history, and personal experience, beginning with comparisons of African and American cultures.

In chapter 15, sociologist Bonnie Winfield makes the case for community-based service in high school curricula, demonstrating that when adolescents develop a sense of community in their neighborhoods their frustrations and frequent violent behavior will be reduced. Co-editor Ian Harris describes in our concluding chapter an ongoing weeklong Summer Institute held at the University of Wisconsin-Milwaukee that teaches nonviolence to inner-city early adolescents, thus preparing them to resist peer pressure for violent behaviors. We believe that this unique Institute can become an important alternative to more traditional methods of addressing violence in the schools. Here again, students are shown the power of nonviolence. Peaceful philosophies, when taught in tandem with peacemaking strategies, help young people act peacefully when faced with conflict. The Institute builds in the minds of the young a peace consciousness that promotes open-mindedness, a deep concern for social justice, the courage to face up to violence, as well as characters that are empathetic, respectful of others, cooperative and caring.

The peacebuilding approach to adolescent violence being advanced by the authors in this volume has recently been championed by winners of the Nobel Peace Prize. They, collectively, want to declare the first ten years of the next century a decade of nonviolence in the hopes of raising interest in strategies of nonviolence as solutions to the problems of youth violence. In the appendices we include their "Peace!" letter of July 2, 1997, first published as a full-page advertisement in *Le Monde*, inviting all of us to join them in an effort to influence all the governments of the world.[25] We also provide a bibliography of age-appropriate books for adolescents that will teach them peacebuilding concepts. These books include histories, biographies, and novels about people who have dedicated themselves to peace.

Linda Rennie Forcey and Ian Murray Harris
April 1998

Notes

1. Mark L. Rosenberg, M.D., Centers for Disease Control. U.S. Testimony, July 23, 1992.

2. Bureau of Alcohol, Tobacco, and Firearms (ATF), "How Many Guns?" ATF News Release FY 91-36, Washington, DC: U.S. Government Printing Office, 1991.

3. Bureau of Alcohol, Tobacco, and Firearms, "How Many Guns?"

4. Louis Harris and Associates, *Between Hope and Fear: Teens Speak Out on Crime and the Community* (Washington, DC: National Institute for Citizen Education in the Law, 1995), 73.

5. Louis Harris and Associates, *Between Hope and Fear*, 6.

6. Louis Harris and Associates, *Between Hope and Fear*, 15.

7. Alexander Cockburn, "The War on Kids," *The Nation*, June 3, 1996: 7, 8.

8. Linda Rennie Forcey, "Peace Studies," in *Protest, Power, and Change: An Encyclopedia of Nonviolent Action from ACT-UP to Women's Suffrage*, ed. Roger S. Powers and William B. Vogele (New York: Garland, 1997), 407-9.

9. Marvin Berlowitz, "Urban Educational Reform: Focusing on Peace Education," *Education and Urban Society* 27, no. 1 (1994): 82-95; Ian M. Harris, "From World Peace to Peace in the 'Hood: Peace Education in a Postmodern World," *Journal for a Just and Caring Education* 2, no. 4 (October 1996): 378-95.

10. See Kenneth Meier, Joseph Stewart, and Robert England, *Race, Class, and Education: The Politics of Second Generation Discrimination* (Madison: University of Wisconsin Press, 1989), 84-86.

11. Harris, "From World Peace to Peace in the 'Hood."

12. Donna Crawford and Richard Bodine, *Conflict Resolution Education: A Guide to Implementing Programs in Schools, Youth-Serving Organizations, and Community and Juvenile Justice Settings* (Office of Juvenile Justice and Delinquency Prevention and Office of Elementary and Secondary Education, U.S. Department of Education, 1996); and Laurie Stavahn, David W. Johnson, Roger T. Johnson, and Don Real, "The Impact of a Cooperative or Individualistic Context on the Effectiveness of Conflict Resolution Training," *American Educational Research Journal* 33, no. 4 (winter 1996): 801-24.

13. Linda Lantieri and Janet Patti, *Waging Peace in Our Schools* (Boston: Beacon, 1996).

14. Crawford and Bodine, *Conflict Resolution Education*, 39-47.

15 See John W. Burton, *Resolving Deep-Rooted Conflict: A Handbook* (Lanham, MD: University Press of America, 1987).

16 Lantieri and Patti, *Waging Peace in Our Schools*, 140.

17 Robert Woito, "Nonviolence, Principled," in *Protest, Power, and Change*, 357–63.

18 Ian M. Harris, "Nonviolence in Education," *Proceedings of the Midwest Philosophy of Education Society 1995–1996*, 154–73.

19 Amy Swerdlow and Linda Rennie Forcey, guest editors, *Women's Studies Quarterly: Rethinking Women's Peace Studies* 23, nos. 3, 4 (fall/winter 1995).

20 Linda Rennie Forcey, ed., *Peace: Meanings, Politics, Strategies* (New York: Praeger, 1989), 3–14.

21 Global Village Portrait from World Development Forum, 15 April 1990, cited in Marion O'Malley and Tiffany Davis, *Dealing with Difference* (1994, compiled by and available from the Center for Peace Education, University of North Carolina, Chapel Hill, NC 27514), 7.

22 *Time*, 9 April 1990, cited in O'Malley and Davis, *Dealing with Difference*, 15–16.

23 Kevin Clements, "Conflict Transformation," *Peace and Conflict Studies* 4, no. 1 (July 1997), 11.

24 Lantieri and Patti, *Waging Peace in Our Schools*, 251–52.

25 Full-page advertisement in *Le Monde*, Paris, 2 July 1997 (translated from the French) and circulated on the Internet.

PART I

CONFRONTING VIOLENCE

Chapter 2

Dr. King's Giant Triplets: Racism, Materialism, and Militarism

Nathan Rousseau and Sonya Rousseau

The stability of the large world house which is ours will involve a revolution of values to accompany the scientific and freedom revolutions engulfing the earth. We must rapidly begin the shift from a "thing"-oriented society to a "person"-oriented society. When machines and computers, profit motives and property rights are considered more important than people, the giant triplets of racism, materialism and militarism are incapable of being conquered.[1]

Introduction

When Dr. Martin Luther King Jr. identified racism, materialism, and militarism as interrelated barriers to peace, it was with the idea that by understanding these roadblocks to peacebuilding we could overcome them. Forty years later the need for learning to overcome these obstacles to peace is just as urgent. If the lessons taught by one of the most insightful teachers of peace in the twentieth century have not yet been learned, those lessons are neither less valuable nor less relevant for today. By understanding the depth and breadth of Martin Luther King's vision, adolescents can begin to see how they, as members of this connected world, have the power to make a positive, peaceful difference.

How are racism, materialism, and militarism related? Racism exists when the worth of a person is evaluated on the basis of physical characteristics rather than the character of the individual.[2] The person ceases to exist and a category is put in his or her place. The person becomes a thing. Materialism places the value of obtaining objects and status-gaining experiences as a, and sometimes the, primary focus of life.[3] As objects gain ascendancy, people become useful means to materialistic ends. Greed, fear, and a misplaced sense of superiority combine to create the fertile ground for militarism to take root and flourish. Militarism could not exist in the modern era if people were considered consistently to be more important than things.

The Drum Major Instinct

Everyone wants what is best for the youth of today. Parents and teachers may stress equality, sharing, and peace, but how effectively are these values communicated to young people? The task of serving as a positive role model is not an easy one. In order to provide an environment that is conducive for the development of peace-oriented adolescents, an awareness of the elements in our society that currently undermine that effort is necessary. Teaching today's youth to be aware of those elements can help them to become active critical thinkers with the tools to improve their future.

The competitive nature of our culture can affect negatively the ability of adolescents to recognize and incorporate peacebuilding skills. By the time students enter middle or high school they have been inundated with messages about what it means to be a success and may already be thinking seriously about what it takes "to get ahead" in their own lives. Parents, who have always hoped that their children will develop into productive, financially secure adults, can see that in the United States a rapidly widening gap between the rich and the impoverished exists and that the nation has lost its position of complete dominance in the world marketplace. In such an environment it is not surprising that the emphasis on competition has grown fierce. Good school grades, involvement in extracurricular activities, and playing sports have long been yardsticks for measuring success in school, but today's uncertain economic climate has increased the intensity of early scrutiny for talents that can lead to a future of affluence. While there is nothing inherently wrong with hoping that our young people will be able to support themselves and become productive members of society, the strong emphasis on economic gain is having an impact on young adults. According to a recent study, high school seniors and college freshmen have shown a steady increase in their emphasis on private material gain over the importance of correcting social and economic inequalities.[4]

Dr. King warned against the dangers inherent in putting personal gain over the public good, an impulse he called the drum major instinct—the need to be first. King felt that, if left unharnessed, this competitive instinct leads people to live beyond their means, spending their time, energy, and money "trying to outdo the Joneses."[5] As we will explore in more detail, this particular aspect gives tremendous power to advertisers selling costly lifestyles to an image-hungry public and provides credit card companies with a lucrative, ever growing market.

The unharnessed drum major instinct leads individuals "to push people down in order to push [themselves] up."[6] A sense of exclusivity and superiority is achieved by viewing people of another race or socioeconomic class or country as inferior or exploitable. In this way racism and segregation gain momentum. By extension, countries vying for world supremacy are likely to act in their own self-interest in other countries regardless of the local impact of those actions. At the global level the drum major instinct can lead to wars, economic exploitation, environmental degradation, and the use of military force to influence foreign, political, and economic policies.

Let us look in greater detail at some aspects of U.S. culture in which the indulgence of the unharnessed drum major instinct has caused us to make our priorities something other than peace and equality.

Militarism and Racism

Throughout history exploitation, violence, and war have been justified because one culture or group of people considered itself superior to another, one religious group felt it was more holy than another, one race felt it was smarter and more capable than another. Recent historical events illustrate that little has changed in that area. One need only study or reflect on media and political portrayals of national enemies when war is being broached or fought to realize that people from other countries are characterized very differently when they are our foes than when they are our allies. Demonizing enemies dehumanizes them, making it possible for people to justify taking violent action against them.

The violent actions people take come in many forms. In order to meet consumers' demands for a steady supply of goods while trying to maximize corporate profits, companies have increasingly begun to use cheap labor forces and raw materials in other countries for production. The perceived need to protect continued access to those products and other U.S. investments has, for example, caused the U.S.

government in recent years to keep a close military eye on petroleum-rich parts of the world, to ignore human rights violations selectively when granting most-favored-nation trading status, and to influence political outcomes in some Third World countries.

> John F. Kennedy said, "Those who make peaceful revolution impossible will make violent revolution inevitable."[7] Increasingly, by choice or by accident, this is the role the U.S. has taken—the role of those who make peaceful revolution impossible by refusing to give up the privileges and the pleasures that come from the immense profits of overseas investment.[8]

The globalization of U.S. investments has caused threats to the economic security of countries that provide cheap labor and materials for U.S. companies. Economic disruption often creates threats to the physical safety of U.S. citizens, sufficient reason, many would argue, to use military force internationally. Every citizen who profits from overseas investments of multinational corporations or who buys products that are available only because of the presence of the U.S. military or because of the exploitation of others contributes to the perpetuation of violence in this world.

At the local level the need to protect one's turf, to preserve or better one's social standing is played out every day. Competition is evident in gang warfare, in the violence sparked by groups of new immigrants settling into areas traditionally dominated by other immigrant or minority groups, in white supremacist groups and black separatist groups. The dynamics of racism are perpetuated both by the dominant group and by the minority groups in a given culture. Sociologist Helga Dittmar points to studies confirming that the dominant group is considered to have more positive attributes than minority groups, even among members of minority groups. The noninclusivity experienced by minority group members tends to promote the accentuation of in-group attributes, thereby providing "at least some comparison dimensions which contribute to a positive social identity" within the minority group.[9] Within minority groups, then, those qualities that are considered to be special are emphasized, further differentiating groups from one another and exacerbating intergroup tensions while continuing to place value on the factors that make the dominant group powerful, even if those powerful factors are ultimately exploitative of and harmful to them.

In the United States, where the dominant group is of European origin and where success is virtually synonymous with power associated with wealth, people of color are left with a dilemma as long as they value what makes the dominant group powerful. If they aspire to achieve power by becoming part of the dominant group, if they want to find success within the dominant culture's definition of the word, they can only seek to strive for the power conferred by conspicuous material gain or by positions considered by the dominant culture to be those of honor and authority. They cannot change their color or heritage. A significant change can occur only when the source and legitimacy of the dominant group's power are questioned and when a reexamination of priorities is thrust upon society as a whole. Anytime that people feel the need to set themselves apart from and above others by reason of race, economic situation, or for any other reason, violence in one form or another becomes a likelihood.

Materialism and the Consumer Role Models

There are forces in our culture that work to deepen the divisions between its citizens. One such force is advertising. The effectiveness of advertising, particularly on television and most recently on the World Wide Web, is evidenced by the financial investment that companies make to promote their goods in those media. Between 1985 and 1993, receipts of taxable advertising firms increased 63 percent, reaching $23.7 billion.[10] In a historical study of twentieth-century advertising, Russell Belk and Richard Pollay found compelling evidence to support the idea that the themes employed in advertising have dealt with "a progressively more luxurious and comfortable lifestyle," one that has "increasingly portrayed consumption as an end in itself rather than as a means to consumer well-being."[11] That study is consistent with this comment by Martin Luther King Jr.:

> Now the presence of this (drum major) instinct explains why we are so often taken by advertisers. You know those gentlemen of massive verbal persuasion. And they have a way of saying things to you that kind of gets you into buying. In order to be a man of distinction, you must drink this whiskey. In order to make your neighbors envious, you must drive this type of car. In order to be lovely to love you must wear this kind of lipstick or this kind of perfume. And you know, before you know it you're just buying that stuff. That's the way the advertisers do it.[12]

Psychologist Philip Cushman contends that advertising, which emanates authority and certainty, is particularly effective in an era when society lacks shared beliefs. "Ads seem to criticize and condemn the average consumer while glorifying the model, extolling a standard of beauty and mastery impossible to achieve." He concludes that "customers buy lifestyle in a vain attempt to transform their lives because their lives are unsatisfying and (without massive societal change) ultimately unfixable."[13] How common is it for people not only to spend money to outdo their neighbors but also to measure their success by how closely their lifestyles can match those in the luxurious commercials they see on television? How many of those people live in credit card debt in order to do so?

Perhaps of even more concern are the many young people who seem to accept the notion that wearing sports gear can somehow help transform them to leading the lifestyles of the sports stars who endorse the shoes, shirts, and hats. Young African-Americans comprise a large portion of the market for the $7.5 million worth of athletic footwear wholesaled in 1996. Bob McGee, editor of the industry newsletter *Sporting Goods Intelligence*, notes that "no company wants to say that they're marketing to the inner city crowd. But they know that [inner-city kids] pay more for their athletic wear and they buy more of it."[14]

The trend is disturbing, not only because young people are spending money that they can ill afford in order to project a particular image, but because the professional sports role models are emulated chiefly because of their wealth and their ability to play games well. This narrow choice of role models, reinforced by a materialistic, exploitative society, reflects a value orientation that is at odds with preparing adolescents to become active, responsible participants in their community and in society at large.

The opportunity to play team sports as an adolescent can teach much about discipline, about working as a group toward a shared goal, and about trust, as well as assisting in the development of physical coordination. In a society that prizes entertainment highly and pays accordingly, the dream to become a professional athlete is powerful, particularly among African-Americans, who still earn considerably less than European Americans but who currently make up the majority of professional football and basketball players in this country.[15] However, journalist John Simons notes that

> the odds that any high school athlete will play a sport on the professional level are remote—about 10,000 to one. . . . Yet according to a recent survey conducted by Northeastern University's Center for the Study of Sport in Society, 66 percent of all African-American males between the ages of 13 and 18

believe they can earn a living playing professional sports. That is more than double the proportion of young white males who hold such beliefs. Black parents also are four times more likely than white parents to believe that their children are destined for careers in professional athletics.[16]

Meanwhile are these young people enriching their minds, preparing for college or careers? Are they focusing their energy on how they can forward their lives, advance social causes, or make the world a better place? If they are coaxed into college with athletic scholarships, where is the support for them if they get injured or fail to live up to expectation? Even if they make it to the National Collegiate Athletic Association Final Four, their chances of ever playing with the National Basketball Association are nearly 250 to 1. "There is an overemphasis on sports in the black community, and too many black students are putting all their eggs in one basket," says Harvard Medical School psychiatrist Alvin Poussaint.[17] The same thing could probably be said today about computers of middle-class residents of the United States who are white. Everyone is trying to find the key that will unlock the box of prosperity, but its source remains elusive.

Fifteen years ago earning an M.B.A. was thought to be the magical answer. The popularity of the catchphrase from the movie *Jerry Maquire*, "Show me the money!" perhaps sums up the nation's obsession with the idea that money will solve all problems. Thirty years ago Dr. King said, "Western civilization is particularly vulnerable at this moment, for our material abundance has brought us neither peace of mind nor serenity of spirit."[18] Today, as prison construction flourishes and as new criminal maintenance positions continue to open, it is clear that the affluence of our country has done little, if anything, to solve the social problems that surround us, much less bring us peace of mind or serenity of spirit.

Revolution of Values

Adolescents learn to be who they are by looking at what is all around them. In this culture, where wealth and personal power are revered and sought at the expense of pursuing the country's stated goals of equality, liberty, and freedom, is it any wonder that our young people are confused? Dr. King said, "Alienation is not confined to our young people, but it is rampant among them. Yet alienation should be foreign to the young. Growth requires connection and trust. Alienation is a form of living death. It is the acid of despair that dissolves society."[19]

Despite the fact that our world seems to be getting smaller and smaller because of advances in telecommunications, it is also becoming more confusing and disjointed. Without a firm sense of shared, people-oriented values, and without a common global priority of peace we cannot expect the world to start making any more sense than it does now, either for us or for the generations to follow. The people of the United States still have the opportunity to take a leadership role in making these priorities global priorities.

If peace is to be the true priority, what must be done to ensure it? As role models, parents, teachers, and community leaders need to recognize that in order to raise children and adolescents who make peace and social justice an integrated part of life, they, themselves, must live their lives in a manner consistent with those priorities; they must make the adjustments and sacrifices necessary to put the common good above personal luxury. Role models who say that they want the world to be a better place have to recognize that the competition inherent in racism, materialism, and militarism cannot lead to peace. As Dr. King noted in 1956:

> First, we are challenged to rise above the narrow confines of our individualistic concerns to the broader concerns of all humanity. . . . Through our scientific genius we have made of our world a neighborhood; now through our moral and spiritual genius we must make of it a brotherhood. We are all involved in the single process. Whatever affects one directly affects all indirectly. We are all links in the great chain of humanity.[20]

Such a turnaround will require the "revolution of values" Dr. King discussed at the opening of this chapter. In a very real way parents, teachers, and community leaders must recognize and teach young people to recognize that individual actions (as well as inactions) have consequences. Truly understanding the idea that the world is interconnected forces a recognition that making as much money as one can, even at the cost of exploiting others, cannot make the world a better place. It forces an understanding that putting anyone down in order to raise oneself up is ultimately a pyrrhic victory. It forces a recognition that one's relationship with the environment is just as much in need of balance as one's relationship with fellow human beings who share the planet. This is not mere sentimental idealism. One need only look at the crises of today that exist because of a blatant disregard of the need to be as concerned with other-preservation as with self-preservation—rising crime rates, increasing poverty levels, widespread species extinction—to understand that the actions one takes need to come into line with shared and peaceful priorities in order to assure a livable future for young people.[21] Dr. King elaborated on this theme in 1965:

> From time immemorial men have lived by the principle that "self-preservation is the first law of life." But this is a false assumption. I would say that other-preservation is the first law of life. It is the first law of life precisely because we cannot preserve self without being concerned about preserving other selves. The universe is so structured that things go awry if men are not diligent in their cultivation of the other-regarding dimension.[22]

Unfortunately, making this revolution of values a reality will not be easy. Helga Dittmar has presented compelling evidence that, at least in Western industrialized nations, "meanings of possessions as symbols of identity are socially constituted, that our own identity is expressed and reinforced by what we have, and that we evaluate others in the context of their material things by drawing on socially shared representations."[23] Studies have shown that people from all economic classes tend to share the view of the affluent individual as "more intelligent, successful and educated, as well as more in control of her or his life and environment" and the poor individual as "warmer, friendlier, and more self-expressive."[24] The dominant shared belief that owning luxurious material possessions is connected with being smarter, more successful, and more in control is a difficult link to break. Somehow a revolution of values needs to involve changing our definition of success. A way must be found to believe and to teach that a person, rich or poor, who lives a life of integrity and service is a greater success than someone who becomes wealthy by lying, cheating, and exploiting other people and his or her environment.

The Peace Offensive

Earlier we discussed what harm the unharnessed drum major instinct can and does do. How can that instinct be harnessed so that it contributes to bringing the world together instead of tearing it apart? In this regard Dr. King exhorted people to "Keep feeling the need for being important. Keep feeling the need for being first. But I want you to be first in love. I want you to be first in moral excellence. I want you to be first in generosity. That is what I want you to do."[25] If the need to be first is projected as the need to be first in service to others, the competitive instinct in all of us can actually be harnessed to achieve positive, peaceful ends through peaceful means. Dr. King argued that a "peace offensive" is necessary in a militaristic world:

> Somehow we must transform the dynamics of the world power struggle . . . to a creative contest to harness man's genius for the purpose of making peace and prosperity a reality for all the nations of the world. . . . If we have the will and determination to mount such a peace offensive, we will unlock hitherto tightly sealed doors of hope and bring new light into the dark chambers of pessimism.[26]

The "peace offensive" spoken of by King will be most effective if people can organize themselves to resist the forces in our world that make peaceful coexistence impossible. Becoming more aware of ways in which racism, materialism, and militarism are "sold" to the public assists in focusing efforts to resist those forces. While competition may stimulate creativity and innovation, recognizing the ways in which negative aspects of competitiveness undermine peace efforts can help in the avoidance of the splintering or infighting in peacebuilding organizations. Ultimately the likelihood is that the revolution in values, the obligation to point out exploitation and inequalities in society, must originate among those who are poor, those who are not in power, those who are young, because for the rich, the powerful, and the established the system is "working," no matter how many problems may exist for the majority.

Nonviolent resistance is the method Dr. King advocated for overcoming the fear and greed that stand between the disconnected world as it now exists and "the beloved community."[27] Because money is such a powerful tool in today's world, he suggested, "Now the . . . thing we'll have to do is this: Always anchor our external direct action with the power of economic withdrawal."[28] He explained the effectiveness of pairing public, direct action with economic withdrawal thus:

> Nonviolent direct action seeks to create such a crisis and establish such creative tension that a community that has constantly refused to negotiate is forced to confront the issue. It seeks so to dramatize the issue that it can no longer be ignored.[29]

If adults want to teach adolescents peacebuilding skills, they must recognize and try to overcome their own inconsistencies in values. They must be aware that their financial and political choices have an impact and can make a difference. This means that their lives must include lifelong learning, including finding out which companies are environmentally and socially responsible and which are not and shopping accordingly. In order to compound the impact of responsible financial and political decisions, organizing with like-minded others can show by example the ways in which nonviolent direct action can make the world a better, more peaceful place.

Besides serving as role models for peace and social justice, how can parents, teachers, and community leaders help young people learn to function creatively and responsibly to improve the quality of life worldwide?

- Teach them critical thinking skills (e.g., promoting discussion rather than rote memorization, building confidence in their ability to comprehend complex issues, stressing writing and the reading of challenging primary texts) to enable them to find innovative solutions to today's problems.
- Encourage them to find a redefinition of success for themselves that is oriented toward service to others rather than just personal gain.
- Teach them that service to others includes service to the environment, for we are ultimately as connected to our environment as we are to each other.
- Show them that they can help to improve the world by becoming informed about a product before they support its production with their money. Furthermore, teach them how to organize economic withdrawal with others so that the impact can be felt even more strongly.
- Talk to them about the opportunity they have to revitalize democracy in the United States by participating at every level from voting to running for office.
- Recognize that internal familial problems are exacerbated by external conditions and work to understand and improve those external conditions to help families to function.
- Make learning relevant to students' lives so they can see the value of making learning a lifelong process.
- Rather than discouraging their dreams to become great basketball players or music stars, provide other meaningful career options. Explain the importance of the many kinds of work that are essential for the productive functioning of this world. Of course choosing a career in peace work is a wonderful option,

but there are many ways in which to lead a proactively peaceful life while pursuing other careers.

In 1959 Dr. Martin Luther King Jr. ended a speech before 26,000 high school and college students with words that are just as relevant today:

> Whatever career you may choose for yourself—doctor, lawyer, teacher—let me propose an avocation to be pursued along with it. Become a dedicated fighter for civil rights. Make it a central part of your life. It will make you a better doctor, a better lawyer, a better teacher. It will enrich your spirit as nothing else possibly can. It will give you that rare sense of nobility that can only spring from love and selflessly helping your fellow man. Make a career of humanity. Commit yourself to the noble struggle for equal rights. You will make a greater person of yourself, a greater nation of your country, and a finer world to live in.[30]

Conclusion

If the world were devoid of war, poverty, hatred, starvation, violent crime, species extinction, discrimination, and despair there would be little reason to question the appropriateness of how the world works. However, given the pressing problems facing most of Earth's denizens, human, plant, or animal, the realization must come that something has to change. To that end we have examined some of the ways in which racism, materialism, and militarism are connected and have shown the negative consequences of unharnessed competitiveness and inconsistent values. A widespread reexamination of values is necessary if peace is to be the true priority.

At this point it is more important than ever to show by example and to teach young people directly that working toward a peaceful, unified world is a worthwhile goal. Disillusionment regarding the efficacy of government to meet the needs of the people is reflected by the fact that less than a third of eighteen- to twenty-four-year-olds voted in the 1996 presidential election.[31] At the same time the belief that money is the only meaningful measure of success and that competition is a positive part of that orientation is more prevalent among that age group than among older generations born in the twentieth century.[32] In a cynical, splintered, materialistic, individual-oriented culture the value of organizing for effective change needs to be reintroduced. Dr. Martin Luther King Jr. still stands as a role model worth emulating. His recognition that only nonviolent means could lead to nonviolent ends combined with the strategies he devised to organize for nonviolent change form a meaningful foundation for reorienting adolescents (and adults) toward the significance of uniting for the common good. King called for "a recognition of the solidarity of the human family . . . because basically we are all one."[33]

If adolescents are to learn that they can make a positive, peaceful difference, they must be shown that true success has little to do with making money, nothing to do with putting themselves above anyone else, and everything to do with devoting their energy to serving humanity in whatever way is meaningful to them. Teachers, parents, and community leaders are responsible not only for teaching those values but for living them as well.

Suggested Exercises

Listed below are some suggested exercises to help adolescents become more aware of how the world is interconnected, how media can glamorize violence and advocate materialistic consumerism, and how people of all ages and from all socioeconomic backgrounds can choose to make peacebuilding differences in the world.

"Connected Lives, Connected World"

Before they come into school one morning, have students write down the country of origin of all of the clothing they are wearing and have them list what they ate and drank for breakfast. As a class discussion, talk about the interrelated, international nature of our everyday lives. Find out what the students know about the countries and cultures from which their clothes and food have come. What are the working conditions for people in those countries? How about the migrant workers in this country? This is an exercise both to increase awareness about how dependent we are on others from countries all over the world and to get students to think about the idea that their consumer choices can affect policies.

"What's News?"

Have students watch a national news broadcast and write down a list of the stories presented. In class, discuss what makes these stories news. What proportion of the stories covers violence? Why do criminals get more media attention than people who work to promote peace or who work for social justice? Does media attention glamorize violence and crime? (This conversation can be generalized to include a discussion of the ways in which violence is presented in commercials, television, movies, and video games.) This exercise is intended to make students aware of how cultural factors can affect what is reported as news, and how the fact that violence "sells" may be a factor in its escalation in this country.

"The Priorities Game"
Ask students for suggestions to explain why entertainers in our culture, such as movie stars and professional athletes, are rewarded with public acclaim, role model status, and wealth, while individuals in the "helping professions" such as teachers, social workers, and firefighters are given scant attention and the problems of poverty and violence in this country continue to escalate. Discuss the role of the media. If students express the idea that the current priorities represented here are skewed, ask them for ideas about what they could do to change the situation. This would be a good opportunity to talk about nonviolent resistance. If students are having a hard time coming up with ideas, ask what impact they could have if they could convince all young people to stop buying expensive, highly-promoted sports shoes and gear (or movie tie-ins or makeup advertised by models) for the sake of highlighting this issue. Or if they could start a campaign to boycott professional sporting events (or high-budget movies, etc.) and the products advertised during those events until salary inequalities are addressed in a serious manner. Get the students to brainstorm about ways to organize. (Start a web page? Throw boycott parties? Write letters to magazines aimed at young people?) This is an exercise to get adolescents to think about the priorities exhibited in society and (a) what role they, themselves, play in perpetuating those priorities and (b) what they can do to try to make a difference using techniques of nonviolent resistance.

Notes

1. All references to quotations from Martin Luther King Jr. in this chapter are taken from Martin Luther King Jr., *A Testament of Hope: The Essential Writings and Speeches of Martin Luther King, Jr.*, ed. James M. Washington (San Francisco: Harper San Francisco, 1991). The date cited is the date of original publication by King. In this instance, then, King, 1967, 629.

2. King, 1967, 251.

3. Russell W. Belk, "Materialism: Trait Aspects of Living in the Material World," *Journal of Consumer Research* 12 (December 1985): 265–80.

4. Richard A. Easterlin and Eileen M. Crimmins, "Private Materialism, Personal Self-Fulfillment, Family Life, and Public Interest: The Nature, Effects, and Causes of Recent Changes in the Values of American Youth," *Public Opinion Quarterly* 55, no. 4 (winter 1991): 499–533.

5. King, 1968, 261.

6. Ibid., 262.

7. King, 1967, 240. King is quoting from an address to Latin American diplomats, the White House (March 12, 1962).

8. Ibid., 240.

9. Helga Dittmar, *The Social Psychology of Material Possessions: To Have Is to Be* (New York: St. Martin's Press, 1992), 173.

10. U.S. Bureau of the Census, *Statistical Abstract of the United States* (Washington, DC: U.S. Government Printing Office, 1995), 796.

11. Russell W. Belk and Richard W. Pollay, "Images of Ourselves: The Good Life in Twentieth Century Advertising," *Journal of Consumer Research* 11 (March 1985): 887–97.

12. King, 1968, 260–61.

13. Philip Cushman, "Why the Self is Empty: Toward a Historically Situated Psychology," *American Psychologist* 45, no. 5 (May 1990): 599–611, 606.

14. John Simons, "Improbable Dreams," *U.S. News & World Report* 122, no. 11 (March 24, 1997): 46–52.

15. African-Americans as a group average 59 cents of income for every dollar of income earned by European Americans as a group. U.S. Bureau of the Census, *Statistical Abstracts of the United States* (Washington, DC: U.S. Government Printing Office, 1995), 469.

16   John Simons, "Improbable Dreams," 46.
17   Ibid., 46, 52.
18   King, 1967, 620.
19   Ibid., 644.
20   King, 1956, 138.
21   Charles Birch and John B. Cobb Jr., The *Liberation of Life: From the Cell to the Community* (Cambridge: Cambridge University Press, 1981).
22   King, 1965, 625.
23   Helga Dittmar, The *Social Responsibility of Material Possessions*, 183.
24   Ibid., 180.
25   King, 1968, 265.
26   King, 1967, 629.
27   King, 1958, 87.
28   King, 1968, 282.
29   King, 1963, 291.
30   King, 1959, 22.
31   Margot Hornblower, "Great Xpectations," *Time* 149, no. 23 (June 9, 1997): 58–68.
32   Ibid., 58.
33   King, 1963, 121.

Selected Bibliography

Belk, Russell W. "Cultural and Historical Differences in Concepts of Self and Their Effects on Attitudes toward Having and Giving," *Advances in Consumer Research* 11 (1983): 754–59.

———, "Wordly Possessions: Issues and Criticisms," *Advances in Consumer Research* 10 (1983): 514–19.

Gould, Kenneth A., Adam S. Weinberg, and Allan Schnaiberg. "Legitimating Impotence: Pyrrhic Victories of the Modern Environmental Movement," *Qualitative Sociology* 16, no. 3 (fall 1993): 207–45.

Levy, Frank S., and Richard C. Michel, "An Economic Bust for the Baby Boom," *Challenge* 29, no. 1 (March/April 1986): 33–39.

Sampson, Edward E. "The Debate on Individualism: Indigenous Psychologies of the Individual and Their Role in Personal and Societal Functioning," *American Psychologist* 43, no. 1 (January 1988): 15–22.

Tashchian, Armen, Mark E. Slama, and Roobian O. Tashchian. "Measuring Attitudes toward Energy Conservation: Cynicism, Belief in Material Growth, and Faith in Technology," *Journal of Public Policy and Marketing* 3 (fall 1984): 134–148.

Terrie, Martha E. "Social Constructions and Cultural Contradictions: A Look at a Christian Perspective on Economics," *Journal of American Culture* 17, no. 3 (fall 1994): 55–63.

Chapter 3

Countering School Violence: The Rise of Conflict Resolution Programs

Molly K. Pont-Brown and John D. Krumboltz

With an estimated fifty million handguns in circulation, a national homicide rate of nine people per 100,000, and headlines of brutality in every major newspaper and magazine, violence is a hot topic in the United States.[1] Violence affects every element of U.S. society. Black and white, male and female, rich and poor, urban and rural, a rapidly increasing number of U.S. residents have witnessed, experienced, or committed violent acts of one kind or another. Perhaps most troubling is the portion of that population under the age of eighteen that has been touched by violence. Adolescence and violence are two words frequently paired together today, and with good reason. Stories and statistics show that violence has permeated U.S. society, leaving no one—including children—untouched.

"This Violence Must Stop"

"My fears for the future are a lot of things. My fears are that I'm not going to live to see the future. I say this because there is so much killing going on in high schools," writes Franchesca Ho Sang, a fourth grader at P.S. 28 in the Bronx.[2] Many children have tales not just of fear, but of experience to relate, such as this Manhattan eighth grader's story:

> My father was singing to me and as we went into the building I asked him for fifty dollars. He asked me for what and I told him for some sneakers. So he gave it to me. I was real happy. . . . And then it happened. A gun went off and I just ducked. My mother came out. [She] asked me, "Where's your father?" . . . That's when I realized that my father had gotten shot. I went crazy. I was

going wild. My brother got my father's gun from the house and went looking for the man that killed my father.[3]

For an increasing number of adolescents, guns are an everyday reality, even a necessity: "I have a gun, but I leave it with my uncle. I only carry it with me to parties," writes another Manhattan eighth grader.[4] Seven-year-old Brandon Green, witness to the bloody shooting of one young man by another outside a movie theater where Brandon's mother had taken him to see *Aladdin* in her effort to provide an alternative to the violence shown on television, states it most simply: "This violence must stop."[5]

Children and Violence: Statistics

The urgency of Brandon's simple plea is confirmed by the statistics regarding children and violence. The Children's Defense Fund (CDF), a nonprofit organization that works to improve the lives of children in the United States and has added violence to its list of major concerns in the 1990s, compiles oft-cited lists of statistics regarding the plight of children today.[6] CDF reports that in 1995, sixteen children and youths were killed by firearms every day in the United States.[7] Since 1979, more children (60,008) have died from gunfire in the United States than U.S. soldiers killed during the Vietnam and Gulf wars and in the U.S. engagements in Haiti, Somalia, and Bosnia combined.[8]

Children in inner cities display symptoms of posttraumatic stress syndrome similar to those experienced by children in war-torn countries such as Cambodia or Bosnia. Dr. James Garbarino, who has studied children in those war-torn countries and in the often violent inner-city neighborhoods of the United States, finds that U.S. children also experience depression, rage, nightmares and sleeplessness, and a bleak sense of their own future; many, when asked what they will be at the age of thirty, simply answer "Dead."[9] Perhaps their responses are not too far off the mark; a study in *The New England Journal of Medicine* found that young men in Harlem are less likely to live to age forty than their counterparts in Bangladesh.[10]

Violence is a part of U.S. pop culture as well; *TV Guide* reports that a violent incident is shown on television, on average, every six minutes. Movies are similarly violent; *Lethal Weapon II*, a movie popular with adolescents, contains over 260 murders in its 114 minutes.[11]

Growing up in a culture in which violence has become commonplace, children have not remained merely on the receiving end of this national epidemic. In 1995, over 1.8 million youths were arrested, one in eighteen of these for violent crimes, and 2,383 of those for murder.[12] A Northeastern University study found that the number of boys twelve years of age and under arrested for murder doubled between 1985 and 1991.[13]

With children both initiating and attempting to protect themselves from acts of violence, accidental and intentional violence has infiltrated the one institution formerly considered a child's safe haven from the perils of the outside world—U.S. schools. Various studies have indicated that anywhere from 9 to 23 percent of students have reported being victims of violent activity at school.[14] On a typical school day, more than 135,000 youths bring weapons to school because they fear for their safety.[15] California schools reported a 200 percent increase in gun confiscations from students between 1986 and 1990, and in a 1987 survey of high school students, 48 percent of tenth-grade boys and 34 percent of eighth-grade boys said they could get a handgun if they wanted one.

Children and Violence: School Stories

The statistics themselves are frightening enough, but the stories coming out of U.S. schools are even more harrowing. Sharon K. Williams writes that "more and more disputes that once ended in playground shouting matches are now ending in shooting matches." In Milwaukee, for example, a twelve-year-old fired a semiautomatic pistol on his school playground in reaction to a slap in the face from a fellow classmate.[16] In a recent Salem, Oregon, playground incident, four second-grade boys were arrested after they held a girl's nose and mouth so that she could not breathe; apparently the victim had been the girlfriend of one of the boys who was angry over their breakup.[17]

In Walton, New York, a fifteen-year-old student was accused of shooting his teacher in the face after she told him to stop talking in class, while a fourteen-year-old girl in Hartford, Connecticut, slashed the throat and head of a teacher's aide whose report landed her in detention.[18]

In Los Angeles, a fifteen-year-old boy who feared street gangs attempted to protect himself by bringing a gun to school; he accidentally fired the gun when reaching into his book bag. The shot killed one classmate and wounded another.[19]

Teachers, astounded and frightened by these and other incidents, are concerned about the children they teach: "I've been teaching for twenty years, and every year it gets worse and worse. There's more fighting. The kids seem to have such short fuses—the least little thing sets them off. They see violence on the street and at home, and they don't know any other ways to deal with conflict," reports one teacher.[20] Concerns such as these, gathered from campus experiences, have led many educators to turn to conflict resolution programs for help in stemming adolescent violence in U.S. schools and society.

School-Based Conflict Resolution Programs

School-based conflict resolution programs find their roots in many societal and educational movements; they are perhaps most closely descended from neighborhood mediation and legal arbitration programs offering alternative ways for adults to resolve conflicts. In a 1984 article describing the increased popularity of community mediation programs, Albie M. Davis noted that similar dispute resolution skills and curricula were increasingly introduced to adolescents through school-based programs. An expert in the field of community mediation, Davis labeled this school-based involvement "a trend [that] deserves to be watched."[21] Two years later, in an article aptly titled "Schools Can Replace Gladiators with Mediators," Moses S. Koch called the introduction of school-based dispute resolution "an approach that may catch on—and deserves to."[22] Today, their predictions appear to have been right on target.

Conflict resolution programs are being demanded and implemented in great numbers by schools across the United States. The explosive growth of these programs in both elementary and secondary settings is almost immeasurable. As early as 1987, Ann Gibson, then director of the National Association for Mediation in Education (NAME), the nation's premiere clearinghouse for school-based conflict resolution information, commented on the growth: "It's really hard for us to know how many programs exist. Every day I find out about programs I didn't know about."[23] According to NAME, students, teachers, staff, and administrators participated in conflict resolution programs at over five thousand schools nationwide in 1994.[24] This constitutes a marked increase from a 1991 count of some two thousand programs in the nation's approximately 80,000 public schools.[25]

The Role of Violence

These numbers reflect a growing trend in education that deserves attention. Despite the ever increasing number of schools that host conflict resolution programs and the rapid spread of such programs today, school-based conflict resolution got off to a slow start. "In the beginning stages," says Gibson of NAME, "programs developed very slowly . . . it was difficult . . . generally to make inroads in schools. For the most part programs developed because community mediation programs approached schools with their ideas and suggested that they work together." Gibson continues, "There was much less [of] the kind of thing that's happening now, where schools are initiating [programs]."[26] Gail Sadalla, formerly of the San Francisco Community Board, a leader in the school-based conflict resolution movement, agrees: "It was really hard in the beginning to get people to go for this."[27] Priscilla Prutzman of Children's Creative Response to Conflict (CCRC) attributes some of the schools' initial hesitancy to a lack of understanding and awareness. "At that time, nobody saw the point of violence prevention—that you teach people the skills before they get into it."[28]

Other factors cited in the recent growth of the conflict resolution in schools movement include increased availability of funding and more opportunities for those in the field to collaborate over the past fifteen years.[29] However, the position of violence as the primary factor in the movement's recent explosion is undeniable. Today, schools are increasingly turning to conflict resolution programs to address problems of violence on campus.

What Does Conflict Resolution Look Like in Schools?

School-based conflict resolution programs vary greatly according to the time and resources available, as well as the interests of those implementing them. A basic goal of most programs is to convey the idea that conflict is not bad; rather, conflict is a natural occurrence that may be addressed in nonviolent ways. School-based programs seek to empower students by teaching them the skills to resolve their conflicts nonviolently through a problem-solving approach. Some programs incorporate broader issues such as diversity appreciation, prejudice and tolerance, critical thinking, communication and listening skills, problem solving, or peaceable alternatives to social and political injustice. In the most generic sense, all programs aim to teach children skills that bring about "positive, non-adversarial relationships with others."[30]

School-based programs generally follow one of three formats. Some are a mixture of all three:

1. Teacher training. Teachers are trained in conflict resolution techniques, then encourage their students to "state their complaints in ways that leave open the possibility of a peaceful settlement." "I" statements such as "I feel angry when you take my pencil without asking" are one example. Teachers also encourage role-playing exercises to develop listening skills and practice "I" statements.
2. Peer mediation. Selected students learn conflict resolution techniques and are on call to mediate conflicts between their peers, whether they be playground disputes in elementary schools or interracial and gang-related incidents in secondary institutions.
3. Curriculum incorporation. Conflict resolution is either introduced as a separate subject or integrated with another subject (such as social studies) for classroom instruction. This is where most diversity appreciation and peace studies learning would take place, and it is most common at the secondary level.[31]

Schools dedicate differing degrees of time and energy to conflict resolution. Some programs may be requested by a school, while others may be mandated by a school district. Some schools involve all staff, teachers, administrators, and even parents in continuous training. Such programs seek a real change in school climate and attitude toward conflict. Other schools implement conflict resolution as a quick-fix solution to increased school violence or as a means of controlling unruly children. Such programs might involve just one two-hour training session for a group of twenty student peer mediators who roam the schoolyard during recess periods. The conditions under which a school program is introduced and implemented have a marked effect on that program's impact.

Most certainly, the various school approaches to conflict resolution render the definition of a school-based program somewhat ambiguous; similarly, the previously cited NAME statistics about the number of programs in schools are less definitive due to the wide variety of activities that fall under the name "program." Nonetheless, countless schools are making conflict resolution a priority. Peer mediation in particular has been popular. One 1989 study of forty inner-city seventh graders interviewed about their experiences with and beliefs about conflict and behavior found that conflicts play a particularly important role for adolescents in that

1. conflicts pervaded adolescents' lives, offering opportunities for self-protection, social status, personal growth, interpersonal insight, conflict resolution, and heroic drama;
2. adolescents lacked conflict proficiency, and reacted instinctively;
3. peer conflict for adolescents had a different meaning than for adults, rendering adult intervention intrusive, among other things.[32]

While incidents involving drugs, assault, or weapons are usually left to school administrators or legal officers to deal with, successful mediation may resolve problems that involve fighting, prejudice, harassment, poor parent-child communication, racial slurs, gang disagreements, dirty looks, jealousy, classroom misbehavior, horseplay, poor sportsmanship, theft, threats, taunting, gossip, and more.[33] The following is an example of one such mediation:

> At lunch a student is wearing a skirt given to her by her boyfriend. The girl next to her in [the] cafeteria line accidentally drops catsup on the skirt. An argument ensues, but as the girls are about to swing at each other, a teacher moves into the scene, and asks the two antagonists if they would like the help of a student mediator in settling their differences. Somewhat reluctantly, they follow her to a predesignated area where a student mediator is on duty. The teacher leaves. In 15 minutes, all three students exit the area with a written signed agreement: "Mabel is sorry she spilled the catsup on Joan. Joan apologizes for having lost her temper."[34]

Simplistic as it may seem, the above mediation would reinforce to the students the idea that their problem can be resolved nonviolently. The actual mediation process is dictated by a set format. Usually it requires that the students agree to several rules, for example, no interruptions, truthfulness, no put-downs. Then the antagonists relate their sides of the story individually and propose various solutions to the problem until they find one or more to which they can agree. Solutions also aim to prevent similar future incidents. The mediator is an active listener who restates the disputants' stories for them; she does not impose any solutions of her own.[35]

Multimedia approaches to conflict resolution are also being tried to reduce adolescent violence. A computer program using games, simulations, graphics, cartoons, and interactive interviews has been designed to teach adolescents how to resolve conflicts without violence.[36] Units include anger management, dispute resolution, and perspective taking. While the results are not yet in, the program represents a creative effort to use technology to advance the cause of peace.

The Resolving Conflict Creatively Program

The Resolving Conflict Creatively Program (RCCP), a collaborative effort of Educators for Social Responsibility (ESR) and the New York City public schools, is one example of a program that introduces both peer mediation and conflict resolution curricula. Begun in 1985 in the New York City schools, the program today operates in eight school systems in five states.[37] Some 150,000 students now participate in RCCP, making it one of the largest programs of its kind in the country.

The program has garnered much attention from the press and the federal government. As Education Secretary Richard W. Riley describes it, RCCP "incorporates the knowledge and skills of conflict resolution, an appreciation for diversity, and attitudes for countering bias into every aspect of campus life."[38] In RCCP, conflict resolution is viewed as an opportunity to grow and learn, to increase community and cultural understanding, to value diversity, and to prevent prejudice by focusing on intergroup relations and creative win-win solutions.[39]

The program's three core components involve a classroom curriculum, peer mediation, and parental involvement. Staff from RCCP train school administrators, staff, and teachers in conflict resolution and intergroup relations skills, paying them for their time spent learning; teachers then instruct students in what they have learned using RCCP's comprehensive curriculum, which includes units such as Communication, Equality, and Preventing Prejudice/Celebrating Differences. Consultants from RCCP visit classrooms regularly, and teachers conduct monthly follow-up sessions once the curriculum has been covered, often integrating creative conflict resolution with other subject matter.

Once students have been instructed in the RCCP curriculum, a group of student mediators is selected by their peers for further training. Peer mediators are on duty to help other students solve conflicts before they become violent. As in the above example, they take parties in conflict to a quiet place and, with a few very basic rules agreed upon by all, find creative ways to resolve that conflict.

Adolescents involved in RCCP become very excited about the new methods that they learn, and take those lessons home with them. To reinforce this, RCCP developed a parental involvement component of the program in which parents are paid for training in peaceful conflict resolution so that they may negotiate with and respond to their children as their children are being taught to negotiate at school.

Are Conflict Resolution Programs Effective?

Julie A. Lam, a sociologist at the University of Massachusetts, examined reports on fourteen conflict resolution programs in 1990 and found that there is "a wealth of anecdotal material from teachers and principals attesting to the merits [of such programs] but scant data showing a statistically measurable effect in reducing fighting or improving rates of suspension, truancy, or attendance."[40]

Such anecdotal success stories from RCCP participants abound. Katherine Augustine, principal of the McDonough No. 38 Elementary School in New Orleans, a school at which 97 percent of students receive free lunch and the federal Chapter 1 funding is schoolwide, praises the program: "There's been a change in attitude in students and the rapport they have with one another and with teachers. Parents are also starting to treat their kids differently. It's done a lot for us. . . . We're in the middle of a combat zone. That's why I know this program works."[41]

"The parent training workshop of the RCCP was a warm, fun, and very rewarding experience for me. It has affected my relationship with my children primarily in regards to conflicts and how to handle them. I have been given tools I can use when there are sibling fights, conflicts between parents and children, and between my children and their friends," says Betsy Biele, a parent in Brooklyn's Community School District 15.[42] Students seem to have learned something, too: "I have learned that you cannot judge a person by their color or what they look like on the outside. People are all the same inside," says Kyle Walker, an eleven-year-old student at Roosevelt Middle School in Vista, California.[43]

These RCCP stories illustrate a great deal of enthusiasm on the part of program participants, and that enthusiasm conveys a large measure of success for the program. The problem, as stated by Lam, is the lack of hard statistical data. RCCP itself commissioned a study of the program from Metis Associates, Inc. in 1990. While the study found that the program had positive effects, its findings were based almost solely on opinion surveys filled out by teachers, administrators, and peer mediators involved in the program. Teachers surveyed answered questions about their own attitudes and about students' attitudes. Examples of those statistics from the study include the following:

- 70.9 percent of responding teachers have observed that to a moderate or great extent, children are demonstrating less physical violence in the classroom;
- 77.8 percent of responding teachers have observed more caring behavior among their children; or
- 71.5 percent of respondents have noticed that children have increased skills in understanding others' point of view. (pp. 6-7)

A student achievement test measured students who had completed RCCP against a control group, finding that the RCCP participants had increased their knowledge of concepts related to conflict resolution and had a greater awareness of conflict resolution behaviors than did the control group. The difference between the mean scores of the program group and the control group was judged to be statistically significant, although the control group may have differed on other unknown characteristics (p. 8). Whether program students always act on their increased awareness of conflict is less quantifiable.

Another survey in the Metis study measured the effect of the program on the attitudes and behaviors of participating teachers. It found, for example, that:

- 87.7 percent had increased their use of specific conflict resolution techniques in the classroom either a great deal or moderately;
- 78.6 percent said that their sensitivity to children whose backgrounds differed from their own had increased either moderately or a great deal; and
- 89.3 percent said that their willingness to let young people take responsibility for solving their own conflicts had increased either moderately or a great deal. (p. 10)

A teacher opinion survey that gave respondents only three options for categorizing their behavior change—"a great deal," "moderately," or none at all—does not provide a completely accurate picture of what occurs in the classroom. No records of specific instances were kept—the number of times a teacher stepped out of a conflict and let the students handle it, for example—and whether teachers really changed their behavior along with their attitudes is not recorded.

In its study, Metis Associates, Inc. also measured the impact of the program on class climate, reporting that 84 percent of respondents found that positive changes had occurred since the introduction of conflict resolution. Another 60 percent noticed positive changes in the school climate since RCCP's introduction there.[44]

Finally, the peer mediation component of RCCP was studied. Statistics similar to those cited above are given in the report, with teachers finding that students had been helped through peer mediation and that the mediators' self-esteem had been aided through participation in the program. Students found mediation helpful, and student mediators believed that their experiences had given them lifelong skills (p. 12).

In summary, the Metis study concluded that RCCP participants rate the program highly, that the program has a positive impact on students, participating staff, and classroom and school climate, that children's attitudes and behavior appear to have changed in a positive way, and that peer mediation has been successfully implemented and fosters more peaceful class and school environments. With its heavy reliance on personal testimonies about the success of RCCP, the Metis study illustrates Lam's point that most support for conflict resolution programs is anecdotal. Another study by Marlene DeMorat et al. relied on teacher ratings to show that an intervention that trains aggressive students to attribute nonhostile intent in ambiguous interactions with peers produced increased self-control.[45]

Yet program successes are hard to quantify. Moses S. Koch does use some numerical data in his evaluation of programs. He notes that "[i]n a multi-ethnic high school in Hawaii, fighting incidents dropped from 83 to 19 in the [mediated dispute resolution] program's first two years" while one New York City high school experienced a 50 percent reduction in suspensions for fighting within one year of a program's introduction there.[46] Many program administrators and participants cite similar numerical reductions; yet, as Priscilla Prutzman, cofounder of CCRC in New York mentions, there are simply too many variables affecting the indicators of success. A reduced suspension rate, for example, may be influenced by many factors, not simply by the introduction of a conflict resolution program on campus. "More research needs to be done," says Prutzman.[47] Her sentiments are echoed by numerous professionals involved with school-based conflict resolution. A more updated study of RCCP's success reducing violent incidents that is currently being finalized and features a sample size of more than 8000 students may offer more of the statistical evidence that seems to be lacking in the conflict resolution field.[48]

Clear experimental studies with behavioral outcome measures continue to be in short supply. In summarizing research efforts to evaluate adolescent violence prevention efforts, Linda Dahlberg wrote, "The fundamental question from the perspective of public health and policy is: 'Do these programs work? Do any of the individual, peer, family, or setting approaches effectively reduce aggressive and violent behavior?' The answer to these questions is not known at the present time."[49] She goes on to point out, however, citing the work of Patrick Tolan and Nancy Guerra, that positive effects have been found for certain types of interventions, for example, cognitive-behavioral interventions, family interventions, school climate programs that involve parents, and interventions that reduce exposure to media violence.[50] The PeaceBuilders program showed some beneficial effects, especially among fourth-grade girls, but the results were based on teacher ratings, which did not consistently agree with student ratings.[51]

An entire issue of the *American Journal of Preventative Medicine* was devoted to youth violence prevention in 1996 that described thirteen evaluation projects, which are currently underway. While final results were not presented, Patrick Tolan and Nancy Guerra in their closing commentary observed that "The next steps for these and similar projects are to determine the program impact and implementation, strive for longer follow-up, document conditions that interact with proximal impact on distal outcomes, and further broaden evaluation efforts into modifying situations instead of modifying only individuals. Finally, we must recognize that the goal of evaluation is not to declare all earnest efforts effective, but to determine which efforts merit further consideration."[52]

Despite the current dearth of hard evidence, "the growth [of conflict resolution programs in schools] . . . is indicative of the success. It's very hopeful. . . . It's a field now, a profession," says Priscilla Prutzman of CCRC.[53] Even emerging criticism indicates the field's prominence. Speaking of conflict resolution in general, Albie Davis states that "the very fact that the movement is attracting criticism is an indication that it is growing up, that it is having an impact and deserves to be taken seriously."[54] Indeed, conflict resolution may soon be as common as reading, writing, and arithmetic—Albie M. Davis has labeled it the "Fourth 'R'."[55] Priscilla Prutzman considers institutionalization a real possibility: "[perhaps] it will be that every school will automatically have a mediation program and conflict resolution will be integrated into the curriculum. It already is the case that conflict resolution is a course of study in colleges."[56]

Those involved in school-based conflict resolution certainly expect no immediate slowdown in the popularity of such programs. "It's growing like crazy. There's no question about it. Everybody can see that it's the wave of the future," says Bob Tafoya, a Sacramento school administrator.[57] Larry Dieringer, the executive director of ESR, stated in 1994 that "the demand for conflict resolution and violence prevention in the last three to four years has gone through the roof. It went from a trickle to a steady flow."[58]

Prospects for the Future of School-Based Conflict Resolution: The Need for Integration

Conflict resolution is increasingly used today with adolescents in educational settings. A wealth of anecdotal information exists attesting to its successes in the schools. Moreover, conflict resolution is recognized as a positive tool by politicians through legislation such as the attempted Safe Schools Act of 1993, and violence prevention and school safety prioritized in the seventh goal of the Goals 2000: Educate America Act passed in 1994.[59] Not surprisingly, then, those in the field of school-based conflict resolution are encouraged. While conflict resolution programs in schools do indeed appear to be having a positive impact, that impact is limited by several factors. Both its frequent detachment from other violence prevention measures and its use as a peacemaking rather than a peacebuilding tool hinder the ability of school-based conflict resolution to effect broad-based change. To make a long-lasting impact beyond the walls of the school, conflict resolution must be integrated with other violence prevention and peacebuilding strategies.

Addressing Violence on a Larger Scale

Conflict resolution in and of itself is not a solution to the problems of violence in society that are spilling over into U.S. schools. Truly, few conflict resolution advocates have ever suggested that school-based programs alone are the answer to problems of violence among children and in society. Ann Gibson of NAME concedes that it is difficult to learn conflict resolution skills in "the bubble of the school," yet maintains that it is an important violence prevention measure.[60] Conflict resolution programs are essential, but they must be viewed and treated as part of a broader set of efforts aimed not only at preventing violence in society but also at eliminating its root causes. Poverty and discrepancies in wealth, racism, injustice, rampant consumerism, and the stresses faced by families must be addressed, according to Larry Dieringer of ESR. "It's got to be more systemic," he says of the conflict resolution effort. "If you're looking at violence in our society, education alone is important, but it's not going to do it alone. . . . Unless we as a society are acting on a number of fronts, I don't think we are going to be able to deal sufficiently with the [violence] problem."[61]

Some programs are beginning to recognize this need for integration. One example is a Violence Prevention Initiative sponsored by Victim Services of New York. The initiative, funded by the Centers for Disease Control, provides an opportunity to test various violence-prevention techniques. Chris Whipple of Victim Services characterizes the project as the organization's attempt to broaden its conflict resolution efforts and place them within a community framework.[62] Conflict resolution is one important component of a campaign against violence in this initiative.

Dorothy Espelage et al. investigated some of the family and environmental factors associated with bullying behavior by middle school adolescents. Bullies were more often male, from stepfamilies or single parent families, had less adult supervision and fewer positive adult role models, were exposed to more television violence and gang members, and had less positive peer influence.[63] Additional evidence associating negative family interactions with conduct disorder in male children is provided by Catherine Morton et al.[64]

Modifications in the school environment still offer the most accessible and powerful hope for change. Caroline Smith et al. studied 772 at-risk adolescents to identify the protective factors associated with reductions in delinquent behavior. They found that the single most powerful resilience factor against delinquency was school success.[65] Specific predictive measures included achievement in reading and mathematics, commitment to school, attachment to teachers, and aspirations and expectations to go to college by both adolescents and parents.

If school success is such a powerful predictor of resilience, one might well ask why schools do not work harder to produce success for every student. Here we face the ultimate irony. Most schools use a competitive grading system that requires teachers to compare students with each other and to award higher grades only to those students who excel their peers. Consequently, as John Krumboltz and Christine Yeh point out, no matter how excellent the teachers' instruction, no matter how hard the students work, half the students will always be labeled publicly as below average. The competitive grading system inevitably discourages and humiliates a large number of students, making it sensible for them to drop out to preserve their self-respect and to seek ways of gaining revenge. Schools could use ways of helping every adolescent to learn by encouraging self-improvement, not by comparing students with each other.[66] Altering the grading system in this way might well have powerful benefits, but the effects on school violence have yet to be demonstrated.

While schools offer an initially powerful intervention venue, conflict resolution interventions need to be applied beyond the educational setting. The Smith et al. study showed that family and peer factors also contribute to adolescent resilience against delinquency.[67] Conflict resolution programs in schools must be integrated with other programs and measures designed to prevent violence and eliminate its root causes in society.

Toward a Culture of Nonviolence: Peacemaking versus Peacebuilding

Ian M. Harris analyzed differences among three educational strategies used to deal with violence in schools.[68] The first is peacekeeping. This strategy seeks to make schools safer places in which to be; it often involves strict rules about behavior on campus and the use of security guards and/or metal detectors at the school site. The second strategy is peacemaking—attempting "to provide students with skills to manage their conflicts nonviolently." It is into this category, of course, that most school-based conflict resolution and peer mediation programs fall. Yet many peace educators would argue that the third response to violence—peacebuilding—is necessary for the efforts of school-based conflict resolution to make a lasting impact. Conflict resolution should not be implemented in isolation as a quick-fix, five-step, talk-it-out solution to playground altercations; rather, the teaching of skills for dealing with interpersonal conflict must be paired with a proactive approach of peacebuilding. Peacebuilding seeks to create a culture of nonviolence by challenging youths not only to reduce violence in society, but also to commit themselves to building peace in all arenas of life—to strive not only for the absence of violence but also toward the presence of peace.

Some school-based conflict resolution programs are incorporating peacebuilding strategies into their curricula. One such example is the Resolving Conflict Creatively Program, which uses a "peaceable schools" model that seeks to transform an entire school culture to one of nonviolence rather than offering quick fixes for daily conflicts.[69] This type of approach is essential for conflict resolution programs to have an impact outside the school. Students must be given not only the strategies to deal with conflicts as they occur, but also the motivation to pursue standards of social justice—to live their lives more proactively in the pursuit of a more just and peaceful world.[70]

High Hopes

Many in the field of conflict resolution have high hopes for its increased use and its success in stemming and preventing violence. "My hope is that it [conflict resolution] will become a real integral part of every school curriculum and that ultimately we will work ourselves out of business because it will become so integral, and that we will be part of changing people's minds about violence," says Ann Gibson.[71] In a country and a world plagued by random acts of violence, ethnic cleansing, and religious strife, the need for conflict resolution programs should not subside any time soon. Ann Gibson and her counterparts will likely not work themselves out of business in the foreseeable future. As they continue to create and implement conflict resolution programs in the schools, all involved should consider the increased success and broader societal impact that might be achieved if school-based conflict resolution is treated as one very important and essential component of a larger approach that includes other violence prevention and peacebuilding measures.

Notes

1 Deborah Prothrow-Stith with Michele Weissman, *Deadly Consequences* (New York: HarperCollins, 1991), 13; U.S. Bureau of the Census, *Statistical Abstracts of the United States: 1996*, 116th ed. (Washington, DC: U.S. Government Printing Office 1996), 201.

2 "Learn to Fly," *New York Times*, 2 January 1993, 21.

3 Stephen O'Connor, "Death in the Everyday Schoolroom," *The Nation* 256, no. 20 (24 May 1993): 702.

4 Ibid., 703.

5 Courtland Milloy, "A 7-Year-Old's Plea for Sanity," *Washington Post*, 3 January 1993, B1, B4.

6 Unless otherwise cited, violence statistics in this section are from Children's Defense Fund, "Statistics on Children and Violence" (Washington, DC: Children's Defense Fund, 1993).

7 Children's Defense Fund, "Every Day in America" [http://www.childrensdefense.org/facts.html], March 23, 1997.

8 Children's Defense Fund, "Gun Deaths" [http://www.childrensdefense.org/gundeaths.html], March 23, 1997.

9 Daniel Goleman, "Attending to the Children of All the World's War Zones," *New York Times*, 6 December 1992, sec. 4, p. 7.

10 C. McCord, M.D. and H. P. Freeman, M.D., "Excess Mortality in Harlem," *New England Journal of Medicine*, 322, no. 3 (January 18, 1990): 173–77.

11 Donald Roberts, "Children and the Media" (lecture presented in Children and Society course, Stanford University, February 2, 1993).

12 Children's Defense Fund, "Safety Facts" [http://www.childrensdefense.org/safefaqs.html], March 23 1997.

13 James Alan Fox and Glenn L. Pierce, "The Young and the Rootless," *USA Today Magazine* (January 1994): 24–26.

14 J. Patrick Kachur, M.D. et al., "School-Associated Violent Deaths in the United States, 1992–1994," *JAMA* 275, no. 22 (12 June 1996): 1729.

15 Linda Lantieri with Janet Patti, "The Road to Peace in Our Schools," *Educational Leadership* 54, no. 1 (September 1996): 28.

16 Sharon K. Williams, "We Can Work It Out," *Teacher Magazine* 3, no. 2 (October 1991): 22.

17 "4 Second Graders Accused of Trying to Kill Girl, 7," *New York Times*, 20 December 1996, B13.

18 William Celis III, "Suburban and Rural Schools Learning That Violence Isn't Confined to the Cities," *New York Times*, 21 April 1993, Education section, B11; "Student Ejected from Detention Slashes an Aide," *New York Times*, 22 November 1996, B4.

19 "Los Angeles Student Is Killed as a Gun Discharges in Class," *New York Times*, 22 January 1993, A16.

20 Nancy Carlsson-Paige, "Children's Understanding of Conflict: A Developmental Perspective" (Ph.D. diss., University of Massachusetts, 1992), 1–2.

21 Albie M. Davis, "Justice without Judges," *Update on Law-Related Education* 8, no. 2 (fall 1984): 57.

22 Moses S. Koch, "Schools Can Replace Gladiators with Mediators," *Education Weekly* 5, no. 20 (2 April 1986): 28.

23 "Schools Borrowing Successful Idea from Labor Negotiations," *Nation's Schools Report* 13, no. 17 (27 October 1987): 1.

24 Annette Townley, telephone conversation with author Molly Pont-Brown, Stanford, CA, 2 March 1994.

25 David Singer, "Teaching Alternative Dispute Resolution to America's School Children," *Arbitration Journal* 46, no. 4 (December 1991): 33.

26 Ann Gibson, telephone interview with author Molly Pont-Brown, tape recording, Stanford, CA, 2 March 1994.

27 Gail Sadalla, telephone interview with author Molly Pont-Brown, tape recording, Stanford, CA, 22 February 1994.

28 Priscilla Prutzman, telephone interview with author Molly Pont-Brown, tape recording, Stanford, CA, 28 February 1994.

29 Gail Sadalla, telephone interview; Chris Whipple, telephone interview with author Molly Pont-Brown, tape recording, Stanford, CA, 8 March 1994.

30 Nancy Carlsson-Paige, "Children's Understanding," 27.

31 Sharon K. Williams, "We Can Work It Out," 22.

32 Susan Opotow, "The Risk of Violence: Peer Conflicts in the Lives of Adolescents" (paper presented at the annual meeting of the American Psychological Association, New Orleans, LA, August 1989, Abstract), Dialog, ERIC, ED 316823.

33 Moses S. Koch, "Schools Can Replace Gladiators with Mediators," 28; Charles T. Araki, "Dispute Management in the Schools," *Mediation Quarterly* 8, no. 1 (fall 1990): 57–58.

34 Moses S. Koch, "Resolving Disputes: Students Can Do It Better," *NASSP Bulletin* 72, no. 504 (January 1988): 17.

35 Albie M. Davis and Kit Porter, "Dispute Resolution: The Fourth 'R'" *Missouri Journal of Dispute Resolution* (1985): 135–36.

36 Kris Bosworth, Linda L. Dahlberg, Dorothy Espelage, Gary Daytner, and Tracy DuBay, "Using Multimedia to Teach Conflict-Resolution Skills to Young Adolescents," *Youth Violence Prevention: Descriptions and Baselines Data from 14 Evaluation Projects*, Supplement to *American Journal of Preventive Medicine* 12, no. 5 (September/October 1996): 65–74.

37 Linda Lantieri with Janet Patti, "Road to Peace," 29.

38 U.S. Department of Education, *Remarks Prepared for U.S. Secretary of Education Richard W. Riley* (remarks presented at the conference "Safeguarding Our Youth: Violence Prevention for Our Nation's Children," Washington, DC, 21 July 1993), 5.

39 Unless otherwise cited, RCCP facts listed in this section are from *Waging Peace in Our Schools*, prod. by Linda Lantieri and Peter Barton, 26 min., Educators for Social Responsibility, 1992, videocassette.

40 Kathleen Teltsch, "Reacting to Rising Violence, Schools Introduce 'Fourth R' Reconciliation," *New York Times*, 26 December 1990, Education section, B15.

41 Mary Massey, "Los Angeles Riots Highlight Need for Schools to address Issues of Racism, Cultural Diversity, Creative Ways to Resolve Conflict," *Education USA* 34, No. 38 (18 May 1992): 217.

42 Resolving Conflict Creatively Program, "Testimonials from Participants" (New York: Resolving Conflict Creatively Program, 1993), 2.

43 Lisa R. Omphroy, "Speak Softly and Carry an Open Mind," *Los Angeles Times*, 24 April 1992, B1, B4.

44 Unless otherwise cited, facts from the mentioned study of RCCP are from Metis Associates, Inc., *The Resolving Conflict Creatively Program: 1988–89, Summary of Significant Findings* (New York: Metis Associates, Inc., May 1990), 1–13.

45 Marlene DeMorat, Su-Je Cho, Brenda Britsch, William D. Wakefield, Tara Smith, and Cynthia Hudley, "Attributional Biases and Reactive Aggression: Teacher and Student Perceptions of Self-Control" (paper presented at the annual meeting of the American Educational Research Association, Chicago, IL, April 1997), 9.

46 Moses S. Koch, "Resolving Disputes," 16.

47 Priscilla Prutzman, telephone interview.

48 Linda Lantieri with Janet Patti, "Road to Peace," 31.

49 Linda L. Dahlberg, "Making a Difference: Current Efforts to Determine What Works in Preventing Youth Violence" (paper presented at the annual meeting of the American Educational Research Association, Chicago, IL, April 1997), 26.

50 Patrick H. Tolan and Nancy G. Guerra, "What Works in Reducing Adolescent Violence: An Empirical Review of the Field" (paper prepared for The Center for the Study and Prevention of Violence, Institute for Behavioral Sciences, University of Colorado, Boulder, F-888, 1994), 1–94.

51 Wendy J. Vesterdal, Alexander T. Vazsonyi, and Daniel J. Flannery, "A School-Based Violence Intervention Program for Elementary Students: Comparisons by Gender and Grade Level" (paper presented at the annual meeting of the American Educational Research Association, Chicago, IL, April 1997), 9.

52 Patrick H. Tolan and Nancy G. Guerra, "Progress and Prospects in Youth Violence-Prevention Evaluation," *Youth Violence Prevention*, 129.

53 Priscilla Prutzman, telephone interview.

54 Albie M. Davis, "Justice without Judges," 56.

55 Albie M. Davis and Kit Porter, "Dispute Resolution," 121–39.

56 Priscilla Prutzman, telephone interview.

57 Robert Tafoya, telephone interview with author Molly Pont-Brown, tape recording, Stanford, CA, 16 February 1994.

58 Larry Dieringer, telephone interview with author Molly Pont-Brown, tape recording, Stanford, CA, 5 March 1994.

59 *Safe Schools Act of 1993*, 103d Cong., 1st sess., S. 1125.

60 Anne Gibson, telephone interview.

61 Larry Dieringer, telephone interview.

62 Chris Whipple, telephone interview.

63 Dorothy Espelage, Kris Bosworth, Kathryn Karageorge, and Gary Daytner, "Family/Environment and Bullying Behaviors: Interrelationships and Treatment Implications" (paper presented at the annual meeting of the American Psychological Association, Toronto, Canada, August 1996), 8.

64 Catherine S. Morton, Thomas V. Sayger, Arthur M. Horne, and Corinna A. Ethington, "Relationship between Family Environment Factors and the Development of Conduct Disorder in Males Ages 6–11" (paper presented at the annual meeting of the American Educational Research Association, Chicago, IL, April 1997), 1–13.

65 Carolyn A. Smith, Alan J. Lizotte, Terence P. Thornberry, and Marvin D. Krohn, "Resilience to Delinquency," *The Prevention Researcher* 4, no. 2 (Spring 1997): 6.

66 John D. Krumboltz and Christine J. Yeh, "Competitive Grading Sabotages Good Teaching," *Phi Delta Kappan* 78, no. 4 (December 1996): 324–26.

67 Smith et al., "Resilience to Delinquency," 6.

68 Ian M. Harris, "From World Peace to Peace in the 'Hood: Peace Education in a Postmodern World," *Journal for a Just and Caring Education* 2, no. 4 (October 1996): 378–95.

69 Linda Lantieri with Janet Patti, "Road to Peace," 29.

70 Ian M. Harris, "From World Peace to Peace in the 'Hood," 386, 392.

71 Anne Gibson, telephone interview.

Chapter 4

Redefining School Violence in Boulder Valley Colorado

Matthew W. Greene

Violence in U.S. Schools

Every day, some teenagers in the United States attend primary and secondary schools that are plagued by violence, fear, and sometimes even loss of life. Violence is not solely a product of inner-city school systems. Rather, violence has spread to suburban neighborhoods and middle-class areas of many ethnicities. Not only crime itself, but also the perception of a threat to one's safety and well-being, is pervasive in today's society.[1] In 1995, 35 percent of tenth graders reported that they had been threatened or injured at school during the previous year.[2] Adolescents who live in the suburbs and small towns of the United States, while statistically less at risk of becoming victims of violence than those in urban areas, nevertheless may perceive danger in their schools and communities.

The current debate over how to solve the violence problem in U.S. public schools includes discussions about the goals of education, the causes of violence, and the role of the school in solving its own and its neighborhood's problems. There is a clear connection between opinions in these areas and acceptance of various policy prescriptions for the schools. Technological security devices and reliance on strict punishment and deterrence through expulsion are countered by proposals for interdisciplinary programs in peace education and training in peer mediation. Some view the violence problem in U.S. society as a public health issue that requires comprehensive treatment. Many are concerned that such behavioral control mechanisms as metal detectors and searches in schools may create a security state environment that impinges on the real sense of security, safety, and self-respect of students, teachers, and administrators.

Certainly, schools are not disconnected from the society in which they exist. Curing violence in schools will not stop all the violence in the school environment. On the other hand, reducing violence in society as a whole may not solve the problem of violent youths acting aggressively toward one another. There is a contrast between those who may see schools as the victims of societal violence, and those who may see schools as instruments for decreasing societal and school violence.

The national debate is inconclusive in terms of defining the school violence problem and evaluating the merits of various approaches to violence prevention.[3] A solid understanding of how much violence occurs in the schools, and what that violence looks like, is lacking, even though many students, teachers, and parents have expressed their concerns over safety and violence in their schools.[4] It is incumbent upon individual communities to come to an understanding of the school violence issue as it exists in their local context. Communities must assess the extent of their own violence problem, and the efficacy and desirability of various prevention alternatives. Doing so before there is a crisis situation will improve the chances of avoiding further problems. The local debate can be informed by the national discussion, but must come to grips with its own lack of information and understanding about school violence.[5] Based on fifty-four interviews in the Boulder Valley School District with stakeholders involved in the school violence problem, this study arrived at a redefinition of the problem in one local context that is more comprehensive than the current formulation of the debate, and shows that preventative alternatives generally are less conflictual than expulsion policies.

School strategies that address peacebuilding and violence prevention face many practical obstacles that mitigate against their successful adoption, implementation, and continuation in school and community settings. There is considerable disagreement about the desirability and efficacy of such policies as violence prevention and conflict resolution programs, police in the schools, mandatory expulsions for weapons, and metal detection equipment, to name just a few. Often, communication and agreement among stakeholders in the schools, the criminal justice system, and mental health and social service agencies, and among parents, students, and elected officials, are blocked by misperception, turf battles, and deeply held value and belief differences. Comprehensive and collaborative efforts at peacebuilding require understanding among stakeholders about areas of conflict and consensus.

This chapter discusses these areas discovered through interviews with teachers, administrators, students, probation officers, attorneys, judges, social workers, and other stakeholders in the schools and community of Boulder, Colorado. It elaborates on the five major viewpoints exemplified by participants in the study, and draws conclusions about ways to expand consensus in local communities involved in the debate over school violence and discipline based on a redefinition of the school violence problem. It presents the school violence problem as one that deeply affects all adolescents, and connects this contextually based research to the broader concepts of Peace Studies and peace education.

The Importance of Problem Definition

Defining a policy problem is both one of the most difficult and one of the most important tasks in any policy area. Errors in problem definition often lead to eventual policy failures, and often the assumptions made in an initial problem definition set limits on the policy alternatives that will be considered. "The problem definition establishes the universe of discourse for the decision-making process. It determines the options and consequences to be considered and the kinds of information and uncertainty to be taken into account. In many cases, the decision has effectively been made once the definition is set."[6] Thus, it is essential to be explicit about the choices made in problem definition, and to be clear as to what is being included or excluded in the definition chosen. Whether one defines the school violence problem as one of "bad" kids with guns or as one of a social culture of violence will influence the selection of policies to deal with violence.

The policies that local school boards, school administrators, states, and the federal government enact will have a great effect upon schools, adolescents, and society. For the optimal policies to be enacted in each school, district, system, or state, those who make, implement, and witness the effects of school violence policies need to share information, identify areas of potential conflict, and realize that there may be areas of substantial agreement among them. Diverse points of view may be reconciled in terms of shared educational goals and the recognition of the needs of disparate groups in the educational process.

Likewise, policymakers and educators may be able to prevent intense conflict if they can anticipate and prepare for areas of potential conflict.

The Boulder Valley Study

The Boulder Valley School District is not contiguous with any one municipality. Rather, it encompasses a diverse group of separate municipalities that includes Boulder, Broomfield, Lafayette, Louisville, Nederland, and Superior. These communities range from a Colorado mountain town, to more suburban "bedroom" communities, to the small city of Boulder, which has approximately 100,000 inhabitants. Boulder Valley is one of two school districts in Boulder County. The other is the St. Vrain School District. Boulder Valley's is not necessarily the most representative school population in terms of ethnicity, class, income, or social diversity. However, sufficient difference of opinion was found within the district to warrant this study and to provide a sample of perspectives on how to resolve the school violence problem.

The Boulder Valley School District has not seen anywhere near the violence present in some urban schools. The scale of the problem is thus significantly reduced in Boulder Valley. However, this study may be particularly relevant to those communities and smaller school districts on the edge of the urban violence problems that are now facing an increase in school violence and that must come to terms with the destruction of their sense of security. The intent of the study was to identify groups of individuals according to shared viewpoints about school violence, to identify areas of conflict and consensus between these viewpoints, and to arrive at a broader definition of the school violence problem in Boulder Valley. This was done through interviewing a diverse selection of participants on this problem, asking open-ended questions, and attaining their opinions on a broad array of statements about school violence. This definition would provide policymakers and interested parties a better understanding of the local issue. It would hopefully prevent increased conflict over policy solutions, and help guide the community toward a more consensual and effective resolution of this problem.

Actual numbers in terms of school-related offenses and juvenile crime in Boulder Valley are difficult to find, and thus confuse the issue. Boulder County has a justice system that covers two school districts and multiple police forces. Records are kept by numerous agencies and are not gathered centrally. In 1993, when this study was conducted, the central school district office did not seem to keep records on individual school or district-wide violence. Individual schools varied in how and whether they kept records detailing school crimes and violence. Site-based management, schools that did not keep track of incidents or report them to police, and the lack of district-wide data gathered centrally made school district school violence information difficult to locate.

Students have brought weapons to school in Boulder Valley, although there has not been a fatal shooting in school in recent years. The rate of violent crime in Boulder County, which includes the Boulder Valley and St. Vrain districts, dropped 11.1 percent from 1982 to 1992. This figure takes into account a population growth of 3,459 people in that period. Of a total of 2,943 arrests for serious violent and property crimes, 38 percent were juveniles.[7] Some identify intrapersonal violence as a key element of the school violence issue. The teen suicide rate in Colorado for fifteen- to nineteen-year-olds in 1989 was almost double the 1988 national rate. Teen suicide is the second leading cause of death for adolescents next to accidents. In 1992 there were forty-five teen suicides in Colorado, compared with twenty-eight in 1991.[8] One prevention specialist reported in 1993 that 30 percent of all high school students in Colorado were contemplating suicide, that 50 percent of all high school students had carried a weapon to school for protection at least one day in the previous year, and that youth violence had increased 120 percent in two years.[9] The Colorado Department of Education reported a 1989 survey conducted in Colorado, but excluding Denver, that showed that 34 percent of males and 9 percent of females had carried a weapon for self-protection during the previous thirty days. Thirteen percent of the students reported having been in a fight that resulted in treatment from a doctor or nurse. Over 25 percent of tenth graders reported being anxious, worried, or upset nearly all the time.[10]

In Boulder Valley, a nonscientific survey conducted by the City of Boulder's Youth Services department in 1993 found that 75 percent of student respondents, most in middle and high schools, felt "pretty safe" or "very safe" at school. Only 4 percent of the Boulder Youth Services respondents felt "pretty unsafe" or "very unsafe" at school. However, 27 percent agreed or strongly agreed that they had often thought about committing suicide, reflecting the numbers given for the Colorado survey. Thirty-seven percent disagreed that youth needs and concerns were taken seriously in Boulder. Twenty percent noticed unequal treatment of low-income teens in Boulder. Twenty percent also noticed ethnic and racial discrimination against teens. Twenty-five percent normally used alcohol or drugs for entertainment, and over half felt alcohol and drugs were a problem at school.[11]

Total juvenile arrests in 1992 for Boulder, Broomfield, Lafayette, Louisville, and Nederland were 1,603. These included two arrests for rape, forty-nine for felony assault, ninety-four for simple assault, and twenty-three for weapons. In all of Boulder County, total juvenile arrests rose 3.5 percent between 1987 and 1992, while total arrests fell 1.4 percent. By 1992, juveniles were making up a larger proportion of arrests made in Boulder County. Teen arrests in the City of Boulder increased from seventy-nine in 1982 to 139 in 1992. This 43.2 percent increase in teen arrests was almost four times as much as the 11.2 percent population increase during the same period.[12]

Thus, during 1993, juvenile crime overall was increasing in Boulder Valley, as were juvenile offenses involving weapons. In terms of violence in schools, adolescents generally reported feeling safe, yet also reported disturbing incidents and serious mental concerns. Trends and hard data on offenses in schools were hard to determine. The biggest violence problems in Boulder Valley, generally a middle-class, politically progressive area, were perceived to be fighting, school disruptions, and truancy. It is clear that more systematic state, district, and school gathering of information and reporting on school violence trends needs to be undertaken. In lieu of such information, this study addressed the participants' perceptions of the problem and qualitative information. This secondary type of data will be important for policymakers and others confronting violence issues.

The School Violence Problem and Adolescents

Many symbols are utilized in discussions of school violence across the country. These key words and phrases condense the school violence debate and are important politically in terms of the power they have to influence a public with limited time and ability to absorb information.[13] The dominant national definition of the school violence problem focuses on what Ian Harris refers to as "peacekeeping" strategies.[14] To keep students "safe" and "secure" so that they can learn, metal detectors, security guards, locker searches, and closed campuses are discussed as possible solutions in the school violence debate. Expulsion of adolescents who bring weapons to school or who cause trouble has become the primary focus of violence debates around the country. This focus has led legislators, school district administrators, and school officials to argue over the transfer of these students to alternative education programs, due process concerns regarding students' civil liberties and rights to a fair hearing, reintroduction of these students into school, and how to improve "order" and "discipline" for all students in school.[15]

Programs that focus on "peacemaking" skills, such as peer mediation and alternative conflict resolution programs, are increasingly popular today, but receive less attention from policymakers and the public.[16] "Peacebuilding" programs, which represent an even greater sort of problem redefinition, or paradigm shift, are even further removed from the dominant policy mindset in this country, even though they are being successfully implemented in a number of local areas.[17] One of the most salient characteristics of the school violence problem is its complexity, a dearth of information as to the extent of the problem, and a lack of systematic evaluations of various policy approaches.

The debate over the selection of alternatives to solve the school violence problem will become ever more intense if funds become scarcer than they already are. Officials may have to make choices between buying metal detectors and instituting curricular and cultural reforms that teach students to solve conflicts nonviolently. They may have to decide between expelling students into the criminal justice system or an alternative education program and hiring additional counselors to talk to children in school. Program evaluation in particular suffers in an environment of tight budgeting. This overall complexity and uncertainty makes values and perspectives even more important in defining the problem, and makes it even more important that educators and community members try to reach informed consensus about appropriate policies.

Violence affects teenagers in many ways, and one does not have to be a physical victim of violence to experience the trauma associated with teasing, racial slurs, bullying, fighting, rape, or shooting. Witnesses and members of the school community will continue to feel the impact of violence long after it has occurred. Teenagers living with the fear of violence may be distracted and prevented from learning, interacting socially at school, and even attending school regularly. If policymakers are to discover and implement positive and successful strategies to reduce school violence, they must understand violence issues from the perspective of those directly involved in and at risk of victimization. Adolescent voices must be included in the debate over what to do about school and youth violence.

Viewpoints on School Violence

Five common viewpoints on school violence emerged in Boulder Valley.[18] These positions represent variations along several lines.[19] These groups were labeled the preventionists, the antiexpulsion preventionists, the expulsion preventionists, the traditional educators, and the conventionalists.

Preventionists

> We need to put more resources into what we can do preventatively when we see a kid falling apart. We're not doing enough. There are not enough resources. Even 10–20 years ago, there was more focus on prevention and early intervention. Now, there is a more crisis response, post hoc-oriented approach.[20]

The preventionists represented a proactive educational viewpoint. Its members generally posited an "empowerment" stance for education. Students should be taught to solve their own problems, and should be given the skills necessary to resolve conflicts without violence. In this view, students joined gangs and committed violent acts because something was lacking in their lives, such as acceptance, and effective strategies to prevent violence would include targeting the family and peer social factors. The preventionists supported almost any educational strategy that involved training kids to solve problems and to deal with each other and society. Overall, the group favored education over punishment in decreasing violent crime. This view accepted most of the prevention strategies that educators are currently discussing: peer mediation, conflict resolution training, and violence prevention curricula.[21]

Antiexpulsion Preventionists

> We need alternatives to expulsion. Kids are not old enough for a job, so they can't get those. The school will provide no alternative program to school violence. There is a lot more to diagnosing a problem and treating it that we need to be doing. Every school violence case I get can be treated. Kids get

labeled, stigmatized. The only case that can't be treated is when the family can't be treated. I know schools have limited resources and must prioritize, but they must pay attention to one kid. They have an obligation to educate all kids. It is a major problem to cast out a kid and give up.

The antiexpulsion preventionists were similar to the preventionists in terms of their preventionist viewpoint and focus on student training and empowerment. However, the antiexpulsion preventionists were more firmly antiexpulsionist and pointed more to the broader social factors involved in promoting violence. This group was also more concerned about the effects of school violence on the education process itself. The antiexpulsion preventionists were even more supportive of peer mediation programs, educational strategies, teaching of interpersonal skills in schools, training youths to defuse confrontations, encouraging trust and friendship in schools, implementing conflict resolution programs, and empowering students through education, than were the preventionists. However, the antiexpulsion preventionists opposed the most strongly of any viewpoint the use of deterrence and control strategies, such as expulsion, to prevent violence and keep weapons out of the school. This viewpoint was even more indicative of a Peace Studies and peacebuilding approach to school violence.

Expulsion Preventionists

There should be a comprehensive approach. We do need alternatives, too. I can go along with a zero-tolerance policy and expulsion for kids with weapons in school. But we need services for the kids who are out. Alternative education needs to be received along the way, starting with junior high.

The expulsion preventionists combined some of the preventative measures advocated by the preventionists with a strong punitive element that included expulsion. They felt that schools should be doing more to train students, but that they should take care of immediate violence problems by removing troublemakers from schools. In addition to this call for an additional role on the part of the school, there was a feeling that schools did not get enough money and were facing significant financial difficulties. Advocacy of both expulsion and educational training was a key characteristic of this group. The alternatives to expulsion that expulsion preventionists advocated included peer mediation, teaching interpersonal skills, and an overall focus on empowerment through constructive nonviolent conflict management. This group showed acceptance of peacekeeping, peacemaking, and peacebuilding strategies. Moreover, it was particularly representative of the perspective that schools needed to be made safe through some initially tough policies before more constructive approaches could be put into place.

Traditional Educators

> Teaching kids to control anger, and to work out problems, will reach some, but there will always be some who skip it, or go home to a lot of crap. Kids are shooting at each other with no provocation. That we can see. If we sit back, and close the doors, and don't say "no" to kids, it will be dangerous for us all. If you say "no," other kids are empowered, and schools are still safe. School violence is where you see a disregard for others, a lack of respect for authority. I know it sounds old-fashioned, but no respect for rules or authority leads to a lack of respect for anyone.

The traditional educators combined a strong pro-expulsion stance with a lack of support for specific violence prevention education programs or actions. While there was agreement with broad goals of teaching social skills and social values, and with taking a comprehensive approach to violence, there was not acceptance of student responsibility for solving problems. Money was somewhat of an issue for this group. The traditional educators took a "disciplinary" and punitive approach to the violence problem in Boulder Valley. They strongly believed in expulsion as a behavior modification technique, and as a deterrent for future gun possession in school. This group's agreement with the need of administrators to protect the safety of the majority of the students, rather than the interests of individual disruptive students, exemplified the reasoning behind their expulsion sentiment. The traditional educators represented a more traditionally conservative viewpoint, in which families were responsible for some violence by not spending enough time with their kids, and in which schools could continue their mission of teaching a standard curriculum and imparting social skills and values throughout the school climate and not through specific classes. The traditional educators represented more of a peacekeeping orientation, and the "conservative" values that they advocated were based on traditional educational approaches.[22]

Conventionalists

> A lot of schools have alternative programs. But you can't isolate kids and expect them to function in society. Our problems aren't kids as much as parents, or lack of parenting. I spend so little time with things I want to teach, dealing with all the other issues.

The conventionalists held a more traditional educational viewpoint, but were not convinced of the merits of expulsion. In their view, local violence was a problem, but it could be handled within the school, where the school focused on teaching the basic curriculum and creating a strong disciplinary structure. In the long term, societal violence would decrease through the gradual reduction of inequalities. For the present, no new programs were needed in the schools. Schools were doing enough, and though they should teach values, this should be done in the context of general subject instruction. This group did not favor punitive measures, but held that the lack of a strong school disciplinary structure contributed to student violence.

Understanding the Sources of Conflict and Consensus

The major points of conflict in Boulder Valley were centered on specific policy alternatives. Broad agreement surrounded trends in violence, forecasts for the future, and general goals. Bringing these points of agreement into a debate on school violence would help to alleviate conflict. Avoiding a stalemate on disagreeable alternatives requires recognizing these points of contention and introducing more amenable alternatives into the decision process. Overall, there was consensus that schools should be safe places and that students should be empowered to solve conflicts without violence. These two goals provide ample opportunity for moving a debate away from expulsion and toward discussion of alternative ways to achieve these goals. Many of the preventative approaches address both goals specifically. The Boulder Valley study illustrated a number of other characteristics of the school violence debate.

What is Violence? A Definitional Issue

> Violence is bringing any kind of weapon to school, whether they use it or not. It would involve any kind of physical altercation or threat thereof. It's a continuum, and would include verbal abuse, racial slurs, sexual harassment. From bringing a gun to school and using it on one end of the spectrum to a racial slur on the other.

One of the biggest issues involved in preventing violence is deciding what constitutes violence. Some include only intentional physical harm against a student in school. Others include verbal threats, or things that make people feel uncomfortable. Some see violence in school as no different from violence in society, and define school violence as any violence involving school-age kids. While it may not be possible to arrive at complete consensus on an exact definition of school violence, it is possible to establish a continuum of violence from lesser to more extreme types. These types might then invoke a hierarchy of responses, depending on the severity of the offense. Defining violence must be an interim goal essential for the prevention of future violence.

The concept of a continuum, or scale, was brought up numerous times in interviews. Where the continuum begins is the subject of debate. Where it ends is generally agreed upon. On the extreme end of the scale we can reliably put serious physical harm, such as someone getting shot. On the other end we have a group that comprises racial slurs, verbal harassment, emotional and mental violence, sexual harassment, or "anything that makes another person feel uncomfortable." Then there are "degrees of violence" which include pushing and shoving, slapping, fistfights, and on to rape and suicide.

One administrator grappled with the question of where violence begins in these terms: "When one individual makes a choice that infringes on the rights of another. Verbal, physical violence. And a mental level. An elementary level. You don't need blood spilled or bruises. Children are capable of a form of violence mentally, such as head games. That can really damage the self-esteem of people." And a teacher stated that "school violence is probably no different than violence period. Any person inflicting verbal or bodily harm with malice is violence. A continuum from verbal assault to the use of a weapon. not a separate definition for school violence from violence within the family, community. It inflicts some kind of harm, is done knowingly." These definitions all accept a continuum that begins with verbal or mental violence, and is not confined to the school. On the other hand, a police officer insisted that: "It's physical. Anywhere from slapping in the face to a coma. There are degrees." A law specialist put it this way: "An out of control physical act that borders on danger. Pushing around, etc., doesn't count. That is just growing up. Where control factors are not present, the teachers don't know what to do. Aggressive behavior that's out of control and borders on danger."

Violence: An Increase in Intensity

Once violence has been defined, the question becomes "Has violence increased?" Statistics are often in short supply, although fortunately some states and districts are moving toward mandatory and comparable incident reporting systems. Beyond these statistics, however, are the qualitative comments of adolescents and those with whom they interact. Many interviewees said that the number of violent incidents overall may not have increased, but that the intensity or degree of each violent act was more severe than in the past, and that they were seeing many more weapons. Weapons had the potential, they said, to make the violence much worse. From a probation officer:

> What I think is happening, is that although there's not more violence, the level of violence has changed. A normal fight turns into serious injury, violence. The degree or intensity of each act is up. They involve weapons, or continuing when the person is down. Kids don't understand death or consequences—bullet or knife damage.

The lack of consequences of violence as shown on television and in the movies was the most important factor identified as desensitizing kids to violence. A prosecutor said: "We're seeing more of violence where the object is more to hurt someone for the sake of hurting. Also, more weapons and guns. That's the type of violence that's increasing." This is a qualitative shift in the type of violence occurring that is difficult to measure statistically or systematically.

Overall in Boulder Valley, there were many accusations of an "ostrich routine," in which school authorities were sticking their heads in the sand and denying that a violence problem existed. One school administrator said, "I want to discuss and admit that there's a problem. We have violence and weapons and we need to deal with it. Until that, what is there to discuss?" People were aggravated that some took an attitude of "it can't happen here," or "that's an inner-city, minority problem." Some portrayed fighting as an everyday, normal experience. Others mentioned drive-by shootings and violence that had gone unreported by the press. One former student claimed that:

> A lot of school violence is taken into the community from the schools. It's harder to get in trouble in the community. It happens the other way too. You know where you can find someone in school. Fighting and violence is a problem in Boulder. It has gotten worse, and is going to get worse. Gangs are starting to move out here and stuff. It's not that big now, but it's a lot bigger than two years ago.

The perception that violence was worse in Boulder Valley was not universal, however. One student said that violence "is not really growing. It's almost decreasing now. You rarely see fighting here. It's not a common thing." He spoke of kids maturing and deciding not to fight. But he also spoke of the peer pressure from teens to fight to impress the opposite sex, or pressure to be macho and not to back down. And he described a twenty-person fight at Boulder High that lasted fifteen minutes and in which someone was stabbed.

Information Sharing and Confidentiality: Help or Hindrance

> People don't realize what the facts are, what's going on out there. The baseline problem is that we don't understand the magnitude.

There was a significant lack of information in Boulder Valley about the extent of the violence problem in schools, what programs were in place to help kids and families, and what agencies were doing in relation to violence. There were also difficulties among agencies in terms of sharing information about kids and in cooperating with one another. Confidentiality rules and turf problems, respectively, were blamed for these problems.

A law specialist had problems with confidentiality being dismissed too easily: "Confidentiality is seen as an obstacle, not as an important protection." Designed to protect kids, confidentiality rules do not allow mental health, or social services, or schools, or doctors, or lawyers, or criminal justice agencies to share information about a child easily, if at all. While this protects the child from discrimination and other labeling problems, it inhibits successful cooperation and coordination between agencies and people who are all serving the same child. The Serious Habitual Offender Directed Intervention Program (SHODI) is one collaborative program in Boulder County that tries to improve services by sharing information. Parents are required to waive confidentiality in this case so that the sharing can occur.[23] Again, there are legal issues involved that should be addressed in terms of whether it is in the adolescent's long-term interest to waive confidentiality in order to get better treatment. As an educator put it, "Do people understand the full consequences of this?" One teacher brought up how confidentiality affected her in school:

> One of my biggest issues is that every time there is a report of a gun in school over the past eight years, it comes to me through the grapevine. I won't know who the kid is. I'm the type to step in the hall and say break it up, and chew them out. If I knew a kid had a weapon, I'd talk differently, be more careful. I'd just as soon come home to my kids every day. I don't want to not know if

the kid's had a gun because of his personal constitutional rights. You forfeit a lot of rights when you bring a weapon to school.

Turf issues, accentuated by budgetary constraints, was the other major inhibitor of interagency cooperation identified by respondents. As a social worker said: "Due to a lack of resources, we're having more difficulty cooperating. I hope it won't get worse, but it could. In the long run it saves money if we work together. Some resources don't overlap. But organizations protect turf and budgets. They pull back, protect themselves. It's getting harder to cooperate."

In the information sharing context, some people identified the district's open enrollment policy, which allows students to transfer to any school in the district, as a contributor to some school administrators' desire not to have statistics or information about violence in their school publicly addressed. One teacher said: "Public image in the district is the biggest thing. With open enrollment, kids can choose their school. Administrators are concerned with PR, not issues." At the school level, some administrators did not want to see violence reported, and disliked the way they perceived the media focusing on the negative events in school, not the positive. "Sometimes I'm discouraged about the amount of press that violence gets," said one administrator.

There were serious concerns among minorities in Boulder Valley about racial discrimination, particularly on the part of the police force and school officials, and a general lack of attention to minority interests. One business person stated: "I've been trying to deal with schools on why children of color in schools are manhandled. There seems to be more aggression against them. People have shared stories with me. My concern is primarily with violence against children of color in schools." A health worker said: "It's very important to me that the issue of institutionalized racism is dealt with." A community worker stated that "One of the biggest problems in the school system is not lack of programs or money, but is a lack of sensitivity from administrators and teachers, a lack of understanding, and the treatment of multicultural students especially."

A comprehensive approach to violence prevention was recognized by many as the best way to treat troubled children. Early intervention, a general balancing of empathy and structure, and sensitivity to different cultures were all seen as ways to better serve students. Interagency cooperation with an overall coordination of resources was perceived as more effective and more efficient in delivering services. Nevertheless, issues of constitutional rights need to be explicit and discussed with teenagers, parents, and teachers.

Family Versus School Responsibility

Is the family or the school primarily to blame for violence? The focus of the family/school debate in Boulder Valley was on who was responsible for instilling values in children, teaching children social skills and discipline, and preparing kids to function in society without hurting other human beings. "There needs to be more community involvement, more school/parent involvement, more partnership with society as opposed to school/parent blame. The community is responsible for raising children." There were three types of views that defined the school violence problem in this way.

One view held that schools were absolutely not responsible for doing a job that should be done by the parents of a child. This view blamed the lack of a family structure, poor parenting skills, a lack of early discipline growing up, and a dysfunctional family for a child's violent outbursts and problems. A police officer stated that violence was caused by "the breakdown of the family . . . one parent families, parents who copped out in the sixties, and give their kids no guidance, respect, moral values, nothing. . . . Schools cannot teach respect. The parents must. It's a social problem." A prosecutor put it this way: "Family. It boils down to this. The overwhelming number of cases comes from screwed-up families. The court system and school system are poor substitutes for effective parenting." One teacher said:

> Our problems aren't kids as much as parents, or lack of parenting. I really sometimes think we should have parenting school, not kid school. . . . Many parents are irate if they're disturbed at work. The philosophy was for years and years, that if there were trouble in school, then there would be double trouble at home. Parents were much more supportive of teachers. There was a lot of respect. I've been called every name in the book, mostly from parents. There's absolutely no confidence or support. Parents call and say, 'Where are my kids this week?' I'm startled, concerned, amazed. How can people have all these kids and value them so little?

The second view on school and family responsibility pointed to a lack of parenting as a major cause of youth violence, and put some of the blame for today's problems on the modeling of violence in the home and a lack of family structure, parental attention, and values and skills instilled by the family. But this group arrived at the conclusion that if parents were not doing their jobs, then the schools should. In this case, the school could be an active player in decreasing violence by teaching conflict resolution, interpersonal relations, and other social skills-oriented topics. A special education teacher said:

> The most important piece is what's going on in the families, how the family affects school. Problems come out in school, but they're not necessarily because of school. Whose responsibility is it to fix it? Schools? Get to families? Ideally, it is not schools, but practically it may be. It was not necessarily the original intent of schools to raise children. We used to have more education stuff at home. Now, there is no base from home when kids get to school. Schools may have to end up doing the job of parenting.

A judge asked and responded, "To what extent should the schools be teaching morality, values? It should be taught in the home, but there are many incompetent parents. It's not an ideal situation, but we must face the fact that many parents are consumed with their own problems. Parents are not enough for kids."

A third line of thought about school versus parent responsibility placed less emphasis on the inability of parents and more emphasis on the ability of schools to do something about violence. This view tended to express the need for conflict resolution skills and violence education for the population in general. This training and information was necessary and good in and of itself, and could only be taught by the school. "We need peer mediation, conflict resolution," said one attorney. "It's beyond me why we're not teaching it from preschool on up. Everyone needs it in this country—families, husbands, wives." Some indicated the success of programs already in place in some schools:

> Counselors, peer counselors, are taking care of some of the steam. Conflict resolution is good decision-making here 10–15 years ago. Some felt it was a personal skill needed through life. We may be seeing less violence because of it. Affective learning skills may be paying off. Boulder has been good on some of the preventative measures. I've seen it pay off. It has worked here.... Modeling of conflict resolution stuff should become second nature.

The question of family versus school responsibility, then, was a strong undercurrent in people's thinking about violence. Relating these conceptions of school/parent responsibility to the five general viewpoints identified in the study, the three preventionist viewpoints tended to favor a strong school role in preventing violence by teaching kids how to deal with conflict. There was not, however, a clear connection between each viewpoint and whether they perceived the school role as ideal or purely a necessary evil. The conventionalists and traditional educators were likely to put more blame and responsibility on parents, but this was not always the case. The middle ground here is the sentiment that the school may not be the ideal place to parent, but that it may be the necessary alternative.

Expulsion: The Dominant Dichotomy

Expulsion was the dominant topic of discussion in terms of the school violence issue. School violence was a less prevalent public debate in Boulder Valley than were such issues as overcrowding, school finances, bond issues, and year-round schools. However, when violence was discussed, the subject often turned to what to do about weapons in schools, whether students who carried weapons should be expelled, and associated issues resulting from expulsion and suspension.[24]

A new state law was put into effect in 1993, and significantly amended in 1996, that, among other things, allows schools to expel students for a calendar year, not just for the remaining part of the current school year. This means someone who is expelled in May cannot automatically return in September. Also, districts have the right to refuse to readmit an expelled student, although by law students must be in school until the age of sixteen. In Colorado in 1995-96, middle/junior high and senior high school expulsions accounted for almost 95 percent of all expulsions.[25] The question is, where do adolescents go who are expelled from school? A bill proposing the creation of alternative education programs for disruptive students was finally passed in 1996. There was little support for this idea among the groups identified in Boulder Valley.

One social worker described the whole issue of suspension and expulsion: "This is a joke. It doesn't do anything. It gets the kids out of school, puts them on the street, alienates them, and gives them an excuse to learn more tricks. At the bottom of this is some kind of rage that needs to be addressed." There were calls for counseling, treatment, education, and structure once kids were expelled, although many of those expressing these ideas were against expulsion in the first place. They felt that the adolescents should be in the schools, not tracked into a "disruptive" program, and that expulsion neither changed behavior nor deterred other kids from causing trouble. A major argument against expulsion and suspension consisted of these objections to a lack of educational and treatment programs once teenagers were expelled.

"Scaring kids does not have a long-term impact on behavior," said one administrator. "Try and fire me if you want to," said another. "I will work with each individual kid, family, and family services. I won't expel, even though the community may want it." One mediator said: "Suspension and expulsion are absolutely counterproductive and ridiculous. Too many at-risk kids see it as an enforced vacation or a counter-motivation. They are not allowed to make up work. We are saying that 'we are punishing you by forcing you to fail.' They should be made to double their work." This idea of kids desiring to get expelled or suspended was echoed by others. As a response, some brought up enforced school or community activities for teens who got into trouble. Others mentioned in-school suspension or other alternative programs within the school.

Opposing the antiexpulsion stance was a viewpoint with two general characteristics. One was a focus on the safety of the majority. The other was a belief in a strong disciplinary stance and "sending a message." These two reasons were not necessarily independent of one another, and often a person who believed in expulsion expressed both ideas. Some of those who believed in expulsion also called for alternative programs and structure once the adolescents were removed from school.

One administrator put it very clearly:

> I know there's a big concern about expulsion. People are asking, where do they go? But as a school, we must get them out. Then it's the parent's problem, not ours. Maybe they'll take more of a role. My concern is for the safety of the school environment. . . . We have expulsion, zero tolerance at [our school] for weapons. We tried to get the District to go for it. We found a loaded gun, knives, brass knuckles. After a really strong action, with the police, weapons left the school. I'm not saying that they're not going to come back. But you must take a zero-tolerance policy. I heard of at least five other guns in school on the day we took the pistol. I feel we've protected the safety of our students. We've checked cars and lockers if we've gotten a tip. We've made it obvious that they weren't going to be there after school.

This statement shows both belief in the efficacy of expulsion and an expressed desire to protect the safety of the majority in school.[26] "The bottom line is safety," said another administrator. "We will have it every time at the expense of the individual." A social worker expressed it this way, joining prevention and expulsion:

> You may need to get the horse back in the barn before you begin the training. . . . I'm a believer in that if a kid has a gun in school, he's out of there. For

how long? I don't know, you must work it out. Immediate, no-questions-asked, mandatory expulsion. Parents absolutely have to be part of the process in terms of getting the kid back in. Therapy for students and parents must happen outside of school. Expulsion for other weapons? I'm unsure. A twelve-inch blade? Probably expulsion. A pocket knife? Probably just as dangerous, but I'm unsure. If you're at a crisis point, you set absolute guidelines and follow them absolutely until the behavior is under control. If you need to, throw kids out for anything weaponish, maybe for a while. Individual schools may need different approaches and rules.

Here we see the belief in the necessity of being firm with kids and setting limits. We also see this idea joined with a call for therapy for both child and family to address the underlying causes of the problem. This is another possible middle ground in terms of expulsion and the school violence issue as a whole.

Expulsion and Violence Prevention: Whose Domain?

Policy issues need to reside with the school board. Certain things are relegated to site-based management. Things that cut across all schools need to have some consistency. We have allowed some variance in some areas, such as attendance. In terms of major policy implications, to ensure a degree of equity, those have to be put with the board. Legal responsibility for policy is at the board level. As long as our policies have had broad enough parameters, schools can work within them. Parameters are consistent with each school. We give serious consideration about delegating a policy role to the school. For example, with weapons, we're not going to. The board maintains a consistent policy. Clearly the responsibility lies with the board. Some things we can delegate, and some things need to be consistent. I'm not sure what they all are, but when we're asked that question, we decide those.

One school board member thus raised a central question. In whose domain should responsibility for making school violence policy reside? Secondarily, what should those policies be? Mandatory expulsion? Mandatory peace education? Mandatory violence prevention curriculum? Mandatory peer counseling?

The recent implementation of site-based management in Boulder Valley raised a number of quandaries, one of which was the balance between central administrative and individual school responsibility for making policy. Throughout the survey discussions, there was wide support for the general concept of site-based management, and a decentralized, grass roots, inclusive approach to policymaking. Yet there were also calls for a certain amount of consistency and guidance from the central administration, within which individual schools would have some flexibility. The question before school districts and states is not only whether they should have "tough" weapons expulsion policies, or should allow schools to consider expulsions on their own. They need also to consider whether the more educational, preventative aspects aimed at school violence should be left to the schools to implement on their own, or should be structured and mandated in some form at higher levels.

A Comprehensive Problem, Requiring Comprehensive Action

> There needs to be a united front on how to treat a kid. Band-Aids won't solve the problem. We need a systems approach.

School violence, and violence among youth in general, was viewed by most participants as a problem with multiple causes that must all be addressed.[27] Some key aspects of the solutions to the problem came from a psychiatric, counseling, or therapeutic standpoint and were particularly espoused by the preventionists and the antiexpulsion preventionists in the Boulder Valley sample. Television and media exposure to violence, alcohol use in the family and by the student, the large size of schools and classes, and access to guns were among the causes of school violence that were mentioned. Early intervention, family counseling, modeling of skills, balancing empathy and structure, conflict resolution training, violence prevention education, and multi-cultural awareness and sensitivity were among the solutions. The fact that there is no one answer was emphasized.

It is clear that no single agency or institution can solve all of these problems. Interagency cooperation then becomes essential. Boulder Valley has two Family Resource Schools that started as pilot programs, and which some supported for their work involving parents, schools, the community, mental health and social services, and students to solve problems. These kinds of programs are expensive, but are potentially effective.

Early identification and intervention for troubled and behaviorally disordered youth was strongly supported, and some questioned the ability of high school programs to make changes. "It's like trying to close the barn door after the animals are out by trying to see what we can do in high school," said one prosecutor. One administrator bemoaned the lack of elementary school counseling and treatment:

> We are losing out so much by not having counseling at the early years. Kids have so much earlier life experience than later. I want early-on counseling, to harness energy, and clear up anger. To head off patterns, at the ground level of developmental stages, for stronger self-esteem, more positive imaging, and more self-worth. We're financially constrained, so we have counselors only at the middle school level. How many individuals can one person handle? What's the ratio of counselors to kids? It concerns me.

Boulder Valley has some limited day treatment programs in the schools, which provide some of the intensive attention required by adolescents who have behavioral problems and their families. Boulder Valley has "interventionists" who work with kids in schools, and has some other collaborative programs, but these may not be sufficient. Some are only available for those who qualify for mental health and social services; some teenagers who need these programs may not be getting them. One therapist referred to a "reactive versus a proactive situation," whereby intervention only occurs when there is an extreme situation. In addition to the general problem of dealing with these children, some interviewees spoke of a disturbing trend among today's elementary school children. They mentioned more problems occurring at a younger age, and children coming to school who were unable to function socially and had a serious lack of discipline and parenting. Some referred to these younger children's exposure to societal and familial violence and lack of support as "baggage."

A good description of the comprehensive, early intervention approach was offered by someone who works with abused children:

> We need close communication between schools, protective services, courts, parents, etc. This has to happen early on, when delinquency occurs. There needs to be attention to restitution from the very beginning, as well as specific plans for individuals who are doing the targeting appropriate to the level of harm committed and chronicity in terms of therapy and counseling, and enrollment in activities which reward them for participation. We need quite often to get police, parents, and social services to help run these activities. There is still a long way to go to get to a planned concerted effort, joining public and private entities. Get rid of corporal punishment. Have 'management of problems' training. Bring in outside help. How to engage parents is crucial. Maybe when kids have difficulties, there is some way to engage, maybe require, the involvement of parents. What no one will say, is that much of the problem must be addressed before kids even get to school. Early child rearing, and focus on abuse, the quality of the relationship between adults and children. Preschool socialization of children must be emphasized. Emotional and social preparation is important. Readiness for school. We all must begin to address this, and get more systematic in thinking about child rearing before kids get to school.

A continual message that came particularly from those involved in the medical and counseling fields was the need for a balance between empathy and structure. In other words, discipline needs to be tempered with caring. One child psychiatrist spoke of society being "more clear about limits and what their structure is." A social worker stated that "a healthy administrator, teacher, parent, or cop, any adult, must balance empathy and structure. Very few can or do do it." This correlates with the idea of modeling nonviolent behavior in society overall, so that kids will learn to function themselves. A special education teacher said: "You need many parts on the same page. With the family, with the kid, with the doctor. Parents must hold up their end. Take a small model into the school. Tight structure and empathetic support."

Conclusions

This chapter has identified five viewpoints regarding the school violence issue. Two are oriented toward prevention, one toward both prevention and expulsion, one toward expulsion and traditional educational values, and the other toward neither prevention nor expulsion. These viewpoints and the specific elements of the debate in Boulder Valley may serve to inform discussions of school violence among students, teachers, policymakers, and community members in other areas. There is a substantial middle ground in the debate surrounding methods of prevention and conflict skills training. Expulsion is a conflictual element, but there is a chance for reconciliation if due process is emphasized and alternative programs and treatment are provided.

Districts, schools, and communities would do well to begin refocusing the school violence debate around prevention issues, publicizing the preventative programs they might currently have in place, creating positive opportunities for adolescents to become involved in addressing violence prevention, and playing a more active role in experimenting with and assessing these types of programs. Policymakers can take into account the areas of conflict and consensus identified here in order to facilitate policy formulation and promotion. That preventative and educational alternatives "work better" than punitive options has not been established, but it is possible to say that the former solutions were more supported by the participants in this study.

The redefinition of the school violence problem moves the debate away from the particular, *post facto* punishment of expulsion, and toward the multifaceted, underpublicized forum of prevention. This chapter has identified much consensus about comprehensive prevention and intervention among professionals and community members. If educators moved these aspects to the front of the debate, the problem would be redefined. From "What do we do with adolescents who carry weapons and disrupt school?" the question would become "What can we do to prevent adolescents from fighting and bringing weapons to the school in the first place?"

This redefinition of the problem along systemic, comprehensive, and preventative lines opens up a realm of possible policy actions and valuable discussions about parental involvement, nonviolent conflict resolution, and modeling of disciplined, empathetic behavior. It allows for the introduction of peace education strategies, with explicit discussions of values, culture, and systems of violence that affect children and communities in many different ways. Shifting to a peacebuilding model requires a real paradigm shift in the sense of a different, and more comprehensive, definition of the school violence problem than currently dominates the media and policy landscape. Understanding viewpoints about the problem and areas of conflict and consensus between them may help to accomplish such a shift.

Notes

1 See, for example, Jackson Toby "Violence in School" (Washington, DC: National Institute of Justice, December 1983); and n.a., *The Los Angeles Times* (26 June 1992), p. A1. This article about crime in Omaha describes the "crime fear/crime risk" paradox: "Although the crime problem is most acute in the inner city, fear of crime is far greater in other parts of the Omaha metropolitan area, where crime is rare to nonexistent..."

2 This is a reduction from 40 percent in 1991 as reported by the same survey. National Education Goals Panel, "The National Education Goals Report: Building a Nation of Learners" (Washington, DC: Author, 1996) 58.

3 Julie Lam, "Evaluating the Program" (unpublished draft chapter on evaluating mediation programs Amherst, MA: National Association for Mediation in Education, 1992); and Patrick Tolan and Nancy Guerra, "What Works in Reducing Adolescent Violence: An Empirical Review of the Field," No. F–888. (Boulder, CO: Center for the Study and Prevention of Violence, July 1994).

4 Louis Harris, "Metropolitan Life Survey of the American Teacher, 1993: Violence in America's Public Schools" (New York: Louis Harris and Associates, Inc., 1993); Louis Harris, "Metropolitan Life Survey of the American Teacher, 1994, Violence in America's Public Schools: The Family Perspective" (New York: Louis Harris and Associates, Inc., 1994); Gale M. Morrison, Michael J. Furlong, and Richard L. Morrison, "School Violence to School Safety: Reframing the Issue for School Psychologists," *School Psychology Review* 23 no. 2 (1994): 236–56; William J. Reese, "Reefer Madness and A Clockwork Orange," in *Learning from the Past: What History Teaches Us about School Reform*, ed. Diane Ravitch and Maris A. Vinovskis (Baltimore, MD: The Johns Hopkins University Press, 1995) 355–81; and Albert J. Reiss Jr. and Jeffrey A. Roth, eds., *Understanding and Preventing Violence* (Washington, DC: National Academy Press, 1993).

5 American School Health Association, the Association for the Advancement of Health Education, and the Society for Public Health Education, "National Adolescent Student Health Survey," *Health Education* 19 (August/September 1988): 6. This survey indicates that many adolescents knew little about violence statistics and which kinds of violence were most prevalent.

6 Baruch Fischhoff, Sarah Lichtenstein, Paul Slovic, Stephen L. Derby, and Ralph L. Keeney, *Acceptable Risk*, New York: Cambridge University Press, 1981, 9. See also Ronald D. Bunner, "Global Climate Change: Defining the Policy Problem," *Policy Sciences* 24 (1991): 291–311; and David A. Rochefort and Roger W. Cobb, eds., *The Politics of Problem Definition: Shaping the Policy Agenda* (Lawrence, KA: University Press of Kansas, 1994).

7 n.a. *Boulder Daily Camera* (12 May 1993).

8   n.a. *The Denver Post* (5 May 1993).

9   The Colorado Crisis Center, "Building Safe Communities" (Denver, CO: Author, 1993).

10 Colorado Department of Education, "A Status Report on Colorado Youth: Trends and Implications" (Denver: Author, August 1992). Note that Denver accounted for some 44 percent of the state's homicides in 1992 [*Boulder Daily Camera* (12 May 1993)]. Thus excluding Denver from the above figure for weapons possession is significant.

11 City of Boulder Youth Initiative, Boulder Youth Services, Boulder, CO, 1992-93.

12 n.a. *Boulder Daily Camera* (16 May 1993), from Colorado Bureau of Investigation Annual Report and Boulder Police Department.

13 Herbert A. Simon, *Reason in Human Affairs* Stanford: Stanford University Press, 1983). See also Ronald D. Brunner, "Key Political Symbols: The Dissociation Process," *Policy Sciences* 20 (1987): 53-76; Murray, Edelman, *Political Language: Words that Succeed and Policies that Fail* (New York: Academic Press, 1977), and Walter Lippman, "The World Outside and the Pictures in Our Heads," in *Public Opinion* (New York: The Free Press, 1965).

14 Ian M. Harris, "From World Peace to Peace in the 'Hood: Peace Education in a Postmodern World," *Journal for a Just and Caring Education* 2, no. 4, (October 1996): 378-95, 383-84.

15 See Jackson Toby, "The Schools," in *Crime*, ed. James Q. Wilson and Joan Petersilia (San Francisco: ICS Press, 1995) 141-70.

16 National School Boards Association, *Violence in the Schools: How America's School Boards Are Safeguarding Our Children* (Alexandria, VA: Author, 1993).

17 See Ian M. Harris, "From World Peace to Peace in the 'Hood", and Peter Hall. "Policy Paradigms, Social Learning, and the State: The Case of Economic Policymaking in Britain," *Comparative Politics* 25 (April 1993): 275-96.

18 Viewpoints were identified through the use of the Q-sort survey and the Cluster Analysis statistical methodology. From April through July 1993, a set of fifty-two school violence opinion statements were administered to fifty-four respondents. Participants arranged the cards on which individual statements were printed along a -5 to +5 disagree to agree scale. Open-ended follow-up questions were asked, scores were noted, and responses were later clustered into viewpoints. See Stephen R. Brown, *Political Subjectivity: Applications of Q Methodology in Political Science* (New Haven: Yale University Press, 1980); Maurice Lorr, *Cluster Analysis for Social Scientists* (San Francisco: Jossey-Bass, 1987). Q-sort statements were organized according to Lasswell's "problem orientation" categories: goals, trends, conditions, projections, alter-

natives. See Harold D. Lasswell, *A Pre-View of Policy Sciences* (New York: Elsevier, 1971). For a discussion on the use of the kind of data produced by clustering "viewpoints", see Ronald D. Brunner, J. Samuel Fitch, Janet Grassia, Lyn Kathlene, and Kenneth R. Hammond, "Improving Data Utilization: The Case-Wise Alternative," *Policy Sciences* 20 (1987): 365-94.

19 Occupation, age, gender, and ethnic background did not appear to have any significant bearing on viewpoint membership. The various viewpoints each included teachers and students, mediators and police officers, politicians and administrators, parents and attorneys, social workers and principals in a seemingly nondeterminate mix. Thus a debate that is structured to oppose such groups as teachers and parents mistakenly dichotomizes the dialogue. There was a lack of communication and shared information among such groups as criminal justice workers and school workers, and this gap should be addressed. Ethnicity, gender, and age were also poor indicators of viewpoints in this study. In some cases, students grouped together with administrators. Minority viewpoints tended to hold certain claims of racial bias in common, but did not fall into the same general viewpoints due to differing specific opinions on school violence. Men and women tended to be rather spread out in the perspectives. Thus, it is possible, at least in this sample, to deconstruct some of the more familiar and common stereotypes based on occupation, age, or race, and to replace them with more accurate viewpoint descriptions based on shared opinions on school violence. Because the purpose of this study was not such generalizations, and due to the nonrandom sampling involved in the selection of participants, one cannot make claims that this lack of correlation would be true in the overall Boulder Valley population or in other school districts.

20 Quotes from Boulder Valley interviews are used anonymously through the text.

21 See Linda Rennie Forcey, "Peace Studies," in *Protest, Power, and Change: An Encyclopedia of Nonviolent Action from ACT-UP to Women's Suffrage*, ed. Roger S. Powers and William B. Vogele (New York: Garland 1997) 407-9.

22 See, for example, Theodore M. Black, *Straight Talk about American Education* (New York: Harcourt Brace, 1982); and Toby, "The Schools," 1995.

23 Colorado passed a law in 1996, SB 96-096, providing for the transfer of such information.

24 Interestingly enough, the most frequent reason for suspension in 1993 was poor school attendance. Behavior accounts for the majority of suspensions in the state today, while behavior and weapons account for the largest number of expulsions. Colorado Department of Education. "State Summary of Pupils Suspended and Expelled by Gender and Ethnic/Racial Group and Counts of Suspensions and Expulsions by Reason" (Denver: Colorado Department of Education, 1996).

25 Colorado Department of Education, "State Summary of Pupils Suspended and Expelled."

26 The zero tolerance for weapons discussion is now moot, given the passage of federal and state legislation mandating expulsion for weapons possession in the schools.

27 For examples of more comprehensive approaches to violence, see David Hawkins and Richard Catalano Jr. *Communities That Care* (San Francisco: Jossey-Bass, Inc., 1992); J. David Hawkins, Jeffrey M. Jenson, Richard F. Catalano, and Elizabeth A. Wells, "Effects of a Skills Training Intervention with Juvenile Delinquents," *Research on Social Work Practice* 1, no. 2 April 1991): 107–21; Deborah Prothrow-Stith, *Deadly Consequences: How Violence is Destroying Our Teenage Population and a Plan to Begin Solving the Problem* (New York: HarperCollins Publishers, 1991); and Reiss and Roth, eds., *Understanding and Preventing Violence*.

Bibliography

American School Health Association, the Association for the Advancement of Health Education, and the Society for Public Health Education. "National Adolescent Student Health Survey." *Health Education* 19, (August/September 1988).

Baker, Keith, and Robert J. Rubel, eds. *Violence and Crime in the Schools.* Lexington, MA: Lexington Books, 1980.

Bastian, Lisa, and Bruce M. Taylor. "School Crime: A National Crime Victimization Report." Washington, DC: U.S. Department of Justice, September 1991.

Black, Theodore M. *Straight Talk about American Education.* New York: Harcourt Brace, 1982.

Brodinsky, Mary, "Reporting: Violence, Vandalism and Other Incidents in Schools." ED 208 603. Washington, DC: American Association of School Administrators, 1981.

Brown, Stephen R. *Political Subjectivity: Applications of Q Methodology in Political Science.* New Haven: Yale University Press, 1980.

Brunner, Ronald D. "Key Political Symbols: The Dissociation Process." *Policy Sciences* 20 (1987): 53–76.

Brunner, Ronald D. "Global Climate Change: Defining the Policy Problem." *Policy Sciences* 24 (1991): 291–311.

Brunner, Ronald D., J. Samuel Fitch, Janet Grassia, Lyn Kathlene, and Kenneth R. Hammond. "Improving Data Utilization: The Case-Wise Alternative." *Policy Sciences* 20 (1987): 365–94.

City of Boulder Youth Initiative, Boulder Youth Services, Boulder, CO, 1992–93.

The Colorado Crisis Center, "Building Safe Communities." Denver, CO: Author, 1993.

Colorado Department of Education, "A Status Report on Colorado Youth: Trends and Implications," Denver: Author, August 1992.

Colorado Department of Education. "State Summary of Pupils Suspended and Expelled by Gender and Ethnic/Racial Group and Counts of Suspensions and Expulsions by Reason." Denver: Colorado Department of Education, 1996.

Edelman, Murray, *Political Language: Words that Succeed and Policies that Fail.* New York: Academic Press, 1977.

Fischhoff, Baruch, Sarah Lichtenstein, Paul Slovic, Stephen L. Derby, and Ralph L. Keeney. *Acceptable Risk.* New York: Cambridge University Press, 1981.

Forcey, Linda Rennie. "Peace Studies," in *Protest, Power, and Change: An Encyclopedia of Nonviolent Action from ACT-UP to Women's Suffrage*, ed. Roger S. Powers and William B. Vogele, 407–8. New York: Garland 1997.

Garofalo, James, Leslie Siegel, and John Laub. "School-Related Victimizations among Adolescents: An Analysis of National Crime Survey (NCS) Narratives." *Journal of Quantitative Criminology* 3, no. 4 (1987): 321–39.

Gaustad, Joan. "Schools Attack the Roots of Violence." ED 335 806. Washington, DC: Office of Educational Research and Improvement, October 1991.

George, Patricia Lucas. "How To Keep Your School and Students Safe. Tips for Principals from NASSP." ED 327 002. Reston, VA: National Association of Secondary School Principals, March 1990.

Goldstein, Arnold P., Steven J. Apter, and Berj Harootunian. *School Violence*. Englewood Cliffs, NJ: Prentice-Hall, 1984.

Gottfredson, Gary D., and Denise C. Gottfredson. *Victimization in Schools*. New York: Plenum Press, 1985.

Hall, Peter. "Policy Paradigms, Social Learning, and the State: The Case of Economic Policymaking in Britain." *Comparative Politics* 25 April (1993): 275–96.

Harris, Ian M. "From World Peace to Peace in the 'Hood: Peace Education in a Postmodern World." *Journal for a Just and Caring Education* 2, no. 4 (October 1996): 378–95.

Harris, Louis. "Metropolitan Life Survey of the American Teacher, 1993: Violence in America's Public Schools." New York: Louis Harris and Associates, Inc., 1993.

Harris, Louis. "Metropolitan Life Survey of the American Teacher, 1994, Violence in America's Public Schools: The Family Perspective." New York: Louis Harris and Associates, Inc., 1994.

Hawkins, J. David, Jeffrey M. Jenson, Richard F. Catalano, and Elizabeth A. Wells. "Effects of a Skills Training Intervention with Juvenile Delinquents." *Research on Social Work Practice* 1, no. 2 (April 1991): 107–21.

Hawkins, J. David, and Richard Catalano Jr. *Communities That Care*. San Francisco: Jossey-Bass, Inc., 1992.

Lam, Julie. "Evaluating the Program." Unpublished draft chapter on evaluating mediation programs. Amherst, MA: National Association for Mediation in Education, 1992.

Lasswell, Harold D. *A Pre-View of Policy Sciences*. New York: Elsevier, 1971.

Lippman, Walter. "The World Outside and the Pictures in Our Heads," in *Public Opinion*, 3–20. New York: The Free Press, 1965.

Lorr, Maurice. *Cluster Analysis for Social Scientists*. San Francisco: Jossey-Bass, 1987.

The Los Angeles Times (26 June 1992): A1.

Mesinger, John F. "Alternative Education for Behaviorally Disordered Youths: A Promise Yet Unfulfilled." *Behavioral Disorders* 11, no. 2 (1986): 98–108.

Morrison, Gale M., Michael J. Furlong, and Richard L. Morrison. "School Violence to School Safety: Reframing the Issue for School Psychologists." *School Psychology Review* 23 no. 2 (1994): 236–56.

National Center for Education Statistics. "Teacher Survey on Safe, Disciplined and Drug-Free Schools." NCES 91–091. Washington, DC: Author, November 1991.

National Center for Education Statistics. "Public School Principal Survey on Safe, Disciplined and Drug-Free Schools." ED 1.328/3:P 96/2. Washington, DC: Author, February 1992.

National Institute of Education. "Violent Schools—Safe Schools: The Safe School Study Report to Congress, Executive Summary." Washington, DC: Author, December 1978.

National School Boards Association. *Violence in the Schools: How America's School Boards Are Safeguarding Our Children*. Alexandria, VA: Author, 1993.

National School Safety Center. "Student and Staff Victimization: NSSC Resource Paper." ED 271 667. Westlake Village, CA: Author, April 1986.

National School Safety Center. "School Crime and Statistical Review." Westlake Village, CA: Author, June 1993.

Prothrow-Stith, Deborah. *Deadly Consequences: How Violence is Destroying Our Teenage Population and a Plan to Begin Solving the Problem*. New York: HarperCollins Publishers, 1991.

Prothrow-Stith, Deborah, Howard Spivak and Alice J. Hausman. "The Violence Prevention Project: A Public Health Approach." *Science, Technology, and Human Values* 12, nos. 3, 4 (1987): 67–69.

Reese, William J. "Reefer Madness and A Clockwork Orange," in *Learning from the Past: What History Teaches Us about School Reform*, ed. Diane Ravitch and Maris A. Vinovskis, 355–81. Baltimore, MD: The Johns Hopkins University Press, 1995.

Reiss, Albert J., Jr., and Jeffrey A. Roth, eds. *Understanding and Preventing Violence*. Washington, DC: National Academy Press, 1993.

Rochefort, David A. and Roger W. Cobb, eds. *The Politics of Problem Definition: Shaping the Policy Agenda*. Lawrence, KA: University Press of Kansas, 1994.

Simon, Herbert A. *Reason in Human Affairs.* Stanford: Stanford University Press, 1983.

Toby, Jackson. "Violence in School." Washington, DC: National Institute of Justice, December 1983.

Toby, Jackson. "The Schools," in *Crime,* ed. James Q. Wilson and Joan Petersilia, 141–70. San Francisco: ICS Press, 1995.

Tolan, Patrick, and Nancy Guerra. "What Works in Reducing Adolescent Violence: An Empirical Review of the Field." No. F–888. Boulder, CO: Center for the Study and Prevention of Violence, July 1994.

U.S. Senate. "Crime and Violence in the Schools: Hearing before the Subcommittee on Juvenile Justice of the Committee on the Judiciary, on the Scope and Severity of Crime and Violence in Schools and on Proposed Initiatives to Combat Juvenile Crime in the Schools." S.Hrg.98-844, 1/25, 1984.

PART II

CLASSROOM STRATEGIES FOR PEACEBUILDING

Chapter 5

Peace and Conflict Curricula for Adolescents

Linden L. Nelson, Michael R. Van Slyck, and Lucille A. Cardella

If creating peace implies developing peaceful people, education is the cornerstone for peacebuilding. While peace education involves learning about peacemaking, peacekeeping, and peacebuilding, its ultimate objective goes beyond transmission of knowledge to development of peaceful people. Developing peaceful people is a legitimate objective for public education at this time in history because, as stated succinctly by Martin Luther King Jr., "We must learn to live together as brothers or perish together as fools."[1]

Peacebuilding also implies developing sustainable economies, democratic societies, and social systems that provide for security and justice. These developments require the efforts of peaceful people who not only know how to promote peace, but who also "strive for peace" and are motivated to "pursue standards of social justice" and "to construct a better world."[2]

It is important to recognize the monumental nature of the educational task implied by defining our goal as peaceful people. Adding instruction to the curriculum about the history of peacemaking, principles of conflict resolution, and multicultural issues will be necessary but insufficient for developing peaceful behavior. More fundamental and pervasive changes in curriculum and pedagogy will be required because social behavior is determined by attitudes, values, social and problem-solving competencies, as well as by knowledge.

Promoting peaceful behavior will require curricula and other methods that affect students' attitudes, values, competencies, and personal and political beliefs.[3] While we focus here on the role of curricula, the importance of other methods will constitute a subtheme of this chapter. Specifically, we will argue for a comprehensive approach to school-based conflict resolution/peace education efforts that includes other methods such as cooperative learning and peer mediation programs, with curricula providing a base for the other methods and activities.

Fortunately, curriculum materials are available for educators who wish to begin or augment efforts to influence adolescents to behave more peacefully. Before describing and evaluating some of these curricula, we will elaborate further on specific objectives of peace education for adolescents. By specifying educational objectives we hope to provide some guidelines for selecting and developing curricula and some criteria for evaluating their effectiveness.

Educational Objectives

According to Judith Filner, past director of the Conflict Resolution Education Network, the essential objectives of conflict resolution curricula include "understanding conflict; mastering problem-solving processes including negotiation, mediation and collaborative problem-solving; internalizing effective communication skills that emphasize the ability to understand the other person's perspective . . .; and understanding and incorporating the underlying philosophy of conflict resolution which is based on . . . meeting the interests of everyone involved."[4]

We appreciate the emphasis in this statement on "mastering" and "internalizing" essential conflict resolution competencies in addition to the goal of "understanding" conflict. However, we believe that this statement does not sufficiently emphasize the importance of attitudes, values, and expectations. Curricula should be designed deliberately to influence such factors. In the following sections we delineate objectives for peace education curricula. These objectives served as criteria for evaluating five peace and conflict curricula in the study we describe later in this chapter.

Knowledge and Understanding
It is impossible to describe all of the knowledge relevant for understanding peace and conflict. Every discipline has something to offer, and every conflict has a different history and unique characteristics. The immensity of this educational objective is reduced somewhat by recognizing that peaceful people are not omniscient and that the pur-

suit of peace is a collaborative activity by which knowledge can be shared. In addition, a growing body of theory and research provides us with a knowledge base concerning peace and conflict. This literature can be drawn upon to inform us about those consistent principles that emerge from the study of social conflict and are thereby recommended as necessary components of peace education curricula.

Our list of educational objectives is influenced by the content of the curricula we reviewed for this project, by our opinions about what seems most essential for peaceful people to know, and by the theoretical and research literature on conflict and peace. While most of the curricula in our project focused on interpersonal conflict, the specific knowledge required for understanding conflict between adolescents is obviously different from the specific knowledge relevant for resolving ethnic conflict in Africa or for international conflict issues. Given the current limitations in time that teachers have for teaching about peace and conflict, instruction should emphasize general principles that apply to nearly all types and levels of conflict.

This generic knowledge includes principles about tendencies toward bias in perceptions of others (e.g., prejudice, ethnocentrism, dehumanization); factors in escalation and de-escalation of conflict; causes and consequences of cooperation, competition, and violence; the role and dynamics of emotion in human relations; the importance of reconciliation following conflict; effective communication, problem solving, and decision making; conflict resolution strategies (e.g., negotiation, mediation, arbitration); and nonviolent methods of social influence (e.g., positive incentives and reinforcement, friendly initiatives, nonviolent activism and resistance).

The high school curriculum should also address the specific topics of interpersonal conflict between adolescents and between adolescents and adults; conflict and violence in the family and community; causes and consequences of war and ecological crises, including nuclear war and environmental degradation; systemic causes of violence (e.g., oppression and injustice); the United Nations and international peacekeeping; theories about national security and defense; nonviolent philosophies; and activities of peacemakers.

These lists of general principles and specific topics are meant to be illustrative rather than complete, and they describe educational objectives for the high school curriculum as a whole. We would not expect every curriculum manual or workbook, nor every teacher, to address all of these principles and topics. Peace education, and peacebuilding more generally, are necessarily cooperative ventures.

The concept of a comprehensive approach to peace education is relevant here. In such an approach, curricula would be implemented at all grade levels. This would mitigate the need for any specific curriculum to cover all topics or issues. Rather through a comprehensive approach all of the principles and topics would be covered in a logical, age-appropriate, sequential fashion.

Competencies

Imparting knowledge is not sufficient to create a peaceful person. Teaching the skills necessary for peacemaking, peacekeeping, and peacebuilding requires providing opportunities for students to learn by doing, to obtain feedback about their performance, and to practice. Indeed it has been argued that peace education efforts restricted to a didactic approach will only have limited effectiveness and that even curricula that include experiential components may be limited in terms of having a permanent effect.[5]

David and Roger Johnson suggest that what is required to make "learning by doing" effective is an outlet for practice such as a peer mediation program.[6] Once again this argues for a comprehensive approach in which curricula serve as a base upon which other such activities such as peer mediation are built. However, curricula should clearly make an effort to include as much experiential opportunity as possible to facilitate the learning process, ideally serving as a training vehicle for peer mediators.

In particular, students should learn how to solve problems by analyzing the causes of conflict, generating appropriate action alternatives, and applying relevant criteria in deciding on a course of action. Students should learn the communication skills of active listening, perspective taking, reflection, and empathy. Students should also learn to use methods of conflict resolution like negotiation and mediation, and techniques for nonviolent social influence. All of these competencies assume self-control and abilities to manage anger and other emotions in oneself and others.

The authors of the curricula we have reviewed for this project describe numerous methods and activities for training these competencies. Many authors have developed prescriptive models for conflict resolution that combine suggestions for emotional control, problem solving, negotiation, and decision making in a step-by-step fashion. For example, one approach uses the acronym "TRIBE" to refer to the suggested steps that should follow after "stop and think," which is step one in the model. The TRIBE steps are "Tell what's up with you; Reflectively listen to the response; Identify what's important; Brainstorm possible solutions; Evaluate solutions and try it."[7]

Perhaps the most common theme of these prescriptive models is known variously as integrative bargaining, principled negotiation, or collaborative problem solving, and was popularized in books by Roger Fisher and William Ury and by Eleanor Wertheim, et al.[8] A good example is the "negotiation process" described by Richard Bodine, Donna Crawford, and Fred Schrumpf: "1. Agree to negotiate, 2. Gather points of view, 3. Focus on interests, 4. Create win-win options, 5. Evaluate options, 6. Create an agreement."[9]

There is quite a bit of evidence demonstrating that social problem solving and conflict resolution competencies can be taught effectively,[10] and there is some evidence that after instruction that included training in these competencies, children and adolescents behaved more cooperatively and less violently in their schools and communities.[11] Assertiveness training can also be an effective approach for teaching adolescents how to influence others without being aggressive.[12] Successful programs for training anger management and emotional self-control have also been developed.[13]

Attitudes and Values

Peaceful people obviously differ from more aggressive and militaristic people in some of their attitudes and values. Adults who rated values related to international harmony and equality as important, compared to adults who rated these values as relatively less important, were more favorable toward social justice policies, more politically active, and more likely to vote for liberal and environmental candidates.[14] Other researchers use the concept of "universalism" to describe a cluster of correlated values including "a world at peace," "protecting the environment," "a world of beauty," "equality," "social justice," and other related values. Adults who rated or ranked the universalism values highly were more willing to have social contact with outgroups (e.g., Israeli Jewish teachers' willingness to have social contact with Arabs), were more involved in antinuclear activism, and had relatively nonviolent dispositions according to a self-report measure of nonviolence.[15]

Researchers have shown that aggressive children and adolescents, compared with less aggressive children, are more likely to select a hostile goal (e.g., "teach the other a lesson") when confronted with a problem, and are more likely to agree with statements that legitimize aggression (e.g., "it's OK to hit someone if you just go crazy with anger").[16] Recent research by one of the authors found a relationship between hostile and violent behavior by adolescents and their self-reported attitudes concerning appropriate ways to respond to conflict.[17] Specifically, adolescents reporting greater levels of hostility and violence in their interpersonal interactions were more likely to endorse a dominating conflict management style as appropriate whereas adolescents reporting low levels of hostility and violence were more likely to endorse prosocial conflict management styles.

Demonstrating the relationship between peaceful attitudes and peaceful behaviors does not prove whether the behaviors are caused by the attitudes, or vice versa. However, the consensus among researchers is that attitudes and values are important causes of behavior, and that behaving often causes a change in attitudes.[18] The implications for peace educators are that (1) curricula should directly address and support the development of peaceful attitudes and values, and (2) curricula that encourage students to take peaceful actions in the school and community will promote development of peaceful attitudes. Research suggests that the second implication will be effective only when students perceive that their peaceful actions are voluntary.[19]

Curricula should provide activities that require discussion between students, and between students and teachers, about attitudes and values. Students' values are likely to be influenced by group norms that develop in the context of group interaction.[20] This assumes that teachers will guide the group discussions in peaceful directions. There is evidence that a high level of student-teacher interaction facilitates students' modeling of teachers' values.[21]

Here again we invoke the concept of a comprehensive approach to peace education. Without formal, official, structured opportunities to voluntarily engage in the learned behaviors beyond the classroom, there is less likelihood that potentially desirable effects on subsequent attitudes will occur. While curricula do suggest activities to engage in, there is the risk that they may be artificial. The more that structured "real world" opportunities are provided for meaningful peaceful behavior, the more likely such behavior will influence the development of peaceful attitudes and values.

If values and attitudes are considered important educational objectives, who has the authority to determine which values will be assigned this status? Obviously, there are conflicting value systems to some extent in all societies. We prefer to confront these conflicts rather than to pretend that peace education could be effective without influencing students' values. We, as citizens in a democratic society, will try to affect the deliberations of our elected representatives and school boards concerning education objectives and policies in public schools, and we will accept their decisions.

Fortunately, the central values and attitudes of peaceful people are widely respected. Although individuals differ in their ratings and ranking of values, few would claim that peace, justice, and equal opportunity are unimportant. Most citizens value both peace and national strength, even though they differ on the relative importance of each.

Valerie Braithwaite asked a large sample of Australian adults and college students to rate the importance of eighteen social values.[22] She identified a cluster of ten correlated values, a factor she called "international harmony and equality." These ten values are listed in table 1, and we believe they would be widely accepted as a statement of educational objectives for peace education.

We also want to make explicit several attitudinal objectives that may be implied by the values listed in table 1. We believe these to be essential attitudes of peaceful people that are widely respected: (1) a preference for nonviolent methods of social influence, (2) a preference for collaborative approaches to resolving conflict, and (3) tolerance and appreciation for human diversity (i.e., individual, gender, ethnic, cultural, and national differences), including diversity in attitudes about conflict and peace.

**Table 1. International Harmony and Equality Values
(from Braithwaite, 1994)**

A good life for others (improving the welfare of all people in need)
Rule by the people (involvement by all citizens in making decisions that affect their community)
International cooperation (having all nations working together to help each other)
Social progress and social reform (readiness to change our way of life for the better)
A world at peace (being free from war and conflict)
A world of beauty (having the beauty of nature and the arts: music, literature, art, etc.)
Human dignity (allowing each individual to be treated as someone of worth)
Equal opportunity for all (giving everyone an equal chance in life)
Greater economic equality (lessening the gap between rich and poor)
Preserving the natural environment (preventing the destruction of nature's beauty and resources)

We acknowledge cultural differences in attitudes and beliefs concerning conflict. Culture influences how conflicts are perceived and handled (e.g., what is regarded as appropriate responses to conflict). As one example, research has found differences in the endorsement of conflict management styles between Israeli and Arab adolescents.[23] Recognizing the growing diversity in the United States, we must keep in mind that there may not be complete consensus on what it means to be a peaceful person.

Efficacy and Outcome Expectancies

A voluminous research literature in psychology demonstrates that people's actions are greatly influenced by their personal and collective efficacy expectancies.[24] Efficacy expectancies involve beliefs about one's capability, or the capability of one's group, to perform actions that would result in desired outcomes. Many studies have found that measures of personal and political efficacy predict an individual's amount of involvement in peace and environmental activism.[25]

Efficacy beliefs develop largely from personal experience, but are also affected by observing the experiences of others. Efforts to increase efficacy are often called "empowerment." If positive efficacy expectancies for peaceful behaviors are an important educational objective, curricula should include many opportunities for students to successfully engage in peacemaking and peacebuilding activities in order to develop confidence in their capabilities. The concept of *small wins* suggests that even big social problems can be redefined in scale so as to identify tasks and actions by which adolescents can experience success.[26] Most of the curricula described below use group activities and role playing to develop confidence in peacemaking, and many curricula suggest activities in the school and community that would provide successful experiences in peacebuilding. Efficacy beliefs may be enhanced by providing very specific information about how citizens can and have affected policymakers, and by showing how citizens can work in groups and organizations to have greater impact. Curricula should provide numerous examples of successful peacemaking and peacebuilding by adolescent and adult models.

Even if students value peace and are confident in their abilities for peaceful behavior, they are unlikely to act peacefully unless they believe that their actions will have positive outcomes. Cooperative behavior is not supported by an environment that rewards only competition. Therefore, the development of cooperative behaviors in adolescents may require adoption of cooperative learning pedagogies and structures in high school classrooms.[27] At the very least, teachers and peers must recognize and reward cooperative behavior when it occurs.

Students' nonviolent responses to conflict will be withheld if they are ridiculed rather than praised. Given the sensitivity of adolescents to peer pressures, the development of norms that allow and foster peer support for nonviolence should be given high priority. As mentioned earlier in the section on attitudes and values, guided class discussions with a high level of interaction between students is probably the most powerful method for influencing group norms. Appropriate activities for promoting class discussion and interaction are offered in many of the curriculum materials described in the next section.

We believe that all of these goals are more likely to be achieved when curricula are part of a comprehensive approach to peace education including cooperative learning, peer mediation, and community involvement. A comprehensive approach includes all children at all grade levels as well as the entire school staff, parents, and other members of the community. Within such a framework, adolescents will have examples of adult cooperative interactions and receive support for embracing norms of peace and nonviolence.

Curriculum Review Project

This section of the chapter describes results of a curriculum review project of the Peace and Education Working Group of the Division of Peace Psychology of the American Psychological Association. Five peace and conflict curricula written for adolescents or for teachers of adolescents were selected on the basis of our perceptions that they were widely used and offered a variety of approaches to addressing the educational objectives discussed in the previous section. One purpose of the project was to provide comparative and evaluative information about peace education curricula to teachers and other educators. Additional purposes, not directly related to our objectives in this chapter, were to investigate the utilization of psychological concepts by authors of the curricula and to give authors suggestions for improving the applications of psychology to curricular content and pedagogy.

There were twenty-one reviewers—a mix of professors, clinicians, school psychologists, advanced graduate students, and other psychologists who work with adolescents.[28] Each curriculum was evaluated by between five and seven reviewers, and each reviewer evaluated one or two curricula. We will first describe the curricula along with summaries of reviewers' comments about strengths and weaknesses. Then, we will report the reviewers ratings of the curricula on various relevant dimensions including the degree to which each curriculum seems likely to promote educational objectives related to development of peaceful people.

Managing World Conflict: A Resource Unit for High Schools[29]

Description: The curriculum addresses the nature of intergroup and international conflict and focuses on international conflict resolution. It does not address interpersonal or community conflict. There are thirty-four pages of instructions for teachers and seventy-six pages of readings and other handouts for students. The learning objectives for each of seven lessons involve skills for preparing and writing essays about conflict, but more generally relate to analyzing and thinking critically about the development and management of conflict. In particular, the curriculum helps prepare students for participation in the National Peace Essay Contest.[30] Methods of instruction include cooperative learning, one large-scale role play, "paired writing" in which students write critical reactions to each other's statements, and other group and individual activities.

Strengths: The lessons are clear, engaging and age appropriate. They offer valuable writing and speaking experiences. The role play in lesson one is particularly well designed. The emphasis on "learn by doing" and the diversity of international conflicts discussed are positive features. The curriculum is unique compared to other curricula we reviewed in its inclusion of the conflict management strategies of diplomacy, balance of power, security alliances, and track-two diplomacy.

Weaknesses/Limitations: While the curriculum teaches analysis of conflict and how to write about conflict, it doesn't provide sufficient instruction in conflict resolution skills or about what citizens might do to promote peace. It is deficient in presentation of major theories about conflict and peace, and about basic principles of conflict resolution, negotiation, and mediation. There is no model presented for problem solving or negotiation, and no attempt to teach principles that would generalize to other levels of conflict, such as interpersonal conflict. There is little discussion of the psychological roots of violence or of peacebuilding. Pedagogical support for teachers is minimal, particularly regarding how to facilitate group interaction and cooperative learning.

Conflict Resolution[31]

Description: This 158-page textbook for students focuses specifically on negotiation, mediation, and arbitration. The subject is primarily interpersonal conflict, including examples of disputes between individuals and companies, landlords, or employers. The author explicitly suggests that the same steps are used for simple and complex disputes, but only a few examples of intergroup and international conflict are mentioned. The topics of war and peacebuilding are not addressed.

The author begins with a brief description of how legal disputes can be resolved through litigation, and she points out the benefits of alternative dispute resolution for each stage of the legal process. Half of the book is devoted to negotiation, described as an eight-step process, with chapters on methods, obstacles, and creative approaches in negotiation. The text also describes six-step mediation and arbitration processes. Most chapters conclude with a list of conflict scenarios and suggestions for using them in class discussions or role plays. A twenty-page teacher's resource manual is also available. It offers additional suggestions for class activities that are similar to those in the textbook.

Strengths: The text is very readable and has a logical and easy-to-follow format. It provides a wide variety of examples of conflict for students to discuss or role play. The sections on obstacles to negotiation and how to overcome them are very good. The author communicates well the advantages of participatory decision making for increasing motivation to abide by decisions.

Weaknesses/Limitations: Although many examples of conflict are provided in order to allow for role plays and practice in applying concepts, the exercises are not well structured. There are insufficient guidelines for students and teachers about how to carry out the role plays. Also needed are exercises in basic communication skills such as active listening. Guidelines for dealing with hostility, bias, and anger management are also insufficient.

The negotiation model has too many steps and doesn't seem user-friendly. The discussion on mediation is limited to one particular model, not the one generally used in high school peer mediation programs.

Although the author suggests that dispute resolution methods apply to all levels of conflict, the curriculum does not provide the necessary background for understanding conflict and applying conflict resolution methods in areas other than interpersonal conflicts. Some of the examples of conflict lack realism for adolescents, and the text may be too simple for many juniors and seniors.

Making Choices about Conflict, Security, and Peacemaking Part I: Personal Perspectives[32]

Description: In this 399-page manual for teachers, descriptions for eighty-one activities are organized into seven chapters on the meaning of security, diversity issues, conflict analysis, interpersonal conflict resolution, anger and violence, war and peacemaking, and group problem solving. The introduction to the book explains its teaching philosophy and methods and offers many suggestions about how to integrate activities into the high school curriculum. The seven chapters consist entirely of activities. Each activity includes sections on objectives or purpose, learning strategies, time requirements, materials needed, and detailed instructions. Most activities include handouts with readings, charts, and/or instructions for students. The broad range of activities includes brainstorming, journal writing, interactive dialogues, role plays, cooperative learning, community action projects, and more.

Strengths: The learn by doing activities are exceptionally creative, interesting, and age appropriate. They clearly implement the teaching philosophy and objectives articulated in the introductory section. The layout for activities is very helpful and the instructions are clear and complete. The activities for developing skills in communication, problem solving, and negotiation are very good.

The curriculum is more comprehensive than most. It addresses peacemaking and peacebuilding, and it covers intrapersonal, interpersonal, intragroup, intergroup, community, and global issues. Suggestions for integrating activities into the high school curriculum are extensive and creative, and helpful suggestions are given for selecting activities that are labeled "academically challenging," "promote positive intergroup relations," "essential" to the chapter, or "liked best by teachers and kids."

Weaknesses/Limitations: While the manual's encyclopedic organization allows great flexibility in selecting activities that stand alone and can be integrated into the existing curriculum, this may result in teachers giving insufficient attention to prerequisite skills and to repetition of basic themes and principles. It is questionable whether the curriculum provides for sufficient practice and reinforcement of basic skills.

The manual fails to establish important connections between topics in different chapters. For example, the relevance of activities in the chapter on security for understanding the subsequent chapters on conflict, war, and peacebuilding is not sufficiently explicit. The curriculum should more directly address obstacles to cooperative problem solving and problems in negotiation such as asymmetry in power and authority.

Workbook for the Course in Peaceful Conflict Resolution "Alternatives to Violence"[33]

Description: This 372-page workbook is designed for use by students participating in the "Alternatives to Violence" course. The course is a highly structured curriculum of twenty sessions described in a *Teacher's Guide*. Only the workbook was evaluated by reviewers in this project, and it can be used separately from the course.

Workbook sections correspond with the twenty course sessions. For each section, the workbook includes learning objectives, a worksheet with questions that personalize the objective, a space for a journal entry, readings and charts, a summary page, and a list of suggested additional readings. The readings and charts comprise the majority of the text. The last 100 pages are brief descriptions of cases of successful application of nonviolent principles. These cases are keyed to the sessions, and case analysis sheets are provided for students to answer analytical questions about each case.

The purpose of the course is to teach nonviolent philosophy and behavior. The *Teacher's Guide* includes detailed agendas and teaching instructions for each session. Sessions require one to two and one-half hours each. A *Materials Kit* costing $195 is needed to obtain master copies for handouts and transparencies, videos, and other materials. The *Teacher's Guide* and *Materials Kit* provide instructions and materials for a wide variety of games, role plays, group activities, and audio-visual materials.

Strengths: The workbook is clearly written, accessible, and interesting for adolescent readers. The sections on communication skills, responses to conflict, active listening, anger management, and group decision making and leadership are very good. There is a well planned progression of topics from interpersonal to global issues. The diversity of readings and numerous case studies allow opportunities for students to conceptually apply conflict analysis and resolution skills.

A number of relevant topics often neglected in other curricula are included: the cycle of oppression, guidelines for interrupting oppression, working the democratic system, how to write letters to representatives and editors, nonviolent self-defense, nonviolent national defense, positions on nonviolence of world religions, and nonviolent philosophies.

Weaknesses/Limitations: Few of the readings or case studies deal with common adolescent conflicts involving sex, drugs, harassment, or gang violence. The workbook would benefit from some readings about nonviolence programs that have been recently created to prevent youth violence. Discussion about the causes of violence seems incomplete. Fear, pride, greed, and developmental causes such as socialization practices could be explored more fully. Material on prejudice, outgroup bias, and ethnocentrism should be expanded. In particular, analysis of the causes of war is inadequate, and there are few examples of negotiation and mediation applied to international conflict.

It may be difficult to incorporate the entire "Alternatives to Violence" course (thirty to forty hours) into the high school curriculum, but the *Teacher's Guide* and *Materials Kit* include many useful ideas and exercises that could be used selectively. The course may be more appropriate for settings other than public schools because of the time it requires and because its bias toward nonviolence is stronger than the attitudes shared by most teachers, administrators, and parents. The workbook can be used effectively apart from the course, but it does not include the role playing and other group interaction activities that are essential for practicing conflict resolution skills.

Conflict Resolution: A Secondary School Curriculum[34]

Description: This 295-page manual for teachers focuses on interpersonal communication and conflict, and does not address the topics of international conflict and peace. It begins with an introductory section including an overview, pedagogical suggestions, and guidelines for conducting role plays. There are five chapters plus appendices. Chapters are titled "Understanding Conflict," "Conflict Styles," "Communication: An Overview," "Skills for Effective Communication," and "Resolving Conflict." Each chapter includes eight to fifteen pages describing basic principles followed by eleven to twenty-eight classroom activities.

The classroom activities are designated as key or supplementary and include statements about objectives, duration, and materials, followed by detailed instructions for teachers' presentations and for students' involvement in activities. Most activities have worksheets, readings, or other handouts to use with assignments, role plays, and structured group interactions.

Strengths: The curriculum is well organized for teaching a progression of skills for self-awareness, conflict analysis, interpersonal communication, and collaborative problem solving and conflict resolution. Although chapters could be taught as independent units, the curriculum's strength is the progressive development of component skills that are necessary to effectively engage in collaborative conflict resolution. The activities are clearly designed to provide opportunities for practicing these component skills.

Other strengths include the emphasis and activities on self-assessment, analysis of conflict, and the individual planning and reflection that should occur in the initial stages of the conflict resolution process. Reviewers described the curriculum as "user-friendly" with easy-to-follow instructions and loose-leaf pages that can be easily removed from the binder for duplication.

Weaknesses/Limitations: The authors fail to capitalize on opportunities to encourage students to generalize understanding of interpersonal conflict to larger conflicts in society at community, national, and international levels. There is insufficient discussion about causes and consequences of violence at all levels from domestic, ethnic, and gang violence to warfare between nations. Students' values related to violence and nonviolence should be explored more thoroughly and the subject of anger management needs greater attention. Some reviewers suggested that the curriculum relies too heavily on role plays, which may be difficult for shy students. Other exercises may be too simplistic for adolescents. The curriculum would benefit from a greater variety of activities including school and community projects.

Reviewers' Ratings

Reviewers estimated the probable influence of each curriculum on various educational objectives related to the development of peaceful people. Table 2 reports the percentage of reviewers expecting various degrees of impact (i.e., considerable, some, or none) on objectives in the categories of knowledge, competencies, attitudes and values, and efficacy expectancies.

The results in table 2 show that for most objectives there were substantial differences in reviewers' expectations about the probable impact on students. This suggests that educators might be able to choose curricula based on the objectives of greatest importance to them. Educators interested in achieving the comprehensive objectives of peace education would, according to the opinions of our reviewers, be advised to consider the curricula written by John Looney or Carol Lieber.

Reviewers also rated the curricula for levels of interest and difficulty. They were asked to "consider the typical interests and abilities of eleventh graders" when making those ratings. They also indicated all of the grade levels for which the curricula would be appropriate. Finally, they evaluated how well each curriculum fulfilled "its particular educational objectives," and they indicated whether they would recommend the curriculum "for teaching high school students the educational objectives for which it was designed." These ratings and evaluations are reported in table 3.

Other Choices

Although we will not attempt to describe all of the curricula available for teaching about peace and conflict, there are a number of other curricula we believe to be particularly worthy of mention.[35]

TRIBE: Conflict Resolution Curriculum for High School is a 223-page teacher's manual with about twenty activities for each grade level from ninth to twelfth.[36] There is a progressively more sophisticated presentation of the TRIBE conflict resolution model for each grade level and an emphasis on communication, problem solving, and negotiation skills at all levels. Additionally, the ninth-grade curriculum focuses on anger and assertiveness, the tenth-grade curriculum includes some applications to global issues, and the twelfth-grade curriculum focuses on conflict in the workplace.

Playing with Fire: Creative Conflict Resolution for Young Adults is an eighty-hour training course described in 172 pages.[37] The course emphasizes self-awareness, personal responses to conflict and injustice, assertiveness, crisis management, mediation, and negotiation. It does not address international conflict or global issues.

We Can Work It Out! Problem Solving through Mediation is a 132-page teacher's manual with handouts for students.[38] It focuses on active listening, problem solving, and mediation. There are sixteen

Table 2. Percentage of Reviewers Rating Curriculum Impact on Objectives as Considerable, Some, or None

	Conflict Resolution (Gordon)	Managing World Conflict (Davis, Eckenrod)	Alternatives to Violence (Looney)	Making Choices (Lieber)	Conflict Resolution: Secondary Sc. (Sadalla, Henriquez, Holmberg)
Knowledge about Interpersonal conflict					
Considerable	20%	0%	50%	71%	67%
Some	80%	60%	50%	29%	33%
None	0%	40%	0%	0%	0%
Knowledge about International conflict					
Considerable	0%	40%	50%	29%	17%
Some	0%	60%	50%	71%	33%
None	100%	0%	0%	0%	50%
Knowledge about Peacebuilding					
Considerable	0%	20%	67%	43%	0%
Some	20%	80%	33%	57%	83%
None	80%	0%	0%	0%	17%
Conflict resolution competencies					
Considerable	40%	0%	33%	86%	83%
Some	20%	80%	67%	14%	17%
None	40%	20%	0%	0%	0%
Critical thinking competencies					
Considerable	20%	20%	20%	57%	33%
Some	60%	80%	60%	29%	67%
None	20%	0%	20%	14%	0%
Ethnocentric attitudes					
Considerable	0%	20%	33%	14%	0%
Some	0%	60%	50%	86%	50%
None	100%	20%	17%	0%	50%
Peace and Justice values					
Considerable	0%	40%	67%	43%	17%
Some	20%	60%	33%	57%	83%
None	80%	0%	0%	0%	0%
Political efficacy					
Considerable	0%	0%	17%	0%	0%
Some	50%	60%	67%	83%	33%
None	50%	40%	17%	17%	67%

Table 3. Percentage of Reviewers Rating Levels of Interest, Difficulty, and Appropriateness

	Conflict Resolution (Gordon)	Managing World Conflict (Davis, Eckenrod)	Alternatives to Violence (Looney)	Making Choices (Lieber)	Conflict Resolution Secondary Sc. (Sadalla, Henriquez, Holmberg)
Interest level					
Exciting	0%	0%	0%	43%	0%
Interesting	20%	100%	100%	57%	67%
Uninteresting	60%	0%	0%	0%	33%
Boring	20%	0%	0%	0%	0%
Difficulty					
Too difficult	20%	0%	17%	0%	0%
Appropriate	20%	80%	83%	100%	83%
Too easy	40%	0%	0%	0%	17%
Unsure	20%	20%	0%	0%	0%
Grade appropriateness					
12th grade	60%	80%	100%	71%	50%
11th grade	40%	80%	100%	86%	50%
10th grade	80%	60%	67%	86%	100%
9th grade	60%	20%	50%	57%	100%
Fulfills objectives					
Excellent	0%	20%	33%	71%	17%
Good	20%	60%	50%	29%	33%
Satisfactory	40%	0%	17%	0%	50%
Poor	40%	20%	0%	0%	0%
Very Poor	0%	0%	0%	0%	0%
Recommendation					
Yes	40%	100%	83%	100%	83%
No	20%	0%	0%	0%	17%
Unsure	40%	0%	17%	0%	0%

conflict scenarios with role-playing parts for practicing mediation. It does not address international or global issues.

Creative Controversy: Intellectual Challenge in the Classroom is a 462-page manual that describes a unique approach to teaching conflict resolution called "academic controversy."[39] This methodology engages students in a structured exchange of ideas about a controversial issue. The objective is not to "win a debate," but to fully explore the issues, to understand opposing positions, and to mutually create a conclusion that reconceptualizes and synthesizes conflicting perspectives.

Some teacher's manuals are designed to be applicable for all levels, K–12. Two examples are *Creating the Peaceable School* and *Teaching Children To Be Peacemakers*.[40] These manuals are more comprehensive than others in dealing with pedagogical issues, classroom climate, and cooperative learning, in addition to covering the usual subjects of anger management, communication, problem solving, and conflict resolution. Most of the activities described in *Creating the Peaceable School* seem too simple for adolescents, whereas more of the activities described in *Teaching Children to be Peacemakers* seem appropriate for the high school level. These curricula focus on interpersonal conflict and have very little material on international or global issues.

Other curricula are directed primarily toward violence prevention, and some are designed specifically for delinquent or gang-involved youth. Examples are *Violence Prevention Curriculum for Adolescents* and *Aggressors, Victims, and Bystanders: Thinking and Acting to Prevent Violence*.[41] Programs in this category have been described and evaluated elsewhere.[42]

Peace and conflict curricula may be ordered from catalogs that describe publications from a number of sources. Perhaps the most comprehensive is the *Conflict Resolution Education Catalogue*, formerly the *NAME Catalogue*.[43] Other useful catalogs include *ESR Resource and Training Catalog* and the *Cooperative Learning Catalog*.[44]

Evaluating Curricula Effectiveness

To the best of our knowledge, none of the five curricula in our project have been evaluated by outcome assessment studies. We are aware of only two studies examining the effectiveness of instruction about peace and conflict in high school settings, and there are only a few published studies with children in grades one through nine or with college students.[45] Although this research has demonstrated that conflict resolution skills can be imparted to students, these interventions were in the form of highly focused and directed training activities as opposed to a more general curriculum about peace and conflict. Also, interventions designed to alter aggressive behavior have been effective with a specialty population of "offender" adolescents.[46]

The lack of outcome evaluation research on curricula raises a set of issues concerning appropriate approaches to such research. From a methodological perspective, a design including simple intervention (i.e., a single curriculum) or comparative intervention (i.e., multiple curricula) plus control group (i.e., no intervention) with pre- and post-assessment would be adequate to establish the general effectiveness of any given curriculum. However other issues arise such as determining what aspects of a curriculum produce any given effect.

Central to this issue is a clear delineation of the effects desired in the youth who would be the targets of such curricula. This suggests that we must articulate a set of factors associated with being a peaceful person. Thereafter, appropriate measures must be found or developed that adequately assess these factors as a basis for determining the effectiveness of any given curriculum. A number of such factors can naturally be derived from our delineation of the educational objectives of the curriculum. These include relevant knowledge, mastery of specific skills, and internalizing certain attitudes, values, and efficacy expectancies. Another source of criteria of effectiveness may be found in the research that has evaluated other types of conflict resolution programs.

Research by one of the authors has attempted to validate the conflict attitude construct, making use of an established and validated inventory, the Rahim Conflict Management Inventory.[47] This measure has been found to consistently relate to measures of conflict behavior (e.g., fighting) as well as other aspects of the adolescent's life (e.g. self-esteem). Thus, this measure suggests itself as a good one to assess any changes in attitude concerning appropriate ways of responding to conflict, with the expectation that any such changes in attitude will be manifested in changes in behavior, which can also be assessed. Other attitude inventories and behavior-rating scales have been used to assess peer mediation programs.[48]

In work on violence prevention, beliefs concerning the acceptability of aggression as a response to conflict were measured.[49] Such beliefs were found to be related to antisocial and aggressive behavior. An intervention designed to reduce violence was found to be effective in altering the aggression-condoning belief system as well as aggressive behavior.[50] It should be noted that these measures were developed with violent offenders and thus would probably be most appropriate for use in schools with high rates of violence.

In the domain of skills, a primary goal of all conflict resolution interventions is to develop cooperative problem-solving abilities. Thus any valid measure of problem solving for conflict resolution would be useful in assessing the effectiveness of peace education curricula, and a number of relevant assessment tools have been developed.[51] Another issue of concern is the level of effect in which we are interested. By that we mean whether we would restrict ourselves to assessing effects that are clearly within and relevant to the issues of conflict and peace, or whether we are interested in what have been referred to as "higher order" effects such as self-esteem and improved academic performance, secondary effects that may also derive from learning the principles and practices of conflict resolution and peace education.[52]

Summary and Conclusion

In this chapter, we have emphasized the need of conflict resolution curricula not only to assist students in mastering conflict resolution competencies but also to influence their attitudes, values, beliefs, and efficacy expectancies. As previously stated, this instruction should encompass general principles that apply to nearly all types and levels of conflict. Through examples, guided class discussion, cooperative group learning activities, and role playing, the opportunities to learn methods of conflict resolution, techniques for nonviolent social influence, and communication skills should ultimately provide successful experiences in peacebuilding and the development of peaceful people.

The five peace and conflict curricula reviewed vary in the degree to which they accomplish these objectives and utilize these pedagogical techniques. The *Making Choices about Conflict, Security, and Peacemaking* curriculum addresses peacebuilding comprehensively using a broad range of activities. Although the *Workbook for the Course in Peaceful Conflict Resolution* also covers the scope of conflicts from interpersonal to global using diverse cases and addressing often neglected topics, it was felt that it might be difficult to incorporate the entire course into a high school curriculum. The remaining curricula, at least according to our reviewers, provide insufficient models for conflict resolution applicable to all the various types and levels of conflict. However, they do incorporate instructional strategies judged to be beneficial for influencing conflict resolution competencies relevant to at least one level of conflict.

However, rather than viewing the curricula as alternative options we can also view them as complementary, with each having a place at different points in time. This brings us back to the concept of a comprehensive approach to the task of peace education in which curricula serve as the cornerstone for a school-wide effort. Several components of a comprehensive approach can be described. These include cooperative learning pedagogies, peer mediation programs, community projects, and parental involvement, perhaps as co-mediators for parent-child conflicts. In addition this approach includes all levels of school personnel as well as participation by the larger community. Finally, in order to allow for coverage of all appropriate topics and conflict resolution practices, peace education should be implemented at all grade levels and for every child and adolescent.

Notes

1 From a speech in St. Louis, 22 March 1964, reported by *St. Louis Post-Dispatch*, 23 March 1964, from *The Oxford Dictionary of Quotations*, 4th ed., ed. Angela Partington (Oxford: Oxford Press, 1992), 397.

2 Ian M. Harris, "From World Peace to Peace in the 'Hood: Peace Education in a Postmodern World," *Journal for a Just and Caring Education* 2, no. 4 (October 1996): 386.

3 Linden L. Nelson and Daniel J. Christie, "Peace in the Psychology Curriculum: Moving from Assimilation to Accommodation," *Peace and Conflict: Journal of Peace Psychology* 1, no. 2 (1995) 161-78.

4 Judith Filner introduction to *Conflict Resolution Education Catalog* (Washington, DC: National Institute for Dispute Resolution, 1997), iii.

5 Michael Van Slyck and Marilyn Stern, "Conflict Resolution in Educational Settings: Assessing the Impact of Peer Mediation Programs," in *The Art and Science of Community Mediation: A Handbook for Practitioners and Researchers*, ed. Karen Duffy, Paul Olezak, and James Grosch (New York: Guilford Press, 1991), 257-74.

6 David W. Johnson and Roger T. Johnson, "Teaching Students to be Peacemakers: Results of Five Years of Research" *Peace and Conflict: Journal of Peace Psychology* 1, no. 4 (1995): 417-38; Van Slyck and Stern, "Conflict Resolution," 272.

7 Kathryn Liss, Dee Edelman, Blythe Tennent, and Jan Bellard, *TRIBE: Conflict Resolution Curriculum for High School* (Chapel Hill, NC: The Mediation Network of North Carolina, 1995).

8 Roger J. Fisher and William Ury, *Getting to Yes: Negotiating Agreements Without Giving In* (London: Hutchinson, 1981); Eleanor H. Wertheim, Anthony Love, A. Littlefield, and Connie Peck, *I Win, You Win: How to Have Fewer Conflicts, Better Solutions, and More Satisfying Relationships* (Melbourne, Australia: Penguin, 1992).

9 Richard J. Bodine, Donna K. Crawford, and Fred Schrumpf, *Creating the Peaceable School: A Comprehensive Program for Teaching Conflict Resolution* (Champaign, IL: Research Press, 1994).

10 Thomas J. D'Zurilla, *Problem-Solving Therapy: A Social Competence Approach to Clinical Intervention* (New York: Springer, 1986); Melisah C. Feeney and John A. Davidson, "Bridging the Gap Between the Practical and the Theoretical: An Evaluation of a Conflict Resolution Model," *Peace and Conflict: Journal of Peace Psychology* 2, no. 3 (1996): 255-69; Linden L. Nelson, Natasha L. Golding, David R. Drews, and Mary K. Blazina, "Teaching and

Assessing Problem Solving for International Conflict Resolution," *Peace and Conflict: Journal of Peace Psychology* 1, no. 4 (1995): 399–416.

11 Nancy G. Guerra and Ronald G. Slaby, "Cognitive Mediators of Aggression in Adolescent Offenders: II. Intervention," *Developmental Psychology* 26, no. 2 (March, 1990): 269–77; Nancy G. Guerra, Patrick H. Tolan, and W. Rodney Hammond, "Prevention and Treatment of Adolescent Violence," in *Reason to Hope: A Psychosocial Perspective on Violence and Youth*, ed. Leonard D. Eron, Jacquelyn H. Gentry, and Peggy Schlegel (Washington, DC: American Psychological Association, 1994), 383–404; Johnson and Johnson, "Teaching Students," 425–33.

12 Kathryn L. Wise, Kaarre A. Bundy, Eugene A. Bundy, and Larry A. Wise, "Social Skills Training for Young Adolescents," *Adolescence* 26, no. 101 (spring 1991): 233–41.

13 Eva Feindler and Randolph Ecton, *Adolescent Anger Control* (Elmsford, NY: Pergamon Press, 1986); Arnold P. Goldstein, *The Prepare Curriculum: Teaching Prosocial Competencies* (Champaign, IL: Research Press, 1988); Raymond W. Novaco, *Anger Control: The Development and Evolution of an Experimental Treatment* (Lexington, MA: Lexington Books, 1975).

14 Valerie Braithwaite, "Beyond Rokeach's Equality-Freedom Model: Two Dimensional Values in a One-Dimensional World," *Journal of Social Issues* 50, no. 4 (winter 1994): 67–94.

15 Shalom H. Schwartz, "Are There Universal Aspects in the Structure and Contents of Human Values?" *Journal of Social Issues* 50, no. 4 (winter 1994): 19–45; Daniel M. Mayton II and Adrian Furnham, "Value Underpinnings of Antinuclear Political Activism: A Cross-National Study," *Journal of Social Issues* 50, no. 4 (winter 1994): 117–28; Daniel M. Mayton II, Rhett Diessner, and Cheryl D. Granby, "Nonviolence and Human Values: Empirical Support for Theoretical Relationships," *Peace and Conflict: Journal of Peace Psychology* 2, no. 3 (1996): 245–254.

16 Di Bretherton, Linda Collins, and Carmel Ferretti, "Dealing with Conflict: Assessment of a Course for Secondary School Students," *Australian Psychologist* 28, no. 2 (August 1993): 105–11; L. Rowell Huesmann and Nancy G. Guerra, "Children's Normative Beliefs about Aggression and Aggressive Behavior," *Journal of Personality and Social Psychology* 72, no. 2 (February 1997): 408–19; Ronald G. Slaby and Nancy G. Guerra, "Cognitive Mediators of Aggression in Adolescent Offenders: I, Assessment," *Developmental Psychology* 24, no. 4 (July 1988): 580–88.

17 Michael Van Slyck, Marilyn Stern, and Salman Elbedour, "Adolescent Attitudes Toward Conflict: Correlates, Consequences and Cross Cultural Issues," in *Children and Adolescents Concepts of War, Peace and Conflict: An International Perspective*, ed. Amiram Raviv, Louis Oppenheimer, and Dani Bar-Tal (Lexington, MA: New Lexington Press, in press).

18 David G. Myers, *Social Psychology*, 5th ed. (New York: McGraw Hill, 1996), 125–43.

19 Ibid., 137–40.

20 Edith Bennett, "Discussion, Decision, Commitment and Consensus in Group Decision," *Human Relations* 8, no. 3 (June 1955): 251–73.

21 Alexander W. Astin, *What Matters in College? Four Critical Years Revisited* (San Francisco: Jossey-Bass, 1992).

22 Braithwaite, "Beyond Rokeach," 73.

23 Van Slyck, Stern, and Elbedour, "Adolescent Attitudes," in press.

24 Albert Bandura, *Self-Efficacy: The Exercise of Control* (New York: W. H. Freeman, 1997),

25 Susan T. Fiske, "People's Reactions to Nuclear War: Implications for Psychologists," in *Psychology and Social Responsibility: Facing Global Challenges*, ed. Sylvia Staub and Paula Green (New York: New York University Press, 1992), 305–26; Douglas McKenzie-Mohr, "Understanding the Psychology of Global Activism," in *Psychology and Social Responsibility*, 327–42.

26 Karl E. Weick, "Small Wins: Redefining the Scale of Social Problems," *American Psychologist* 39, no. 1 (January 1984): 40–49.

27 Johnson and Johnson, "Teaching Students," 419–20.

28 We are grateful to the following members of the Peace and Education Working Group, Peace Psychology Division of the American Psychological Association, for serving as reviewers (the numeral "2" in parentheses indicates having reviewed two curricula): Teresa Rose Banghart, David Boyer, Diane Bretherton, Dan Christie (2), John Dempsey (2), David Drews, Lili Goodman, Susan Heitler, Cosima Krueger (2), Marc Martin (2), Howard Mausner, Thomas Milburn, Carol Mitchell (2), Connie Mogg Davis, Francene Orrok, Stephanie Paravicini (2), Paul Pedersen, Johanna Tabin, Wendy Theobald (2), Janet Walker (2), and Lisa Webne-Behrman.

29 James E. Davis and James S. Eckenrod, *Managing World Conflict: A Resource Unit for High Schools* (Washington, DC: United States Institute of Peace, 1994): Available at United States Institute of Peace, 1550 M Street NW, Suite 700, Washington, DC 20005-1708. Phone: (202) 457-1700. Cost: Free.

30 The National Peace Essay Contest is open to all students in grades nine through twelve. More than fifty college scholarships totaling about $50,000 are awarded each year. For information, call United States Institute of Peace; phone: (202) 457-1700.

31 Vivian E. Gordon, *Conflict Resolution* (Florence, KY: ITP West Publishing, 1988): Available at ITP West Publishing, 7625 Empire Drive, Florence, KY 41042. Phone: (800) 354-9706. Cost: $30.95 ($22.75 for student copies).

32 Carol M. Lieber, *Making Choices about Conflict, Security, and Peacemaking. Part I: Personal Perspectives* (Cambridge, MA: Educators for Social Responsibility, 1994). Available at: Educators for Social Responsibility, 23 Garden Street, Cambridge, MA 02138. Phone: (800) 370-2515. Cost: $28.

33 John Looney, *Workbook for the Course in Peaceful Conflict Resolution "Alternatives to Violence"* (Akron OH: Peace Grows, Inc., 1995). Available at: Peace Grows, Inc., 513 W. Exchange Street, Akron, OH 44302. Phone: (330) 336-8031. Cost: $25.

34 Gail Sadalla, Manti Henriquez, and Meg Holmberg, *Conflict Resolution: A Secondary School Curriculum* (1987). New edition was published in 1998. Available at The Community Board Program, Inc., 1540 Market Street, Suite 490, San Francisco, CA 94102. Phone: (415) 552-1250. Cost: $44.

35 The curricula described here may be ordered from the *Conflict Resolution Education Catalogue* that is available without cost from NIDR, 1726 M Street, NW, Suite 500, Washington, DC 20036. Phone: (202) 466-4764.

36 Liss et al., *TRIBE.*

37 Fiona Macbeth and Nic Fine, *Playing with Fire: Creative Conflict Resolution for Young Adults* (Philadelphia: New Society Publishers, 1995).

38 Judith A. Zimmer *We Can Work It Out! Problem Solving through Mediation* (Culver City, CA: Social Studies School Service, 1993).

39 David W. Johnson and Roger T. Johnson, *Creative Controversy: Intellectual Challenge in the Classroom* (Edina, MN: Interaction Book Company, 1992).

40 Bodine, Crawford, and Schrumpf, *Creating the Peaceable School*; David W. Johnson and Roger T. Johnson, *Teaching Children to be Peacemakers* (Edina, MN: Interaction Book Company, 1991).

41 Deborah Prothrow-Stith, *Violence Prevention Curriculum for Adolescents* (Newton, MA: Education Development Center, 1987); Ronald G. Slaby, Renee Wilson-Brewer, and Kimberly Dash, *Aggressors, Victims, and Bystanders: Thinking and Acting to Prevent Violence* (Newton, MA: Education Development Center, 1994).

42 Guerra, Tolan, and Hammond, "Prevention and Treatment."

43 See note 35.

44 The *ESR Resource and Training Catalog* may be obtained from Educators for Social Responsibility, 23 Garden Street, Cambridge, MA 02138. Phone: (800) 370-2515. The *Cooperative Learning Catalog* may be ordered from Kagan Cooperative Learning, 27134 Paseo Espada, Suite 303, San Juan Capistrano, CA 92675. Phone: (800) 266-7576.

45 Bretherton, Collins, and Ferretti, "Dealing with Conflict"; Quanwu Zhang, "An Intervention Model of Constructive Conflict Resolution and Cooperative Learning," *Journal of Social Issues* 50, no. 1 (Spring 1994): 99–116. Johnson and Johnson, "Teaching Students;" Feeney and Davidson, "Bridging the Gap;" Nelson et al., "Teaching and Assessing."

46 Guerra, Tolan, and Hammond, "Prevention and Treatment."

47 Van Slyck, Stern, and Elbedour, "Adolescent Attitudes."

48 Jeffrey Jenkins and Melinda Smith, *School Mediation and Evaluation Materials* (Albuquerque, NM: New Mexico Center for Dispute Resolution, 1995).

49 Slaby and Guerra, "Cognitive Mediators . . . Assessment."

50 Guerra and Slaby, "Cognitive Mediators . . . Intervention."

51 Feeney and Davidson, "Bridging the Gap;" Johnson and Johnson, "Teaching Students," 422–25; Nelson et al., "Teaching and Assessing."

52 Michael Van Slyck and Marilyn Stern, "A Developmental Approach to the Use of Conflict Resolution Interventions with Adolescents," in this volume.

Chapter 6

The Speak Your Piece Project: Exploring Controversial Issues in Northern Ireland

Alan McCully, Marian O'Doherty, and Paul Smyth

In a survey of peace education in the postmodern United States, Ian M. Harris opens with a frightening portrayal of levels of violence on the campuses of some U.S. high schools.[1] Outsiders to Northern Ireland might think that such scenarios should hold little terror for educators who have worked with young people in the midst of community violence that spans the last twenty-eight years. Yet, in a survey of research into the impact of "the troubles" on children, Edward Cairns and Tara Cairns conclude that the "prophets of doom," who at the outbreak of the unrest in 1969 predicted that community violence would result in spiralling increases in youth crime and in instances of young people with mental health problems, have largely been proved wrong.[2] However, in their conclusions the authors also note concerns and call for further research:

> Although a proportion of children in Northern Ireland have had personal experience with political violence and some feel anxiety symptoms as a result, nevertheless most of these children seem able to cope and do not suffer serious psychological impairments. However there are worrying indications that political violence may be linked to variations in the level of certain aspects of anti-social and sociopathic behaviour.[3]

The task of investigating the impact of violence on young people in Northern Ireland is a complex one, made difficult by local variations in the instances of acts of violence, the need to distinguish between those affected directly and those affected indirectly, and the impact of other socioeconomic factors that have contributed to violent behavior in other societies. In many aspects Northern Ireland is a conservative society as reflected in its comparatively high levels of church attendance.[4] One early study even suggested that the outbreak of communal violence had actually directed "the young away from rebellion against the adult world characteristic of their age group towards conformity with their parents."[5] This conservatism is also reflected in the Province's school system. It is characterized by segregation:

> It is segregated by religion in that most children attend predominantly Protestant (controlled) schools or Catholic (maintained) schools; by ability (and some would say by social background) in that a selection system operates at age 11 to decide which children attend grammar schools (more than one third at second-level education); and often by gender (particularly at second-level where a quarter of the secondary schools and almost half of all grammar schools are single-sex).[6]

It is popularly argued that schools have been a stabilizing influence throughout the years of the "troubles." The new Labour Party minister with responsibility for education in Northern Ireland recently described the high levels of performance achieved by Northern Irish second-level students in external examinations in a United Kingdom, compared to their peers in the United Kingdom, as a source of pride.[7] He also noted that a greater percentage of the Province's young people leave formal schooling with no qualifications than elsewhere in the United Kingdom. In recent years, there are indications, for example in the resolutions passed at teacher trades union conferences and in the use of exclusion as a disciplinary measure, that a rise in the frequency and intensity of disruptive behavior by students is perceived as an increasing problem in some schools, particularly those in urban settings.[8] It is difficult to quantify the extent to which "the troubles" have retarded the economic and social life of the Province, but factors common to other areas of the British Isles and beyond, such as poverty, deprivation, and family breakdown, have also contributed to social dislocation. Any peacebuilding program in Northern Ireland is bound to address itself primarily at the level of community conflict. This paper concentrates on one such initiative, the Speak Your Piece project, but it should be noted that some schools in Northern Ireland are also experiencing incidents of violent disruption not directly related to the wider conflict.

The Origins of Education for Mutual Understanding

Before examining the origins, philosophy, and work of Speak Your Piece to date it is important to chart the attempts made by educators in both the school and youth work sectors to intervene to try to defuse conflict. Over the past three decades many of those who have sought solutions in Northern Ireland have cited education as a source of hope in attacking the bigotry and prejudice that underlies sectarian tension.[9] Early work in the field was carried out by committed individuals, sometimes supported by projects based in the higher education institutions, and by voluntary agencies. Norman Richardson documents the various approaches, including those that sought to work primarily in the formal curriculum and those that put their energies into cross-community interschool contact and residential work.[10] Some saw schools as offering "oases of calm," in which emphasis was placed on what young people had in common. Others thought it imperative that the young seek understanding of those contentious issues that contribute to conflict. These developments "represented a patchwork of small, relatively isolated projects, geographically dispersed, each making a contribution toward the evolution of a more coherent and developed programme of work."[11]

In the 1970s the Northern Ireland Department of Education adopted what a senior school inspector recently called a "benign neutrality."[12] In the 1980s government educational policy became more proactive in community relations. This was partly in response to more cohesive pressure from diverse groups working in the field and to research that highlighted the extent of the divisions in the educational system.[13] In 1982 the Department of Education of Northern Ireland (DENI) signalled formal support for work in the community relations field when it issued Circular 82/21, *The Improvement of Community Relations: The Contribution of Schools*. This stated that, "every teacher, every school manager, Board member and trustee, and every educational manager within the system has a responsibility for helping children learn to understand and respect each other."[14]

With support from the Northern Ireland Council for Educational Development (NICED), a quasi-governmental curriculum agency, Education for Mutual Understanding (EMU) emerged as the nomenclature under which educational work in the community relations field was carried forward. When, for the first time, a statutory curriculum was introduced into Northern Ireland in 1989, EMU and a related theme,

Cultural Heritage, were two of six compulsory cross-curricular themes.[15] It was envisaged that these themes would be embraced by all teachers and would infuse work done across all subject areas of the curriculum. EMU is defined as being "about self-respect, and respect for others, and the improvement of relationships between people of differing cultural traditions."[16] Its four objectives are

- fostering respect for self and building relationships
- understanding conflict
- interdependence
- cultural understanding

Cultural Heritage is defined as "enabling pupils to know about, understand and evaluate the common experiences of their cultural heritage, the diverse and distinctive aspects of their culture, and the interdependence of cultures."[17] Both have an obvious focus on the Northern Ireland conflict. They also have objectives that address the whole range of social relationships and interaction of cultures at family, peer group, community, and international levels. Labels such as Peace Studies, which might be perceived as having overt political implications, are avoided. The emphasis is very much on a process whereby, through rational inquiry and the fostering of relationships, greater understanding and tolerance might result. In turn, this should contribute to more constructive attitudes in society.

There were parallel developments within the Northern Ireland youth services during this period. The youth services include all those working educationally with young people outside the formal school system. The 1987 Policy Document which included a youth work curriculum, states that its first objective is

> To promote *greater understanding* of a society with diverse traditions by engaging where at all possible in programmes where there is a *strong cross-community involvement*.[18] (original emphases)

It was not until 1992 that guidelines for this work were outlined.[19] Funding was moved from the Department of Education to the Youth Council for Northern Ireland and the youth departments in the five regional educational boards to establish the Community Relations Youth Service Support Scheme (CRYSSS) within which is contained the Cross-Community Contact Scheme (CCCS). The CCCS gives funding to youth organizations to run cross-community projects with other groups, covering a proportion of program and residential work costs. CRYSSS has allowed wider access to funding for special events, projects, research, and even the employment of key personnel.[20]

EMU in Practice

In the school sector the statutory provision of the EMU program has been in operation since August 1992. Researchers into its initial statutory years recognize its substantial achievements but ask fundamental questions about its structure, operation, and philosophy.[21] The program has done much to raise the profile of community relations work in schools, and many have become more conscious of creating a positive and open ethos conducive to this type of work. However, they also identify limitations. The implementation of a cohesive strategy has suffered because teachers tend to interpret the nature and scope of EMU in widely different ways. Too often it is defined in terms of cross-community contact rather than as an integral part of the formal curriculum. A heavily laden, subject-driven curriculum, combined with inadequate structural support and a lack of training and professional development for teachers involved in the implementation of EMU, is resulting in some schools taking a minimalist approach to the statutory requirements. Sharper and, potentially more contentious, cultural, religious, and political issues are often avoided.

As a consequence of their research Alan Smith and Alan Robinson made a number of recommendations for the future direction of EMU, summarized below:

- the amalgamation of EMU and Cultural Heritage with a single set of four objectives
- the development of strategies that address more challenging and controversial issues
- the underpinning of the work with concepts such as human rights, civic responsibility, democracy, and justice
- the creation of more supportive management and training structures[22]

Within these, there is recognition that if education is to contribute to a sustained improvement in community relations, the underlying tensions and inequalities in society must be addressed and young people empowered to affect change. There are echoes here of Johan Galtung's "positive peace."[23] Smith and Robinson concluded that there is some evidence to suggest that government support for Education for Mutual Understanding, along with a range of other community relations initiatives, has helped change the discourse in Northern Ireland by introducing a language which allows people to express their support for cultural pluralism and political dialogue rather than sectarianism and political violence. The challenge now is whether initiatives can help young people move beyond the "polite exchange" so that they engage with each other in meaningful discussion of controversial social, cultural, religious and political issues.[24]

Speak Your Piece was initiated to address these controversial issues and associated training needs. Channel 4, a British Television network, committed approximately $350,000 to commission a series of five programs entitled *Off the Walls,* to facilitate the exploration of contentious cultural, religious, and political issues with young people in the fourteen to seventeen age range. To give the series every chance to realize its potential European Union money was secured to establish a research and development support team based at the University of Ulster in Coleraine. Initially, the emphasis was placed on work in twenty pilot schools but it was clear that, as students in schools reflect the attitudes fostered in the wider community, it was also important to engage young people in less formal environments.

In the informal youth sector, too, research revealed that only a minority of youth workers (27 percent) operating in the community relations field, had moved beyond placing an emphasis on commonality and interdependence in society to focusing on division, inequity, difference, personal encounter, and conflict resolution,

> Youth workers had creatively incorporated a community relations dimension into a wide range of program areas, highlighting the fact that there is no single blueprint for the work. Whilst the programme areas were found to be diverse it was noted that most of the work did not go beyond the stage of addressing non-controversial issues. Thus there is much scope for the development of more complex work that addresses personal and controversial issues.[25]

Similar patterns were emerging in the youth services to those outlined by Smith and Robinson in schools. With support from the Youth Council of Northern Ireland, a parallel strand of Speak Your Piece undertook to work with twenty pilot youth workers.

The Philosophy of Speak Your Piece

Speak Your Piece began formally in September 1995, with an initial commitment to run for two years. The television series was entrusted

The Speak Your Piece Project

to an independent production team, which took early guidance from the project initiators but was then given the artistic freedom to shape the programs as it wished. The series was first broadcast in May and June 1996 and has since been made available on video. Each of the five programs takes a theme around which there is controversy in Northern Ireland:

1. Identity
2. Culture
3. Religion
4. Politics
5. The Choice (where do we go from here?)

Each consists of three strands; a comparative commentary from Jerusalem on the Israeli/Palestinian conflict, drama sequences featuring four characters and their friends, and a studio debate involving young people. Rather than attempting to provide answers, each program poses questions. The programs seek to provide complexity on issues that are often interpreted from a narrow perspective.

The time available prior to broadcasting gave the project team the opportunity to do preparatory work with the pilot groups. Previous experience has shown the importance of practitioners in this field working through the processes involved and clarifying their own perceptions on the issues before they engage with groups of young people. Participants in both pilot groups brought varying levels of experience to the project but both groups were characterized by a high level of commitment to community relations work. The professional interaction, stimulated by input from the project team and viewing of the programs helped establish a philosophy and a framework for handling controversial issues.

Three principles emerged from Speak Your Piece's early engagement with its pilot groups:

- enabling dialogue that is forthright and inclusive
- providing alternatives to violence and avoidance as ways of responding to conflict
- facilitating participatory decision making which encourages democratic processes

Inclusive dialogue is one of the most-used phrases of the Northern Ireland peace process yet it is illusive in practice. It seems vital that if the concept is to become embedded, young people have the opportunity to expose their views to others, and are prepared to have those views challenged. While acknowledging the reality that some may see violence as one response to their situation, the project must counter by providing nonviolent alternatives. Equally vital, there is a need to challenge those who choose to ignore or avoid controversy. Having encouraged young people to engage in dialogue and clarify their positions, it is important that they have the opportunity to utilize the skills and understanding acquired to respond creatively to conflict in their lives.

These are grand objectives but how can inclusive dialogue be practically sustained? The model promoted by Speak Your Piece presents a framework of dialogue. This attempts to identify those factors which both help sustain and impede discussion: communication and social skills; emotions and feelings; decision making and democracy; relationships about power and respect (gender, status, wealth, age); and past experiences, biography.

The critical factors that individuals bring to discussion are positioned around the controversial issue. Facilitators must be aware of how these impinge on the dynamics of the dialogue. It is important to nurture the social and communication skills of participants to enable them to communicate at the same level as others. Other potential imbalances are those relating to power, gender, and status. For example, a teacher has to recognize the effect of his or her authority in the classroom and compensate for this when facilitating discussion. Facilitators must also recognize that when exchanging views on deeply held attitudes, possibly involving those who may have suffered directly from the conflict, a misplaced, or misunderstood, word or gesture has the potential to severely alter the dynamics of the discussion. Conversely, past experiences and personal biographies, handled appropriately, can inform and enrich. The decision-making dynamics of the group should also reflect the democratic objectives of the process.

In order to overcome possible barriers there are important implications for the approaches and role of the facilitator. Where possible groups should be given opportunities to build up familiarity with the skills required to discuss controversial issues in an open and trusting atmosphere. It is vital to generate respect for the right to express points of view and to show sensitivity to personal biographies. Challenging opinions requires the facilitator to use appropriate resources, ask probing questions, and ensure that young people are involved in a process of inquiry that takes a critical account of the evidence presented. Concepts such as democracy, justice, and human rights should be fostered as ways of anchoring the debate when emotions run high. From the outset the project rejected the notion of "neutral chairmanship."[26] No one in Northern Ireland is immune from the forces that have shaped their background. Hence, the project places emphasis on practitioners working through the resources and associated activities to examine their own attitudes and prejudices before carrying the work to young people. In so doing they are better prepared to understand the feelings of young people working through the same process and are less likely to abuse their position.

In summary, within the framework of the core values outlined in the three principles, practitioners should:

- work through activities that encourage an open sharing of biographies
- inform young people of a range of other views and opinions
- show that there are multiple perspectives on any issue
- clarify and help to resolve internal personal conflict
- support fair (fairer) outcomes
- encourage creative thinking in responding to controversial issues

To help them in their task the project team brought together ideas that emerged from the training workshops with sound existing practice to produce a thirty-two-page guidance booklet to the series.[27] This was designed to provide practitioners with a structure, questions, ideas, and activities to tease out the issues contained in the television programs. The methodology places emphasis on an active experiential approach, and owes much to the participation of youth workers in the project. Teachers in Northern Ireland, even those operating in the field of social education, have a tendency to be more formal in their methodological approaches.

The Experience of Speak Your Piece

During 1996–97 teachers and youth workers from the pilot groups explored the potential of the programs with young people, mostly utilizing and adapting the guidance booklet. The project adopted an action research approach that included semi-structured interviews with practitioners, monitored student evaluations, reflective participation, and the observation of sessions. Research is continuing. The pilot teachers and youth workers were brought back together in the fall of 1997 to draw on their experiences of Speak Your Piece and to push forward thinking on the teaching of controversial issues. Findings are emerging in four areas: (1) Resources and methodology; (2) Institutional support structure; (3) Appropriate curriculum provision; and (4) Training.

Resources and Methodology

Television, coupled with an open, experiential pedagogy is proving an effective resource as a means of engaging young people in dialogue on controversial cultural and political issues. Detailed evaluations from sixteen- to seventeen-year-olds in two schools in Northern Ireland (eighteen students in a mainly Protestant school, and thirty-three students from a mainly Catholic school) and one school in the Republic of Ireland (involving twenty-one students), completed after structured modules of work, are encouraging. In each case, over two thirds of those surveyed are generally positive about the experience. Many of the comments refer to a widening awareness, a greater clarity of thinking and a more questioning attitude,

> After watching the series of videos over five weeks my overall reaction was that it was very useful and helped me to think about my beliefs and challenged my opinions. It has made me think very clearly and the main thing that has stuck in my head is, "should religion influence your political opinions?"

The project has some reservations about the applicability of the series in the Republic of Ireland but here, also, there is evidence that the work is informing, challenging, and clarifying opinions,

> Not in the strictest sense of the word an educational video, more an informative watch. You don't have a five-minute reaction to this video.

In all three evaluations the negative responses tend to focus around declarations of apathy toward the conflict,

> My culture has nothing to do with the British/Irish debate so I found this irrelevant. I belong to the teenager culture . . . this was all stuff I'd heard before about dialogue, etc., so it was easy to switch off and ignore.

Or a perception that young people are impotent to influence the situation:

> There isn't much point in doing things in the classroom when it is up to the politicians what happens.

Contrary to that, the evaluations contain several comments that suggest that the work is succeeding in getting some young people to re-examine their social responsibility,

> I realised that in order to make an agreement we all have to listen to other people's point of view and we cannot move away or turn our back on the situation and think that it will go away because what these programmes made me realise is that it affects us all.

The evaluations and classroom observation point to the potential of television as a positive agent for injecting a range of opinions and perspectives into a debate, thus setting a framework for the skillful practitioner to move quickly into work that allows an open exchange of views and clarifies individual positions. Encouraged by the impact of the *Off the Walls*/Speak Your Piece experiment, Channel 4 has commissioned two additional series with an EMU theme for younger students in the four to eleven and eleven to fourteen age groups.

Institutional Support Structures
Ian Harris talks of peace education as being a "holistic philosophy" that embraces all aspects of school life.[28] In the past, workers in the field of community relations often lamented that they worked alone without institutional support.[29] Recent thinking on EMU very much endorses Harris's view in the guise of "the EMU promoting school":

> an ethos which embraces EMU and Cultural Heritage requires schools to go that extra mile in fostering an explicit and visible commitment to better relationships within the whole school and with its broader community.[30]

For practitioners to be effective it is of great importance that they are supported within the culture of the institution in which they work. The experience of Speak Your Piece also indicates the crucial importance of the work being taken up by the committed practitioner who is prepared to take risks with appropriate support. The optimum conditions for the work to become embedded are likely to occur when the energy of the committed practitioner is harnessed to clear lines of communication and supportive management structures.

Appropriate Curriculum Provision

Speak Your Piece has worked within the cross-curricular context of EMU. Amongst its pilot schools group it attracted teachers of English, History, Religious Education and those involved in Personal and Social Education. To date those who have tried to locate the work within the crowded, tightly structured subject programs of study of the Northern Ireland curriculum have had limited success. The work has flourished best when allowed to stand on its own as a self-contained module, either as part of a Personal and Social Education course or as an enhancement module for older, academically-orientated students. Speak Your Piece acknowledges the contribution that can be made by all teachers to fulfil the objectives of EMU but contends that when handling sharper more contentious cultural and political issues, the practitioner requires specific skills and the young people need time and space for debate and reflection. In any future review of the Northern Ireland Curriculum the project would argue for designated timetable space in which issues related to civic, social, cultural, and political education can be dealt with sensitively and reflectively.

The Youth Service curriculum is currently under review and the recent "Review of the Youth Work Curriculum" document includes the suggested program areas of "Values and Beliefs, Political Education and Active Citizenship, and Community Action and Community Involvement."[31] Speak Your Piece sees the potential for complementary developments in the content and ethos of the formal and informal curricula.

Training

In its efforts to disseminate its work, Speak Your Piece has provided training days in a variety of settings for teachers and youth workers. Those who attend come with a desire to make some contribution diffusing the conflict. Often participants draw attention to the inadequacy of their training for equipping them with the necessary skills. This youth worker's comment is typical of the views expressed:

> I will use the activities in any cross-community work if I have a very confident co-facilitator. Further support . . . would be particularly relevant. I feel I would

really need to have to do more research into both traditional backgrounds before undertaking such a programme.

This confidence factor is a critical barrier that practitioners must overcome before they feel able to engage in the risk taking necessary to handle more controversial topics. Speak Your Piece envisages a training structure that extends from initial training, through early in-service work, to the opportunity to complete higher degrees with an emphasis on critical, reflective practice.

Innovative Practice

Speak Your Piece has identified a clear position in relation to the role of educators in the conflict in Northern Ireland. Whatever the professional backgrounds of the practitioners the emphasis is foremost on engaging with the issues of identity, culture, religion, and politics, but it is also important that they bring their specialities and their particular circumstances to the work. A number of innovative developments have stemmed from the interests of project teachers and youth workers: school disciplines, political education, cross-community contact, computer conferencing, and peer education.

Subject Disciplines

In the formal sector some teachers of English have taken a Media Studies critique to the work that has complemented the project's inquiry approach. Teachers of History have taken contemporary comments expressed in the drama sequences and studio debates (for example, a comment by an Irish Republican, "*This is not of our choosing. We never wanted this state. It was forced upon us and now we are forced to shake it off*") and, using the context of their students' study of Irish history, explored the origins and validity of such statements. Teachers of Religious Education have focused their involvement around the extent to which religious belief should influence politics.

Political Education

The lead in Political Education has been taken by a group of youth workers who have explored the potential of the Speak Your Piece resources to foster democratic processes. A recent report into the attitudes of young people to politics in Northern Ireland showed that 75 percent are interested in what is happening politically (in Northern Ireland), yet only 3 percent are involved in a political party (1 percent amongst young women), and only 12 percent are involved in any kind of campaigning group. Asked whether young people should have the opportunity to learn about the political process in schools, 79 percent agreed that they should.[32] The Speak Your Piece group envisages a course that positions the concepts of justice and democracy at its core; and that provides young people with opportunities to actively participate in nonviolent political action. With the emphasis on experiential learning practitioners are encouraged to open the dialogue to voices not always heard, or accessible, in their community.

Cross-Community Contact
Much of the work of Speak Your Piece takes place with groups of young people from one of the main cultural traditions. A considerable amount can be achieved in these circumstances, particularly in clarifying and challenging personal positions in a secure environment, and in fostering the confidence and skills to engage with divergent opinions. However, it is also vital that they have the chance to encounter a full range of views only available when they come into contact with those from the other tradition. Cross-community contact schemes are an established dimension of both the formal and informal sectors but research has shown them to be uneven in their provision.[33] Youth groups keen to explore serious cultural and political issues have found it beneficial to use the Speak Your Piece resources as a way of developing communication skills and confidence before coming together in a residential setting to build on their common experience of the project.

Computer Conferencing
Face-to-face contact is not always easy to sustain on a regular basis. Also, logistical constraints limit the number of young people that can be involved in cross-community work of substance. Speak Your Piece has sought to explore the potential of information technology to enable young people from widely different backgrounds to exchange ideas. The main vehicle for this is a Computer Conference run through British Telecom's *CampusWorld*. For several years a researcher at the University of Ulster, Roger Austin, has been facilitating conferences involving academically-oriented seventeen- and eighteen-year-olds studying aspects of European and Irish History.[34] Questions are placed in

the conference, groups of students within a class debate the issues and respond both to the initial question and to the opinions of others. An academic historian moderates the debate, injecting information, ideas, and challenges when appropriate.

Speak Your Piece has established a conference that asks young people from both schools and youth groups to respond to key questions arising from the television programs, and these are moderated by an experienced practitioner in the community relations field. In contrast to Austin's work the issues being debated are contemporary and potentially more emotionally charged, and the process less defined by an academic subject discipline. The young people involved come from a wide range of social backgrounds, a greater age range and with varying levels of educational achievement. Given these factors, and the easily ruffled sensitivities surrounding the Northern Ireland situation, important questions have surfaced relating to the regulation of the students' input to the conference. Ground rules have been established that place the responsibility on participating groups to monitor their own contributions.

In the four months the conference has operated technical difficulties have curtailed its effectiveness, but there are encouraging signs that the young people participating are taking the process seriously. The involvement of a youth group from an isolated border village, perceived by Protestants as a stronghold of Republican activity and therefore a no-go area, is an indication of the possibilities technology holds for overcoming obstacles to more inclusive dialogue.

Peer Education

In examining schools' responses to violence Harris emphasizes the importance of conflict resolution and peer mediation in developing peacemaking skills.[35] Innovative work has been done in schools with elementary and junior secondary students by the EMU Promoting Schools Project.[36] It has concentrated on developing in students the skills to participate in the resolution of disputes that occur daily in schools. In the process it seeks to alter the climate in schools toward a more open and peaceful ethos.

Peer education as a structured approach is a recent development in Northern Ireland. Much of the work has concentrated on health issues and drug-related education. Under the auspices of the Speak Your Piece project, a number of specialist youth workers are engaging with a group of twenty young people. The aim is to develop a peer-led model for community relations work adapting the project's resources and approach. Brian Murtagh has outlined the potential impact of peer education,

> Adolescence is a time of enormous change when young people struggle to leave childhood behind and take on their new identity as young adults. In the process of taking on a new identity they increasingly look to their peers for acceptance and affirmation. The relationship with peers often assumes a dominant position in their lives. For this reason they learn more easily and more readily from each other than from parents or other adult figures. If provided with positive role models from peers, young people are likely to listen to and to learn positive messages.[37]

Equipped with the necessary skills and confidence, we anticipate that these young people will be able to draw out young people's views and feelings on sensitive cultural and political matters more naturally than the "authority figures" of teachers and youth workers by building on the relationship they have with their peers. This autumn, the trainees will start working with groups of young people in the youth and community sector, and in schools across Northern Ireland.

This paper has outlined the context, philosophy, and practice of one educational initiative seeking to contribute to a more peaceful society in Northern Ireland. The project began during a period of real hope when the paramilitary ceasefires were in place and expectations for peace were high. Its brief life has witnessed the breakdown of the IRA truce and the upheavals resulting from the Orange march disputes in the summer of 1996. Both events clearly demonstrate the failure of all of us in Northern Ireland to come to terms with dialogue, negotiation, and the democratic process as ways of moving our society forward. They also illustrate latent aggression that too frequently surfaces in relationships in Northern Ireland whether emanating from the political situation or from other sources. Education has a responsibility to address all aspects of this violence, however daunting the task.

Speak Your Piece has brought together committed and skilled practitioners from both the formal and informal sectors to support one another and to share expertise and approaches. Returning to the responses of peace educators in the United States to violence in the community and schools, there is much there that practitioners in Northern Ireland recognize as effective practice including: creating supportive environments where young people can vent their deeply held thoughts and feelings; equipping young people with personal and interpersonal strategies to cope with conflict nonviolently; using experiential teaching approaches; and underpinning practice with the concepts of justice and democracy.[38] Practitioners in both countries would benefit from sharing their experiences.

Notes

1 Ian M. Harris, "From World Peace to Peace in the 'Hood: Peace Education in a Postmodern World," *Journal for a Just and Caring Education* 2, no. 4 (October 1996): 379–80.

2 Edward Cairns and Tara Cairns, "Children and Conflict: A Psychological Perspective," in *Facets of the Conflict in Northern Ireland* ed. Seamus Dunn (Basingstoke: St. Martin's Press, 1995), 97–113.

3 Ibid., 101–2.

4 Ibid., 98–99.

5 David Jenvey, "Sons and Haters: Youth in Conflict," *New Society* 21, 125–27.

6 Alan Smith, "Education and Conflict in Northern Ireland," in *Facets of the Conflict in Northern Ireland*, ed. Seamus Dunn (Basingstoke: St. Martin's Press, 1995), 186–88. Smith also makes reference to the establishment of integrated schools attended by both Protestants and Catholics in roughly equal numbers and promoting an ethos that embraces both cultural traditions. Since the establishment of the first school in 1981, thirty-three integrated schools have opened (twenty-two first level, eleven second level), catering for a little under 3 percent of school provision.

7 Tony Worthington, speech to NAS/UWT Conference, 22 February 1997, issued by the British Labour Party Media Office.

8 Rosemary Kilpatrick, Alexandra Barr and Caroline Wylie, *The 1996/97 Northern Ireland Suspension and Expulsion Study* (Bangor, DENI Research Report Series No. 13, 1999).

9 Malcolm Skilbeck, "The School and Cultural Development" in *Curriculum Design*, ed. M. Golby (London: Croom Helm, 1975), 27–35. Skilbeck initiated the Schools Cultural Studies Project at the New University of Ulster, which advocated a reconstructionalist philosophy, renewing Northern Irish culture by taking what was best from each tradition.

10 Norman Richardson, *Roots if Not Wings: Where Did EMU Come From?* (Belfast, Churches Education Centre, n.d.) 1–6.

11 Alan Smith, "Education and the Conflict in Northern Ireland," 170.

12 Maurna Crozier and Richard Froggatt ed., *Cultural Traditions in Northern Ireland: Cultural Diversity in Contemporary Europe* (Belfast: Queens University, 1998).

13 John Darby, Don Batts, Seamus Dunn, Joe Harris, and Sean Farren, *Education and Community in Northern Ireland: Schools Apart?* (Coleraine: New University of Ulster, 1977) concluded that the education system was genu-

inely segregated and that there was very little crossover or interaction between the two sectors. Seamus Dunn, John Darby, and Kieran Mullan, *Schools Together?* (Coleraine: New University of Ulster, 1984) confirmed that very little meaningful contact existed between the two sets of schools despite claims to the contrary. Dominic Murray, *Worlds Apart? Segregated Education in Northern Ireland* (Belfast: Appletree Press, 1985), in a survey of life in two first-level schools (one Protestant, one Catholic) in a rural town, found that there was little different in the formal curriculum taught but that in the hidden curriculum each strongly reflected the cultural tradition from which its students came.

14 DENI, Circular 82/21. *The Improvement of Community Relations: The Contribution of Schools* (Belfast: 1982).

15 HMSO, *Educational Reform* (Northern Ireland) Order 1989 (Belfast: 1989) 15.

16 DENI, *Educational (Cross Cultural) Themes* (Belfast: HMSO, 1992) 5.

17 Ibid., 8.

18 DENI, *Policy for a Youth Service in Northern Ireland* (Belfast: 1987) 16.

19 Clem McCartney, *Community Relations Guidelines* (Belfast: Youth Council for Northern Ireland, 1992).

20 This includes the funding for the Speak Your Piece project officer with responsibility for youth service developments.

21 Alan Smith and Alan Robinson, *Education for Mutual Understanding: The Initial Statutory Years* (Coleraine: The Centre for the Study of Conflict, University of Ulster, 1996).

22 Ibid., 81–90.

23 Linda Rennie Forcey, "Peace Studies" in *Protest, Power, and Change: An Encyclopedia of Non Violent Action from ACT-Up to Women's Suffrage*, ed. Roger S. Powers and William B. Vogele (New York: Garland), 407–8.

24 Smith and Robinson, *Education for Mutual Understanding*, 82.

25 McCartney, *Community Relations Guidelines*, 7. For similar findings see Youth Service Partnership Group, *Reconciliation-Cross Community Project Report* (Belfast: European Bureau, 1995).

26 In Britain the role of teacher as "neutral chairman" when facilitating discussion on controversial issues was pioneered in the 1970s by the Humanities Project. See Lawrence Stenhouse et al., *The Humanities Project: An Introduction* (London: Heinemann, 1970).

27 Alan Smith, Alan McCully, Marian ODoherty, and Paul Smyth, *Speak Your Piece: Exploring Controversial Issues* (Coleraine: University of Ulster, 1996).

28 Harris, "From World Peace to Peace in the 'Hood," 387.

29 Richardson, *Roots If Not Wings*, 5.

30 Northern Ireland Council for The Curriculum, Examinations and Assessment, *Mutual Understanding and Cultural Heritage: Cross-Curricular Guidance Materials* (Belfast: CCEA, 1997), 5.

31 Youth Council of Northern Ireland, *Review of the Youth Work Curriculum: Report of the Curriculum Review Working Group* (Belfast: YCNI, 1997), 15.

32 Kate Fearon ed., *Politics: The Next Generation* (Belfast: Democratic Dialogue, 1997), 8–11.

33 See Smith and Robinson, *Education for Mutual Understanding*, 40–49. Also for the youth services YSPG, Reconciliation-Cross-Community Project Report.

34 Roger Austin, "Computer Conferencing in History: A Pilot Study at 16–18" *Teaching History* 75 (1994), 33–35.

35 Harris, "From World Peace to Peace in the 'Hood," 387.

36 Jerry Tyrell and Seamus Farrell, *Peer Mediation in Primary Schools* (Coleraine: Centre for the Study of Conflict, University of Ulster, 1995).

37 Brian Murtagh, *Peer Education: A Manual* (Dublin: National Youth Federation, 1996), 4–5.

38 Harris, "From World Peace to Peace in the 'Hood," 378–95.

Chapter 7

How Can Caring Help? A Personalized Cross-Generational Examination of Violent Adolescent Experiences in Schools

Barbara J. Thayer-Bacon

Adolescents in the United States are growing up surrounded by violent acts of aggression. We can read about attempts to injure or harm others in the news, see examples in the movies and television shows, and hear violence in teenagers' music and on MTV. We come face to face with the violence our children grow up with when researchers tell us the three most frequent causes of death for adolescents are accidents, murder, and suicide.[1] It is not surprising to find that children's lives are affected when they grow up with violence all around them, and they potentially become violent themselves, even to the point of owning guns and killing each other. What can schools do, particularly teachers and students, to help curb the violence we live around? How can we help to create safe, peaceful environments in our schools in which adolescents can learn to be peaceful themselves? These are the questions to be explored in this article.

Before we can explore these questions, however, we must define what we mean by violence and peace. If we define violence in terms of the use of extreme physical force, as in war situations, then peace is defined simply as "the absence of extreme physical force (war)." However, if we define peace to include "the presence of social justice" then we expand what we mean by violence.[2] In this article I embrace a "positive peace" definition to include issues of social justice. I wish to distinguish violence in terms of levels and degrees, so that acts of aggression that are physical (e.g., assaults, rapes) are considered overt forms of violence, and acts of aggression that violate individuals' dignity (e.g., verbal harassment, belittlement, and threats) are viewed as covert forms of violence. In this way, violence is "a behavior that violates other individuals" and that violation can by physical (overt violence) or mental, emotional, even spiritual violence (covert violence).[3]

Now that we are able to talk about violence in terms of levels and degrees, let us move to place schools within their larger social context. Schools are just one social institution among many that affect the qualities of our lives. Other social institutions include the government, the economy, families, religions, cultural communities, the expressive arts, and the media. Schools fulfill many purposes for society, too. Traditionally we have asked schools to pass on the knowledge of our society and to help inculcate our young so they will be prepared to participate and contribute to our society as adults. In a democratic society such as the United States, we ask our schools to prepare democratic citizens for the future of our country.

As other institutions struggle with changing roles due to events and changing factors in our lives, so too do our schools. In the twentieth century we have asked our schools to take on roles that have historically been the responsibility of other institutions. For example, in the past, our churches and families have mainly taught children about right behavior, and how to live a moral life. Now changes in economic institutions, as well as in cultural communities have caused families and churches to change their roles in our lives. Schools are called on to fill a gap in teaching morality that families and churches traditionally filled. Schools are also called on to assume parental roles in actual physical care of children, including making sure our children are fed, clothed, rested, and protected from physical harm.

Because our schools are one among many social institutions in our society, they reflect whatever conditions the larger society is experiencing. When our society feels tensions due to racial or sexual discrimination, these same tensions are experienced in our schools. When our society struggles with economic loss, due to changing economic conditions and the loss of jobs which results in the lowering of income levels, our schools show the wear and tear signs of a society in economic decline. When adults in our society cope with their problems by using drugs and alcohol, our youth model their behavior, and drugs and alcohol are then found in our schools. And when our society experiences an increase in violence, as can be seen by an increase in crimes and the purchasing of arms, for example, then these same conditions are reflected in our schools. Racism, sexism, and poverty manifest themselves in overt forms of violence such as gang fights, and in covert forms such as sexual harassment.

In order to consider how teachers and community leaders can help our schools be peaceful environments in which adolescents can learn to be nonviolent, peaceloving, and peacebuilding individuals, it will be fruitful to consider what are necessary qualities of peace. This is a philosophical question, and as a philosopher of education, this is what I hope to contribute to the larger discussion on peacebuilding for adolescents. While schools clearly cannot eradicate violence, they can foster a more peaceful environment. If we can better understand the essential ingredients for peace to occur, then we can explore ways to ensure these ingredients are present and thriving in our schools. It is my contention that one vital quality of a peaceful environment is that it is a *caring* environment. When we examine examples of overt and covert violence in any setting, we always find that the setting lacks genuine forms of caring. In order to defend this contention, I must thoroughly explore what caring means, how it relates to other qualities, and how it effects all of us.

I use my own experiences as an adolescent and as a teacher, as well as my three teenage children's experiences, as autobiographical and biographical narrative to help us look at caring in our schools. I do not wish to imply by the use of this personal data that my family's experiences are representative of others' experiences, or even that they are more significant in terms of the covert violence they describe: they are not. Rather, I tell our stories as a way of contextualizing myself as a writer, by exposing my subjective voice. I want the reader/hearer to know who I am. I am a unique, qualitative being. I am not an abstract, third-person, objective, neutral, anonymous philosopher. I speak from the first-person perspective to remind you (and myself) that ideas do not have a life of their own. They do not sprout out of the ground drawing nourishment from the soil, water, air, and sunlight. Ideas are *peoples'* ideas, and that means they are influenced by such contextual variables as social, political, psychological, economic, and historical forces. Theory that is estranged from the empirical world and social contexts runs the risk of being universalist or dogmatic. I also hope that these particular stories will serve as metaphors to the reader's own stories, for all of us have experienced covert violence in school, with a teacher toward a student, and between students.

I tell a story from my teenage years and one from my daughter's adolescence in order to help us make a cross-generational, personalized examination of adolescent experiences. This autobiographical and biographical narrative approach makes it possible to contextualize schools within our larger society, as well as compare how things have changed over the past thirty years. By drawing on real peoples' experiences, I will also be able to speak philosophically about what happens in our schools in terms of *caring* in a concrete fashion that teachers, guidance counselors, and school administrators will be able to understand. It is important to remember, though, that the data I present through these stories are unique, as with any qualitative study, and are not generalizable to all people. Still, they should bring out some general points about caring and how it relates to peacebuilding that are applicable to all of us in our own unique situations.

These stories will serve as examples of a lack of caring and they will help us understand how lack of caring results in covert and/or overt violence. I then describe how caring could have helped, or did help. It is my hope that through an examination of caring we can look at ways schools already care for their students, examine structures and factors that get in the way of schools doing a better job of caring for students, and make suggestions for ways in which schools can improve their caring capabilities. Schools can be more caring places, and they can teach people to be more caring of each other. Understanding *caring*, teaching people the value of *caring*, and helping people experience *caring* and its effects will go a long way toward lessening the violence we currently experience in our society at large.

What is Caring?[4]

What is caring and how does it function as an emotional feeling that helps us in our efforts to inquire? Maxine Greene presents the case that caring involves a form of "attachment to those one is serving or working with."[5] It is possible, however, for people to form attachments in ways that are not caring, as we will find later. Jane Roland Martin looks to the home and parenting to help define caring and Sara Ruddick defines caring in terms of "mothering" in *Maternal Thinking*.[6] However, placing caring in a domestic domain, even a redescribed domestic domain, risks reinscribing a false dichotomy between private and public domains. Thus, caring is allowed to remain hidden from public sight, and caring remains devalued as private and personal. Carol Gilligan and Belenky et al. describe caring as being a feminine ethical orientation that is relational, based on a concept of self that is rooted in a sense of connection and relatedness to others. Nel Noddings describes caring in terms of feminine qualities.[7] These ways of defining caring leave us vulnerable to the false conclusion that caring is feminine, and therefore, gender-specific. Feminist scholars such as Jean Grimshaw, as well as the above-named authors, have warned us *not* to link caring to only girls and women.[8]

Milton Mayeroff describes caring as "recognizing the intrinsic worth of the 'other' and being committed to promoting its growth for its own sake."[9] Nel Noddings also describes caring as always being relational, between the carer and the one cared-for. Caring involves a "feeling with" the other (other people, other life forms, or even inanimate objects), and it stresses attending to the other. All caring involves presence (being present), generosity, and acquaintance. Noddings does not describe caring in terms of "empathy," for empathy can be taken to mean a projecting of oneself onto others. For her, caring is a move away from the self toward being receptive of the other. We will find that this relational quality of caring is very important for it helps us identify and understand false forms of caring.

Joan Tronto[10] agrees with Noddings that caring is necessarily relational, it must have an object. In her earlier work, however, she disagrees that the object of caring occurs with abstract ideas as well as with living beings. Tronto distinguishes between "caring about" and "caring for" based on the objects of care, arguing the "caring about" refers to "a specific, particular object that is the focus of caring. Caring for involves responding to the particular, concrete, physical, spiritual, intellectual, psychic, and emotional needs of others." Tronto presents the case that "traditional gender roles in our society imply that men care about but women care for."[11] In making this distinction Tronto reveals more about caring and traditional assumptions of gender difference. Like Jane Roland Martin's analysis of domesticity, Tronto points to political issues involved with caring in her discussions.[12] Unfortunately, by distinguishing "caring for" from "caring about," Tronto reinscribes a traditional philosophical assumption about people and ideas being separable. Let me explain.

From an epistemological standpoint, emotional feelings like caring affect us, as inquirers, because our emotional feelings help us choose what questions we want to address and try to understand. They also affect how we address the questions on which we choose to focus.

Emotional feelings such as caring are what motivate us and inspire us. They are what make us feel unsettled and troubled about issues and problems. They are what make us feel excited and give us the desire to carry on with our efforts to understand. When we attempt to divorce reasoning and critical thinking from emotional feelings, we make the mistake of separating ideas from people. This is the mistake Tronto makes in distinguishing between "caring about" and "caring for." Just as violence is not just an idea, but an action done by people which affects other *people*. When I care about ideas such as peacebuilding, I do so because I understand the abstract concept of peacebuilding in relation to real peoples' lives for whom I care. An important necessary ingredient toward helping us change violent situations into peaceful ones is learning how to care for and about, to attend to and value peoples' problems in relation to ideas that help give meaning to peoples' experiences.

People do not have to like or love each other in order to care. People do need to develop the ability to be receptive and open to other people and their ideas, willing to attend to them, to listen and consider their possibilities. Care does *not* entail that people agree with each other. Care does mean people are open to possibly hearing others' voices more completely and fairly. Caring about other people (and in agreement with Noddings, other people's ideas, other life forms, or even inanimate objects) requires respecting others as separate, autonomous people, worthy of caring. It is an attitude that gives value to others by denoting that others are worth attending to in a serious or close manner. Attitudes of acceptance and trust, inclusion and openness are important in all caring relationships.[13] My position is that without caring, one cannot hope to understand the violence in our society, let alone change it. Let's begin to explore caring for people in our schools.

Teachers and Students in the 1960s

> When I think back on all the *crap* I learned in high school,
> It's a wonder I can think at all
> Paul Simon, *Kodachrome*

Now as a teacher and mother of three teenage children, I look back on my high school years as violent times. The civil rights movement was in full force and I watched rioting on my television screen and experienced racial strife in my school. Black, white, and Hispanic students struggled to understand each other and appreciate each other's anger, fears, and hopes for a better life. At the same time that racial tensions were high, so was the fear of war, and I spent my teenage years watching daily body counts on the television news concerning the Vietnam War. This war kept escalating while I was in high school, and my friends had to face the reality of potentially dying in a war we did not understand. The Vietnam War affected me at a personal, family level for my father was a career officer in the Air Force, a refueling pilot who spent two tours of duty in Vietnam and the surrounding regions. On top of all this confusion, anger, and frustration, we were also part of the sexual revolution. We expressed our feelings and coped through drugs, alcohol, and rock 'n roll. I know what it is like to be a teenager living in violent times.

Let me share a story that illustrates a lack of caring between teachers and students, resulting in covert violence. I tell this story from my perspective as a teenager. My story is not one of verified overt violence, physical acts of aggression intended to injure or harm others physically, but rather covert violence, in terms of verbal harassment, belittlement, and threats which harm others' self-esteem and self-dignity. Most children and teachers in schools, past or present, do not regularly experience physical threats to injure or harm them, but implied threats such as I will describe are common occurrences. If we can explore the lack of caring demonstrated in this story, and describe how caring could have helped, then perhaps we will have a clearer understanding of ways we can help build peace in our schools.

When I was a senior in high school I made the cheerleading squad along with six other girls. Seven of us were required to spell out "BOMBERS," our school team's name. We lived at Ramey Air Force Base in Puerto Rico, where our fathers worked as career officers or enlisted men. This was the only Department of Defense (DOD) school I ever attended, and it represents an example of one kind of implied threat with which students live. Our schools, and societies at large, threaten adolescents by insinuating that they need to follow the rules or they will bring dishonor and disgrace to their families. Their parents' jobs could be jeopardized, depending on how the students conducted themselves. In my case, this was literally true. I learned there was a double meaning to DOD schools, for if students made mistakes or caused problems in school their actions could be written up in their father's annual reviews, as the school board was comprised of the base commander and his senior staff of officers. Everyone knew that a bad or even a lukewarm review in the military meant no more promotions and an end to a parent's career. We were dependents being defended by the Department of Defense, and we were on the defensive.

The seven of us fortunate enough to be chosen for the cheerleading squad began to experience another form of covert violence many students experience on a regular basis, in the form of bullying behavior from teachers. Many students experience teachers who intimidate, frighten, and/or attempt to manipulate them on a regular basis, for the teaching role is one that involves power. Our cheerleading sponsor, Miss Taylor, was an unusual person.[14] As a cheerleading sponsor she looked unusual because she was overweight and not very physically attractive. She lived with another teacher, a frail, delicate, quiet woman, Miss Snyder, and together they were partners in love and work, traveling and teaching for DOD schools. What makes Miss Taylor an example of covert violence in our schools is not her appearance or love life. It is the manner with which she coached us, her pedagogical style, which was covertly violent. She had a way of addressing us that was more typical of a sadistic football coach or drill sergeant than a cheerleading sponsor.

As I remember, things pretty quickly began to unravel for our cheerleading squad. At first we were bribed to put up with Miss Taylor's overbearing, demeaning approach by promises of beautiful uniforms and state-of-the-art equipment. This is not an uncommon tactic bullying teachers, or students, use. We practiced two-three hours, five days a week, all summer long with a sponsor who screamed at us, belittled us, or locked us in our practice room when she was not there "to make sure the boys wouldn't bother us." When Miss Taylor was not there we complained bitterly about her and plotted her demise. The first girl to quit the squad was Chris, one of the returning seniors. Chris had put up with Miss Taylor as a sophomore but did not try out as a junior because of her abusive pedagogical style. She was talked into trying out for her senior year with the promise that things would be different with Miss Taylor. When she discovered that this was not true, she quit in August before school even started. An alternate replaced her, a sophomore named Cindy.

Miss Taylor's bribery lost its impact when the uniforms and equipment arrived and we discovered that our uniforms were handmade in Aquadilla, Puerto Rico, not what we had chosen from the catalogs we had pored over. We also found out that the school was not paying for our equipment, we were. This ushered in Miss Taylor's second set of tactics to keep us in line, also commonly used by bullies, overt threats and covert subterfuge. Two of the seniors on the cheerleading squad were Puerto Ricans, Maria and Roberta, whose fathers were enlisted men. They could not afford to pay for their uniforms and equipment. Miss Taylor paid for their bills with the understanding "they owed her." This exchange meant she could ask them to do favors such as run errands or wash her car, and treat them however she wanted. She harassed and bullied them mercilessly. Rumor had it she was sexually involved with Maria, but that was never confirmed. It was confirmed, however, that Miss Taylor expected Maria to spy on us and give regular reports back to her. We began to mistrust each other and be careful about what we said. Our misery increased as the football season progressed.

Then came the final tactic Miss Taylor used on me, to try to keep me quiet and in line. I was someone she did not harass very much, but my best friend, Vanessa, was one of her main targets of verbal abuse. I went to talk to Miss Taylor about her treatment of Vani, and her response was to tell me that Vani had not legitimately qualified with the judges to make the cheerleading squad, but that Miss Taylor had made an "executive decision" and placed her on the squad anyway. This was our little secret and in her mind it gave her the right to treat Vani however she wanted. She threatened to tell Vani of her status as a team member and remove her from the squad if I complained to higher authorities. Miss Taylor was counting on our dreams to be cheerleaders and on our friendships to conceal her antics.

Miss Taylor represents a dangerous, violent form of false caring that is found in our schools, as well as our homes and other social settings. It is an infantile, hedonistic form of false caring that I call "mirror caring," in which people act as though they care for another, only as long as the cared-for person fulfills a need of the one caring. We see this false form of caring in schools with teachers who attempt to see themselves through their students' eyes. They want their students to mirror their own image back as a way of reaffirming the value of who they are. Mirror caring is an infantile demand for more love, in which teachers call to their students for needed attention. This demand for love from students is a way of seeking confirmation of our wholeness. The issue is one of identity, and teachers are in a position to require students to affirm their own identity by demanding and insisting students reflect what teachers want to see. As Jo Anne Pagano has perceptively noted, talented students "reflect us back to ourselves as twice our size by seeming to become us or like us."[15] Without that affirmation, the hedonistic desire to have students be mirrors can turn sadistic, as it did with Miss Taylor when the girls who were not willing or able to reflect her identity back to her became the targets of her wrath.

Scholars such as Jo Anne Pagano are concerned about caring as "love" and describe a hedonistic, indoctrinating side to teachers who love their students too much. The erotic side of teachers' loving their students is a danger no matter what sexual orientation the teachers or students have. Pagano worries about the dangers of coercions that act upon the bodies of students as teachers perceive themselves as loving their students as disembodied minds. This is an illusion of innocence because in fact students are embodied, sensual beings, as are their teachers. Pagano notes that teachers' desire to be loved "seems too large for the student-teacher relationship to bear. Certainly too large for any student to bear."[16] The dangers of teachers desiring to be loved by their students were apparent on Miss Taylor's cheerleading squad. We suffered the kinds of consequences students suffer in violent situations (whether they be covert or overt): loss of physical and mental health, lowered self-esteem and depression, loss of friendships, and isolation from our peers.

Did Miss Taylor really care for us? If caring means one tries to apprehend the reality of the person cared for, and support that person by being receptive to his or her needs, then certainly Miss Taylor failed to care for Vani, Roberta, Maria, Chris, Cindy, Susie, Tara, or me. I am sure Miss Taylor perceived herself as caring in her relationship with her cheerleaders, because she was willing to be the sponsor and devote a great deal of her time to make sure we did a good job and represented the school well. However, Taylor's acts of care were not perceived as such by us, because she was manipulating and using us for her own needs, and she was unable to develop a reciprocal relationship with us at any level. It is important to remember that while we as teachers may perceive ourselves as caring, that unless that caring is perceived as caring by our students, it is not caring.

What happened with the Ramey Bomber cheerleaders? When Miss Taylor told me that she did not intend to change her violent style of teaching, I turned to my fellow cheerleading friends to try to solve our situation. At this point I organized my first rebellion. We met and decided to resign in mass. We figured that if we all resigned the adults would have to realize there was a problem and the problem did not rest with us, but rather with our cheerleading sponsor. We were hoping to get Miss Taylor replaced by anyone else. It is interesting to note we did not turn to other adults for help. In the middle of football season I turned in a letter of resignation and went home, announcing to my parents I had resigned. I waited to see what would happen.

What happened? Nothing. No one else turned in a letter of resignation. Miss Taylor remained the cheerleading sponsor and the cheerleading squad went on without me. Vani resigned at the end of football season when her nerves could not take it anymore and she became physically ill. Roberta resigned in the middle of basketball season, having a nervous breakdown. However, it was too little, too late. All pictures of Chris, Roberta, Vani, and myself were removed from the school yearbook when they were mailed to the publisher, and all records of us as cheerleaders are gone.

My parents tell me I never told them what was going on. I do not remember. They say that I just came home one day and announced I had resigned. They knew something was terribly wrong because they knew how much I had wanted to be a cheerleader. My parents went to the school superintendent and requested an investigation. Because my father was a lieutenant colonel, the school administration moved to comply with their request. They called us into the superintendent's office in pairs to ask what was going on, a younger girl with an older girl, a Puerto Rican girl with a White girl. Nobody said anything, except me. I watched in amazement as my friends remained silent in intimidation and my career as a cheerleader came to an end. My parents tried unsuccessfully to get Miss Taylor fired; they were only able to have an incident letter placed in her file. At the end of the year she transferred to another DOD school to continue her teaching career.

What was hardest for me to understand, and therefore forgive, at the time of this experience was how my own friends responded to our cheerleading sponsor dilemma. Why were we unable to help each other? Why were they unable to stand beside me, rather than capitulating and leaving me hanging there alone? Is it because they did not care? They never offered me their reasons for changing their minds. Because they were not able to be open and honest with me, their actions betrayed my trust, and I perceived them as falsely caring. Now I realize that most of them probably did care about me to some level or degree, but their kind of caring was weak and ineffectual, a kind of "timid caring." We were teenagers with very little political sway in a scary situation, and it would have taken all of us standing together to solve the problem of our cheerleading sponsor. My friends' fears outweighed the courage they needed to be able to show they cared for me. While it is not always necessary, courage can play a very important role in acts of care. To different levels and degrees, we all lacked self-confidence, which affected our courage. (How many teenagers really do feel good about themselves?) We also lacked self-awareness and an understanding of how our society's rules shaped our lives. We were acculturated to be respectful of adults, and as girls, to be quiet and not complain. For my friends to be able to speak up meant going against their cultural beliefs which had surrounded them since birth. This is extremely difficult for anyone to do, especially people who are not yet adults, still trying to develop their voices.

This story represents many forms of covert violence, with overt violence possibly mixed in (if Miss Taylor was in fact having sex with a minor). It also is a story that helps us understand how caring plays an important role in eliminating violence and building peace. The Ramey Bomber cheerleaders needed some teachers (and more parents) who were able to be receptive to our situation and generous in their efforts to try to understand and believe us. We needed teachers who cared about us and had the courage to act on our behalf. We also needed to be brave, ourselves, and act together.

Why did we feel we only had each other to turn to as a way of solving our problem? What about the other adults in the cheerleading story, the students' parents and other teachers? As the mother of three teenagers, I know it is hard to have a caring relationship with teenagers. They strive to break free from their parents and be autonomous and independent. Often they experience problems in their lives of which parents are not even aware. Apparently, we did not talk to our parents about what was going on with Miss Taylor, so they were removed from being able to help us. As for the other teachers at the high school, I cannot imagine that they were not aware of problems with Miss Taylor, but maybe I am wrong. Maybe they really did not know. Still, I think there were missed opportunities and a failure occurred for the adults, both parents and teachers, with whom we spent so much time.

Teenagers do talk, mostly to each other. We talked to each other continually about what we were experiencing. Were the adults just not listening carefully to what we were saying? I suspect more adult effort to attend to our situation and be receptive to what *was* being communicated would have given us a sense of being cared for and would have encouraged us to open up and seek more help. Why seek help from adults who will not believe your word over another adult's, and who make you feel devalued, immature, and deceitful?

As it was, when I did talk to my parents, they were not able to help me solve my problems. This is a hard lesson for any child to learn. However, I remember feeling tremendous relief when my parents finally knew what was going on, and I greatly appreciated their efforts to help remove Miss Taylor as our sponsor. I knew that they believed me and they supported my efforts, unlike many parents and teachers who doubt children's words. I felt validated and strengthened in my resolve to not just let things be. Their caring had a powerful effect on me.

The Ramey Bomber cheerleaders needed the adults in our lives to help us solve our problem, especially the teachers who worked on a daily basis with Miss Taylor and knew what she was like with her students. Most of our teachers maintained an uninvolved, neutral stance throughout the year. Some of them actually began to intimidate us in their interactions with us as a way of helping Miss Taylor and further harming our resolve. I was president of the Honor Society that year, and Miss Snyder, Miss Taylor's roommate, was the sponsor of that organization. My ability to serve as president came into question after I resigned from the cheerleading squad. I was also in the honors senior English class with a teacher who had taught with Miss Taylor at her previous DOD school assignment, as well as in Puerto Rico, and I began to be belittled in his class, and received the first C I ever received in high school that next grading period. The guidance counselor called me into his office and advised me not to go to college as I would probably not have the resolve to complete it. When I applied to college and saw that I had to have letters of recommendations from my guidance counselor and senior English teacher, I remember a sinking, panicky feeling that I was in serious trouble, and might not get admitted into college, even though I had a GPA of around 3.8 and I graduated fourth in my class. My teachers' protection and support for their colleague were terrifying to me!

What does this story teach us about caring and peacebuilding? As adults, we have opportunities to teach children how to communicate and relate to each other, and to us. We have chances to set up environments in ways that encourage interaction and responses from others. However, we must be careful to not abuse our powerful roles as authority figures. We have responsibilities to ensure that environments are safe, so that immature, fragile, and contrary voices are heard. We must try to protect those who have less power and authority (e.g., children, students), and we must commit ourselves to genuinely caring about them. This means we must really try to listen, and hear what they have to say. And when there are acts of violence, we must be stirred to action, to try to help them. As Paulo Freire points out in *Pedagogy of the Oppressed*,[17] there cannot be a neutral stance in oppressive situations. If a person is involved in an oppressive, dehumanizing condition, either that person is working to help transform the situation or she or he is supporting the efforts of the oppressor, even if she or he is doing nothing. Freire warns teachers:

> The educator does not have the right to be silent just because he or she has to respect the culture. If he or she does not have the right to impose his or her voice on the people, he or she does not have the right to be silent. It has to do precisely with the duty of intervening, which the educator has to assume without becoming afraid. There is no reason for an educator to be ashamed of this.[18]

I hope you are beginning to understand the power of caring and the destruction or ineffectuality that comes from false forms of caring or lack of caring. Genuine caring is necessary to help prevent or end harmful, oppressive behavior. I move on to story two and concerns about peacebuilding in relation to caring in our schools today.

Teachers and Students in the 1990s

> Here we are now, entertain us!
> I feel stupid and contagious!
>   Kurt Cobain of Nirvana, *Smells like Teen Spirit*

My children attend high school during another violent time in our society. I teach in these current times of fear for one's safety and well-being, with students coming to school with knives and guns and becoming members in gangs as ways to protect themselves and help them feel like they have some control over their lives. In the 1990s, we still live with discriminatory tensions related to racism, sexism, and poverty, and the expressive release of those tensions through crime, drugs, alcohol, rock 'n roll, and new forms of music such as rap. While my children say they have never been in a fight, or experienced direct physical harm, they have seen fights, and have had times when someone verbally or physically threatened them, and they were afraid.

They consider these experiences routine, however, and typical behavior of adolescents who are trying everything out for the first time. They have found their friends to be their best sources of help in times of need, not their teachers or other adults. When adults are the aggressors, students may need other adults to help them solve their problems, but when the aggressors are peers, students can help each other pretty effectively, though not without some false starts or mistakes along the way.

I am in the unique position of being able to affirm my children's claims, for I was a teacher for two of my children at different times in their school careers, and my daughter experienced an unusually aggressive and hostile school year while she was a student in my class. This was my most volatile teaching experience, and it occurred in an exclusive resort town on the coast of California, not in an inner city, and not with the lower-income, minority children often portrayed in the media as instigators of violence. The children I taught that year were from wealthy or middle-income families, the class size was small (nineteen students), and there were sixteen white students in the class. In my daughter's situation she had two teachers in the classroom who both cared a great deal about her, and were well aware of the aggressive, intimidating behavior she was being confronted with on a daily basis, and still we were not able to help her or her colleagues in the room. I learned a lot that year, and found it a very humbling experience. I worried all year about its affects on my daughter, but she brushes it off as not being that significant of an experience.

I tell my daughter's story as I remember it, for it represents a lack of caring between students, and the overt and covert violence that was the result. It also will help us understand how caring can help build peace in our schools, for in this story the students were able to end the violence and be successful peacebuilders. They used their ability to care for my daughter as a way of helping them understand how she might be feeling, and therefore move to end their aggressive, harmful behavior.

What happened? My daughter was new to this school, as I had just accepted a teaching position. As an attractive girl, she was the center of the boys' attention. She enjoyed their attention and did not want to hurt any of their feelings, so she tried to be friends and flirt with all of them. This was a mistake. There was one particular male in the class who already had a girlfriend, and often she would do things with Thad, his girlfriend Sara, and one of the other boys. Halfway through the year Sara moved away and Thad was alone. There was a turning point when Thad seemed to feel left out and excluded from my daughter's attentions, and the other boys seemed to tire of her trying to be friends with all of them. Their caring for her was another false form of caring, "amorphous caring," one that changes as peoples' needs dictate. Thad rallied the other boys to join him in excluding my daughter and harassing her. She began to experience sexual harassment that became more aggressive and intimidating as the year progressed and her teachers continued to try to resolve the problem.

The boys began by teasing and belittling my daughter verbally and gossiping about her. This is a kind of harmful behavior that adolescents experience as well as participate in on a daily basis. She did what most teenagers do to cope; she ignored them and spent her time with the girls in the class. My co-teacher and I ignored them as well, knowing that often the best course of action is no action that draws attention to their behavior, since attention is what they are seeking. Indirectly, though, we talked to the whole class about "caring community" kinds of issues and ways to model this. We also talked privately to my daughter, so she knew we were aware of what was going on. We gave her advice on how her friendly flirting had probably caused jealous feelings to be aroused, and what she could do to prevent this from occurring in the future. We also offered advice on how to handle the situation she was now in, and we offered emotional support. If I had not been her parent, we would have also called her parents at that point so they were aware of the situation and would be able to offer their daughter support at home as well.

Because I *was* the parent, as well as teacher, my co-teacher and I shifted responsibilities so that I was not directly teaching my daughter in case that was exacerbating the situation for her. The boys became more aggressive and intimidating, and scared the other girls in the class into avoiding my daughter, with threats of reprisals to them if they did not. The girls stopped being my daughter's friends in class, although some of them would occasionally call her at home. This action on the girls' part hurt my daughter a great deal, as she lost the protection of her peers. She also lost respect for the girls and their apparent lack of courage and concern for her well-being. Again, as I had at her age, she found that it is very difficult for teenagers (especially girls who have been acculturated to be submissive) to stand up and offer help under potentially violent, abusive conditions. They have not had the opportunity to develop their self-esteem, as well as make decisions concerning their values and beliefs, to the point that they can express their voice and act in times of fear and distress. We see them again representing timid caring, which can be found in adult relationships as well. The girls' withdrawal and decision to not act in support of my daughter added to the power of the impact of the boys' threatening behavior. It also seemed to open the door on the boys' aggressive behavior, because they shifted from verbal harassment to more physical harassment.

The boys began to knock my daughter's books off her desk when they would walk by, or pinch her or jab her with their elbows. They were physically attempting to intimidate her. My daughter held her ground and continued to ignore them, refusing to let them know that they were getting to her. Most often she would not show that she was upset with what was going on until she got home, where she would cry. Occasionally she would confront them when they did something to her. My co-teacher and I stepped up our surveillance of the room, and began punishing the boys for what they were doing. This created a backlash effect. The boys seemed to gather strength from knowing their actions were causing a rise, and they became more subversive but also more threatening with their tactics. When our punishing did not stop matters, we turned to our administration for assistance, and were advised to call the parents of the boys who were doing the harassing, to enlist their support by talking to their children about their behavior. This created an even bigger backlash effect. After calling parents, my co-teacher and I walked into a classroom that we could see was excited to know they were creating enough concern to have their parents called. Thad pulled a knife on my daughter outside of the classroom within a week of our seeking parental support. She was terrified. He was suspended, but when he returned to school he proceeded to do the same thing to her again. Neither the school, teachers, nor parents were able to end this violent behavior.

In the end, the students themselves solved the problem and came to my daughter's aid. When Thad's behavior became so extreme that even they could see it was dangerous and scary, they started to step in, speak on her behalf, and offer her protection. The support came first from one of the boys who had participated in the sexual harassment. He was one of the minority students in the class, and he was finally able to empathize with how my daughter might be feeling when he started to experience exclusion himself by the other boys. José spoke up to the whole class at a class meeting and told them that what they were doing was wrong and shared how painful it felt to be excluded. This brave action seemed to break the resolve of the group and open up space for others to begin to show my daughter that they cared. They began to see that while my daughter might have made a mistake in terms of flirting with the boys, what Thad was doing was violent and an extreme overreaction. They stopped trying to hurt her emotionally or physically, apologized to her, and began to try to win back her friendship. My daughter struggled to trust those students again. She was leery of their offers of friendship, but she kept that to herself, and tried to act like she was willing to be friends. They all began the painful process of forgiving.

Once my co-teacher and I knew we had the aggressive behavior of the group under control, we were better able to focus on Thad's needs and try to find out what else might be going on in his life to cause him to act violently. We found out that Thad's parents had gone through a bitter divorce, and that his father, who was apparently very wealthy, had moved away. Thad rarely saw him at a time in his life when he may have really needed him. We also found out that the parents had a serious drug problem and, as Thad was old enough to know what was going on with his parents, it is possible he was using drugs as well. Overall, Thad seemed to have parents who were struggling to cope with their own problems and were unable to attend to Thad's needs as they should.

Thad's story is typical of the aggressive, violent students I have taught. Children learn how to be aggressive because their social institutions (including their families, extended families, and friends, their neighborhoods and larger communities, their expressive arts and media, and their schools) teach them how to be violent. If we want to help our children be able to live in peace with their environment and each other, we have to teach them about peace, and treat them in a peaceful manner. Caring is an important and necessary ingredient for peacebuilding, for caring is what helps us understand others' perspectives. Our ability to care is also what moves us to action. If we can show our students that we genuinely care about the situations in their lives, and that we genuinely care for them as people living in these situations, we will empower them to help find solutions to their problems.

We also need to take responsibility for the way things are, even as we recognize that institutions that shape and affect our lives are ones we have socially constructed.[19] Once we are able to recognize and begin to understand our own responsibilities for current conditions, we can stop blaming others and work together to change things in a more peaceful direction. It takes a lot of courage, as we saw with José in story two, and myself in story one, to claim responsibility and move to act in ways that change things in positive directions. There is no guarantee that our actions will be successful; in story one, mine were not, but in story two José's were. Not to act in a caring manner, however, does guarantee that violence will continue to prosper.

What does story two teach us about how caring can help build peace? We learned in this second story that students are abler to help each other against aggressive peers, although not without some mishaps along the way. Adults can certainly help adolescents gain the skills they need to be successful builders of peace by helping adolescents develop their abilities to communicate and relate to each other. Students also need chances to develop their abilities to constructively think about ways to creatively solve their problems. Tools that all people have available to help them constructively think are reason, intuition, imagination, and emotional feelings like caring.[20] As Maxine Greene reminds us in *Releasing the Imagination*:

> All we can do is to speak with others as passionately and eloquently as we can; all we can do is to look into each other's eye and urge each other on to new beginnings. Our classrooms ought to be nurturing and thoughtful and just all at once; they ought to pulsate with multiple conceptions of what it is to be human and alive. They ought to resound with the voices of articulate young people in dialogues always incomplete because there is always more to be discovered and more to be said. We must want our students to achieve friendship as each one stirs to wide-awakeness, to imaginative action, and to renewed consciousness of possibility.[21]

Conclusion

We learned that violence is reflected in our social institutions: abuse in our homes, crime in our neighborhoods, physically and verbally damaging behavior on our televisions, distrust for our public officials, and disrespect for our school personnel. Schools are only one of many social institutions. They cannot solve all the problems of our society. These problems are much too complex and interrelated to be taken care of by one institution. However, schools can be a site where people can come together to study and learn about our problems, attempt to generate possible solutions to our problems, and model for our larger society and our other social institutions ways to solve our problems.

We can begin to build peace through acts of genuine caring. We found through the stories shared that there are many forms of false caring, such as mirror caring, timid caring, and amorphous caring.

Genuine caring involves an attitude of respect and trust; it is a receptive valuing of others in a generous manner. I have made the case here that caring is vital to help us turn acts of aggression into peaceful acts, for without a caring attitude we cannot hope to understand others and what they are experiencing. It is only through their willingness to tell us that we can hope to enlarge our own views and gain more insight. We can hope to have others open up to us and share their lives with us when we show them we care. Caring is *not* a panacea—it will not solve all of our problems. But caring is a starting place. Without it we cannot even begin to lessen the violence we currently experience in our schools, homes, places of work, communities and neighborhoods, on our televisions and radios, all around us.

Notes

1. Compiled by John McIntosh for the American Association of Suicidology: National Center for Health Statistics, Washington, DC (1996).

2. Scholars in the field of Peace Studies debate how to define peace. Kenneth Boulding represents a narrow definition of peace, which Johan Galtung labeled "negative peace" in contrast to his broader definition of peace that includes social justice, which Galtung called "positive peace." See Linda Rennie Forcey, "Peace Studies," in *Protest, Power, and Change: An Encyclopedia of Nonviolent Action from ACT-UP to Women's Suffrage*, ed. Roger S. Powers and William B. Vogele (New York: Garland Press, 1997).

3. Ian M. Harris, "From World Peace to Peace in the 'Hood: Peace Education in a Postmodern World," *Journal for a Just and Caring Education* 2 no. 4, pp. 378–95, 381 (October 1996).

4. This section overlaps with my paper "The Power of Caring," *Philosophical Studies in Education* (1997): 1–32.

5. Maxine Greene, "The Tensions and Passions of Caring," in *The Caring Imperative in Education*, ed. M. Leininger and J. Watson (New York: National League for Nursing, 1990): 29–44.

6. Jane Roland Martin, *The Schoolhome* (Cambridge, MA: Harvard University Press, 1992); Sara Ruddick, *Maternal Thinking: Toward a Politics of Peace* (Boston: Beacon Press, 1989).

7. Carol Gilligan, *In a Different Voice* (Cambridge: Harvard University Press, 1982); Mary Field Belenky, Blythe McVicker Clinchy, Nancy Rule Goldberger, and Jill Mattuck Tarule, *Women's Ways of Knowing* (New York: Basic Books, Harper Collins Publisher, 1986); Nel Noddings, *Caring* (Berkeley: University of California Press, 1986). See also Nel Noddings, *The Challenge to Care in Schools: An Alternative Approach to Education* (New York: Teachers College Press, 1992).

8. Jean Grimshaw, *Philosophy and Feminist Thinking* (Minneapolis, MN: University of Minnesota Press, 1986).

9. Milton Mayeroff, *On Caring* (New York: Harper and Row, 1971).

10. Joan C. Tronto, "Women and Caring: What Can Feminists Learn about Morality from Caring?" in *Gender/Body/Knowledge*, ed. Alison M. Jaggar and Susan R. Bordo (New Brunswick, NJ: Rutgers University Press): 172–187. See also Joan C. Tronto, *Moral Boundaries: A Political Argument for an Ethic of Care* (New York: Routledge, 1993).

11. Tronto, "Women and Caring," 174.

12 Tronto, "Women and Caring."

13 Barbara Thayer-Bacon, "Caring and Its Relationship to Critical Thinking," *Educational Theory* 43, no. 3 (summer 1993): 325.

14 All names are changed to protect the anonymity of the people involved in the stories.

15 Jo Anne Pagano, "Taking our Places," Keynote Address, Ohio Valley Philosophy of Education Society, Indianapolis, IN, 1994, 18.

16 Ibid., 11.

17 Paulo Freire, *Pedagogy of the Oppressed* (New York: The Seabury Press, 1968). See chapter one.

18 Paulo Freire and Myles Horton, *We Make the Road by Walking*, ed. Brenda Bell, John Gaventa, and John Peters (Philadelphia: Temple University Press, 1990), 138.

19 Peter L. Berger and Thomas Luckmann, *The Social Construction of Reality: A Treatise in the Sociology of Knowledge* (Garden City, NY: Anchor Books, 1996).

20 Barbara Thayer-Bacon, with Charles Bacon, *Philosophy Applied to Education: Nurturing a Democratic Community in the Classroom* (Columbus, OH: Prentice-Hall, 1997). See chapter four.

21 Maxine Greene, *Releasing the Imagination* (San Francisco: Jossey-Bass, 1995), 43.

Chapter 8

Adventure-Based Learning in the Name of Peace

Nadja M. Alexander and Teresa B. Carlson

In a world catapulting into the twenty-first century amidst growing youth disorientation, discontent and violence, adventure-based learning (ABL) offers a nature-based alternative to classroom peace education curricula. This essay will explain how ABL can be used as an effective teaching strategy in peace education. In particular, the authors will focus on peacemaking skills that foster caring, trust, cooperation and tolerance. While the focus will be on schools, the philosophies and strategies are equally applicable to youth leaders and community programs. Further, this chapter concentrates on young adolescents at the junior high or middle school level as research has indicated that this is a crucial time when values, attitudes, and skills are developed.[1]

To become peacemaking citizens, adolescents need to develop certain skills. These skills include effective communication, an ability to cooperate with others, an awareness of how they and others respond to frustration or stress, a tolerance and understanding of individual differences, and problem-solving skills. This chapter begins by describing the philosophy behind ABL. The authors then discuss the need for adolescents to learn peacemaking skills and demonstrate how the experiential educational model, ABL, can contribute in this regard. Subsequently, practical strategies for implementing ABL activities into peace curricula are discussed.

What Is ABL?

The theoretical foundations of ABL are closely linked to the work of John Dewey, the American educator and philosopher who promoted the importance of teaching youth the skills of peacemaking through experiential learning.[2] The development of "interpersonal and global peace" was central to Dewey's concept.[3] As a form of experiential learning, ABL harnesses the intimate learning experiences of youth during outdoor adventure programs in order to develop peacemaking skills in adolescents.

ABL has been defined by Latess as "the process of eliciting, in a learner, cognitive [knowledge], affective [feeling] and psychomotor [skills] outcomes by using physical and social challenges and perceived risk [disequilibrium] which can be controlled by individual(s), circumstances and/or equipment and paraphernalia."[4] Subsequent reflection and processing help participants make meaning out of the experience in order to apply their learnings to the next activity and a new environment.[5] The "adventure" element refers to the challenge of stepping outside one's comfort zone to grapple with the unknown and face a sense of disequilibrium or, in Latess's terms, perceived risk. In doing so, participants are encouraged to harness conflict and uncertainty and transform them into positive catalysts for change. The teacher must believe that students can make meaning out of their own experiences rather than relying on interpretations of others' experiences which are then written down and communicated to students (traditional learning).

The word adventure immediately conjures up images of rock climbing, rappelling, and rafting down rapids. While these are valuable additions to the program, many other strategies can be adopted that allow ABL to be used within a school or community setting. Adventure-based learning comprises a sequence of activities that move from low-risk icebreakers through games that require trust and cooperation and place the participants in situations that require increased perceived physical and emotional risk. These activities use easily obtained equipment such as ropes, planks, blindfolds, tennis balls and nature itself. The degree of risk will depend on the aims of the program, the facilitating skills of the instructor, the availability of access to "wilderness" environment and the needs and readiness of the participants.

The Need to Develop Peacemaking Skills in Adolescents

Adolescence is a time of great risks and opportunities. The changes adolescents undergo, both biologically and socially (e.g. moving from elementary school to junior high or middle school and then on to high school) create stress and tension. Further, the ground rules have changed. Statistics indicate that adolescents spend only 4.8 percent of their time with parents while 40 percent of time is spent in leisure activities. Jobs are no longer guaranteed, regardless of obtained qualifications. In fact, African-American adolescents *with* a high school diploma have a 54 percent unemployment rate.[6]

A proactive approach to tackling the problems that this shift in society has created for youth demands innovative and challenging educational methods that have the ability to affect behaviors and attitudes. Accordingly, this chapter concentrates on opportunities for building positive relationships and partnerships between those who work with adolescents and the adolescents themselves. Unfortunately, in many schools adults and students are not members of the same community. Rather, "They exist in two unconnected communities inhabiting the same building."[7]

A considerable amount of teaching at the middle and high school levels is verbal (didactic), abstract, and covers substantial material that from an adolescent's perspective may appear meaningless and "boring." In contrast, programs and curricula that engage students and respond to their needs, interests, and strengths have been identified as resulting in highly effective learning outcomes.[8] Within the context of a peace curriculum, learner-centered structures in which students feel that they are contributing members of a community of learners and teachers are most likely to be successful. Ian Harris espouses an experiential model: "In a postmodern world, peace educators get students to examine violence in their own personal lives, conflicts that exist in their neighborhoods, homes, and personal relations. Peace education implies drawing out of students their innate desires to live in peace."[9]

Adolescence is a time of taking risks and experimentation, and a time when tensions are often created by uncertainties about knowing who one is and where one belongs. Often the combination of these aspects, combined with ready access to drugs, vehicles, and weapons, result in behaviors such as smoking, drinking alcohol, drug taking, risking early pregnancy, high-risk driving, and violence. Recognition of the need to belong, to be trusted, and to be able to make one's own meaning out of life provide the fundamental building blocks in the teaching of peacemaking skills. This desire to belong, however, can also result in the establishment of adolescent gangs. Often these gangs offer what schools and communities do not: a sense of belonging, involvement, and challenge.

Nevertheless, when challenged appropriately this willingness to take risk, experiment, and rise to challenges can result in a positive, productive environment in which skills such as communication, negotiation, and conflict management can exist and, indeed, flourish. Research suggests that students trained in the skills of peacemaking, such as cooperating, communicating, and negotiating, are less likely to engage in harmful behaviors that result in destructive outcomes.[10] A supportive learning environment provides an atmosphere in which honest communication exists, trust between class members and the teacher has been developed, and grounds for conflict management can be laid. ABL is one teaching and learning technique that, used in conjunction with other proactive strategies, can create an environment in which participants feel comfortable in accepting new challenges.

Why Does ABL Work?

Within the skills context, ABL works for three primary reasons. First, the philosophy of ABL takes us back to basics. Second, it incorporates play, and finally, it penetrates cultural barriers.

ABL Takes Us Back To Basics

There are four key features of ABL. These features are the removal of participants from centers of population, if possible in a natural environment; the introduction of disequilibrium and uncertainty; the fact that involvement is undertaken voluntarily (challenge by choice); and the fact that each activity is followed by a structured reflection.[11] An explanation of the legitimacy of these features and their relationship to the teaching of peacemaking skills follows.

Element 1: Participants are removed from centers of population and unique challenges are presented by the environment. Adventure-based learning is based on the belief that we are able to identify and recognize our own values through our focused and "pure" interaction with nature. David Yaffey advocates that "raw, hands-on experience is the soundest foundation of a system of values."[12] Others who argue for the importance of using the natural environment believe that "the manner in which the program forces students to interact with the environment . . . requires certain responses that are of value: cooperation, clear thinking and planning, careful observation, resourcefulness, persistence and adaptability."[13]

Although the ideal setting for adventure-based learning is in the outdoors in an environment away from the school buildings and grounds, the fact that we live in a less than ideal world often makes this option impractical or nonfeasible. The authors have successfully facilitated ABL programs "on-site," that is, on the school grounds, in a gymnasium, or even in the classroom setting. Thus, this form of teaching and learning should not be rejected even if the "ideal" is not available. Nevertheless, it remains important that wherever possible students are taken into a new environment (away from the classroom), even if that is simply a park nearby or the school oval. If the environment cannot be changed, the disequilibrium can be introduced through other means such as using blindfolds and adapting activities to suit the environment available.

Elements 2: The introduction of disequilibrium and uncertainty. By adding the element of disequilibrium, activities in adventure programs become less predictable and therefore more "real." Disequilibrium can be defined as an individual's awareness that a mismatch exists between old ways of thinking and new information.[14] Disequilibrium is a curious concept because its reality depends on perception. If students feel at risk when temporarily blindfolded during an activity, then they are at risk, despite the fact that they are, in an objective sense, completely safe. ABL elicits real responses from students rather than potentially programmed responses that more easily occur in popular forms of experiential learning such as the role play. In this way ABL moves beyond teacher-student rhetoric to enhance deep learning within students.

Adding a dimension of reality to activities means that the emergence of real conflict within the student group must be reckoned with. For example, adolescents often develop defense mechanisms to assist them to cope with the anxiety ABL can raise. These defenses commonly include "denial, blaming others, taking control, anger, aggressiveness, being super responsible, perfectionism, intellectualizing, charming others and humor."[15] Defense mechanisms provoked during ABL activities are similar to reactions and feelings that students are also likely to experience in their personal lives.

Element 3: The activity is undertaken voluntarily (challenge by choice). No one should be forced to participate in an adventure. This would be detrimental to the empowerment process, as success or failure could too easily be attributed to the facilitator. Saying "no" and making choices are fundamental to the development of original thought and one's own systems of values and beliefs.

Element 4: Each activity is followed by a structured reflection (processing). Actual achievements realized during adventure programs often reflect potential that participants did not know existed within themselves. Experiences can be intense and can trigger developmental processes within participants. With effective guidance by the facilitator (otherwise these moments can be short-lived), adolescents recognize the potential within themselves to develop both as an individual and as a contributing member of a school community.

ABL Incorporates Play

ABL works through play that remains in most cases an undervalued part of the learning culture in schools. Plato was once quoted as saying, "You can learn more about an individual during an hour of play than in a year of conversation."[16] In play, experimentation and creativity are encouraged and "failing" is less evident. Play should be fun (the antithesis to boring). Fun involves spontaneity, energy, and laughter and invites involvement. Fun "is what makes the experience come alive. It keeps people focused, engaged and connected to each other and the activities."[17] There are many examples of how using the concept of play and working through the physical can achieve successful changes in youth.[18]

By working through the medium of play and then asking students to transfer what they have learned to other more "real life" situations, ABL offers the best of all worlds: fun, challenge, involvement, belonging, and positive risk taking, as well as the ability to learn from the experiences.

The connection to the development of peacemaking skills becomes self-evident when one considers that a peacemaking environment is one that allows students to take positive risks, and which promotes an enjoyable, supportive environment in which people feel accepted, involved, empowered, and a part of a community. The "gang" can become a positive word and lose its negative connotations; the belonging, the fun, and the risk taking can be a positive, productive experience.

ABL Penetrates Cultural Barriers

ABL has the ability to move beyond the cultural barriers that limit our learning potential. The "hate groups" that are now becoming more prevalent in both rural and urban communities work on fear of others different from themselves.[19] Stereotyping prevents individuals from seeing beyond the obvious: differences in color, accent, race, religion, or age. Within an ABL setting, adolescents are presented with the opportunity to interact and see beyond the "obvious." Similarities are noted while differences are celebrated as they assist in the solving of difficult problems. Further, overcoming difficult tasks can bind groups together and help individuals to feel they are valuable members of a community, regardless of the heterogeneous nature of the group.

ABL activities do not re-create scenarios within a particular culture as role plays do. ABL goes beyond the acted out words of a role play by focusing on a situation that results from participants' actions and reactions to real events, thus providing real experiences participants from all cultural groups. As most activities take place in a displaced environment (outdoors), much of the "culture" that individuals carry around with them is left behind in the classroom and a new group culture usually develops in the course of adventure program.

Incorporating ABL into the Peace Curriculum: Practical Strategies

Newcomers to ABL may find it difficult to envisage how it could work in a school or community context. This section is designed to offer concrete examples and resources for running adventure programs and to explain how this teaching and learning strategy can be incorporated into a school program. Those wishing to implement adventure programs in schools will find the references provided at the end of this chapter an invaluable and apparently limitless source of practical ideas.

Before beginning any program, effective leaders or teachers determine the current climate within the group and the demonstrated capabilities of the participants. The role of the "facilitator" should to be to support, encourage, and coach, rather than to teach or direct. Factors to consider when determining the level of entry and teacher involvement are the age and maturity of the group, the readiness of the group, and the length and goals of the program.[20]

Four important aspects of any ABL program are trust, communication, cooperation, and fun. Most peacemaking strategies include the first three of these elements but because peacemaking is a "serious" business, the last is sometimes ignored. Yet fun helps reduce tensions, encourages a feeling of belonging, and as a result may reduce antisocial behaviours.

Trust is the key to an effective ABL program and it is essential if peacemaking skills are to develop. This quality allows people to share without fear of being ridiculed. It is essential to remember, however, that trust must move in both directions. Teachers cannot expect students to move beyond their comfort zones if they are not prepared to do the same. Although this may appear to be a great risk, it grants teachers the freedom to experiment, get things wrong, and relate to students on a more human level.

The sequencing of the program is one of the most vital considerations to take into account when designing the ABL experience because inappropriate sequencing of activities can result in loss of trust and involvement. The first series of activities should be "*icebreakers.*" These introductory activities establish an atmosphere that encourages students to interact, frees them from common classroom inhibitions, and establishes an environment that allows them to say what they think and ask questions and listen to each other. Activities such as this also encourage students and teachers to laugh at themselves and laugh with (not at) others. In addition, icebreakers emphasize the learning of names. When a person moves from being "hey you" to being acknowledged as someone in her or his own right, an identity and a relationship begin to develop. Additionally, icebreakers encourage participants to physically move closer to others. They are often asked to link arms, hold hands, and move in close proximity to others. It is important that this type of activity be conducted with a sense of "fun" so that the awkwardness and discomfort can be overcome.

Accordingly, a supportive environment begins to develop. An example of an icebreaking activity and document resources can be found at the end of this article.

Trust and cooperation activities are sequenced to follow the introductory games. How fast the participants are moved along the trust continuum depends on the demonstrated abilities of the group. Trust and cooperation activities build awareness, teamwork, and confidence in the group. They should be introduced and facilitated with care. Creating the environment in which participants can trust each other is a precarious business, particularly when dealing with adolescents who may have had little experience of trusting and being trusted.

An example of a trust and communication exercise is the minefield activity (A description of this acitvity is included at the end of this article). It is a useful activity from which to launch a discussion on communication as the basis for listening, negotiating, or mediating skills. Students work in pairs; one is blindfolded and the partner is required to verbally lead their "blind" partner though a series of obstacles without being "blown up." The processing session that follows encourages awareness of how vital the peacemaking skills of effective communication, trust, and cooperation are to the successful completion of any task.

As students become more comfortable with the other members of the group, the program sequence moves on to include *problem solving or initiative activities*. These tasks offer increased challenges and are complex and potentially frustrating. The qualities needed to solve these tasks include effective communication skills, particularly an ability to listen to the ideas of others, and require patience, tolerance, and an awareness of the needs of the group.

An example of an initiative activity is the raft activity (located at the end of this article) in which six or more participants are placed on a "raft" and asked to move successfully to the other side of the river. Successful completion of the task requires considerable cooperation and trust among team members, as well as some innovative thinking. The task becomes increasingly difficult, and frustration can often result as sections of the "raft" are "swept away." The processing session that follows can raise many valuable considerations. For instance, questions may provoke the following issues: the different responses to frustration, the different levels of frustration and different "triggers"; how others dealt with these reactions; the cheating that may have occurred and when cheating is "OK" and when and how it can affect the development of trust; responsibility to others in the group; and how cooperation (or lack of it) affected the result.

From these reasonably low-key activities, more "risk" challenges could be added. These challenges could include wilderness pursuits and high rope challenges. Often, however, these involve expertise, expense, and many practical stumbling blocks. While moving on to this level is ideal, it is not often possible. Nevertheless, inclusion of similar activities to the ones used in this chapter illustrate that an ABL program can be implemented with limited resources and can have considerable impact on peacemaking skills such as communication, tolerance, cooperation, and trust.

The final aspect of ABL emphasized throughout this article is the need for *fun and play* in the lives of our youth. Many adolescents are bored and unhappy at school and with many aspects of life itself. The medium of ABL offers challenges within a supportive environment but also offers both the facilitator and participants fun. How many teachers and adolescents can return home after a day and honestly state, "I had a really enjoyable day today. I laughed a lot." Laughter with others reduces the feeling of alienation often experienced by adolescents, contributes to a shared understanding, and increases the possibility that peacemaking skills can develop.[21] In many of our schools often there is a substantial division between the two communities: teachers and students.[22] One of the most effective ways to reduce this "them and us" division is to share experiences, overcome challenges together, and share laugher.

By exposing the fundamental underpinnings of ABL, the authors have argued for its application to the development of skills to build caring, cooperation, trust, and tolerance amongst adolescents in their school, their community, and in their world. We are not advocating the ABL is a panacea of all ills. We are arguing that ABL, if introduced sequentially, taking into consideration the needs and readiness of the learners, can be a very effective addition to a peacebuilding curricula.

ACTIVITIES

Icebreaker Suggestion
Warp Speed
This is an icebreaker that involves learning names, working together, thinking and laughing, without any major upheaval. A more comprehensive description can be found in Karl Rohnke's book *The Bottomless Bag Again*, 2nd ed. (pp. 53–54).

This activity requires minimal equipment (a ball and a stopwatch) and can be done inside or outside the classroom depending on available space. Students form groups of approximately twelve. Within each group they are given the task of moving a soft, "grabbable" throwing object in a particular sequence. Each time they throw the ball they must say the name of the person to whom they threw the object. When everyone has touched the object, challenge the group to repeat the same sequence in the fastest possible time. Don't be strict with the rules and persist in challenging them to decrease the time.

Processing the experience allows students to consider the interactions within the group; whether all voices were heard; the development of breakthroughs and why and how these occurred; the need to listen to others and to be assertive about one's own communication so that all voices are heard. Finally the importance of clarifying rules for group communication can be emphasized.

Trust and Communication Exercise
The Minefield
The two main objectives of this activity are to highlight the importance of communication and provide an environment in which trust is an important focus. A more comprehensive description can be found in Karl Rohnke's book *The Bottomless Bag Again*, 2nd ed. (pp. 52–53). Equipment includes a long rope to form the boundary of the field and a range of objects (balls, frisbees, cardboard boxes, etc.).

Miscellaneous objects are scattered within a space approximately 15" × 40". Outline the area with rope. Divide the group into pairs: one will be sighted and verbally guide the "unsighted" (blindfolded) partner across the field. Touching a "mine" could result in a time penalty or a return to the beginning. The processing could include: the relevance of body language in communication; awareness of the potential (mis)reception of their message by others; how the participants would have felt if their partner deliberately gave faulty directions; and the increase of empathy once the activity has been experienced.

Initiative or Problem-Solving Activity
The Raft
The equipment required for this activity are a minimum of 6 blocks (5" × 3" × 12") 2 planks (3' × 5.5"), and 2 ropes for markers (stretched out approximately 45' apart) per 6–8 participants. Each raft consist of 6 blocks and 2 planks, the planks rest on top of the blocks so it appears that the raft consists of only 4 planks (see diagram below). The game begins with six people "aboard" the raft. The object is to get the group from one river bank (designated by ropes) to the other without falling into the river. Pressure must be applied to all parts of the raft at all times, otherwise they will float away (be removed). That is, any equipment that is left unconnected with at least one person on the raft, will be taken away by the facilitator. While the blocks will float (and therefore can be stood on directly when in contact with the ground), the planks will not (and therefore must be placed on a blocks as they will "float"). Rafts can be placed opposite each other (allowing the participants the opportunity to join as one team when they reach the middle) or side by side. Usually, regardless of position the participants compete, rather than cooperate. Processing ideas were listed in the text.

Block placement

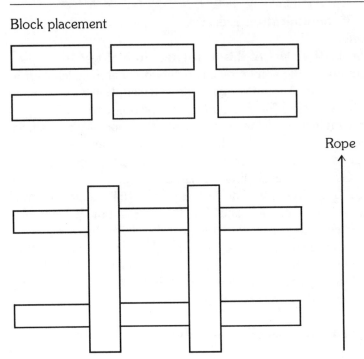

Planks over blocks so it appears there are only 4 pieces of equipment, not 8.

RESOURCES

Macbeth, Fiona, and Nic Fine. *Playing with Fire: Creative Resolution with Young Adults*. Philadelphia: New Society, 1995.

Orlick, Terence. *The Cooperative Sports & Games Book: Challenge without Competition*. New York: Pantheon Books, 1979.

Rohnke, Karl. *Bottomless Baggie*. Dubuque: IA: Kendall/Hunt, 1991.

———. *The Bottomless Bag of Tricks*. Dubuque, IA: Kendall/Hunt, 1988.

———. *Challenge by Choice*. Beverley, MA: Wilkcraft Creative Printing, 1987.

———. *Cowstails and Cobras: A Guide to Ropes Courses, Initiative Games, and Other Adventure Activities*. Hamilton, MA: Adventure Press, 1977.

———. *From Cowstails and Cobras II: A Guide to Games Initiatives, Rope Courses and Adventure Curriculum*. Dubuque, IA: Kendall, 1989.

———. *Silver Bullets*. Hamilton, MA: Adventure Press, 1984.

Schoel, Jim, Dick Prouty, and Paul Radcliff. *Islands of Healing: A Guide to Adventure-Based Counseling*. Hamilton, MA: Project Adventure. 1998.

Notes

1. Fred M. Hechinger, "Schools for Teenagers: A Historic Dilemma," *Teachers College Record* 94 (Spring 1993): 522-39.

2. Ted Woodward, "Breaking Barriers through Adventure-Based Citizen Diplomacy," *The Journal of Experiential Education* 14 (May 1991): 14-19.

3. C. F. Howlett, *Troubled Philosopher: John Dewey and the Struggle for World Peace*. (Port Washington: Kennikat Press, 1977), 62, 148.

4. Dennis Latess, "Outdoor Adventure Education: The Potential Benefits," *New Zealand Journal of Health, Physical Education and Recreation* (1992): 15-25.

5. Fred M. Hechinger, "Schools for Teenagers: A Historic Dilemma," *Teachers College Record* 94 (Spring 1993): 522-539.

6. Elena Nightingale and Lisa Wolverton. "Adolescent Roleness in Modern Society," *Teachers College Record* 94 (Spring 1993): 472-86.

7. Deborah Meier, "Transforming Schools into Powerful Communities," *Teachers College Record* 94 (Spring 1993): 654-58.

8. Cecile Cullen, "Membership and Engagement at Middle College High School." *Urban Education* 26 (1991): 83-93.

9. Ian M. Harris, "From World Peace to Peace in the 'Hood: Peace Education in a Postmodern World," *Journal for Just and Caring Education* 2 no. 4 (October 1996): 378-95, 382.

10. David Johnson and Roger Johnson, "Conflict Resolution and Peer Mediation Programs in Elementary and Secondary Schools: A Review of the Research." *Review of Education Research* 66 (winter 1996): 459-506.

11. Dave Yaffey, "Outdoor Pursuits and Adventure Experience," *The Journal of Adventure Education and Outdoor Leadership* 8 (1991): 22; Flor, "Building Bridges," 27.

12. Yaffey, "Outdoor Pursuits and Adventure Experience," 25.

13. John Hattie, Herb Marsh, James Neill and Garry Richards, "Adventure Education and Outward Bound: Out-of-class Experiences that Make a Lasting Difference," *Review of Educational Research* 67 (spring 1997): 43-87.

14. Reldan Nadler and John Luckner, *Processing the Adventure Experience*. (Dubuque, IA: 1992), 7-14.

15. Nadler and Luckner, *Processing the Adventure Experience*, 16.

16 Authors' recollections.

17 Karl Rohnke and Steve Butler, *Quick Silver: Adventure Games, Initiative Problems, Trust Activities, and a Guide to Effective Leadership* (Dubuque, IA: Kendall/Hunt, 1995).

18 Teresa Carlson and Nadja Spegel, "Adventure into Education: Innovation in Teaching in Tertiary Setting" (paper presented at Australian Education Research Conference, Singapore, November 1996): 1–18; Dona Carson and H. L. "Lee" Gillis, "A Meta-Analysis of Outdoor Adventure Programming with Adolescents," *The Journal of Experiential Education* 17 (May 1994): 40–47; Don Hellison, Tom Martinek, and Nicholas Cutforth. "Beyond Violence Prevention in Inner City Physical Activity Programs," *Peace and Conflict: Journal of Peace Psychology* 2 (1996): 321–37; Tom Martinek and Don Hellison, "Fostering Resiliency in Underserved Youth through Physical Activity." *Quest* 49 (February 1997): 34–49.

19 Harris, "From World Peace to Peace in the 'Hood," 378–95.

20 Rohnke and Butler, *Quick Silver*, 25.

21 Raymond Calabrese, "Adolescence: A Growth Period Conducive to Alienation," *Adolescence* 22 (October/November 1987): 929–38.

22 Meier, "Transforming Schools," 654–58.

PART III

SCHOOL STRATEGIES FOR PEACEBUILDING

Chapter 9

A Developmental Approach to the Use of Conflict Resolution Interventions with Adolescents

Michael Van Slyck and Marilyn Stern

Overview: The Emergence of Youth-Oriented Conflict Resolution (YOCR)

Over the last twenty years, the Western world, notably the United States, has been witness to what is referred to as the alternative dispute resolution (ADR) movement, which involves the application of such dispute processing modalities as negotiation and mediation to virtually every manifestation of social conflict.[1] One of the major applications of ADR has been to disputes involving minors who are in conflict with their peers in school, their parents at home, and people in the general community.[2] This application of ADR has been labeled youth-oriented conflict resolution, hereafter referred to as YOCR.[3] A number of different forms of YOCR have emerged. Three major forms are briefly described here.

One manifestation of YOCR has been the development and implementation of largely didactic educational curricula focusing on teaching the conceptual issues of peacemaking and dispute resolution through negotiation and mediation.[4] Another development has been the establishment of school-based peer mediation programs in which youth, from elementary to high school, are trained in the skills of dispute resolution and thereafter function as mediators in the resolution of disputes between their peers.[5] Yet another form of YOCR is the use of mediation in community settings for resolving conflicts between adolescents and their parents or persons from the community when such disputes have intersected with the juvenile justice system.[6]

Despite the procedural differences in implementation of these various forms of YOCR, their general goals are similar. On the surface they all aim at promoting constructive conflict management through the use of prosocial dispute resolution techniques. Underlying this overarching goal is the desire to impart the concepts, skills, and behaviors that constitute what is referred to as a problem-solving orientation to the resolution of interpersonal conflict. This orientation is based on such principles as defining conflict as a mutual problem that should be resolved in a fashion that integrates the needs and interests of all of the parties involved in the conflict.[7]

In addition to these basic goals concerning the resolution of conflict, the possibility that broader "higher order" effects may be achieved through YOCR has also emerged. On an immediate level the hope is that YOCR can produce better school environments and thereby improved circumstances for learning. On a more long-term level is the notion of developing better citizens (e.g., "peaceful people"—see Nelson et al., this volume) who in turn will help to create a more peaceful world.

However, it has also been suggested that the impact of YOCR may be even more fundamental and includes such effects as a positive influence on aspects of adolescent adjustment, which may facilitate optimal development.[8] If these assertions are valid, YOCR may in fact produce "better people," that is, better functioning, more adaptive individuals. The basis of these latter claims for a developmental impact of and approach to YOCR is explored in this chapter.

Empirical Background: The Impact and Effectiveness of YOCR Programs

Overall, the research on the various forms of YOCR is limited in terms of both quantity and quality. Some applications of YOCR have received virtually no attention (e.g., curriculum), while other applications have been the subject of increasing attention (e.g., peer mediation). A brief synopsis of the findings of these research efforts is provided as a basis for understanding some of the assertions made concerning the potential of YOCR for a broader effect on a developmental level. It should be noted that the majority of YOCR activity and research focuses on adolescents (from early to late) and thus this age group is the primary focus of our thinking and discussion.

No full-fledged evaluative research that we are aware of has examined the efficacy of the curriculum-based educational approach in the field. A recent effort has attempted to evaluate the content of such curricula for their potential effectiveness in terms of meeting their educational goals and with regard to their psychological content.[9] These authors conclude that a number of the existing curricula suggest themselves as potentially effective in teaching the concepts of a problem-solving orientation to dispute resolution, with the goal of creating "more peaceful people."

One study did examine the impact of a YOCR intervention in a school setting that included a curriculum component.[10] This research found that learning conflict resolution principles and techniques increased social support and decreased victimization. These changes in the students' interpersonal relations led to higher self-esteem, more positive attitudes toward life, less depression or anxiety, and enhanced internal locus of control. However, the lack of systematic field research on the curriculum approach precludes any definitive conclusions about the independent impact and efficacy of this type of YOCR intervention.

An increasing number of studies have been conducted on YOCR in the form of school-based peer mediation programs. Some have argued that this research has not been systematic or rigorous enough to clearly demonstrate the impact and efficacy of this type of YOCR. However, this body of research has delineated a consistent set of positive effects associated with this type of YOCR that we believe provide a basis for drawing some initial conclusions.

These effects include a reduction in disciplinary problems and improvements in "school climate under some circumstances,"[11] enhancement of self-image in such areas of importance as educational and vocational development,[12] increased academic performance,[13] and cognitive complexity skills,[14] as well as the transfer of skills to settings outside of the school, including to the home setting[15] and interactions with parents.[16]

More generally, this type of YOCR has also been credited with enhancing the development of abilities associated with social competence, including cognitive and affective perspective taking, critical thinking, and language development.[17] As a result of these positive findings, school-based peer mediation programs are increasingly being recognized as viable violence prevention programs that promote positive youth development, community peace, and the reduction of prejudice.[18]

Only a limited amount of research has examined the use of YOCR in the form of mediation for parent-child conflicts to determine its impact and efficacy. However, the findings from this body of research are reasonably consistent and offer support for the conclusion that parent-child mediation can be an effective intervention modality for helping distressed families in conflict.[19] Specifically, these studies consistently report improvement in one or more indices of family interaction or functioning, including such factors as manageability of the child, occurrence of family conflict, communication, expressiveness, independence, and achievement.

These results suggest that mediation can both resolve specific parent-child disputes as well as have a positive impact on the general quality of (often dysfunctional) family interactions. Finally, one study examined a community-based program designed to divert adolescents out of the juvenile justice system for minor criminal infractions (e.g., shoplifting).[20] This study found more positive relationships between the youth and the victims of their offenses subsequent to mediation than justice system processing.

Overall, research on the use of conflict resolution interventions with adolescents indicates that this intervention modality can be an effective alternative to such standard approaches as the juvenile justice system, counseling, and normative school-based disciplinary procedures for resolving conflicts.[21] Perhaps more important, this research has suggested the potential for a more fundamental positive impact resulting from these intervention approaches. The nature and basis of this impact is discussed in the next sections.

Theoretical Background: A Developmental Approach to YOCR

We have argued elsewhere that, on a general level, the primary impact of YOCR interventions is to alter adolescents' attitudes and behaviors relevant to conflict.[22] Support for this conclusion comes from a recent review of the research on peer mediation.[23] This view is in line with others who have suggested that a major goal of peace education is to move children from negative to positive attitudes toward conflict as a basis for preventing violence.[24]

However, we have suggested that perhaps more important than the resolution of specific conflicts or the prevention of violence, as beneficial as that may be, the changes in attitudes and behaviors resulting from the process of learning the principles and practicing the skills associated with the prosocial conflict resolution approaches used in YOCR (i.e., the "problem-solving" approach to conflict), have positive effects that transcend the issues of conflict. Specifically, the results from research on YOCR suggest that in addition to having an effect in the domain of conflict (e.g., reduced disciplinary problems), it also has effects beyond this domain (e.g. on self-esteem) which have implications for the adjustment and development of the youth involved.

In an initial theoretical statement on this topic, we argued that the research on YOCR suggested two major explanations with regard to the apparent positive impact on aspects of adjustment of these interventions on adolescents: the first explanation took a developmental orientation and the second, an attitudinal approach.[25] Recent research and additional consideration of the issues has led us to modify this explanatory model, especially with regard to the attitudinal approach, which while retaining its attitudinal emphasis, we now believe also includes a developmental component. This revised explanatory model for the positive impact of YOCR is briefly described here.

The first factor in our model is based on stress and coping literature and attempts to explain why learning about and using prosocial conflict resolution skills would be associated with such positive effects as enhanced self-image and improved cognitive skills. This factor takes an explicitly developmental perspective. In our initial statement the second factor sought to explain how (i.e., the circumstances under which) the attitudes and behaviors transmitted in conflict resolution intervention efforts were optimally acquired and generalized to other aspects of the adolescent's life, embracing an attitude change perspective in trying to understand this issue.

However, our recent research on adolescent attitudes toward conflict suggests that the attitude construct has an even more fundamental relationship to the positive effects associated with YOCR. Specifically, this research suggests that what we have come to refer to as conflict attitude is associated with aspects of adolescent adjustment and therefore also fits within a developmental framework. Each of these factors receives more extensive attention in the following sections.

Conflict, Coping, and Optimal Development

In terms of the first factor (i.e., the "why" question), we have argued that the effects on aspects of adjustment found in the research stem from the fact that the orientation and skills associated with YOCR processes such as mediation are "developmentally appropriate." We contend that such YOCR processes emphasize the development of attitudes and behaviors that are consistent with a set of coping skills, the acquisition of which has been associated with positive adjustment and optimal developmental outcomes in adolescents.[26]

Adolescence is marked by the testing of limits and boundaries, and inevitably, a greater range of stressors, including interpersonal conflicts, with which adolescents must cope. Faced with these circumstances, adolescents must necessarily develop a larger repertoire of effective coping responses to meet the demands of these stressors.[27] Coping behavior has been conceptualized as a central element of adolescent psychosocial competence, and thus understanding how adolescents cope with stressors such as conflict is important. This is especially critical since research suggests that the types of coping strategies employed by adolescents are not only related to adolescent adjustment, but also to those coping strategies which emerge in adulthood, and therefore have implications for adult success.

A good deal of attention has been given to the identification of those factors believed to enhance adolescents' ability to effectively cope with various stressors. Some of the major factors identified are an internal locus of control orientation, a sense of mastery of the environment, and the use of an active oriented problem-solving approach to managing stressful events. In addition, a stable and well-structured support system and greater family cohesion have also been associated with more effective coping and better adjustment among adolescents. We believe that YOCR interventions promote these factors in a number of significant ways.

One of the central goals in the process of conflict resolution is to help people learn to define conflicts as mutual problems, which are best resolved cooperatively. As such, conflict resolution is both theoretically and practically aimed at the development of a personal sense of responsibility for the existence of the problem as well as for resolving the present and future conflicts. This emphasis on personal responsibility for the resolution of the conflict should in turn promote an internal locus of control orientation. This assertion has been supported by at least one study that found such an effect.[28] Similarly, the successful use of conflict resolution skills in resolving disputes, either as a disputant or a mediator, should promote a sense of self-efficacy and mastery of the environment.

On an even more basic level, conflict resolution is focused on promoting problem-solving behavior and increasing its use as a means of resolving conflicts. Thus, the orientation inherent to conflict resolution promotes the use of that coping strategy most often associated with optimal adolescent adjustment and positive developmental outcomes. The belief that one can effectively engage in problem solving has been associated with more optimal adjustment through its impact on self-esteem, affective well-being, and actual problem-solving performance.[29]

In addition, the approach taken by YOCR emphasizes enhanced communication and greater concern for the needs and interests of others, effects that are likely to enhance interpersonal interactions. As noted earlier, research has indicated that the use of conflict resolution techniques such as mediation is associated with increased positive interactions between family members, including a greater sense of family cohesion. These various effects can be expected to promote a more reliable support system for the adolescent. The study by Zhang also provides support for this contention.

We believe that this line of reasoning and related research findings support our assertion that the approach offered by YOCR is consistent with those factors associated with an adolescent's ability to cope more effectively with the major stressors in her or his life. In turn, the development of more effective coping abilities should promote adjustment and the attainment of positive developmental outcomes. In terms of the stress and coping literature, these various effects can be viewed as enhancing what is referred to as the youth's "resilience" in meeting the challenges of the major stressors of the developmental period. Specifically, the possession of problem-solving skills and the development of a more stable support system, can be viewed as promoting what are referred to as "protective mechanisms" that form the basis of competent coping underlying resilience. Thus, this analysis suggests that adolescents are prime candidates for deriving beneficial developmental effects from the process of learning and using the skills of youth-oriented conflict resolution.

Conflict Attitudes and Adolescent Adjustment

With regard to the second factor in our explanatory model (i.e., the "how" question), we argued that a necessary component to attaining the positive effects of conflict resolution interventions is an active applied component, for example, a peer mediation program. Indeed, it has been argued that simple exposure to the principles of conflict resolution, even through experiential training, may be insufficient to have a permanent and meaningful impact on attitudes and behaviors concerning conflict.

Rather it has been argued that an ongoing opportunity to make use of conflict resolution skills by establishing and maintaining such activities as peer mediation programs is necessary to achieve permanent changes in both attitudes and behaviors.[30] This line of reasoning is consistent with attitude change literature, which suggests a greater likelihood of significant and permanent attitude change following and resulting from changes in related overt behavior, when that behavior is viewed as voluntary.[31]

However, as noted earlier, recent research by the authors suggests an even more fundamental importance of the attitude construct in terms of adolescent adjustment.[32] Attitudes can be defined as tripartite mental structures that provide the basis for an evaluative reaction toward an object (e.g., an individual) and include cognitive, affective, and behavioral intention components (i.e., a response tendency).[33] Attitudes and behaviors have been demonstrated to have a reciprocal relationship whereby, in addition to attitudes influencing behavior, behavior can influence or even change existing attitudes. In addition, attitudes are thought to exist in associative networks and therefore can be expected to influence and be influenced by other attitudes held by the individual.

These attributes of attitudes suggest that the attitude an individual has toward conflict will not only influence behavior in response to conflict, but also attitudes and behaviors in other domains of the individual's life. It also suggests that behaviors engaged in as a response to conflict may influence underlying attitudes toward conflict as well as other attitudes. Such effects, one can hypothesize, are particularly likely when repeated often and when negative as in chronic conflict that is responded to in a contentious or violent fashion.

This theoretical analysis is supported by developmental research on adolescent conflict. In a review of this literature, Laursen and Collins suggest that "although single conflict episodes rarely have a significant impact on close relationships, the cumulative effects of contentiousness are detrimental."[34] Among the effects found are that frequent conflict has adverse implications for developmental outcome and that high rates of contentious conflict have been found to be associated with greater rates of adolescent delinquency, behavioral disorders, and incidence of runaway and suicide attempts. Laursen and Collins also note that although limited in quantity, this research suggests a positive impact on adolescent development of the use of prosocial conflict resolution strategies by adolescents.

In this theoretical context a multistudy program of research was developed by the authors that takes this conflict attitude approach to understanding the impact of YOCR. The research program includes a study on parent-child mediation in upstate New York, and a series of studies assessing adolescent conflict attitudes and their correlates in high schools in the Middle East, a study at an adolescent educational facility in a New York State prison, and a study in a middle and high school setting in upstate New York. The results from the five studies are highly consistent in terms of the relationship found between conflict attitude and indices of adolescent adjustment and are briefly summarized here.

Conflict Attitudes, Their Correlates, and Consequences

In all five studies, conflict attitude, operationalized as self-reported conflict response tendency as measured by the Rahim Conflict Management Inventory (RCMI), was found to be related either to conflict behavior or to attitudes and behaviors in other domains of the adolescent's life.[35] The RCMI assesses individuals' inclinations to respond to conflict on five standard dimensions that have been identified in research about how individuals manage conflict; specifically, avoidance, compromise, domination, integrating, and obliging. Other measures employed in these studies included assessments of the quality of family relationships and level of family conflict, self-esteem, mental health distress, and various personality traits.[36]

Among the findings were that conflict attitude was associated with the self-reported likelihood of witnessing or engaging in physical violence, with the general level of conflict and hostility in the family and the seriousness of the incidents of family conflict, and with the level of violence of criminal behavior. In all cases, endorsement of a "prosocial" conflict resolution style (i.e., integrating, compromising, and obliging) was related to reports of less negative conflict behavior, whereas endorsement of a dominating conflict management style was related to greater levels of negative conflict behaviors (e.g., hostility and violence).

On a more global level, conflict attitude was related to the adolescents' general relationships with their parents and their overall life satisfaction. Specifically, adolescents who endorsed prosocial conflict resolution styles reported greater satisfaction with their relationship with their parents and with the quality of their lives on a variety of dimensions. In terms of attitudes and factors in other domains of the adolescent's life, conflict attitude was consistently found to be related to a number of indices of adjustment. With a significant exception discussed below, the endorsement of prosocial conflict response tendencies was associated with greater levels of self-esteem, better mental health adjustment, and the endorsement of positive personality traits as representative of the self. In contrast, the endorsement of a dominating conflict response tendency was negatively associated with these factors.

The exception to these general findings highlights the potential importance of the developmental approach to YOCR. As is clear from our delineation of the sites of our research, the populations examined are highly diverse in nature. Perhaps the major distinguishing factor among them, even greater than culture, was the circumstances in which they lived and grew up. Specifically, one set of our samples grew up in explicitly or relatively benign environments (e.g., as part of the middle class of the United States), whereas our other set of samples grew up in explicitly difficult, often violence-plagued environments (e.g., Palestinians from Gaza and incarcerated adolescents in the United States from severely disadvantaged backgrounds). The pattern of results described above obtained for the members of the group of samples containing those from explicitly or relatively normal environments, and the exceptions were from members of the group of samples containing those who grew up in "difficult" circumstances.

Those adolescents from the samples containing individuals who grew up in difficult circumstances, the tendency was to endorse a dominating conflict response style. This endorsement was related to two seemingly dichotomous patterns of relationships to the other measured factors. For these samples, as with our other samples, endorsement of a dominating style was related to greater levels of emotional distress.

However, unlike our "benign circumstance" samples, for these "difficult circumstance" samples, endorsement of a dominating style was related variously (depending on sample and measures used) to higher self-esteem and the endorsement of positive personality traits, whereas the endorsement of an integrating style was associated with lower self-esteem and negative personality traits. We note that the similarity in the pattern found for our samples from such apparently diverse cases as Palestinian adolescents growing up in warlike situations such as Gaza Strip and incarcerated adolescents from severely disadvantaged backgrounds in the United States is consistent with arguments made that the circumstances of U.S. minority youth is not dissimilar from those of adolescents growing up in war-torn or warlike circumstances.[37]

Overall, the results of our research suggest that what adolescents think about conflict (i.e., their attitude), at least in terms of how they report they respond to it, has implications for a variety of other factors related to adjustment and developmental outcome. The emergence of two distinct patterns, one for adolescents from benign environments, the other for adolescents from adverse environments, fits and supports a developmental approach to the use of YOCR. In this regard, our results are consistent with developmental research in demonstrating a positive relationship between prosocial conflict management styles and positive adolescent adjustment and developmental outcomes and a negative relationship between antisocial conflict management styles (e.g., domination) and these factors.

These results suggest that establishing YOCR interventions in a systematic way, such as in school settings, would present possibilities for several levels of impact. First, YOCR interventions offer the opportunity for "natural" interventions that establish positive or alter negative conflict attitudes and behaviors through curriculum and peer mediation program implementation. Such efforts would be expected to have a salutary effect on levels of conflict and violence within these schools and such ancillary effects as an improved learning environment.

However, such an approach seems warranted for reasons that are perhaps even more important. That is, as the basis for the enhancement of positive developmental outcomes through the inculcation of prosocial conflict attitudes and behaviors, and the prevention of negative developmental outcomes that seem to result from the repeated manifestation of contentious responses to conflict. Such an approach to the use of YOCR is described in the next section.

YOCR Programs as a Developmental/Preventive Approach to Intervention

Current thinking in the field of adolescent mental health intervention argues for a comprehensive prevention-oriented approach as most likely to have the greatest positive impact, as well as being most cost-effective on a long-term basis.[38] The argument for the comprehensive approach suggests that isolated programs implemented in a piecemeal fashion without total institutional support (e.g. a curriculum here, a peer mediation program there) are not likely to have a significant impact on the problems that they are designed to address. Rather it is suggested that programs should be implemented in a comprehensive fashion that involve all components of the system in which they are being implemented (e.g., a school).

Taken together, our developmentally-oriented theoretical model and research results on adolescent attitudes toward conflict, as well as the results from other research on YOCR suggest its use in such a fashion. Specifically we argue for the application of YOCR in terms of what can be labeled a comprehensive developmentally-oriented prevention model approach to intervention. This approach, some aspects of which have been articulated elsewhere, suggests that, depending on the nature of the population, YOCR interventions can be viewed as fitting into one of three levels of prevention each of which is discussed below.[39]

For those adolescents in our research who grew up in positive or reasonably decent environments, the relationship between conflict attitude and other factors was straightforward and "normative." Specifically, prosocial attitudes toward conflict were related positively to indices of adjustment and "antisocial" conflict attitudes (i.e., domination) were related negatively to such indicators. This pattern argues for the use of YOCR on an educational/developmental or primary prevention basis in schools with this type of population. This approach is aimed at enhancing abilities that prevent the development of problems. Thus, in this instance the goal of YOCR would be to inculcate students with a prosocial conflict resolution orientation to enhance the likelihood that all or at least the majority of students develops the positive pattern of adjustment and developmental outcomes associated with such an orientation.

Secondary prevention aims at dealing with incipient problems and attempts to mitigate them before they become exacerbated and perhaps intractable. For children and adolescents from disadvantaged or difficult environments, but not as extreme as in our "difficult circumstance" samples, school-based YOCR may serve as a mitigating force, preventing or if caught early enough, reversing the negative pattern of development and adjustment observed in our findings. Specifically, by teaching and encouraging prosocial attitudes and behaviors toward conflict and providing forums within which to exercise them, it can be hoped that a greater inclination toward their use would occur, thereby preventing the emergence of the negative pattern observed or altering this pattern if still in its early stages.

The second, and more complex pattern found in our samples from difficult environments, raises the issue of the use of YOCR on a tertiary prevention level. Such prevention focuses on extreme problems that have become exacerbated and seemingly intractable and attempts to make the best of them. We have argued elsewhere that such ADR applications as divorce and custody mediation are examples of this approach applied to families.[40]

For adolescents from populations such as our "difficult circumstance" samples, whether the problems resulting from negative attitudes toward conflict (which according to recent research are likely to have developed from exposure to violence) can be remediated by exposure to YOCR alone is open to question, especially if the underlying circumstances (e.g., ongoing exposure to violence) are not altered.[41]

However, by teaching and encouraging prosocial attitudes and behaviors toward conflict, it can be hoped that a greater inclination toward their use would occur, with a reversal of the obtained relationships such that the endorsement of prosocial conflict response styles would become associated with greater levels of self-esteem and positive personality traits. However, for adolescents from such populations, an even more comprehensive, perhaps therapeutically oriented intervention would probably be necessary.

Conclusions and Implications

We have argued here for a developmentally-oriented approach to the use of conflict resolution interventions with adolescents. This call is based on several factors. Evidence suggests that the attitudes adolescents have regarding conflict are associated with their behavior in response to conflict (e.g., endorsement of a dominating conflict management style was related to engagement in violent behavior) and that such behavior is in turn related to behavioral indices of adjustment (e.g., chronic engagement in contentious conflict is related to behavioral disorders). In addition, evidence suggests a relationship between conflict attitudes and a number of indices of adjustment such as self-esteem, mental health status, and personality traits (e.g., endorsement of prosocial conflict management styles was related to higher self-esteem, lower levels of mental distress, and positive personality traits in adolescents from benign environments with a generally inverse relationship for adolescents from difficult environments.

These findings suggest that the attitude an adolescent has toward conflict influences behaviors in response to conflict and is also related to various aspects of adjustment. The research also indicates that having prosocial attitudes toward conflict and engaging in prosocial conflict behavior is related to better adjustment. Given that the primary effect of YOCR is to alter adolescents' attitudes and behaviors toward conflict in the direction of a problem-solving orientation, YOCR interventions seem ideally suited to addressing these critical aspects of adolescent adjustment and development.

We have further suggested that the approach offered by YOCR is developmentally appropriate because it provides an orientation toward resolving conflict that is consistent with those coping skills which promote adjustment and enhanced developmental outcomes. By inculcating the problem-solving orientation to conflict resolution, this approach provides youth with a set of skills that should enhance their ability to cope more effectively with other aspects of their lives, thereby promoting optimal adjustment. Finally, we have argued that YOCR fits a developmental prevention model approach to intervention, whereby, depending on the population to which it is applied, it can prevent, remediate, or ameliorate problems associated with conflict and adjustment.

Notes

1. Kenneth Kressel and Dean G. Pruitt, *Mediation Research: Studies in the Process and Effectiveness of Mediation* (San Francisco: Jossey-Bass, 1989).

2. Michael Van Slyck, Marilyn Stern, and Helena Desivilya, "Resolving Adolescent Conflict in the Home, School, and the Community: Mediation as an Alternative Intervention" (paper presented at the International Conference "The Family on the Threshold of the 21st Century," Jerusalem, Israel, May 1994.)

3. Melinda Smith, "Mediation for Children, Youth, and Families: A Service Continuum," *Mediation Quarterly* 12 (summer 1995): 277–83.

4. Ian M. Harris, "From World Peace to Peace in the 'Hood Peace Education in a Postmodern World," *Journal for a Just and Caring Education* 2, no. 4 (October 1996): 378–95; Linden L. Nelson, Michael Van Slyck, and Lucille Cardella, "Conflict Resolution Curricula: An Assessment of Psychological Content and Potential Effectiveness" (Chapter 5 in this volume).

5. Robin Hall, "Peer Mediation In Schools: A Review and Bibliography" (School of Teacher Education, Charles Stuart University, Bathurst Australia, 1996), Mimeo 44 pp; Linden L. Nelson, Michael Van Slyck, and Lucille Cardella, "Conflict Resolution Curricula: An Assessment of Psychological Content and Potential Effectiveness"); Molly K. Pont and John D. Krumboltz, "Countering School Violence: The Rise of Conflict Resolution Programs" (Chapter 3 in this volume); David W. Johnson and Roger T. Johnson, "Teaching Students to Be Peacemakers: Results of Five Years of Research," *Peace and Conflict: Journal of Peace Psychology* 1 (1995): 417–34; Michael Van Slyck and Marilyn Stern, "Conflict Resolution in Educational Settings: Assessing the Impact of Peer Mediation Programs," in *The Art and Science of Community Mediation: A Handbook for Practitioners and Researchers*, ed. Karen Duffy, Paul Olczak, and James Grosch (New York: Guilford Press, 1991), 257–74.

6. Michael Van Slyck, Laurie Newland, and Marilyn Stern, "Parent-Adolescent Mediation: Integrating Theory, Research, and Practice," *Mediation Quarterly* 10 (winter 1992): 193–208.

7. Harris, "From World Peace to Peace in the 'Hood," 382.

8. Michael Van Slyck, Marilyn Stern, and Jennifer Zak, "Promoting Optimal Adolescent Development through Conflict Resolution Education, Training, and Practice: An Innovative Approach for Counseling Psychologists," *The Counseling Psychologist* 24 (July 1996): 433–61.

9. Nelson, Van Slyck, and Cardella, "Conflict Resolution Curricula."

10 Quan Wu Zhang, "An Intervention Model of Constructive Conflict Resolution and Cooperative Learning," *Journal of Social Issues* 50 (Spring 1994): 99–116.

11 Hall, "Peer Mediation."

12 Van Slyck and Stern, "Conflict Resolution in Educational Settings," 262–66.

13 Johnson and Johnson, "Teaching Students," 417–34.

14 Pamela Lane-Garon, "Social Perspective Taking in Student Mediators" (Ph.D. diss., Arizona State University, 1997).

15 Deborah B. Gentry and Wayne A. Benenson, "School-age Peer Mediators Transfer Knowledge and Skills to Home Setting," *Mediation Quarterly* 10 (winter 1992): 101–9.

16 Julie E. Miller, "Peer Mediation in Orange County Middle Schools: Transferring Conflict Management Skills Learned in Schools to Home," (Masters thesis, University of Central Florida, 1993).

17 Pamela Lane and Jeff McWhirter, "Creating a Peaceful School Community: Reconciliation Operationalized," *Catholic School Studies* 69 (October 1996) 31–34.

18 William DeJong, "School-Based Violence Prevention: From the Peaceable School to the Peaceable Neighborhood," *National Institute for Dispute Resolution Forum* (spring 1994): 7–14; Pamela Moore and Deborah Batiste, "Preventing Youth Violence: Prejudice Elimination and Conflict Resolution Programs," *National Institute for Dispute Resolution Forum* (spring 1994): 15–19.

19 Van Slyck, Newland, and Stern, "Parent-Adolescent Mediation," 195–99.

20 Van Slyck, Stern, and Desivilya, "Resolving Adolescent Conflict."

21 Marilyn Stern and Michael Van Slyck, "PINS Diversion Research Project: Final Report" (Washington, DC: Fund for Research in Dispute Resolution, 1993).

22 Michael Van Slyck, Marilyn Stern, and Salman Elbedour, "Adolescent Attitudes toward Conflict: Correlates, Consequences and Cross Cultural Issues," in *Children' and Adolescents' Understanding of War, Conflict and Peace: International Perspective*, ed. Dani Bar Tal, Amiram Raviv, and Louis Oppenheimer (Jossey-Bass, in press).

23 Hall, "Peer Mediation."

24 Harris, "From World Peace to Peace in the 'Hood," 387.

25 Van Slyck, Stern, and Zak, "Promoting Optimal Adolescent Development," 439–41.

26 Ibid.

27 Bruce E. Compas, Nancy L. Worsham, and Sydney Ey, "Conceptual and Developmental Issues in Children's Coping with Stress," in *Stress and Coping in Child Health*, ed. Annette La Greca, Lawrence J. Seigel, Jan L. Wallander, and C. E. Walker (New York: Guilford Press, 1992), 7–24.

28 Zhang, "An Intervention Model," 99–116.

29 P. Paul Heppner, Janet J. Hibel, Gary Neal, Charles L. Weinstein, and Frederic Rabinowitz, "Personal Problem Solving: A Descriptive Study of Individual Differences," *Journal of Counseling Psychology* 29 (November 1982): 580–90.

30 Van Slyck and Stern, "Conflict Resolution in Educational Settings," 269–72.

31 Phillip G. Zimbardo and Mark R. Leippe, *The Psychology of Attitude Change and Social Influence* (New York: McGraw-Hill, 1991).

32 Van Slyck, Stern, and Elbedour, "Adolescent Attitudes toward Conflict."

33 Zimbardo and Leippe, *Psychology of Attitude*, 30–37.

34 Brett Laursen and W. Andrew Collins, "Interpersonal Conflict during Adolescence," *Psychological Bulletin* 15 (March 1994): 197–209.

35 M. Af"zalur Rahim, *Rahim Organizational Conflict* (Palo Alto, CA: Consulting Psychologists Press, 1983).

36 Van Slyck, Stern, and Elbedour, "Adolescent Attitudes toward Conflict."

37 James Garbarino, Kathleen Kostelny, and Nancy W. Dubrow, *No Place to be a Child: Growing Up in a War Zone* (Lexington, MA: Lexington Books, 1992).

38 Roger P. Weissberg, Marlene Caplan, and Robin L. Harwood, "Promoting Competent Young People in Competence-Enhancing Environments: A Systems-Based Perspective on Primary Prevention," 59 (December 1991): 830–41.

39 Van Slyck, Stern, and Zak, "Promoting Optimal Adolescent Development," 441–51.

40 Van Slyck, Stern, and Zak, "Promoting Optimal Adolescent Development," 441–51.

41 Melanie Duckworth, Sarah Moody-Thomas, Ana C. Fick, Jennifer Hayden, Lieu T. Nguyen, and D. Danielle Hale, "The Impact of Violence Exposure on Coping Responses of Children and Adolescents" (paper presented at the Society for Research in Child Development, Washington, DC, April 1997), 1–6.

Chapter 10

Nonviolent Interventions in Secondary Schools: Administrative Perspectives

Robert C. DiGiulio

As I was verifying sources for this contribution at the Yale University Library, I came across the local newspaper. Its lead article stated that thirty girls at a Connecticut middle school had been strip-searched by an assistant principal, gym teacher, and security guard in an effort to locate $50 a student claimed was missing. Threatened with arrest if they refused to take off their clothing, all thirty students complied, yet no money turned up. The three women who conducted the strip search have been suspended, and the school's superintendent apologized to the girls and their parents.[1] Upon reflection, the article seemed to highlight the incongruous position public schools find themselves in today: Expected by a larger society to teach students to solve differences peacefully and nonviolently, schools fail to model those behaviors when they use interventions that violate students' dignity.

Indeed, any nonviolent intervention program or curriculum may be doomed to failure in schools in which abusive behavior is sanctioned by administrators, including strip searches, verbal abuse, paddling, and other forms of corporal punishment. Although the crime-and-punishment paradigm is the norm in our legal system outside-of-school (witness capital punishment as the ultimate corporal punishment), inside school, programs that purport to teach prosocial behavior cannot work when delivered in an environment laden with fear and permissive of insults to human dignity. In other words, schools must move away from adversarial, crime-and-punishment paradigms before they can successfully model nonviolent ways to resolve conflict.

There is little doubt that today's school leaders—particularly those in middle schools and high schools—are well aware of the propensity for violence by some students. There is also little argument with the idea that school leaders must address adolescent violence. Yet, school administrators seem to approach the question of how their school should address violence (ranging from misbehavior to assault) in one of two ways: On one hand, some administrators advocate a crime-and-punishment position, ready to expel or suspend students who stand in the way of other students "who come to school to learn." This position is similar to peace-through-strength strategies, which identify enemies and criminals, and then seek to deter them through the use of threat and force. Used in both the international and domestic arenas, this position holds that violence can be avoided (and stopped) by frightening people away from violent behavior. Recent "zero-tolerance" legislation also embodies this stance, for it not only prescribes the punishment (expulsion, usually) but also makes it both automatic and unconditional.

On the other hand, there are administrators who acknowledge that although schools must sometimes exclude students, their goal is to keep students in school—and safe there—in order to be able to teach them to act prosocially. Their stance emphasizes education, not expulsion, and they typically place more emphasis on prevention and support instead of reaction and retribution. Unfortunately, of the two stances, the crime-and-punishment model is easier for schools to employ. Because it is fashioned on our criminal justice system, we are "used to" it: it is an understandable (or at least, a more easily defensible) model. As a result, the idea of "school-as-prison" is becoming less farfetched today. Lately, there has been a dramatic increase in the construction of maximum security prisons, and an accompanying expansion of the legal system to accommodate the now over one million U.S. residents who are either in prison or awaiting trial.[2] However, we know that the threat of prison is not preventive, and has little or no effect on the crime rate.[3] We also know that laws do not teach, and that there can be a significant difference between what is legal and what is right. For example, there is no law mandating that students respect each other, yet every teacher who ever attempted to teach prosocial behavior knows that respect must be present as a basic underpinning of human interactions. There are no laws against violating a student's dignity; those who strip-searched the Connecticut students probably felt the ends (possible recovery of money; possible "lesson to others") justified the means (stripping and searching students). Conversely, there are violent school interventions that are explicitly legal in many states—such as the use of corporal punishment—that serve to perpetuate and teach violence with ringing clarity.

It is particularly crucial today for U.S. schools to emphasize nonadversarial interventions and prosocial education because *schools are the only institutions we have in which that can happen.* Aside from criminal lawyers, educators (and a few social workers) are the only professionals who stand between many adolescents and prison. If students do not learn prosocial behavior at home (and many do not), they will learn prosocial behavior nowhere else. The maxim "it takes a village to raise a child" may be romantic and fetching, but U.S. villages are gone, and its communities are fast disappearing. Nonetheless, even in the largest cities in the United States, public schools still hold the potential to be that "village"; to be a community; to be a place where strangers can still come together and do constructive things, bound by their mutual interest in young people and the neighborhood. Particularly for those students whose home and neighborhood lives are filled with violence, schools can hold the necessary conditions—and perhaps even the sufficient conditions—to disrupt the cycle of violence-to-incarceration-to-recidivism. Indeed, Emile Durkheim wrote that schools were the best places for students to become prosocial; to become oriented toward the good of others, even for those students who come from loving, prosocial families.[4] Toward this end, school administrators can advocate for and foster prosocial behavior among staff and students. They hold a key role toward altering the cycle of violence.

Three Approaches to Keep the Peace in School Settings

The types of interventions made by middle and secondary school administrators can be designated as "corrective," "preventive," or "supportive" approaches. Corrective approaches are reactive, after-the-fact responses to student misbehavior and violence, including time-out, suspension, and expulsion, as well as a number of forceful interrogations (such as strip searches). Correctives seek immediate results.

Preventive approaches are designed to preclude; to be before-the-fact, heading off student misbehavior or violence before they occur. There are numerous preventive programs, often focused on a specific aspect of school violence, such as those seeking to prevent weapons from being brought into school, or "Just Say No" drug prevention programs.

In contrast to corrective and preventive approaches, supportive approaches are not reactive, nor do they focus on preventing something from happening. Supportive approaches are more holistic, providing a framework of nonviolent alternatives for students that can supplant violent behavior. For example, after-school and summer recreation programs do not by themselves prevent violence, but they work well toward supporting the reduction of tensions in school and community.[5] Programs in peace education and conflict resolution can be supportive as well. While all three approaches have played a part in the way traditional schools address violence, the approaches most likely to alter violent adolescent behavior lie in preventive, and particularly, supportive approaches.

Corrective Approaches

Perhaps the oldest school interventions are the corrective interventions of exclusion and expulsion. Prior to the turn of the century, students considered to be "incorrigible" were either refused admission to school, or once admitted, were expelled upon commission of an offense or upon demonstration that they were, indeed, "incorrigible." Such students simply stayed home or worked. The first effort toward providing for these sometimes-violent "incorrigibles" came about prior to World War I, when alternative public schools were established to provide education for "not only the truant and the incorrigible, who under former conditions either left early or were expelled, but also many children of the foreign-born who have no aptitude for book learning, and many children of inferior mental qualities who do not profit by ordinary classroom procedure."[6] However, public opinion and court decisions lent impetus toward closing many of these alternative schools, with students gradually moved into the regular classroom in mainstream public schools. Today, schools find themselves having gone full-circle with a return to expulsion and exclusion. Today's emphasis is on zero tolerance, by which student behaviors are recast as criminal offenses, subjecting the student to automatic expulsion or other punishment upon the first commission of the offense. Supported by the American Federation of Teachers and championed by its late president, Albert Shanker, the backdrop for zero tolerance is found in the Gun-Free Schools Act of 1994, which placed an automatic, one-year expulsion from school on any student carrying a weapon.[7] In addition, the act mandated the referral of offending students to the criminal justice system, tightening the connection between the legal system and the U.S. public schools (and forcing the hands of schools and administrators who in the past could have chosen nonjudicial, nonpunitive consequences for its students).

Another traditional corrective school intervention is corporal punishment. Still legal in over twenty states, corporal punishment is a violent response to student misbehavior, often done in the hope that it will serve as a preventive. After punishment, the student will no longer engage in undesirable misbehavior. Typically, corporal punishment consists of spanking or paddling, and is usually confined to elementary-school-age populations.

Of course, physical contact with a student is not always corporal punishment, or a violent intervention. In middle and secondary schools there are times when the school administration is called upon to intervene in order to stop violence to prevent student or staff injury. Breaking up fights is an example, and contemporary schools must provide key personnel with crisis intervention skills. These include nonviolent restraint, where an out-of-control student needs to be restrained, yet at the same time reassured that she or he will not be hurt by restraint. Aside from these stronger interventions, corrective interventions in middle and secondary schools typically do not involve physical contact or force. In fact, the most effective interventions are nonviolent, and do not destroy student or teacher dignity. These interventions are meant to teach, and not to hurt or punish.

In fact, correctives do not have to take the form of strip searches, intimidation, or suspension or expulsion. There are a number of other, nonviolent corrective interventions available to educators,[8] many of which are more appropriate for a teenager's needs and level of moral, cognitive, social, and emotional development. Adolescents have a strong sense of justice and fairness, as well as a normal egocentric focus on themselves—"everyone is looking at me." Cognitively, many are now capable of greater abstract thinking, as well as hypothesizing "what-if-I-did/had-done" alternatives. Thus, schools can use correctives that go beyond simplistic crime-and-punishment stances. These nonviolent interventions include:

Talking to the student. "I messages" are very effective when clear: "I am disappointed by (specify misbehavior). I cannot allow it to continue."

Loss of school privileges. This is useful when the student already knows the limits, what the consequence of disregarding the limit will be. Loss of privileges works best when the loss of privileges is directly related to the misbehavior.

Exclusion. In a prosocial school, this is potentially a powerful consequence, particularly to adolescents whose identity hinges on belonging. (The reason suspensions or expulsions are often taken lightly by some students is because they do not feel part of the school to begin with, so a suspension or expulsion merely confirms for the student this alienation.)

Reflective activities. These involve thinking about, then writing about, one's behavior. Reflection is effective in that it is noncoercive, and allows the student to self-monitor. Anyone who has read Salinger's classic *Catcher in the Rye* knows that adolescents can be particularly astute using reflection. Reflective activities are especially advantageous interventions when an adult provides one-to-one guidance in carrying it out.

Parental involvement. Even if parents cannot remedy their teenager's behavior (and they often cannot or will not), parental involvement is an important part of any nonviolent corrective school intervention. (Care must be taken, however, to guard against parents acting out their anger, beating, or berating the student.)

Contracts. Contracts can be particularly effective for preadolescents and adolescents. Contracts should be written as clearly as possible, stating the goal and what credit the student will earn as a result.

Self-instruction strategies. Self-instruction strategies are also useful nonviolent interventions. These involve teaching the student a set of responses to engage in when the risky situation again arises. For example, a middle-school student who has thrown food in the cafeteria at the urging of other students could be given—or asked to come up with—a specific strategy to use the next time she or he is urged to throw food.[9]

More serious offenses such as fighting and threats of assault require careful but swift intervention, and it is important for the school administration to set up a plan before serious incidents occur. Having a plan (or "crisis intervention plan") in place is essential, as is a meeting of minds reviewing strategies for handling violence and potential student violence.[10] In general, when teachers are faced with serious misbehavior that is more than disruptive and potentially violent, they should not attempt to impose immediate consequences upon a student who is armed or distraught, visibly angry, or "fresh from the fray." There is no "quick fix" possible at those times, only the requirement to act reasonably and firmly to protect the safety of the students and adults (including that of the student) within the classroom and school building.

Preventive Approaches

David Hamburg, President of the Carnegie Corporation, wrote recently of the important role of prevention in adolescent violence. He drew a parallel between successful public health preventive efforts (such as those aimed at reducing smoking by teenagers) and the prevention of violence: "Adolescent experimentation with behavior patterns and values offers an opportunity to develop alternatives to violent responses."[11] Truly, adolescent behavior is not carved in stone; teenagers don "different hats" during adolescence, and this propensity toward experimentation can be put to good use by having students "try on" different responses to conflict, and explore options other than violent responses.

It makes sense that preventing adolescent violence is much simpler and less painful (and less expensive) to the individual and society than correcting it after it has occurred. There are numerous books and resources available for administrators on how to address violence proactively and in addition to resources, many in-school violence prevention programs have been launched, particularly over the past decade.[12]

Early reviews of violence prevention programs were mixed. Some programs did yield results, yet others were not effective when applied to new and different situations. Researcher Renee Wilson-Brewer et al., surveyed over fifty violence prevention programs, and found that fewer than half of the programs actually resulted in a reduction of violence.[13] Daniel Webster reviewed three curricula specifically designed to prevent violence, yet found that there was no evidence of a long-term change in violent behavior.[14]

However, some programs have been successful. Public health administrator Deborah Prothrow-Stith developed the "Violence Prevention Curriculum for Adolescents" that created a nonviolent classroom ethos, and helped students develop a larger repertoire of responses to anger. Her curriculum was being used in schools in 400 cities.[15] In his recent article "From World Peace to Peace in the 'Hood," researcher Ian M. Harris describes how, in Chicago, "a three-tiered violence prevention course involving students, teachers, and parents is being used by 4,000 students in inner-city schools."[16] Linda Lantieri cofounded the Resolving Conflict Creatively Program in New York City in 1985, seeking to teach "intergroup understanding, alternatives to violence, and creative conflict resolution among students, teachers, parents, and administrators" in five demonstration public school districts.[17] By 1995, the program grew to involve 300 schools. The part of the program that works well is its emphasis on conflict resolution, including the use of student mediators, and creation of a "peaceable school" environment.

The American Psychological Association recently issued a report called *Violence and Youth* that enumerated several more aspects of violence prevention programs that work. These include home visitation components, programs that support social and cognitive skill-building, including peer negotiation skills, problem-solving training, anger management, and skills in generating alternative solutions, and perspective taking.[18] In addition, Professors David W. Johnson and Roger T. Johnson state that successful school programs look past violence prevention and incorporate conflict resolution; they create a cooperative context in the school; they decrease in-school risk factors (such as academic failure and alienation); and they recognize the importance of explicitly teaching students sharing, cooperative learning, and working together.[19]

One of the more promising approaches to violence prevention involves creative ways to address violence without relying on coercion and insults to dignity. Pedro Noguera described how an Oakland, California, junior high school opted to hire not a security guard but a local grandmother to monitor students. Instead of relying on strip searches and "instead of using physical intimidation to carry out her duties, this woman greets children with hugs." And when the hugs prove to be insufficient to maintain prosocial behavior, instead of punishments "she admonishes them to behave themselves, saying she expects better behavior from them."[20] While some might chuckle at the seeming naïvete of hiring a grandmother instead of an armed guard, this junior high school was the only school in the district at which no weapons were confiscated from students. Professor Noguera also visited a "continuation" high school. (Continuation high schools are special schools for students who have been forced out of the regular high school, or have chosen to leave, or have been remanded to the continuation high school as a condition of probation.) Although efforts to close a high school campus for security reasons are often met with opposition by students, in one continuation high school visited by Noguera the principal closed the campus during lunch time, "without installing a fence or some other security apparatus, but simply by communicating with students about other alternatives for purchasing food so that they no longer felt it necessary to leave for meals. Now the students operate a campus store that both teachers and students patronize."[21]

There is much that the individual teacher can do to promote violence prevention in the classroom. High school English teacher Barbara Stanford integrated conflict management into her unit on the short story.[22] Her unit begins with activities through which the students look at conflict in their lives. They develop a safe "fictional conflict diary" for a fictitious student, and the class constructs entries to that group diary each day. At the same time, each student keeps his or her own diary, analyzing ways they address conflict, and contributing to the class diary. Gradually, the teacher leads the students to look at conflict outside themselves; through the short story they explore ways to deal with conflict, such as "fight, flight, and think." The class uses role plays and empathy-building activities. Barbara Stanford's work has been successful, particularly because she extends the learning outside the classroom to the students' lives.

In sum, whether initiated by school administrators or individual teachers, violence prevention programs are worthwhile efforts, particularly new and creative approaches. Toward that end, programs should strive to be realistic in their expectations for success, and include sufficient assessment procedures to identify aspects of the program that are particularly useful, and aspects that are or may be transferable to other settings.[23]

Supportive Approaches

Perhaps the most promising territory for effective nonviolent intervention lies in the area of supportive approaches. Unlike corrective approaches, supportive approaches do not emphasize punishment or reaction, and unlike preventive approaches, they are not narrow in focus but more holistic in nature and comprehensive in scope. Supportive approaches teach from a proactive stance, emphasizing *what students can do* instead of emphasizing the negative, as in "Just Say No." The most viable school-based supportive approaches appear to include peace education curricula, conflict resolution training, and the building of learning communities. The three are not mutually exclusive; conflict resolution is an integral part of peace education, and both work well in a learning communities context.

Peace education is part of the broader canvas of Peace Studies. Professor Linda Rennie Forcey described the birth of Peace Studies after World War I, and its blossoming after the Vietnam War. She described certain assumptions that underlie Peace Studies, including "an orientation to nonviolent social change; a belief in interdisciplinary study; a concern for policy formulation; and a willingness to be value-explicit."[24] In practice, and at the school level, Peace Studies is embodied in peace education curricula. Indeed, peace education has come to be seen as an essential component of nonviolent interventions, as well as a catalyst for "raising the sights" of schools to the larger question of human survival. Investigations into school-based peace education programs have been promising. Researcher Ian Harris looked at a peace education curriculum in urban Wisconsin public schools. He found that students in classes that used peace education practices scored higher than control classes on measures of certain prosocial behaviors including tolerance, compassion, communication, listening, caring, and touching. Compared to control groups, peace education students also showed higher levels of conflict resolution skills, and learned more nonviolent responses to conflict.[25] Ian Harris also wrote of the recent program at the University of Wisconsin at Milwaukee's Summer Institute on Nonviolence, which trained peer leaders in nonviolence in order to promote peace and nonviolence when they returned to their schools.[26] The program was a success, and follow-up revealed that the trained students were continuing to work as peer leaders in their respective schools.

Another widely recognized supportive approach is conflict resolution. Authors David Johnson and Roger Johnson have written extensively on the subject, and advocate conflict resolution training over traditional violence prevention programs. They caution that to be successful, conflict resolution programs must recognize that school conflict need not be eliminated; indeed, conflict can be a positive force in the synthesis of new ideas. "How conflicts are managed, not their presence, determines if they are destructive or constructive."[27] Accordingly, they advocate that students should be taught conflict resolution skills, either in the "cadre approach," by which a few students are trained to serve as the school's peer mediators, or the "total student body approach," where each student in school learns how to manage conflict constructively through negotiation and mediation skills. Other programs have shown success, such as "Conflict Resolution: A Secondary School Curriculum," developed by the Community Board Center for Policy and Training in San Francisco.[28]

Professor Thomas Sergiovanni has written of the important role schools can play in helping students repair the sense of loss of community so keenly felt by many adults as well as adolescents. He speaks of schools as a community of place, but more important as a "community of mind." Shared values are essential. "The message for schools is clear: Emphasize the creation of classrooms in elementary and secondary schools that resemble small family groups. Within these classrooms provide for table groupings of students. Connect these family groups into clusters to create neighborhoods of classrooms.[29] Sergiovanni explains that the key to stopping violence is to restore "community of mind," because when students lose a sense of that type of community, they either substitute for this loss (through gang or cult membership), or they live alone, without a sense of community. Connection is either "distorted" or "absent," and violence occurs with unfortunate effortlessness in such an environment.

Furthermore, when violence (and death) occur, such cohesive communities are the best intervention/postvention to help individuals deal with loss. Researcher Joan Ablon interviewed survivors of a Samoan-American social club fire that claimed seventeen victims. She was impressed and amazed by the rapid and healthy recovery of the survivors who had lost close, loved ones.[30] Yet when, in the course of Ablon's interviews, the Samoan survivors heard of the posttraumatic stress symptoms of the survivors of a similar social club fire years earlier (the 1942 Coconut Grove fire in Boston), the Samoans were unable to identify with the acute and morbid grief persisting in the lives of the Boston survivors.[31]

The main difference in recovery between the Boston and Samoan-American groups was attributed to the tremendous cohesion and support inherent in the Samoan-American community. They were not expected to fend for themselves, and the grief, by virtue of being shared, was lessened. In a similar context, I conducted research into widowhood at the University of Connecticut. After interviewing over one hundred widowed persons in the northeastern United States and Canada, I found that bereaved women made the best adaptations when they had sources of support, typically in the form of a confidante or close friend. Indeed, of all factors influencing healthy individual adaptation, I found the presence or absence of that support to be the single most important factor affecting adaptation in widowhood.[32] This may be true also for children and adolescents. For if "it takes a village to raise a child," then it surely "takes a village to mourn a death." In times of bereavement and grief, community schools can be those "villages," but not if they are built on premises of exclusion, nor when they tolerate or sponsor abuses to human dignity (such as strip searches and corporal punishment).[33]

The learning communities approach has worked well, particularly in smaller, family-like school settings. Some middle schools and high schools have purposely created smaller "school-within-a-school" units, to achieve just that sense of community.[34] In such settings, schools can more capably concentrate on building on students' strengths—*what students can do*—instead of documenting *what they cannot do*. Almost twenty years ago, as a school principal working closely with my middle-grade teachers, we asked the questions: "What are our students good at? How can we give them a chance to be good?" Our program became called "A Chance to be Good," after an article I had written urging parents to look at their children's strengths.[35] We won funding for the program from the state's education department and got positive reviews from parents and students. More recently, Stanford professor Henry Levin developed a similar model for education of at-risk, disadvantaged students that seeks to transform schools to honor what students can do instead of what they cannot do. Calling his process "problem-based learning," Professor Levin focused on involving teachers and parents as well as students. His "Accelerated Schools" model has spread to schools in over twenty-five states, and appears to be successful in meeting its stated goals.[36] Even ideas as simple as holding a series of family involvement workshops at an inner-city middle school can be extremely beneficial toward reducing violence and increasing understanding. Joan Goodman, Virginia Sutton, and Ira Harkavy created a series of family workshops involving African-American families with middle school-aged adolescents. As program leaders they found that a tone of care and respect from the workshop leaders toward both parents and students produced a very strong bond between staff and families. Parents were pleased not only to be able to vent their concerns, but to also have their thoughts and feelings heard and understood by other parents and school officials.[37]

Finally, it must be acknowledged that we cannot hope to address adolescent violence with a paintbrush, as it were, dabbing paint only onto the "adolescent" bare spots of the human canvas. While it is true that high schools, middle schools, and junior high schools must deal with the violence in the present, the more durable solution lies in acting on clear evidence that adolescent violence is best addressed *earlier than in the adolescent years*. For instance, we know that early intervention does make a difference. The strongest predictor of violent adolescent and early adult behavior is antisocial behavior (lying, stealing, dishonesty, bullying, etc.) during late childhood and early adolescence.[38] Researchers Stephen Buka and Felton Earls reached the same conclusion about the value of early intervention. Following a thorough ten-year study they conducted at the Harvard School of Public Health, the authors concluded that "more and more evidence seems to suggest that successful efforts to curb violence should begin early in a child's life."[39]

Conclusion

Although some school administrators see nonviolent interventions and violence prevention narrowly, in terms of rules and school board policy, there is another, deeper dimension to the role of the school administrator in creating successful nonviolent schools. At the building level, the school principal has often been identified as the key person. In *Miracle in East Harlem*, author Sy Fliegel summarized the idea well: "Over the past twenty-five years, innumerable studies have been done by countless researchers to find out what makes for truly effective schools. . . . Nearly all these studies, for example, agree that the principal is a crucial factor."[40] This seems to be particularly true when we speak of schools that honor the humanity of each student. Fliegel concluded: "Treat a classroom full of inner-city kids like a bunch of uneducable future criminals, and they won't let you down. Treat them with love, respect, and dignity, however, and watch them bloom."[41]

It is indeed ironic then to see the role of school administrator (notably, principal and assistant principal) evolve away from the traditional, humanitarian leader to a law enforcement official; from a leader in student recognition to a leader of strip searches; from one attesting to student achievement to one testifying against students; from an advocate to a litigant. Sustaining this evolution is a corrosive cynicism that holds that humanitarian, prosocial measures are naive and simplistic. It is true that they are not quick fixes, but neither is the criminal justice approach to schools a fix. Humanistic approaches take time, but they endure outside the walls of the school. It is simplistic to think that if we simply identify, catch, and then throw out all the bad people, we will have a safe school. Or if we treat students aggressively, forcing them to shed their clothing and their dignity, others will fall into line. It just doesn't work that way.

The leadership of school administrators is particularly important in promoting peace education curricula, and programs that advance social justice and conflict resolution. While reactive, corrective approaches must be taken at times (such as in peacekeeping), effecting change that will impact on the society outside the school resides in supportive approaches to school intervention. U.S. middle and high schools can no longer carry on as quasi-police, quasi-judicial and penal agencies. There is far too much other, pressing work to do.[42] Work that only schools can do well, if freed from adhering to society's "crime-and-punishment" model. This means that schools must be free to emphasize not crime detection but how we can and should treat each other well, and how we can and should deal with the inevitable conflicts that arise in our human interactions. Schools need to be able to do all this not after-the-fact of violence, but long before violence occurs.

Professor Noguera sums up these points quite well: "The urban schools that I know that feel safe to those who spend their time there don't have metal detectors or armed security guards, and their principals don't carry baseball bats. What these schools do have is a strong sense of community and collective responsibility. Such schools are seen by students as sacred territory, too special to be spoiled by crime and violence, and too important to risk one's being excluded. Such schools are few, but their existence serves as tangible proof that there are alternatives to chaotic schools plagued by violence."[43]

Ultimately, peace education and conflict resolution are incompatible with the crime-and-punishment model, and the sooner school leaders, administrators, and teachers can free themselves from that archetype, the sooner we will begin to see a prosocial dividend outside of school.

Notes

1 Karla Schuster, "Schools Suspend Trio," *New Haven (Connecticut) Register*, 30 March 1997: 1.

2 California now spends more on building and running its prisons than on its public college and university system, according to Fox Butterfield, writing in *The New York Times*, 2 June 1966: 16E; Allen J. Beck and Thomas P. Bonczar, "State and Federal Prison Population Tops One Million," *United States Department of Justice Press Release*, Annapolis Junction, MD: Bureau of Justice Statistics Clearinghouse, 27 October 1994.

3 "America's predominant response to violence has been a reactive one—to pour resources into deterring and incapacitating violent offenders by apprehending, arresting, adjudicating, and incarcerating them through the criminal justice system. This approach however has not made an appreciable difference. Although the average prison time served for violent crime in the United States tripled between 1975 and 1989, there was no concomitant decrease in the level of violent crimes." James A. Mercy et al., "Public Health Policy for Preventing Violence" *Health Affairs* 12, no. 2 (winter 1993): 7–29.

4 Emile Durkheim, *Moral Education*, trans. E. K. Wilson and H. Schnurer 1925 reprint (New York: Free Press, 1961), 144–57.

5 Wendy Schwartz, "A Guide to Community Programs to Prevent Youth Violence," For *Parents/about Parents* (New York: ERIC Clearinghouse on Urban Education, Accession Number ED396009).

6 Ellwood P. Cubberley, *Public Education in the United States* (Boston: Houghton Mifflin, 1919), 381.

7 Albert Shanker, "Restoring the Connection Between Behavior and Consequences," *Vital Speeches of the Day* 61, no. 15 (New York: The City News Publishing Company, 15 May 1995).

8 Robert DiGiulio, *Positive Classroom Management* (Thousand Oaks, CA: Corwin/SAGE, 1995).

9 More useful information on self-instruction strategies is available from B. W. Camp and M. S. Bash's *Think Aloud*, (Champaign, IL: Research Press, 1981).

10 A practical guide for principals is *Creating Safe Schools: What Principals Can Do*, by Marie Somers Hill and Frank W. Hill (Thousand Oaks, CA: Corwin/SAGE, 1994). Also, chapter 11 of Charles H. Wolfgang's book *Solving Discipline Problems* (Boston: Allyn & Bacon, 1995) contains specific information on nonviolent restraint of students.

11 David Hamburg, "Education for Conflict Resolution: Can We Learn to Live Together?" in "Report of the President," *Carnegie Corporation Annual Report* (New York: Carnegie Corporation of New York, 1994), 4–15.

12 One excellent resource is *Violence in the Schools: How to Proactively Prevent and Defuse It,* by Joan L. Curcio and Patricia F. First (Thousand Oaks, CA: Corwin/SAGE, 1993).

13 Renee Wilson-Brewer et al., "Violence Prevention for Young Adolescents: A Survey of the State of the Art" (Cambridge, MA: Education Development Center, 1991). Also available from the ERIC Clearinghouse, Accession Number ED356442.

14 Daniel W. Webster, "The Unconvincing Case for School-Based Conflict Resolution Programs for Adolescents," *Health Affairs* 12, no. 4 (winter 1993): 126–40.

15 Deborah Prothrow-Stith, *Violence Prevention: Curriculum for Adolescents* (Newton, MA: Education Development Center, 1987).

16 Ian M. Harris, "From World Peace to Peace in the 'Hood: Peace Education in a Postmodern World," *Journal for a Just and Caring Education* 2, no. 4 (October 1996): 384.

17 Linda Lantieri, "Waging Peace in Our Schools," *Phi Delta Kappan* 76, no. 5 (January 1995): 386–92.

18 American Psychological Association, *Violence and Youth: Psychology's Response* Vol. 1. (Washington, DC: American Psychological Association, 1993).

19 David W. Johnson and Roger T. Johnson, "Why Violence Prevention Programs Don't Work and What Does," *Educational Leadership* 52, no. 2 (February 1995): 63–68.

20 Pedro A. Noguera, "Preventing and Producing Violence: A Critical Analysis of Responses to School Violence," *Harvard Educational Review* 65, no. 2 (summer 1995): 206.

21 Ibid.

22 Barbara Stanford, "Conflict and the Story of Our Lives: Teaching English for Violence Prevention," *English Journal* 84, no. 5 (September 1995): 38–42.

23 See the highly informative "Kappan Special Report" entitled "Standing Up to Violence" by R. Craig Sautter, *Phi Delta Kappan* 76, no. 5 (January 1995): K1–K12.

24 Linda Rennie Forcey, "Peace Studies," in *Protest, Power, and Change: An Encyclopedia of Nonviolent Action from ACT-UP to Women's Suffrage,* ed. Roger S. Powers and William B. Vogele (New York: Garland, 1997).

25 Ian M. Harris, "Teachers' Response to Conflict in Selected Milwaukee Schools" (paper presented at the annual meeting of the American Educational Research

Association, San Francisco, CA, April 18–22, 1995), ERIC Clearinghouse Accession Number ED393855.

26 Ian M. Harris, "Assessing the Effectiveness of the UWM Summer Institute on Nonviolence" (paper presented at the annual meeting of the American Educational Research Association, New York, NY, April 8–12, 1996), ERIC Clearinghouse Accession Number ED398283; and see chapter 16 in this volume.

27 David W. Johnson and Roger T. Johnson, *Reducing School Violence Through Conflict Resolution* (Alexandria, VA: Association for Supervision and Curriculum Development, 1995), 13.

28 Joan Gaustad, "Schools Attack the Roots of Violence," *ERIC Digest* 63 (1991): 1–3 (Eugene, OR: ERIC Clearinghouse on Educational Management Accession Number ED335806).

29 Thomas J. Sergiovanni, *Building Community in Schools* (San Francisco: Jossey-Bass, 1994), 127–28.

30 Joan Ablon, "Bereavement in a Samoan Community," *British Journal of Medical Psychology* 44 (November 1971): 329–37.

31 Erich Lindemann, "Symptomatology and Management of Acute Grief," *American Journal of Psychiatry* 101 (September 1944): 141–48.

32 Robert DiGiulio, "Identity Loss and Reformulation in Young, Middle-Aged, and Older Widowed Women," *Dissertation Abstracts International* 42, no. 04, 1984, 1217A. (University Microfilms No. DA8416087); Robert DiGiulio, *Beyond Widowhood: From Bereavement to Emergence and Hope* (New York: Free Press, 1989).

33 Because U.S. culture prizes solitary self-reliance and individuation ("self-help") for bereaved adolescents, schools can provide a particularly important source of support not otherwise easily available in contemporary U.S. communities. See chapter 2, "Teenagers' Experiences with Death," in Robert DiGiulio and Rachel Kranz's *Straight Talk about Death and Dying* (New York: Facts on File, 1995).

34 One notable example is the "School-Within-a-School" at Brookline (Massachusetts) High School, described by Sara Lawrence Lightfoot in *The Good High School* (New York: Basic Books, 1983).

35 Robert DiGiulio, "A Chance to be Good," *The Single Parent* 21, no. 8 (October 1978): 9–11, 13.

36 Ron Brandt, "On Building Learning Communities: A Conversation with Hank Levin," *Educational Leadership* 50, no. 1 (September 1991): 19–23.

37 Joan Goodman, Virginia Sutton, and Ira Harkavy, "The Effectiveness of Family Workshops in a Middle School Setting," *Phi Delta Kappan* 76, no. 9 (May 1995): 694–700.

38 Rolf Loeber and Magda Stouthamer-Loeber, "Family Factors as Correlates and Predictors of Juvenile Conduct Problems and Delinquency," in *Crime and Justice: An Annual Review of Research*, ed. M. Tonry and N. Morris (Chicago: University of Chicago Press, 1986), 29–149; Rolf Loeber and Magda Stouthamer-Loeber, "Prediction," in *Handbook of Juvenile Delinquency*, ed. H. Quay (New York: John Wiley and Sons, 1987), 325–82; S. Mitchell and P. Rosa, "Boyhood Behavior Problems as Precursors of Criminality: A Fifteen-Year Follow-Up Study," *Journal of Child Psychology and Psychiatry*, 22 (January 1981): 19–33.

39 Stephen Buka and Felton Earls, "Early Determinants of Delinquency and Violence," *Health Affairs* 12, no. 4 (winter 1993): 46–64.

40 Sy Fliegel, *Miracle in East Harlem* (New York: Times Books, 1993), 24.

41 Ibid.; I would add that if a teacher helps students discover what they like and what they do well, and encourages them to do it, students will flower for life.

42 An eloquent argument for creating a prosocial "marketplace of learning" in place of our public school system is presented in educator Robert Smilovitz's *If Not Now, When? Education not Schooling* (Kearney, NE: Morris, 1996).

43 Noguera, "Preventing and Producing Violence," 207.

Chapter 11

Integrating a Multicultural Peacebuilding Strategy into a Literacy Curriculum

Rebecca Wasson, Rebecca Anderson, and Melanie Suriani

Violence is a part of the contemporary landscape and a reality for adolescents both at home and at school. Incidents of school violence occur most frequently among low-achieving middle and high school students who lack the social skills to interact peacefully with teachers and peers.[1] Other factors that are reported as contributing to incidents of adolescent violence in schools include the low socioeconomic status of students and authoritative and punitive attitudes and behaviors on the part of professional staff members.[2]

Schools have traditionally addressed discipline problems through the use of corporal punishment, suspension, and expulsion. Opponents of the use of corporal punishment argue that corporal punishment, like suspension and expulsion, is an ineffective means of discipline, producing only short-term compliance. They maintain that corporal punishment inhibits development of self-discipline, fails to teach appropriate behaviors and social problem-solving skills, and more important, models institutional acceptance and use of violence.[3] Many opponents of corporal punishment, suspension, and expulsion are practicing teachers and administrators who are instead embracing or beginning to explore violence intervention programs as a means of addressing discipline problems that result from interpersonal conflicts. It was reported in 1994 that over 5000 elementary and secondary schools across the country were using some form of violence intervention program to address school discipline problems.[4]

Evaluations of violence intervention programs suggest that prosocial behavior can be influenced through school curricula designed to encourage positive interpersonal relationships.[5] The literacy program we discuss was adopted to eliminate reactive disciplinary practices of the past that had depended on the use of corporal punishment. We view this program primarily as a prevention rather than intervention model. The purpose of this chapter is to describe the strategy that uses a combination of multicultural literature, storytelling, and after-reading activities to build a classroom environment that enhances interpersonal relationships and encourages students to value peace.

The Implementation of the Strategy

School Context

The campus is located in a moderate-income residential area only two streets away from a thoroughfare, zoned light industrial. Grades kindergarten through six are housed in one building and the adjacent building houses grades seven through twelve. The school's population draws from two very large government-subsidized apartment complexes. The statistics related in the following section profile the student population in the 1994–95 school year. Free or reduced lunches are based on the family's income being at or below the poverty level. Sixty-four percent of the kindergarten through sixth-grade students qualify for free or reduced lunch while 61 percent of the higher grade students qualify.

Many of the students are low achievers and have experienced more than one grade failure. Consequently, it is possible to see twelve- and thirteen-year-old youth in a fourth-grade classroom or a persistent twenty-year-old graduating senior. Among the kindergarten through sixth grade students, 27 percent are overage for grade. By the time students reach the higher grades the percentage of students overage for grade increases to 42 percent.

Student ethnic composition is representative of the metropolitan area. Seventy-nine percent of the kindergarten through sixth grade population is African-American. The remaining 21 percent are classified as "white" although some of the children referred to themselves as Asian or Hispanic. In addition, the category of "white" contains children who identify themselves as Irish Travelers. Irish Travelers tend to discontinue formal education before the seventh grade. Therefore, the seventh through twelfth grade population is 95 percent African-American.

Dropout rates are only recorded for the senior grades. However, they are especially telling. In the 1994–95 school year, 16.7 percent of the ninth grade, 13 percent of the tenth grade, 10.6 percent of the eleventh grade, and 10.3 percent of the twelfth grade dropped out of school. Low academic achievement, gangs, the necessity of maintaining a full-time job, and the perception that schooling is irrelevant in their lives takes its toll.

Strategy Foundation

The strategy we propose reflects the thinking expressed in the works of Mahatma Gandhi and Paulo Freire, illustrated by the use of multicultural literatures that raise issues of racism, sexism, and economic inequality. This strategy is not characteristic of the traditional teaching/learning paradigm frequently referred to as "the banking concept of education" in which it is assumed that teachers possess the *currency* of literacy that is *deposited* into students' empty minds.[6] Rather, this strategy is consistent with the cognitive approach to understanding adolescent behavior. This approach acknowledges that adolescents make sense of their life experiences through the use of rational thought—that adolescents do make valid conclusions about reality as it is and how it should or could be.

We agree with Freire and Gandhi that education is political in nature and that the proper role for teachers is to facilitate students' dialogue on controversial themes. Through dialogue students develop the skills that are required to establish and maintain a peaceful and democratic community. These skills include the ability to present a well-developed argument based on evidence and logic, and on concern for justice and the awareness of one's own bias. For, as Freire contends,

> There is no such thing as a neutral educational process. Education either functions as an instrument which is used to facilitate the integration of the younger generation into the logic of the present system and bring about conformity to it or it becomes 'the practice of freedom,' the means by which men and women deal critically and creatively with reality and discover how to participate in the transformation of their world.[7]

Further, we assert that if we are to live together peacefully we must be able to not only understand, but empathize with others' history, values, needs, and resources. This assertion echoes Gandhi's approach to peacebuilding and social change through nonviolent action.[8] Gandhi believed that in order to gain a more complete understanding of the correctness, or truth, of any action or position we are obligated to seek out, respect, and consider others' perspectives, for as individuals we are limited in our ability to see the whole reality. However, if others are to share their perspectives with us we must provide a nonthreatening and democratic environment for that sharing. Gandhi also believed that *ahimsa*, or nonviolence, is best learned through practice in an intimate setting such as a family or family-like institution.[9] Ultimately, peace may be achieved by having strong positive relationships with others, a rich feeling of personhood, and a sense of participating in a democratic and caring community.

The instructional strategy itself is grounded in a kindergarten through twelfth-grade multicultural, ethics, and literacy program that was developed by Dr. Pat Walker, University of Massachusetts, and Dr. Robert Selman, Harvard University.[10] The program is based on the research of Selman and others that supports the hypothesis that students' social behavior and values are influenced by their social context.[11]

In its promotional literature, the program claims to increase literacy and multicultural awareness, to promote students' positive interpersonal relationships by increasing ethical awareness, to develop literacy and perspective-taking skills, and thus to decrease students' risk-taking behavior. The program defines "risks" as those interpersonal behaviors that (a) inhibit or disrupt the learning process of a student or a class, and/or (b) threaten the student's physical well-being. Specific examples of risk-taking behavior include fighting, bullying, ostracizing, stealing, breaking promises, tattling, and overt and intentional challenging of authority. Other risk behaviors more commonly identified by society include substance abuse and criminal activity. According to Levitt and his associates, there are three psychosocial components of human development that influence risk-taking behaviors: knowledge of risk taking, social and self-management skills, and personal meanings attached to the risk.[12] These three components undergo transformation as an individual acquires new information, skills, and experiences.

Literacy Lessons in Practice

Our literacy strategy is comprised of five components: connecting, reading, discussing, practicing, and expressing. Although teachers have flexibility in how they implement the components, it is important that each component is included in each lesson.

Connecting

In the classroom, the teacher first connects with students by sharing a personal story that relates to a salient peacebuilding issue that later will be addressed in a book that the teacher and students read. For example, an African-American teacher introduced the theme of prejudice when she told about how, when she was a child, she had to sit at the back of the bus and drink from water fountains labeled "Colored Only." Immediately following the teacher's example, the students are expected to disclose their own personal stories with a partner, in a small group, or to the whole class.

In connecting, teachers move away from traditional classroom practices that are characterized by a lack of student-student interaction and student-teacher interaction. The teacher is no longer the sole disciplinarian, authoritarian, and manager of the classroom environment. Rather, the teacher takes on a new role of participant in a democratic classroom and develops a stronger emotional bond with the students. Both the teacher and the students gain tolerance, even empathy, for each other while they develop skills for creating a peaceful atmosphere for the promotion of interpersonal and intercultural peace.

Reading

After the personal connection has been made, the teacher expressively reads a book aloud. Books are selected specifically to facilitate development of prosocial skills and perspective taking. For example, early adolescents are encouraged to consider an immigrant's perspective of the United States in *In the Year of the Boar and Jackie Robinson*, by Bette Bao Lord.[13] *. . . And Now Miguel*, by Joseph Krumgold, tells of a Mexican-American boy's rite of passage into manhood on a sheep-raising farm in New Mexico.[14]

Prior to implementing this program, classroom libraries were rare and even the school library had a scarcity of multicultural literature. Most library books reflected only white characters and noncontroversial themes; most library books were extremely dated. However, locating books appropriate for peacebuilding is not a problem. They may be obtained from the public library or purchased from local bookstores. Trade books that address diversity issues or issues of gender and economic inequities are also appropriate and are topics in which adolescents are especially interested.

Discussing

After reading the book, a variety of activities contribute to furthering the understanding of problematic issues and peaceful solutions. For instance, teachers may facilitate classroom discussions that encourage the use of high-level cognitive thinking skills by asking open-ended questions. It is important that teachers not make judgments during the discussion, or impose their own values on the judgments made by the students. Rather, the intent is to foster students' ability to take the diverse perspectives of the characters presented in the story. For example, *The Friendship* and *The Gold Cadillac*, both by Mildred D. Taylor, facilitate discussions of race relations before and after the civil rights movement of the sixties.[15] Another of Mildred D. Taylor's books that appeals to African-American students is *Role of Thunder, Hear My Cry*.[16]

Other examples of ways to encourage discussion of peacebuilding issues include invitations to community leaders to tell their personal stories, student development of questions to take home for interview with parents, participation in multicultural events in order to report to the class, and on-line book chats with e-mail partners.

Practicing

The next component of the strategy continues discussion of issues, but differs from the previous activity in that students engage with each other to practice the values and skills they learn from the story. For example, the students can role play, talk with a partner, or interview a partner about the story.

In traditional classrooms, students generally work independently in a competitive manner. Pairs and small groups, on the other hand, provide students the opportunity to engage in tasks without concern for adult assessment. Such work allows students to develop intimacies with other students and thus contributes to creating a caring classroom environment. It also fosters the development of interpersonal skills of conscious deliberation, giving and receiving feedback, listening, and communicating, and assuming responsibility. For example, in *My Brother Sam is Dead*, by James Lincoln Collier and Christopher Collier, students debate the justification of the Revolutionary War.[17] In the book, *Cousins*, by Virginia Hamilton, students explore the emotional issues that surround the guilt of a jealous girl when her cousin drowns saving another child.[18]

Expressing

Discussion and practice with a story is followed by the students' making connections between their own lives and what they have read through story or journal writing, drawing, oral or dramatic presentations, as well as other forms of artistic expression. Long before the written language humans gave shape to their experiences through the arts. Adolescents find drama especially appealing. One teacher had the students role-play "in my shoes, in your shoes." She described many benefits for her students:

> That's what gets them to see both perspectives. They put themselves in that character's shoes. They switched roles. Why does this boy feel that way? Was he really being mean? And they brought out a lot of things. Believe it or not the students will express themselves in ways you never thought about. They brought out that it wasn't the boy's fault because he was brought up that way. His parents had taught him. So that was a very good point that he wasn't being ignorant because he wanted to be ignorant. This is how he was taught. And that brought out the fact in the classroom and even in society how we are discriminated against and it's because we're brought up that way.

In the connecting and discussing components of this strategy students learn that their judgments and opinions are valued both by the teacher and other students. Emotional trust, critical to the establishment of family-like relationships, is further reinforced in the expressing component as they share their talents and abilities as well as their interpretations and appraisals of their social world.

Benefits

Teachers using this strategy can expect several benefits: (a) more reading about peacebuilding issues; (b) creation of a classroom community; (c) reduction of violent acts in school; (d) improved student relationships; and (e) improvement of literacy skills.

More reading about peacebuilding issues. Students like to have teachers read aloud. This strategy not only encourages reading, but also emphasizes the need to read stories on controversial themes to which adolescents can relate. Students make sense of their life experiences by connecting to similar stories—they learn alternative ways of dealing with social issues by being exposed to multiple perspectives.

Creation of a classroom community. The connecting component is especially helpful in creating a democratic and intimate classroom community. The disclosure of the personal stories creates an environment whereby students feel safe and empowered to allow their own voices to be heard. The stories keep students' attention and interest and enhance students' understanding of one another.

This strategy creates a classroom environment whereby teachers establish rapport and feel closer to their students. One teacher explained it this way:

> I think it has made me a better teacher as far as being more compassionate with the students and putting myself in that student's shoes. A lot of children come to school with a lot of problems and before this, I guess you don't realize that. This has made me take a look, you know, being in that student's shoes. And I think that's very helpful. It makes the student feel that I'm more on his side and I understand his problem. And then he understands me. That's one of the important things.

Reduction of violent acts in school. The students learn acceptable behavior options. For instance, talking about the first story he read on the first day of school, one teacher said:

> You know, the very first story I read was about a girl who ran away from home. And you would be surprised how many kids had thought about it, or wanted to. Oh yeah. It was like a bulb just blew up. You know, 'Bing!' And once I get them to thinking about that and realizing the consequences for it, you know, it somewhat changed their philosophy.

Another teacher added examples of how the strategy makes a difference: "I can really tell a difference in them. In their behavior. Socially. Academically. They try harder. The strategy gives them an appreciation for other people. And they're not as bitter and they're more compassionate."

Another teacher provided a specific example of how the strategy is effective in reducing violence in the schools:

> I had one kid that was really a problem. This kid was fighting every day. He was very bitter and I understand that he came from a background of abuse. We teach the students to attack the problem not the person. But he came to me at the beginning of the school year and he fought for the first month. By November, he had zero fights.

Improved student relationships. The teachers also perceived that the students were closer to one another. For instance, one teacher noted how the group work was affecting peer relationships:

> I think pairing the students is very good. It makes the students close to each other, and I never pair them with the same person all the time. You have to make friends with another person. And that's teaching them that you cannot only work with just one person. We must be flexible in life and be able to work with one another.

Similarly, another teacher added: "I think it really teaches them to get along. It teaches them how to interact with other kids their own age."

Improvement of literacy skills. Another benefit of the strategy is it facilitates student learning. It encourages the student to go beyond acquiring traditional reading skills toward the critical literary analysis Freire advocated. As one teacher explained:

> I believe for the students it fosters independence. It gives them a critical thinking avenue. It broadens their thinking abilities. It does. You know, some kids have told me, "Well, I haven't thought about that. That's a good idea. I was going to do that, but since you revealed another option to me, now that sounds better."

Challenges

Although there were benefits to using the strategy, as noted in the previous section, there were tensions associated with the implementation as well. Most notable were the tensions created when addressing Friere's admonitions to allow the students to develop their own personal meanings from the literature. The personal meanings students expressed forced teachers into an unconventional role of counselor and friend.

Many of the teachers felt that the strategy was different from the way instruction is normally carried out in their classrooms and different from their personal philosophy about teaching. In identifying the connecting component as being the "most challenging" aspect of the strategy, one teacher pointed out: "It's kind of hard to come up with a story." She added that while she saw the value in sharing personal stories with her students, it was not her normal disposition to do so: "It's hard for me to share a personal story. It's hard for me because I'm not the type of person to share the personal things with anybody." Indeed, many teachers questioned whether disclosing personal stories with students is appropriate for them to do. As one teacher expressed it:

> I had problems with that [connecting], because I think a lot of times, if you disclose too much it makes you, I don't know, I think that there's a limit to

what you should tell kids in your class. Because I think that you still need to be a certain type of role model for them.

What we usually observed, however, were teachers sharing rich and powerful stories with their students. They were very effective in both the choice of personal stories and in their actual telling. Storytelling is after all the oldest form of human communication, in the home, in religious institutions, and in the community. We found that many teachers have also found a place for storytelling in the schools.

Results of Program Implementation

An instrument designed to assess students' ethical awareness was administered pre- and post-intervention to classes where the program had been implemented, with control classes matched by grade. The data analysis and comparison of treatment and control classes indicated that students could indeed be taught prosocial behavior.[19] Data analysis also indicated that students who were not exposed to the program became more prone to value the use of force and the exhibition of antisocial behavior as they matured. These same students also reacted with punitive behavior toward peers and adults for perceived insults.

Other sources of data included the analysis of a class climate inventory, which when compared with similar schools in the school system, indicated that students perceived less friction in their classrooms.[20] Middle school records indicated a dramatic decline in violent acts. In the school year 1993–94 an excess of 320 fights occurred. One hundred four fights were recorded in 1994–95, and in 1996–97 only eight fights were recorded. These numbers reflect the actual number of fights, though in some cases the same student was involved in multiple conflicts.

At the end of the 1994–95 school year students' academic improvement was indicated by higher scores on standardized tests. One of the teachers implementing the program reported standardized test scores that were significantly higher than those of other classes that had not implemented the strategy at that grade level. They were also significantly higher than this particular teacher's previous year's class scores. The efficacy component of the evaluation indicated that this teacher perceived the role of the teacher as a facilitator fostering relationships in the classroom.

Conclusion

As teacher educators and researchers who evaluate instructional programs in public schools with kindergarten through grade twelve, we are often impressed with the strategies that teachers use to create classrooms that can be described as peaceful exemplars of participatory democracy. Such classrooms contrast dramatically with classrooms disrupted by discipline problems resulting from students' low literacy rates, lack of prosocial skills, or insensitivity to racial and ethnic diversity.

The insights provided by peace education have contributed to programs of school-based conflict management, multicultural awareness, peer mediation, and violence prevention.[21] However, as Ian Harris contends, youth often find too much talk about violence depressing and they are turned off to the messages adults promote. This is especially true when the focus is on creating safe schools with its too easy implication that the students are the problem.

Schools cannot avoid teaching values. Schools will either foster peace or perpetuate structural violence.[22] What do schools contribute to youths' understanding of human rights? How do the years spent in schools contribute to the acceptance of violence and the promotion of social norms of racism, sexism, and responses to unreasonable authority? What stories do we tell, what books do we read that relate to these issues?

By the time youths enter high school, social patterns and pressures have made it difficult for them to listen to adult admonitions on violence. Caring relationships can fill the emotional voids created by chaotic family life in which no adult-child bonds are formed. We believe the strategy outlined in this chapter can foster relationships between adolescents and caring adults. This is the only weapon we adults have to fight the violence that coexists with adolescents seeking rewarding familial relationships and power over their environment.

Our observations, in sum, suggest that the greatest benefit associated with this strategy is that it forces traditional classrooms to take on a more Freireian approach. Both teachers and students are expected to assume new roles. Teachers are expected to share stories of their personal lives with their students, an activity that is not typically done in classrooms. No longer is reading aloud just for the primary grades. Books are to be read aloud to students at all grade levels, and the books selected should focus on cultural differences and ethical and emotional issues. No longer is it taboo to talk about diversity and the issues associated with it. Instead it is recognized that gaining understanding about diversity is needed and valued. The questions asked after the reading are open-ended, without right or wrong answers. The purpose of the discussion is to get students to think, not to evaluate whether they can answer literal and factual questions. Student presentations are no longer limited to formal themes and papers. Communication abilities and skills are witnessed through a wide array of projects that incorporate individual interests and talents.

The goal of peace education is not just to make schools safer. The goal of peace education is to create communities that focus on caring for others and on the democratic principles of the rights and responsibilities of participating members. As educators our task is to model trust and provide our youth with opportunities and skills to explore peaceful options to violence. We have found that the use of this strategy not only stimulates teachers' and administrators' discourses about and reflection on the values and diversities that are fundamental in a democratic society, but also strengthens students' prosocial attitudes, behaviors, and interpersonal relations communication, while better developing all academic skills.

Notes

1. W. H. Evans and S. S. Evans, "The Assessment of School Violence," *The Pointer* 29 (1985): 18–20.

2. R. H. DuRant, C. Cadenhead, R. A. Pendergast, G. Slavens, and C. W. Linder, "Factors Associated with the Use of Violence among Urban Black Adolescents," *American Journal of Public Health* 84 (1994): 612–17; J. M. Haviland, "Teachers' and Students' Beliefs about Punishment," *Journal of Educational Psychology* 71 (1979): 563–70.

3. Evans and Evans, "The Assessment of School Violence"; Haviland, "Teachers' and Students' Beliefs about Punishment."

4. Kathleen K. Shepherd, "Stemming Conflict through Peer Mediation." *School Administrator* 514 (1994): 14–17.

5. William DeJong, *Building the Peace: The Resolving Conflict Creatively Program RCCP* (Washington, DC: National Institute of Justice, 1993); N. D. Feshbach, "Learning to Care: A Positive Approach to Child Training and Discipline," *Journal of Clinical Child Psychology* 123 (1983): 266–71; Annette Kessler, "Peaceful Solutions to Violence." *Principal* 732 (1993): 10–12.

6. Paulo Freire, *Pedagogy of the Oppressed* (New York: Seabury Press, 1970).

7. Ibid., 13–14.

8. Michael W. Sonnietner, *Gandhian Nonviolence Levels of Satyagraha* (New Delhi: Abhinav Publications, 1986).

9. Raghavavan Narusimhan Iyer, *The Moral and Political Thought of Mahatma Gandhi* (New York: Oxford University Press, 1973).

10. Pat Walker, *Voices of Love and Freedom: A K–12 Multicultural Ethics and Literacy Program: Program Training Manual* (Jamaica Plain, MA: Family, Friends, and Community, 1993).

11. R. L. Selman, L. H. Schultz, M. Nakkula, D. Barr, C. Watts, and J. B. Richmond, "Friendship and Fighting: A Developmental Approach to the Study of Risk and Prevention Violence," *Development and Psychopathology* 4 (1992): 529–58.

12. M. Z. Levitt, R. L. Selman, and J. B. Richmond, "The Psychosocial Foundations of Early Adolescents' High-Risk Behavior: Implications for Research and Practice," *Journal of Research on Adolescence* 1 (1991): 349–78.

13. Bette Bao Lord, *In the Year of the Boar and Jackie Robinson* (New York: Harper & Row, Publishers, 1984).

14 Joseph Krumgold, . . *And Now Miguel* (New York: Thomas Y. Crowell Company, 1953).

15 Mildred D.Taylor, *The Gold Cadillac* (New York: Dial Books for Young Readers,1987); Mildred D.Taylor, *The Friendship* (New York: Dial Books for Young Readers, 1987).

16 Mildred D. Taylor, *Roll of Thunder, Hear My Cry* (New York: Penguin Books USA, Inc., 1991)

17 James Lincoln Collier and Christopher Collier, *My Brother Sam is Dead* (New York: Scholastic, Inc., 1974)

18 Virginia Hamilton, *Cousins* (New York: Philomel Books, 1990).

19 Rebecca Wasson, Suzanne B. Huffman, Blake Burr-McNeal, and Gordon E. Kenney, "Development and Piloting of the Prosocial Attitude Blank" (paper presented at the annual meeting of the Mid-South Educational Research Association, Nashville, TN, 1994).

20 Melanie M. Suriani and Rebecca Wasson, "Assessment of an Intervention Addressing Literacy and Ethics" (paper presented at the annual meeting of the Mid-South Educational Research Association, Nashville, TN, 1994).

21 Ian M. Harris, "Peace Education: A Modern Educational Reform" (paper presented at the Annual Meeting of the American Educational Research Association, 1993) ED 362458.

22 D. J. Owens and M. A. Straus, "The Social Structure of Violence in Childhood and Approval of Violence as an Adult," *Aggressive Behavior* 1 (1975): 193–211.

Chapter 12

Disturbing the Peace: Multicultural Education, Transgressive Teaching, and Independent School Culture

Peter Adam Nash

> Any situation in which some (people) prevent others from engaging in the process of inquiry is one of violence.
> Paulo Friere, *Pedagogy of the Oppressed*

Multiculturalism and Independent School Culture

Violence is not a word commonly associated with elite private schools. Indeed, implicit in the physical and philosophical affect of independent schools today is the virtual absence of physical violence.[1] The likelihood is that a student's educational experience will be free of gang intimidation, crimes associated with poverty and drug abuse, and weapon-carrying adolescents that popularly characterize the public school world. To an appreciable degree, this perception of independent schools is warranted by the facts: independent schools generally do provide a physically safe environment. By virtue of their wealth, they usually are able to provide a materially secure environment too, an environment free from the institutional stresses caused by underfunding, overcrowding, shortage of teachers and staff, and lack of equipment. This, of course, is also true for most wealthy suburban public schools.

Yet it would be a grave mistake to conclude that such communities function without structural violence. As Johan Galtung has pointed out, structural violence is built into the very structure of institutions where "good" people, considering themselves to be peacebuilders, may participate in "settings within which individuals may do enormous amounts of harm to other human beings without ever intending to do so."[2] It is in this sense that peace educators with their orientation to multicultural education argue that the defense of the status quo can be a form of violence. In this very sense one could argue that schools that do not espouse multicultural education promote a certain kind of violence.

Carl A. Grant, President of the National Association for Multicultural Education, offers a definition of multicultural education that best encapsulates the articulated and published beliefs of many educators:

> Multicultural education is a philosophical concept and an educational process. It is a concept built upon the philosophical ideals of freedom, justice, equality, equity, and human dignity. . . .
>
> Multicultural education is a process that . . . prepares all students to work actively toward structural equality . . ., to help students to develop philosophical self-concepts and to discover who they are, particularly in terms of their multiple group memberships.
>
> Multicultural education acknowledges that the strength and richness of the United States lies in its human diversity. It demands a school staff that is multiracial and multiculturally literate . . . a curriculum that organizes concepts and content around the contributions, perspectives, and experiences of the myriad of groups that are part of United States society. It confronts and seeks to bring about change of current social issues involving race, ethnicity, socioeconomic class, gender, and disability. . . . It teaches critical-thinking skills, as well as democratic decision-making, social action, and empowerment skills.
>
> Finally, multicultural education cannot be truncated: all components of its definition must be in place in order for multicultural education to be genuine and viable.[3]

It is not that independent school culture altogether lacks good intentions or critical ambiance about multiculturalism. The growth of cultural diversity in the United States is evident in the populations of independent as well as public schools. On a surface level at least, multiculturalism is very much on the minds of their leaders these days. Classes about the history and cultures of people who have migrated to the United States are offered in many schools, and one finds a wide array of workshops for faculty and students offered across the nation on matters of race and gender. For all such timely, cutting-edge thinking, however, the vast majority of today's independent schools continue to offer educational programs designed to replicate an existing power structure of values, resources, and practices that is based upon violence. Historically, these schools have been administered with little tolerance for conflict, dissension, and change. Real social transformation, the kind that is mandated by proponents of multicultural education, is not the goal of independent schools.

This preference for stasis arises partly from the ardent cultivation of the individual as the ideological foot soldier upon which independent schools have always set their sights. The emphasis on individualism is reflected in independent school curricula in the reification of Western enlightenment interpretations of democratic values, universal truths, and public service ideals. With this emphasis, teachers are expected to inculcate generation after generation of students, which include many destined for positions of extraordinary power and influence, with an intellectual and moral determinism that precludes provocative critical inquiry or any genuine desire for social change.

Many independent schools do show appreciation for the human potential in multicultural reform. But few encourage in their teachers the kind of radical pedagogy that must be part of the reform package. Even schools seemingly seeking truly judicious and meaningful integration of alternative voices and perspectives into their programs are coercive about the type of instruction and learning they value and reward. Radical inquiry, essential for peacebuilding in the academy as well as everywhere else, is curbed and curtailed with a reflexive force that is deeply institutionalized, overwhelming the best intentions of even progressive leaders.

Traditionally, those opposed to multicultural peacebuilding stifle radical discourse and practice by publicly equating any challenge to the existing order, be it in the school at large, one's department, or one's classroom, with disturbing an otherwise munificent peace. The renowned theologian Rheinhold Niebuhr, in his book *Moral Man and Immoral Society*, catches this tactic deftly:

> Perhaps a more favorite method is to identify the particular organization of society, of which they are beneficiaries, with the peace and order of society in general and to appoint themselves apostles of law and order. Since every society has an instinctive desire for harmony and avoidance of strife, this is a very potent instrument of maintaining the unjust status quo. No society has ever achieved peace without incorporating injustice into its harmony. Those who would eliminate injustice are therefore always placed at the moral disadvantage of imperiling its peace. The privileged groups will place them under that moral disadvantage even if the efforts toward justice are made in the most pacific terms. They will claim that it is dangerous to disturb the precarious equilibrium and will feign to fear anarchy as the consequence of the ef-

fort. . . . Every effort to disturb the peace, which incorporates the injustice, will therefore seem to them to spring from unjustified malcontent.[4]

Peacebuilding and Transgressive Teaching

Peacebuilding for adolescents that embraces multiculturalism requires that teachers transgress the bounds of independent school harmony; that is, that they go beyond accepted limits, that they disturb the peace. bell hooks describes in her book *Teaching to Transgress: Education as the Practice of Freedom* how actually to teach and model transgression is to make oneself vulnerable through experimentation, advocacy, and the practice of candor. For hooks, peacebuilding cannot come from liberal multicultural fluff in which we romanticize the lives of people on the margins and hold hands as we sing "We are the World."

Rather, hooks demands a political and pedagogical practice that rips into dominant educational paradigms. She insists that all of us engage in serious discourse and struggle to eradicate domination. Only then can one embody "a vision of liberatory education that connects the will to know with the will to become."[5] She writes:

> I am grateful to the many women and men who dare to create theory from the location of pain and struggle, who courageously expose the wounds to give us their experience to teach and guide, as a means to chart new theoretical journeys.[6]

To follow such courageous theorists, as most radical teachers in both private and public schools well know, is to risk harsh, even though unspoken, censure and ostracism. Such reprobation follows the independent schools' consensus on educational protocol, values, and practice. It constitutes what Foucault calls a "regime of truth," one that continues to undermine some of the most exciting efforts of secondary school teachers.[7] Indeed, the regular chastisement of transgressive teachers is built into their very jobs. It accompanies every viable means of school recognition including the yearly renewal contracts, membership on policymaking committees, promotions, and access to professional development funds. Put another way, despite all the truly momentous ongoing changes of private high school education today (such as new texts; teacher workshops on class, race, gender, and sexuality issues; community service programs; student awareness groups; and plans for attracting students, faculty, and administrators of color), the basic power structure of most of the schools remains firmly intact. Private school culture remains fundamentally inviolable.

Thanks to the conservative backlash of the past decade, the silencing of transgressive teachers may be more frequent than ever before. It is my personal observation, over twelve years teaching English in three prestigious schools, that such schools now seem preoccupied with notions of order, legitimacy, standards, and discipline. While I, a prep school-educated white male, have often been praised for helping to formulate and realize alternative teaching methods and a multicultural pedagogy, I have also experienced both censure and marginalization. It has usually come subtly. Although in evaluations of my teaching there has been no evidence of weak student skills, I have been encouraged to "prevent students from floundering" by spending more classroom time on traditional writing skills, having more "academic" conferences with students, while doing more "tracking" and "evaluating" of student progress in reading comprehension and writing. When I have attempted to talk to my evaluators about the nature of school culture and the importance of multicultural reform, I have been made to feel as if I have bitten the hand that feeds me. I can only imagine how a radical educator must feel who is a woman, a person of color, a gay, bisexual, or lesbian person in other such schools these days.

Strategies for Multicultural Reform

As radical teachers are always forced to profess, I do not belittle the importance of teaching English grammar, the skills of good writing and careful reading. Neither do I deny the need for "standards," or the virtues of mastery, obedience, respect, and accountability. I am not given to condoning emotional self-indulgence, pampering, sentimentality, or specious cultural relativism. We must understand, however, how these traditional and seemingly politically neutral educational goals are routinely paraded to stifle pedagogical experimentation by teachers. The result is an oppressive uniformity of teaching and learning styles for even our privileged children. Through the standardization of skills, assessments, and means of expression, administrators and teachers hostile to or fearful of radical pedagogy and the revolutionary tide of multicultural reform are able, seemingly legitimately, to reassert control over their departments. All the while they appear, even to themselves, to be advocates of the sort of vigorous, dialectical reform movement their schools profess to support.

E. D. Hirsh, for example, argues that there is value in multicultural education because it "inoculates tolerance and provides a perspective on our own traditions and values." But, he adds, "it should not be allowed to supplement or interfere with our schools' responsibility to insure our children's mastery of American literature culture."[8]

The stand-pat culture of the independent schools has powerful national spokespersons too. Former Secretary of Education William Bennett recently attended one of President Clinton's panels on race relations. According to the Associated Press, Bennett declared: "'Race matters less than family,' trying to steer the meeting toward his own social message of traditional values and rigorous educational standards. An audience member suggested that local schools should invest more in conflict resolution. 'I'd get the math scores up before we talk about conflict resolution,' Bennett retorted."[9]

By holding fast to traditional methods of instruction, by insisting upon the primacy of traditional skills and traditional forms of assessment in measuring and defining the parameters of student expression, such educators sustain their operative paradigms. These critics who profess to believe in multicultural education have a vision that adheres to Western enlightenment thought and ideology that perpetuates institutions as they now exist. What Henry Giroux has called "the language of possibility"[10] at the heart of multicultural reform is thus circumvented.

Strategically speaking, then, multicultural reform as a major component of peace as we have broadly defined it at all social levels requires a new formulation of what it means to be an educator in both private and public high schools. This is not an impossible task. Many teachers are, in fact, vulnerable, humble, responsive intellectuals in pursuit of peace. As Lisa Maria Hogeland recognizes, many feminists have come to appreciate multicultural reform and the need for transgressive teaching. "Feminism requires an expansion of the self—an expansion of empathy, interest, intelligence, and responsibility across differences, histories, cultures, ethnicities, sexual identities, othernesses."[11] Such teachers need not be overly pessimistic about the chances for the changes in the academy called for by feminists and other reformers. bell hooks eloquently writes:

> The academy is not paradise. But learning is a place where paradise can be created. The classroom, with all its limitations, remains a location of possibility. In that field of possibility we have the opportunity to labor for freedom, to

demand of ourselves and our comrades, an openness of mind and heart that allows us to face reality even as we collectively imagine ways to move beyond boundaries, to transgress. This is education as the practice of freedom.[12]

Educators today can work to rethink their curricula; decentering, reframing, and reconsidering traditional texts within the context of a multicultural reality. That reality makes multiculturalism a major component of peacebuilding at all levels. It requires the development of teaching and assessment strategies commensurate with the awakenings that precede profound ideological shifts. Such peacebuilding will expand radically when teachers are no longer rewarded for intellectual and moral complacency, for teaching that is neither responsive, nor vulnerable, nor engaged. Just as with students, teachers themselves can be encouraged by their administrators and by their colleagues to disturb the peace as a prerequisite for truly meaningful peacebuilding. They can dare to transgress routinely the boundaries of their own comfort, training, and expertise, for a goal all profess to admire, but few truly seek. How better to communicate the critical thinking skills we profess to value as educators than to model them ourselves, peacefully, humbly, in our own imperfect ways?

Education for peace is, like war, about contested territory; that is what can make it compelling, that is what can give it its power to liberate and to transform. The controversy over multicultural education as a component of peacebuilding is not simply a matter of the politics of race and gender. Rather, as Paul Robeson Jr. tells us, it is "at the heart of a profound ideological struggle over the values of American culture and the nature of U.S. civilization." Above all, Robeson argues, "it is a debate about whether the melting-pot culture, which is the foundation of the American way of life and imposes its Anglo-Saxon Protestant values on our society, should be replaced by a mosaic culture incorporating the values of the diverse groups that make up America's population."[13] Multicultural education for peace demands a transgressive pedagogy that disturbs the peace. No program, no curriculum, no matter how diverse or seemingly bias-free, can ever be effective in its absence. It is only through the practice of radical inquiry that the ongoing definition of what it means to be a citizen in any given time period can be responsibly engaged. Henry Giroux writes "Citizenship, like democracy itself, is part of a historical tradition that represents a terrain of struggle over the forms of knowledge, social practices, and values that constitute the critical elements of that tradition."[14]

When administrators are willing to see radical discourse and practice as necessary and creative components of the life of a school that give its peace a meaning that can transform society, and when teachers are willing to speak out and negotiate their own pedagogical autonomy, independent schools will transcend their intellectually crippling legacy of privilege and parochialism. Then will they be able to "sustain and struggle within a project of possibility that enhances rather than diminishes the traditions of democracy, community, and hope."[15]

Notes

1. "Independent school" is the term by which private elite schools now prefer to be called.

2. Johan Galtung, "Twenty-Five Years of Peace Research: Ten Challenges and Responses," *Journal of Peace Research*, 22 (1985): 414-31.

3. Carl Grant, "Challenging the Myths about Multicultural Education," *Multicultural Education* (winter 1994): 4-9.

4. Rheinhold Niebuhr, *Moral Man and Immoral Society* (New York: Charles Scribner, 1960), 129.

5. bell hooks, *Teaching to Transgress: Education as the Practice of Freedom* (New York: Routledge, 1994), 18, 19.

6. Ibid., 74.

7. Michael Foucault, *Beyond Structuralism and Hermeneutics*, 2d ed. (Chicago: University of Chicago Press, 1983), 131.

8. E. D. Hirsh, *Cultural Literacy* (New York: Houghton Mifflin), 18.

9. *Binghamton Press & Sun Bulletin*, 16 December 1997, 15A.

10. Henry A. Giroux, *Teachers as Intellectuals* (New York: Bergin and Garvey Press, 1988), 135.

11. Lisa Maria Hogeland, "Fear of Feminism: Why Young Women Get the Willies," *Ms. Magazine*, November/December 1994, 18-21.

12. hooks, *Teaching to Transgress*, 207.

13. Paul Robeson Jr., *Paul Robeson Jr. Speaks to America* (New Brunswick, NJ: Rutgers University Press), 1.

14. Henry A. Giroux, *Schooling and the Struggle for Public Life: Critical Pedagogy in the Modern Age* (Minneapolis: The University of Minnesota Press, 1988), 5.

15. Ibid., 52.

PART IV
SCHOOL AND COMMUNITY

Chapter 13

Stop the Violence: Conflict Management in an Inner-City Junior High School through Action Research and Community Problem Solving

Arjen E. J. Wals[1]

Introduction

In this chapter an approach to education will be outlined that provides a bridge between school and community on the one hand, and between learning for school and learning for life on the other: action research and community problem solving (AR&CPS). So far AR&CPS has been applied in the context of community-based environmental education mostly in inner-city settings.

After discussing community-based environmental education and its relationship to other emerging educations such as development education, human rights education and peace education, the components of AR&CPS will be described. AR&CPS and its various steps will be illustrated by the case of the Pistons Middle School which is located in inner-city Detroit.[2] In this case, not surprisingly, the students elected school safety as their main topic of investigation. So, based on our experiences with AR&CPS and community-based environmental education, the chapter will close with recommendations for school and community-based development of strategies for conflict management and peacebuilding.

Community-Based Environmental Education

Community-based environmental education is education with strong roots in the community, in the existential world of the learner and in democratic environmental change thought. Community-based environmental education is defined broadly here to include all learning that enables students and teachers to participate in the planning, implementing, and evaluating of educational activities aimed at resolving a local environmental issue that they themselves have identified. What an "environmental issue" is, then, depends on the perceptions and experiences of the learner as well as on the context in which education takes place.

Ideally, community-based environmental education is a continuous learning process that enables participants to construct, critique, emancipate and transform their world in an existential way.[3] *Construct* in the sense of building upon the prior knowledge, experiences, and ideas of the learner. *Critique* in the sense of investigating underlying values, assumptions, worldviews, morals, etc., as they are a part of the world around the learner and as they are a part of the learner himself or herself. *Emancipate* in the sense of detecting, exposing, and, where possible, altering power distortions that impede communication and change. *Transform* in the sense of changing, shaping, and influencing the world around them, regardless of scope or scale.

Community-Based Education and Other Emerging Educations

The above description of environmental education holds that the term "environment" should be defined broadly to include political, social, economic, and bio/physical aspects (figure 1).

Community-based environmental education cannot be seen in isolation from other emerging fields in education that focus on human rights issues, development issues and peace and conflict issues. Environmental issues, for instance, involve ethical questions regarding the injustice in the ways the use of the world's natural resources is shared. We do not know the answers to these questions and should not pretend that we do, but we do know that they cannot be found without also looking at issues of development, peace and conflict, and human rights (not to mention the rights of other species). The relationship between the forms of education that are emerging around these issues is shown in figure 2. Where Greig, Pike, and Selby speak of a narrow focus there is little overlap, where they speak of a broad focus there is much overlap.[4]

Harris, in describing a culture of peace, implicitly refers to links between the four educations sketched in figure 2: "Such a culture pre-

Figure 1 The Environment and Environmental Issues

THE ENVIRONMENT

POLITICAL
Power, policy and decision making

SOCIAL
People living together

ECONOMIC
Jobs and money

BIO/PHYSICAL
Materials, organism, and life support systems

Wide-Ranging Environmental Stress Leads to a Declining Quality of Life in a Degraded Environment

---
Source R. O'Donaghue and C. MacNaught, "Environmental Education Curriculum Development: Towards a Revised Framework of 'Grass-roots' Reconstructive Action," in *Proceedings of the International Symposium on Fieldwork in the Sciences*, ed. J. van Trommel (Enschede, Netherlands: Institute for Curriculum Development, 1990), 23–45.

serves the natural and spiritual environment of human beings and respects the inherent dignity of each person. It is profoundly democratic based on rights. It encourages people to handle conflict in constructive ways. . . . Traditionally peace studies have contributed to building this peace culture by teaching about threats to the environment and interstate rivalries that lead to war and by promoting concepts of world citizenry and ecological security."[5] Harris also considers the study of "ecological sustainability" to be an essential part of the content of peace education.[6] One could argue that in Harris' article on peace education in the postmodern world and in Greig, Pike, and Selby's comparison of four emerging educations, other species are noticeably missing from their environmental education perspective. One could even think of species rights education and violence against other species as themes for these emerging fields and, indeed, they sometimes are. Similarly, one should include the rights of future generations and the way these rights might be violated by our present lifestyles.

Another link between environmental education and peace education is highlighted by research that shows that safety, security, and being at peace are important prerequisites for exploring the community environment or natural areas in the community.[7] In many urban

Figure 2 Four Emerging Fields in Western Education

DEVELOPMENTAL EDUCATION	ENVIRONMENTAL EDUCATION
Narrow focus 1. Problems of third world countries 2. Implicit acceptance of Western view of development 3. Solutions lie in providing aid 4. Student involvement: charitable collections (Teaching *about* development)	**Narrow focus** 1. Local environment 2. Traditional biological and geographical emphasis 3. Implicit acceptance of Western perspective on the environment 4. Developing caring interest in environment and practicing study/research skills (Teaching *about* the environment)
Broad focus 1. World development/interdependencies 2. Non-Western perspectives given due emphasis 3. Solutions lie in reforming economic/political arrangements within and between societies 4. Student involvement: developing skills for participation in decision-making processes (Teaching *for* development)	**Broad focus** 1. Local/national/global environmental interdependencies 2. Exploring relationships between human behavior and global ecosystems 3. Serious exploration of non-Western perspectives on the environment 4. Developing concerned awareness and participatory skills (Teaching *for* the environment)

communities people tend to associate parks and the people "hanging out" there with drugs and violence. In other words, a place you stay away from. Peace in the community could be a key factor in determining the extent to which people have access to their community and the natural and human resources it houses. Many children today are still deprived of a basic right of childhood: the right to experience and explore the world around them safely, spontaneously, and on their own terms.[8]

I will now turn to a pedagogical approach to environmental education which could be utilized just as well by the other emerging educations and mimics the idea, described earlier, of community-based environmental education.

Action Research and Community Problem Solving

In 1985 the University of Michigan's School of Environment and Natural Resources developed, in conjunction with Deakin University (Austra-

Figure 2 Continued

HUMAN RIGHTS EDUCATION	PEACE EDUCATION
Narrow focus 1. Teaching based on key international documents 2. Emphasis on civil and political rights 3. Implicit acceptance of Western view of rights 4. Teaching *about* rights (history of rights, case studies, etc.)	**Narrow focus** 1. Absence of war 2. Disarmament, gun control 3. Limited concept of peace 4. Study/research skills in traditional classroom (Teaching *about* peace)
Broad focus 1. New rights, e.g. environmental rights also included 2. Social and economic rights given equal emphasis 3. Serious exploration of non-Western perspectives 4. Teaching *for* rights (i.e. developing skills) and *in* rights (i.e. democratic and open classroom climate)	**Broad focus** 1. Absence of war and injustice 2. Disarming/dismantling oppressive structures globally 3. Extended concept of peace, including ecological balance 4. Participatory skills within democratic classroom (Teaching *for* and *in* peace)

Source: This figure represents a slightly modified version of one in S. Greig, G. Pike, and D. Selby, *Earthrights: Education as if the Planet Really Mattered* (London: World Wildlife Fund/Kogan Page, 1987).

lia), an approach to education, the aforementioned AR&CPS, that takes the world as perceived by the students as the starting point of their learning. I will first discuss the two main components, before describing the result of their synthesis.

Action Research (AR) is both a methodology and a way of thinking. Kurt Lewin is generally considered to be the founding father of the approach.[9] Action research can be described as ". . .a form of self-reflective inquiry undertaken by participants in social (including educational) situations in order to improve the rationality and justice of their own social or educational practices, their understanding of these practices and the situations in which the practices are carried out."[10] Action research is rooted in "praxis," the process of reflection and action, and is a means for teachers to improve their own practice, to help students acquire knowledge and personal empowerment, and to adjust administrative policies to improve the learning environment.[11] In education, the approach has a dual purpose; the improvement of the learning environment and the empowerment of teachers and students. Hence, its overall purpose is the enhancement of the quality of education itself. Applied to environmental education, action research enables students to participate more fully in the learning process. They come to assume greater responsibility for learning as they become engaged in tackling and acting upon an environmental issue that they themselves have identified and recognized to be important.

Community Problem Solving (CPS) describes the realm in which action research can be employed in the context of environmental education. Lewin's methodology, adapted to schools, revolves around articulating and acting upon a local environmental issue in cooperation with students and other affected people. Important elements of community problem solving are: recognizing a problem; collecting, organizing, and analyzing information; defining the problem from a variety of perspectives; identifying, considering, and selecting alternative actions to take; developing and carrying out a plan of action; and evaluating the outcome and the entire process.[12] In all steps the human and material resources present in the community are utilized whenever possible.

The synthesis, AR&CPS, represents an inquiry process that enables teachers and students to participate more fully in the planning, implementing, and evaluating of educational activities, aimed at resolving an environmental issue that the learners themselves have identified. The definition of an environmental issue largely depends on the perceptions and experiences of the learner and on the context in which education takes place. Throughout the process members of the school community ideally come to interpret their situation as requiring intervention, especially their own intervention. During AR&CPS university participants play the dual role of external researcher and facilitator. AR&CPS has been developed in the late eighties and early nineties in junior high schools in the Detroit metropolitan area, some of these being located in some of the poorest areas of the city itself.

All participants operate within a so-called action research triangle which refers to research carried out simultaneously by students, teachers, and outside facilitators/university researchers.[13] In the context of environmental education this means that *students* investigate a local environmental issue of their own interest (e.g. water quality, school beautification, school violence), *teachers* investigate ways to improve their own teaching (e.g., working in groups, utilizing community resources, conflict management), and *outside facilitators*, who coordinate the research triangle, investigate contemporary issues in environmental education research (e.g,. students' perceptions of nature, student empowerment, curriculum design). Although the focus of the research varies within the triangle, the research process is similar in that all parties are engaged in an inquiry process that at least contains the following elements: *identifying* issues of mutual concern, *analyzing* one particular issue, *generating* potential solutions, *implementing* a selected solution in the real-world and *evaluating* the results (figure 3). This spiral is normally repeated until a situation emerges that is satisfactory to all participants. However, here I will limit myself to the route and perspective within the triangle of students (aged 12–14) from the Detroit public school system.

Figure 3 Simultaneous Improvement of the Community and Learning Environment through AR&CPS (Cycle Shown Is One of Many)

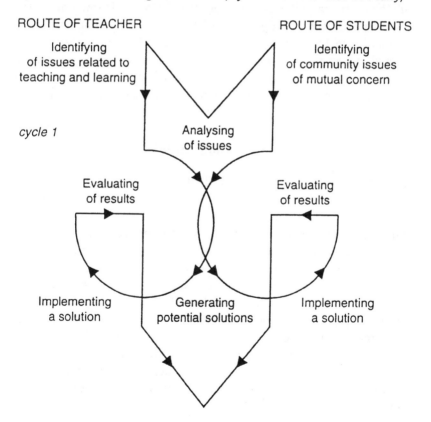

During the AR&CPS process, students are given responsibility in the planning of educational activities and provided with the opportunity to take responsible action within their community environment.[14] Several key assumptions underlie the AR&CPS scheme. First, it is crucial for society to solve critical issues with the full participation of its young members. Second, students need to know that they can be forces of constructive change, and that their involvement is indeed needed in the world. In other words, education should be geared toward replacing feelings of apathy and "powerlessness" with the feeling that one, be it as an individual or in a group, indeed can make a difference. Therefore, AR&CPS emphasizes that students must be given more responsibility in the planning of educational activities and should be provided with the opportunity to take responsible action to improve the quality of their school and community environment. Third, giving students a chance to investigate and act upon a problem of their own choice will increase their motivation to learn. Lastly, the school and its community contain an untapped abundance of rich material for making education more meaningful to the students. Rich material in terms of printed matter (i.e., newspapers, books, magazines), human resources (i.e., students, teachers, parents, and other community members), and equipment (i.e., monitoring devices, computers, Internet access).

The Context: Pistons Middle School

Because of the importance of context in developing programs like these, I will provide a brief, and therefore somewhat narrow, description of some of the school, students, and community that focused on community violence and safety within the framework of AR&CPS.[15]

Although an AR&CPS project can be done in any setting—rural, suburban, and urban alike—the city environment is an especially fertile ground for such a project to take place.[16] City residents live with some of the most pressing problems faced by our society: crime, drugs, poor housing, pollution, poverty, homelessness, and sanitation problems, among others. Urban dwellers who are victims of these social ills often feel powerless to change them. At the same time the schools are trying hard to redefine their role in educating young people in an attempt to fill the gaps created by the unstable environment in which the students grow up.

Pistons Middle School, located in Detroit, a city rich in cultural and ethnic diversity, has also burdened it with many of these societal problems listed on page 246. High school and junior high school drop-out rates rank as some of the highest in the United States. Infant mortality rates are comparable to those of developing countries. Much of the financial community has moved to the suburbs along with most of Detroit's white population.

At the time AR&CPS was first introduced at Pistons Middle School in Detroit, the school could be regarded as a bunker in an urban war zone. The problems that permeate the neighborhoods and the school force the school to focus on safety issues, and to teach a double curriculum that in essence includes the performing of many tasks which ordinarily are considered to be the tasks of parents and/or guardians. Additionally, budget constraints, lack of equipment, and a perceived need to teach students the basic subjects before they drop out of school, put added pressure on the school and its curriculum.

When looking at the students' descriptions of their world, we see a dynamic world full of contrasts and extremes. On the one hand many of the students find themselves fortunate; they live on a relatively nice block, still have some parental guidance, are not involved in drugs, and are still in school. On the other hand they find themselves in a community that is almost saturated with problems, often drug-related, such as street violence, teen pregnancy, and, what they regard as a failing justice system. To cope with the violence in their community they have developed a variety of survival strategies: they know what to do when they hear gunshots, are able to suppress their emotions and to ignore parts of their reality, know how not to draw attention to themselves, know what places to avoid, spend a lot of time indoors mostly using the outdoors to get from one place to another and they have developed their own dreams and fantasies to provide a mental shelter.[17]

School is important to many of the city students who took part in AR&CPS, but not for school learning, which appears to be mostly irrelevant. School instead performs many other functions for them; it brings some stability to their lives; it provides a shelter in a troubled neighborhood; it is a place where groups of students can socialize—something which they can hardly do outside—and, finally, it provides the education needed, if not to fulfill their dreams, then at least to keep them out of the cycle of drugs, gangs, and violence. So, even though many students criticize some of the content of the subjects they are taught and the way some teachers teach, they still value school. They are definitely at an advantage compared to those of their peers who have already left school.

The eighth-grade students (13-14 years old) at Pistons Middle School are acutely aware of many of these community problems. They express frustration and anger at having to deal with them, and do not seem to have much hope that things can get better. Few feel they can do anything about the problems.[18] Meanwhile the Detroit Board of Education and the administrators and teachers of its school, by trying innovation after innovation, have been trying for years to better accommodate the needs of the children and to improve the learning environment. AR&CPS thus represents for many Detroit schools yet another innovative approach. This time, however, they have one that specifically aims to include community issues in the education of the children in an attempt to make their education more meaningful and empowering. This case should not be regarded as model of a successful AR&CPS project, but rather as uses of a point of reference for developing similar programs.

Steps in the Pistons Middle School Project

The steps below describe the project at Pistons Middle School in a more orderly fashion than the reality presents. Most project steps occur simultaneously and not necessarily in the order given. It is important that the participants enjoy the actual nonlinear nature of AR&CPS in order to assure a more natural learning process. This means a learning process in which students and teacher continuously reevaluate: the course and direction of the project, the information needed to continue, the scope and limitations of potential actions taken by the students, and the definition of when the project can be considered a success. This is not to say that the AR&CPS project is open-ended— it has a beginning and an end—but rather that participants have to be able to cope with uncertainty. Uncertainty about when exactly the project will end, uncertainty about the topic of investigation, uncertainty about what the students will learn and uncertainty about what will happen next week.

Planning the Process
After the Detroit Board of Education had identified Pistons Middle School as a try-out school, and the principal had recruited a Science teacher and a Social Studies teacher who had expressed interested in

the project, the outside facilitators set up initial meetings with the administrators and the teachers involved. These initial meetings focused not so much on the question: what exactly is AR&CPS?, but rather on: what are some of the shortcomings in our educational program and how can we address them? During the discussions, the underlying principles and guiding assumptions of AR&CPS emerged and were adapted to the special needs and requirements of school and its community.

The teachers participating in the Pistons Middle School project, perhaps conditioned by past experiences with outsiders bringing a new approach to the school, expected that the facilitators would know exactly what would happen and that all they needed to do themselves was implement the program. The first hurdle for the facilitators, therefore, was to change this image by making clear that by its nature an AR&CPS project is developed by the teachers and students themselves, with only the help of the facilitators and other resources. Once the teachers became aware of their key role in developing the program—as opposed to merely implementing it—they had to decide whether they had the time, energy, and desire to still be a part of it. The Pistons Middle School teachers, partly driven by their eagerness to try something new and much encouraged by the knowledge that they could count on the outside facilitators and the support of the school administration, decided that they would go ahead with the project.

The group decided to have a one-day workshop in which past AR&CPS projects were shared and related to the context of Pistons Middle School. The teachers and the outside facilitators, the school librarian, the principal (on and off) and a parent (all parents of the selected class were invited to attend, but only one showed up) participated in the workshop. The workshop culminated in several decisions that the teachers felt needed to be made before going into the classroom. These decisions included: selecting a rough time line of two-hour sessions twice a week for initially twenty-three months, deciding elements they considered crucial to the project such as faculty orientation, parent notification/involvement, topic generation and selection, and opting for only one topic for student investigation. Much consideration was also given to how to introduce the project to the class.

Prior to starting the project in the classroom, as well as during it, the teachers assessed the students' information gathering, communication and group process skills, of course, needed throughout the project. The teachers found that it would be problematic to work in small groups, or to ask the students to reflect on their learning experience in a journal. Special activities, however, were introduced at various points in the process to work on specific skills needed for environmental problem solving.[19]

After redefining the AR&CPS process with members of the school community and assessing the various skills students needed to develop in the project, the actual classroom work could begin.

Step 1: Identifying Issues of Mutual Concern

The teachers and students at Pistons Middle School agreed that a community walk would be the best way to generate ideas for a research topic. One of the teachers provided a map of the neighborhood and the students split up in five small groups that were familiar with a particular area within the school's surroundings (usually the blocks they themselves lived in). Each group was accompanied by an adult for obvious reasons. The adults and in some cases the students took pictures of points of interest encountered during the two-period walk. One of the groups, consisting of students who had not obtained parental permission to leave the school building, explored the school and school grounds. Students brought notebooks to write down their observations. Our past experiences with community walks had taught us not to focus solely on the negative aspects of the neighborhood, so students were encouraged to write down things they liked as well.

Naturally there was some concern about the idea of going around the neighborhood taking pictures, making observations, and interviewing people on the street. One of the teachers feared that the walk would lead to conflicts with gangs. It is a sad observation that going outside the school building does leave one vulnerable to the ills of the streets: the students have to do this every day. Some of the students were concerned about the community walk (figure 4); the teachers and facilitators had to take several precautions to assure as much safety as possible.

Fortunately it has been our experience that the students know best where to go and where not to go, and that many of the community residents—especially the elderly—are eager to talk about the neighborhood and how it has changed. Many of the students expressed feelings of empowerment in their journals after the community walk and enjoyed leaving the building tremendously. The community walk not only energized the participants but formed a great starting point for soliciting ideas for a topic.

Figure 4 Journal Excerpts from Pistons Middle School Students (Literal Transcriptions)

> "I think that when we go on our trip for a walk, someone is going to get hit by a car or is going to get into a fight, maybe even get lost. That's what I think is going to happen. Or somebody might snatch us little people off, or shoot us or something. That's why I am glad we have guardians and teachers walking around with us."
>
> ". . . If we go out and ask people questions about drugs people will get hurt. My uncle's hand was cut off by a dealer 'cause he couldn't pay him. We are just kids."

Back in the classroom the students of all groups reported their findings. A long list of problems/issues appeared on the blackboard varying from AIDS, drugs, prostitution, violence, and gangs, to toxic waste, air pollution, health care, and homelessness. The teachers asked the students to reflect on the topic that concerned them the most in their journal. The next session, students were asked to share their journal entries with each other. This sharing led to a discussion as to why certain topics might be more pressing than others. Unlike the experience of some of the other AR&CPS projects the students were able to reach consensus about a topic in the relatively short time period of two weeks. Unanimously they decided to investigate the issue of school safety or lack thereof. In their eyes the school no longer formed the safe haven it was said once to have been, but was threatened by outsiders coming in with violent intentions.

Interestingly enough the students' concern about school safety was trivialized by the principal when they interviewed him. Disappointed by his lack of support, the class decided to survey a sample of students, teachers, administrators, and parents, to find out whether his point of view was shared. One of the teachers pointed out that the information obtained through the survey would give them power: "Mr. Johnstone cannot deny something is a problem when eighty percent of the students, teachers and parents think it is!" The students, excited by the prospect of setting the principal straight, energetically became engaged over several sessions of generating survey questions and surveying the school community. The results strengthened their conviction that school safety was an important issue. They showed the results to the principal who then acknowledged it to be a topic worth investigating.

Step 2: Analyzing a Particular Issue

After selection of the safety topic, the first problem became defining the issue of investigation. The students had a tendency to define the problem in terms of seemingly short-sighted solutions. For instance, they would define the problem of lack of safety in the school building as "No metal detectors in the school to keep guns and knives out," or "Students have no identification passes on them." In so doing, the students focused on the symptoms of the problem and not its causes. At the same time they became fixed on ad hoc solutions (get metal detectors, get a student identification system). Much research of the topic was needed to develop a problem statement that defined the project clearly. In order to avoid disappointment and find workable solutions it is important that the students' research build a deeper understanding of the problem. They thought that because they already knew what the problem was they had the solution! It became clear to the teachers and outsiders that successful investigation meant that the students had to slow down.

Up until this investigation phase, the students' project had moved along at a quick pace, arousing their curiosity, an essential element of good education, but now the teachers and facilitators with their slowdown, disrupted the flow of the project. Students were asked to find more information in the library, interview more people, and collect current newspaper articles. Many of them, not convinced of the need for this, lost interest in the project. Forcing the students to gather more information in order to define the problem seemed to them to be keeping them from taking badly needed action. The teachers and outside facilitators thus struggled with a question: do we let them go ahead and discover their ignorance for themselves, with all the risk of serious disappointment, or do we hold them up until they have done enough research for effective action, perhaps losing many students in the process?

Action-oriented environmental education approaches always seem to have both an "information first" side and an "experience first" side. Our experiences with AR&CPS in Detroit schools, however, have shifted us from favoring information gathering first toward emphasizing a simultaneous occurrence of practical experience and information gathering. When students try taking action in the early stages of a project they discover their lack of information or set unrealistic goals. The feelings of disappointment are assuaged for truly concerned students by the sense of purpose they gain from additional information gathering. A mere linear approach that requires students to have all "the facts" before going out to interview figures like the principal, for instance, may well destroy this sense of purpose.

Step 3: Generating Potential Solutions

As a result of this "'information versus experience discussion," therefore, students were soon allowed to pursue some of the tentative solutions. They investigated, for example, the pros and cons of providing everybody with identification passes. They looked at some Detroit schools that already had such systems. They put together recommendations for implementing a pass system and presented them to the principal, only to hear that they had not looked at the costs of such an idea and that there was no money for it. This inspired several students to find out what the costs would be and how to raise money for them. Other students went through a similar process while exploring such ideas as having more and better security guards and student monitors.

Nonetheless, as the students pursued these actions, they came to realize that the issue of school safety was directly related to safety in the community. If the surrounding neighborhoods were safe, the school would be safe too. So attention shifted from looking at ad hoc solutions to seeking the roots of such problems as: "Why do people become violent? Why are so many conflicts 'resolved' with violence? Are there other ways to resolve conflict? What happens to students who get in trouble with the law?" The class decided that they needed more time for finding answers to these questions. Two mothers whose sons had been killed by guns came to the school to talk about the situations that led up to the deaths and share the trauma. A speaker from the Center of Peace and Conflict Studies came to suggest alternative ways to deal with conflict. The class visited a court to see for themselves what happens to those who have committed violence. They also interviewed a judge. Such experiences gradually led the students to redefine the project. No longer was the goal merely getting metal detectors or identification systems (something the administration was willing enough to take under advisement), but rather the students wanted to find a way to teach the whole school about the destructiveness of violence to school and community and about alternative ways to deal with it.

Step 4: Implementing a Selected Solution

The students' shift from trying to implement ad hoc solutions to raising awareness among their peers meant that they needed an effective way to communicate their research findings. Inspired by rap music they chose to use it as background for a set of skits. Small groups worked for several weeks on different skits that portrayed how conflicts start, escalate, and sometimes come to be resolved. They showed the drawbacks of resolutions that rely on violent ways and the advantages of resolving conflicts that nonviolently allow both parties to keep face. The entire class eventually worked on a "Stop the Violence" rap/skit that was acted out before all the students in the school's auditorium. Several individual students also participated in a march against violence in downtown Detroit that had been organized by a local group called Save Our Sons and Daughters (SOSAD).

It is important to emphasize that in most AR&CPS projects, the point is not that students actually completely resolve a problem, although this has been done, but that they learn to take some effective actions to alleviate it. Taking action can be achieved in many creative ways, as is indicated by the actions of this particular AR&CPS project listed in figure 5. The actions reported on here are only the most

Figure 5 Some Visible Outcomes/Actions of AR&CPS at the Pistons Middle School

---

Grade Level: Junior high (8th grade)
Setting: inner-city
Curriculum Subjects: Social studies and science
Project Title: School Safety
Time Period: 48 class sessions (3 sessions per week)
Project Outcomes and Community Actions:

1) school survey on students' and teachers' perceptions of school safety;
2) students submit to the principal a plan for obtaining student ID's to keep outsiders from entering the school;
3) students arrange for the director of Save Our Sons and Daughters
4) (SOSAD) and a representative of the Center for Peace and Conflict Studies to discuss violence in the community and conflict resolution strategies with the students.
5) students participate in SOSAD's annual memorial service to remember Detroit's slain children.
6) students visit Court House, attend several arraignments and interview a judge.
7) students perform and videotape a rap/skit on self destruction in the African-American community in order to raise awareness in the (school) community about the dangers of violence.

visible outcomes of some of the projects. Many actions, in fact, are neither measurable nor observable, others may not be taken until later in life. The Pistons Middle School Project illustrates that action taking can occur at several stages of a project and does not have to occur only at the end.

Teachers facilitating action taking should become familiar with some strategies that can provide students with an "action-perspective" or "the perspective to act" as well as a sense of accomplishment. One strategy that might work is to investigate cases or examples of environmental problem solving carried out elsewhere. Careful investigation of such cases could reveal that resolving an environmental issue requires an amalgamation of a variety of smaller actions and a number of critical decisions.[20] Social psychologist, Karl Weick notes that since smaller problems are more easily solved, framing an environmental issue in pieces may provide enormous psychological benefit.[21] By providing students with examples of successful action taking, ideally involving students as well, they develop confidence that it is possible to change and shape their world, while also discovering some critical steps in the problem-solving process. Some environmental education programs have begun to collect examples of environmental success stories for educational purposes.[22] Other teachers may help students build bridges with the scientific community, the local community, governmental groups, and nongovernmental organizations.

Step 5: Evaluating of Results

Evaluation of the project was an ongoing element of all phases of the Pistons Middle School Project. During the meetings between the teachers and the outside facilitators the process as a whole was frequently evaluated and specific dilemmas, such as their "information or experience first" dilemma, were addressed. Reflection is a key element of AR&CPS students' individual journals served as a medium for them to express their feelings, as well as reactions to the AR&CPS process. These often helped the teacher in modifying the project and assessing both their writing skills and commitment to the project. On several occasions, the students were asked to reflect on key questions that deal with the origins and resolutions of conflict.

- What parties are involved in the conflict?
- What are the interests of the parties which are involved?
- What are the motives to start a conflict?

- What are the power relations?
- What are feasible settlements and/or solutions of the conflict?[23]

Journal entries addressing questions like these illustrated how students' perceptions of conflict and peace changed during the course of the AR&CPS project.

Observation of students' level of participation also helped in evaluating both the project and the students participating. In addition, so called "plus, minus, change" sheets were used periodically to find out specifically what the students liked and disliked about the project as well as to solicit their suggestions for change.

Discussion

The strong problem-solving and action-taking dimension of AR&CPS is still somewhat controversial and needs a proper justification. Three arguments seem to make a good case for an emphasis on problem solving and action taking. First, many young people, as is the case with many adults, are overwhelmed by the community problems they find in real life. It is important to help them explore such existential issues and to provide them with an understanding of their nature and complexity. However, environmental education, or peace education for that matter, should not be limited to raising awareness and increasing understanding. Such can easily feed feelings of mere apathy and powerlessness. It would be dangerous if community-based environmental education would provide students only with an understanding that their the community environment is in bad shape, the root causes of such badness are complex, and improvement is very hard.[24] By bringing in the action-taking component students can, given the right conditions, begin to take charge of some of these issues and develop a sense of power and control.

A second argument for including action taking in a community-based environmental education project has its roots in experiential learning thought. Such thought shows that one never comes to understand a problem fully with all its nuances and complexities, until one fully immerses oneself in it, identifies all the players, and begins to work within a "force field" or field of interferences toward a shared solution. This is a way of saying that we may never really understand a problem until we try to actually implement some solutions.

Finally, it could be argued that without the ability and willingness to act it is impossible to participate in or in any way contribute to a democratic society. As Jensen and Schnack point out a concern for the environment should be connected to a concern for democracy.[25] Vriens, in referring to a work by Johan Galtung, suggests that much education implicitly carries a message of structural violence if it can be characterized as one-sided communication, as promoting inequality between teachers and students, or teachers and administration.[26] In such cases, students receive the message that they are inferior to the educator because of what they don't know and have to learn. This conveys a message of teacher power and student dependency that obstructs learner emancipation, while preventing real self-possession.[27]

The spin-offs of the Detroit AR&CPS projects can be found at different levels. Although no systematic study has been conducted, anecdotal evidence suggests that the involved teachers have changed their teaching style to accommodate the ideas and experiences of the students and allow for more community-based learning. There are also indications—again anecdotal, but statistically plausible—that the level of community violence has gone down in the neighborhoods of Pistons Middle School. It is impossible, however, to attribute this to the one case of AR&CPS. For AR&CPS to actually prove such an impact it would have to become a fully integral part of the school curriculum. Even so, at the level of the schools and the community, many of the basic ideas of the AR&CPS—most notably the utilization of community resources for educational purposes and the focus on local environmental issues—are being used in ongoing projects. These are the Rouge River Interactive Water Quality Monitoring Project and a community organizing project called "The Greening of Detroit." Recently descriptions of the various ways in which AR&CPS has been used in the North America generally have been collected in a practical guide for schools and community groups.[28] It is interesting to note that in Europe the OECD's Environment and School Initiatives Project (ENSI), which developed independently of the AR&CPS, shows many similarities in philosophy and educational approach.[29]

My own immersion as a facilitator/researcher in the AR&CPS projects in Detroit, revealed that the outside facilitator initially had little understanding of the way the students experiences their world. Freire once wrote: "It is not our role to speak to people about our own view of the world, nor to attempt to impose that view on them, but rather to dialogue with the people about their view and ours. We must realize that their view of the world, manifested variously in their action, reflects their situation in the world. Educational and political action which is not critically aware of this situation runs the risk either of 'banking' or of preaching in the desert."[30] Freire's warning tells us that if outsiders are to contribute at all to both educational reform and the creation of a peaceful and sustainable community, they will have to be sensitive to all members of the school and community. Much time must be spent early-on in projects like these getting to know the school community, keeping fully open-minded, overcoming and putting aside our own prejudices and preferences, and, perhaps most important, by being there as much as we can. Education for peace requires an understanding of the way people "define" their own situation. We have to become critically aware of the way others perceive their world and ours. Fortune may dictate some situation that requires the peacebuilder's intervention. If the need for change uncovered by peace education is ignored, for whatever reason, then the educational process inevitably will fall short, will fail to help people understand the roots of oppression, inequality, violence, and environmental deterioration on the one hand, and fail as well in empowering them to become agents of peace, social change, and sustainable development.

As far as the potential role of AR&CPS in helping people create a more peaceful and sustainable community, it can be argued that the "model" offers an educational strategy for involving schools in the community (and vice versa). AR&CPS's emphasis on simultaneous action research and community problem solving, linking schools with community organizations, local government, and interest groups, and development of nonprescriptive empowerment and action competence in learners could all be essential ingredients to the development of community-grounded peace and sustainability.

Notes

1 I wish to thank the teachers and administrators of Pistons Middle School in Detroit for their contribution to the development of AR&CPS. Futhermore I am grateful to William Stapp and James Bull, two former colleagues at the University of Michigan who cofacilitated the Detroit AR&CPS-projects. I also thank Lennart Vriens, who occupies a special chair in Peace Education at Utrecht University in the Netherlands, for sharing some of his own work that allowed me to update this contribution.

2 In earlier publications about AR&CPS narrative accounts of students were prominently used to illustrate their perceptions of their world. See A. E. J. Wals, "Young Adolescents' Perceptions of Nature and Environmental Issues: Implications for Environmental Education in Urban Settings" (Ph.D. diss., University of Michigan, 1991) and the popular version A. E. J. Wals, *Pollution Stinks! Young Adolescents' Perceptions of Nature and Environmental Issues with Implications for Education in Urban Settings* (De Lier, Netherlands: Academic Book Center, ABC, 1994), which can only be obtained through Opulus Press, v/d Bouwmanweg 180Y, 2352 JD Leiderdorp, The Netherlands.

To preserve anonymity, the names of both the students and the school were changed. To avoid confusion I will keep using the fictional name used in past publications.

3 For a basic outline of this approach to environmental education see W. B. Stapp, A. E. J. Wals, and S. Stankorb, *Environmental Education for Empowerment: Action Research and Community Problem Solving* (Dubuque, Iowa: Kendall/Hunt, 1996). For a concrete case of environmental education that follows this approach see A. E. J. Wals, "Backalley Sustainability and the Role of Environmental Education," *Local Environment* 1, no. 3 (1996): 299–316. This case also makes up the core of this contribution.

4 See S. Greig, G. Pike, and D. Selby, *Earthrights: Education As If the Planet Really Mattered* (London: World Wildlife Fund/Kogan Page, 1987), for an educators' guide to four emerging educations: peace education, human rights education, development education, and environmental education.

5 See Ian M. Harris, "From World Peace to Peace in the 'Hood: Peace Education in a Postmodern World," *Journal for a Just and Caring Education*, 2, no. 4 (October 1996): 382.

6 Ian. M. Harris, *From World Peace to Peace in the 'Hood*," 387.

7 See A. E. J. Wals, *Pollution Stinks!*

8 See also M. Berg and E. A. Medrich, "Children in Four Neighborhoods: The Physical Environment and Its Effect on Play and Play Patterns," *Environment and Behavior* 12, no. 3 (1980): 320–348.

9   Although some argue that the early roots of action research can be traced back to John Dewey, Kurt Lewin's 1946 article is most often cited as the first documented description of action research as both a methodology and a philosophy. See K. Lewin, "Action Research and Minority Problems," *Journal of Social Issues* 26 (1946): 3–23.

10 S. Kemmis, "Action Research," in *International Encyclopedia of Education: Research and Studies, Volume I, A–B*, ed. T. Husen and T. Postlethwaite (Oxford: Pergamon, 1986), 42.

11 See W. Carr and S. Kemmis, *Becoming Critical: Education, Knowledge and Action Research* (London, Falmer Press, 1986). For some of the earlier writings on the use of action research in the context of education within the United States see S. M. Corey, *Action Research To Improve School Practices*. (New York: Teachers' College Press, 1953).

12 See W. B. Stapp and A. E. J. Wals, "An Action Research Approach To Environmental Problem Solving," in *Environmental Problem Solving: Theory, Practice and Possibilities in Environmental Education*, ed. L. V. Bardwell, M. C. Monroe and M. T. Tudor (Troy, Ohio: NAAEE, 1994), 49–66 or A. E. J. Wals and W. B. Stapp, "Education in Action: A Community Problem Solving Program for Schools,", in *Building Multi-Cultural Webs through Environmental Education*, 1988 NAAEE conference proceedings, ed. L. A. Iozzi and C. L. Shepard (NAAEE, Troy, Ohio, 1988), 235–240 for one of the first descriptions of AR&CPS.

13 A. E. J. Wals, "Action Taking and Environmental Problem Solving in Environmental Education," in *Action and Action Competence as Key Concepts in Critical Pedagogy*. B. B. Jensen and K. Schnack (Eds), Didaktische studier, Volume 12. (Kopenhagen, Royal Danish School for Educational Studies, 1994), 135–163.

14 See James N. Bull et al., *Education in Action: A Community Problem Solving Program for Schools* (Dexter, Michigan: ThomsonShore, 1988) and A. E. J. Wals, A. Beringer and W. B. Stapp, "Education in Action a Community Problem Solving Program for Schools," *Journal of Environmental Education*, 21, no. 4, (1990): 13–20.

15 For a detailed description of the school and the community I refer to A. E. J. Wals, *Pollution Stinks! Young adolescents' perceptions of nature and environmental issues with implications for education in urban settings*. (De Lier, Netherlands: Academic Book Center, ABC, 1994), 27–44.

16 For other examples of ways of using AR&CPS in urban, suburban and rural environments at different school levels I refer to W. B. Stapp, A. E. J. Wals and S. Stankorb, *Environmental education for empowerment: action research and community problem solving* (Dubuque, Iowa: Kendall/Hunt, 1996).

17 Garbarino even suggests that children growing up in situations like these must turn off their feelings in order to survive. See J. Garbarino, J., K. Kostelny

and N. Dubrow, *No Place to be a Child: Growing Up in a War Zone* (Lexington, MA, D.C. Heath and Company, 1991). For thick descriptions of the students' lives I refer to A.E.J. Wals, *Pollution Stinks!*

18   See also J. M. Bull, "The effect of participation in an environmental action program on empowerment, interest and problem solving skills of inner city students' (Ph.D. diss., University of Michigan, 1992).

19   W. B. Stapp, A. E. J. Wals and S. Stankorb, *Environmental education for empowerment: action research and community problem solving* (Dubuque, Iowa: Kendall/Hunt, 1996) contains a section on skill-building activities which can be infused in the AR&CPS process should a lack of specific skills prevent the process from progressing.

20   See M. C. Monroe, "Converting "It's no use" into "Hey, there's a lot I can do:" A matrix for Environmental Action Taking," in *Setting the EE Agenda for the '90's*, 1990 NAAEE Conference Proceedings, eds. D. A. Simmons, C. Knapp and C. Young (Troy, OH: NAAEE), 141-148.

21   See K. E. Weick, "Small Wins: Redefining the Scale of Social Problems," *American Psychologist*, 19, no. 1 (1984): 40-49.

22   For examples see James N. Bull et al., *Environmental Endeavors: Examples for Student Problem Solving* (Ann Arbor, Michigan: Global Rivers Environmental Education Network, 1990) and L. V. Bardwell, M. C. Monroe and M. T. Tudor, *Environmental Problem Solving: Theory, Practice and Possibilities in Environmental Education* (Troy, Ohio: NAAEE, 1994).

23   See also L. Vriens and J. Grootscholten, "Peace Education and Teaching Conflict in School: An Action Research Project," Unpublished paper presented at the Third International Conference on Education for the Role of Civil Society in Cultures of Peace, University of Cincinnati, April 15-20, 1997. Copies available from the author upon request.

24   An observation made earlier by M. C. Monroe, "Converting "It's no use" into "Hey, there's a lot I can do: "A matrix for Environmental Action Taking," in *Setting the EE Agenda for the '90's*, 1990 NAAEE Conference Proceedings, eds. D. A. Simmons, C. Knapp and C. Young (Troy, OH: NAAEE), 141-148.

25   B. B. Jensen and K. Schnack, "Action Competence as an Educational Challenge," in *Action and Action Competence as Key Concepts in Critical Pedagogy*. B. B. Jensen and K. Schnack (eds), Didaktiske studier, Volume 12. (Kopenhagen, Royal Danish School for Educational Studies, 1994), 5-19.

26   Vriens and Grootscholten, *Peace Education and Teaching Conflict in School: An Action Research Project*. Reference is made to J. Galtung, "Probleme der Friedenserziehung," in *Kritischer Friedenserziehung*, ed. C. Wulf, (Frankfurt am Main: Suhrkamp, 1973).

27   Vriens and Grootscholten, *Peace Education and Teaching Conflict in School: An Action Research Project*, 3-4. In a footnote Vriens remarks that he does

not agree with Galtung that unequal power in the pedagogical relationship is necessarily violent. Parents and teachers, he argues, often use their power to help the child. Vriens does agree with Galtung that the message of the form of peace education often precedes that of the content.

28   W. B. Stapp, A. E. J. Wals and S. Stankorb, *Environmental education for empowerment: action research and community problem solving* (Dubuque, Iowa: Kendall/Hunt, 1996).

29   Organization for Economic and Cultural Development-Center for Educational Research and Innovation, *Environment, schools and active learning*, Final report of the environment and schools' initiatives project (ENSI) (Paris: OECD, 1994) and Organization for Economic and Cultural Development-Center for Educational Research and Innovation, *Environmental learning for the 21st century* (Paris: OECD, 1995).

30   P. Freire, *Pedagogy of the Oppressed* (New York: Continuum, 1986), 85.

Chapter 14

Special Needs, Special Measures: Working with Homeless and Poor Youth

Dé Bryant, Jennifer Hanis, and Charles Stoner

Homeless families (defined as parents with children) are the fastest-growing segment of the homeless population. A 1996 estimate places the number of homeless families in the United States at over 40 percent of all homeless people.[1] Working with homeless and poor populations involves special issues, especially when working with youths. Traditional psychological methods and measures are inadequate to describe their plight—and even less adequate to explain it. Using conventional art or drama therapy when working with homeless youths presents problems due to the transient nature of the population, the unusual living conditions in which these children find themselves, and the special psychological needs such circumstances create. The use of qualitative methods and other community psychology research tools is a more successful approach to addressing the needs of this disenfranchised population. These findings are similar to the findings of earlier research conducted in a southwestern lower Michigan city experiencing urban decline.[2]

The Social Action Project

The Social Action Project (SOCACT) is an action research project to foster empowerment among youths in urban communities. The SOCACT operates in the United States and in Nigeria, allowing for comparative study of the psychological problems of living associated with urban decline. In the United States the project is conducted in two medium-sized, Midwestern communities; in Nigeria the site is a comparable community in Oboland. Researchers collaborate with the client community to define the problem, develop action plans, and implement solutions.

The SOCACT began in 1984 as a part of an initiative between Michigan State University and a nearby community. In 1990 the SOCACT moved to Indiana University, South Bend, and was housed in the Psychology Department, where it remains today. The principal investigator responds to calls for assistance from community groups or individuals by sending in teams of practitioners and scientists. The teams talk with people in the community to understand the problem, decide the best approach to bring about change, and work with residents to make it all happen. When the residents have learned to protect themselves, the teams move on to answer the next call.

Along the way, the teams conduct important research on problems faced by people in communities. The findings from these studies have been presented at professional conferences in the United States, Canada, and Nigeria. They have also appeared in lay and professional outlets—all to try to close the gap between what social scientists believe they know and what happens to real people. Most important, people in the communities also receive the findings and the teams work with them to implement next steps, enabling them to gain mastery over their life situations. SOCACT is composed of five joint community-university components; the Youth Community Theater (YCT) is the subject of this writing.

The intervention strategy used in SOCACT places the principal investigator at the nexus of concentric circles of influence (see figure 1). She trains a team of scientist-practitioners, who then go out and train others, who will go out in their turn and train the local people they know. Data comes back following the same paths, in reverse. Through this approach, the SOCACT team members are participant-observers in the quest to understand the unspoken issues that always underlie events unfolding in a community. It is these issues that help shape the psychological development of individuals such as the youths in the study reported here.[3]

The SOCACT team is an interracial team of United States and Nigerian students, community residents, and professionals from various disciplines. As the project operates, the components that comprise SOCACT remain the same, but the faces of the team members change. Team members cycle onto the team, work in a component for a num-

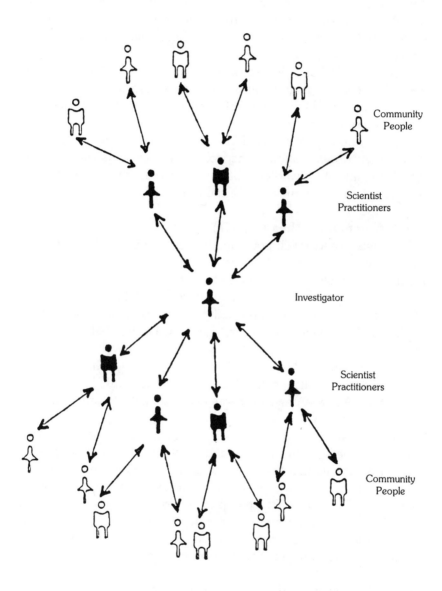

Figure 1 Intervention Team

ber of years, then exit the team. Once a team member exists, the project they were involved with continues with a new set of faces. Team members are required to remain an average of two years. SOCACT is an official course in the psychology curriculum at Indiana University. Students receive three credit hours per semester for participation on the research team.

The SOCACT has a diverse network of supporters, including academic sources, religious organizations, civic associations, and individual donors. In addition, the project receives a steady measure of in-kind resources to cover operational needs. International travel and expenses have been supported by university grants and global nongovernmental organizations. The work is further supported by individual team members who have been willing to use their own financial resources to advance the goals of the project.

Youth Community Theater (YCT)

YCT targets underserved, poor, and homeless youths (whose average age is twelve years old). The focus of this theater is to encourage multicultural explorations of heritage, history, and personal experience beginning with comparisons of African and U.S. cultures. The theater group provides an opportunity for youths in the community to express hidden talents and artistic abilities that will help build self-esteem and self-efficacy. Parents can become involved, thereby enhancing relationships among family members through shared activity and established mutual goals. Through its productions the YCT educates about African-American heritage and its links to other cultures at home and abroad.

The YCT was created after talking with youths and parents about what they believed would make the greatest impact on their quality of life. Residents said that their greatest desire was to be heard, to have some forum in which to express their ideas or dreams without fear of censorship. There is a YCT group in the local neighborhood and a second in a homeless center. To date the youths have performed two original plays, an adaptation of "Hansel and Gretel," and original vignettes for hand puppets at venues around the area.

Action Research: Intervention and Science

The YCT is both an intervention and a research project. As an intervention, it is a creative channel, a safe outlet for expressing thoughts, ideas, and fears. Art and drama are used to develop a positive self-concept, to improve peer interaction and cooperation, and to function as a learning tool for peacebuilding. As youths in the YCT write the scripts for their productions, they explore the nature of violence in their lives.

As a research study, the YCT is a primary prevention project designed to address a problem before its effects become debilitating. The SOCACT team seeks to learn more about what motivates the youths and what shapes their choices when faced with conflict. The SOCACT tries to identify ways to understand self-esteem (confidence and satisfaction with oneself) and improve self-efficacy (belief that one's actions make an impact) among homeless and poor youths. As the stories take shape, SOCACT team members are able to correlate the youth's perceptions about life with their choices for resolving the conflicts of life.

Data for the project is collected using a cluster of instruments: standardized inventories, project-generated process logs, network analysis, and content analysis of artistic products. Findings from these multiple sources are triangulated to identify consistencies, which are then interpreted in the context of prevailing theories of homelessness, psychological development, and primary prevention.

Theoretical Framework

Homelessness

The literature search for this project focused on homeless youths and their families. The literature dealt primarily with theories about the causes of homelessness, focusing on demographic characteristics, risk factors, broad patterns of welfare use, and public policy recommendations.[4] A national conference on homelessness held in 1996 focused on the numbers of homeless people and the burden they place on existing services.[5] A search for regional sources showed that among homeless people violence is found within the family unit itself. In reporting her study of homeless youths in Indianapolis, Barbara Lucas wrote:

> Over two-thirds of the youth reported being neglected by the people who raised them, three-quarters reported being hit, and one-fourth reported being tied up or locked up, one-fourth reported being sexually assaulted by those who raised them.[6]

Other studies report findings of violence as a fact of life for many of America's homeless and poor. In many cases this is second-generation violence, as mothers and fathers repeat the actions of their own parents and other caregivers.[7] This lack of compassion and nurturing plays a role in the lack of interactional social skills in poor and homeless youth. A personal communication with Beth Morlock, Assistant Director of Family Services at the Center for the Homeless in South Bend, Indiana, observes:

> I do not know how many times I have seen a mother carry a child up the stairs by the arm, never carrying that child, never being nurturing. These children are sponges for nurturing and compassion, to the point of trying to fill up other holes in their lives with it.[8]

A comparable finding was reported by Ellen Bassuk and E. M. Galagher, noting that homeless children search for adults to nurture them, turning to siblings for support and nurturing.[9]

Art and Drama
Few writings were available that showed how art therapy is used as an intervention with homeless persons. The use of art and drama as mechanisms for social change is well documented in social movement literature. Examples include urban guerilla theater in the United States, Mexican muralists, and the theater of the oppressed in South Africa.[10] In psychology literature, art therapy is used almost exclusively for diagnosis and treatment of individuals suffering from abuse or similar deep-seated trauma rather than as a preventive strategy.[11] The search did not reveal an intervention that used art therapy to address the needs of the homeless.

Individuals and the Collective
To accomplish a primary prevention—such as peacebuilding through social justice—it is necessary to understand the culture in which people are embedded. Culture exists at different levels, each a concentric circle moving further away from the individual. Peace, defined by its positive connotation of bringing about social justice, is conceptualized as working in a bottom-up rather than a top-down fashion. This means changing how individuals respond to violence in order to ultimately change general cultural norms about dealing with violence.

At an individual level observational learning allows intrinsic rewards from within the individual (self-esteem) to combine with extrinsic rewards originating outside the individual (self-efficacy) to support new, nonviolent behaviors.[12] Because people do not exist within a vacuum, the larger culture must also be included in the intervention. When individuals define their own issues and press for social change to address these issues, a sense of personal power results in collective action.[13]

Violence: Pervasive and Powerful

Homelessness and poverty are complex social conditions that have a direct impact on personality development. Because of the nature of today's society, homeless and poor people deal with violence on a daily basis. Young people start developing violent behavior at an early age, and violent behaviors continue, often escalating, through adulthood.[14] Findings from the youths involved in the SOCACT's Youth Community Theater illustrate the pervasiveness of violence in their lives.

Theater in the Neighborhood

Youths working with the SOCACT team in the low-income neighborhood have written, staged, and performed three plays. Two of the plays described life in their community and spoke of violence as a daily fact. The portrayals went beyond shootings on the playground and drug deals in the local parking lot. The vignettes depicted domestic violence and violence in the schools—followed by descriptions of how they made life fun even with the violence as a backdrop.

The young people wrote stories of a harsh world. They wrote about life with shootings, drugs, gangs. Even in all this mayhem, they were still able to find the stuff of childhood good times: skating, fairs, and parades.

> Story #1
> My name is ———. B. H. is the most dangerous place to lie. You can't even sleep 'cause every 5 minutes you hear an ambulance or police car. But it is not as bad as you think it is. B. H. is a city of dreams. Every year there is a parade and carnival. You will have a great time and leave with a big smile on your face.
> Story #2
> B. H. is dangerous. The reason why it is dangerous is because [sic]. There is always people shoot other stupid people. Sometimes B. H. can be really fun. Some of the fun places are the show, playground, and the skating ring. But more important I will never leave B. H.
> Story #3
> B. H. is a very nice place to stay in. We tike tom [sic] play basketball at the park. We like to go to the YWCA. We like to go shopping. We play a lot of games. People sell drugs. People be shooting in the streets.

These writers are sixth graders in a community that has had its social fabric ripped apart. They live in a city that leads the nation in crime and violence per capita and has one of the highest teenage pregnancy rates in the nation. This violent world for many youths exists not only in this community but in many others in this nation. This is where we need to focus our attention in any effort to "build peace," that is, to help restore the social fabric in this and other communities before they are torn beyond repair.

Theater in the Homeless Center

Young people at the homeless center have begun to write stories for hand puppets made from old socks, buttons, and an assortment of fabric pieces. Interviews with the children about their puppets revealed stories about power struggles between siblings and parents. More strikingly, the interviews also demonstrated the difficulty some children had with the concept of "excessive" violence. To them, violence is how conflicts are resolved, and they cannot envision any other standard of justice.

During interviews at the Center for the Homeless, children told stories using puppets they had made during earlier visits. These stories included many references to violence as a problem-solving mechanism:

> Story #4
> One child related a story that involved a challenge to the power structure between the puppet and its siblings. The names used were the same as this child's actual siblings, including an older brother that he was also having problems with in the same areas. It soon became clear after continued questioning that this child was experiencing similar power struggles in his own life and that he and the puppet were using the same violent tactics in overcoming these conflicts, such as sneak attacks while his brother slept and mutual biting. He claimed that the conflict was resolved by his striking his brother in the head and both agreeing to stop and not to tell their mother about the incident.

During the telling of this story the child displayed two bite marks (one on his upper arm, one on his forearm) that were inflicted by his older brother. He also displayed several bruises on his arms. Though it was not clear from the child's presentation exactly how these marks were produced, they were clear evidence of the violence in real life that the child transferred to the story of his puppet's life.

The characters in another child's story all had weapons as a part of their essential identities. The story about the characters used excessive violence in the main storyline within an "us against them" framework.

Special Needs, Special Measures 271

> Story #5
> Max the superhero had claws that came out of his knuckles and had a laser beam in his eye that zaps people into ashes. He was a wimp in the beginning who got beat up a lot. His enemies are also now super-villains who used to be normal and always used to beat on Max. He (Max) has a son who is half superhero and has powers. Jr's hands can turn into anything. Max has a normal wife and several brothers and sisters who are normal as well as having special powers. One sister Beth crushes people's heads by squeezing them. Her hair barrettes fly off and can cut people's heads off. His son's eyeball also serves as a weapon and can be removed and thrown as a bomb. His hand can also serve this same purpose.

The names of these characters are drawn from this child's own siblings and in many ways mimic her own life. This child was separated from her parents at age seven and had constant fights with her siblings involving physical violence, hitting, biting, and sneak attacks while they slept. The parallels with the storyline illustrate the violence pervasive in these children's lives.

Theater across an Ocean

Youths in the United States participated in an exchange program, writing letters and sending mementos to youths in Iboland, Nigeria. They wrote and recorded a radio play to send overseas to their new friends in another culture. Their stories consistently depicted violent encounters, but they also displayed youthful simplicity. On the same audiotape the youths described muggings committed by crack addicts and tried to describe snow to people who had only seen it in pictures.

> Log Entry #1
> Children sent drawings that also described common elements of their daily lives. In the Ibo culture, family and social relationships provide the social context for how the children think about themselves. As a result, their pictures depicted the extended family of grandparents and distant relatives as the central part of the composition. Children also drew their physical surroundings: cars, homes, or vegetation.

The most notable difference between the two sets of stories was that the Ibo youths did not talk about violence or crime. This was very consistent with the norms of their culture. Socialization emphasizes personal honor and integrity, especially in terms of considering the impact of one's actions on the family or the larger community. Traditional notions of social responsibility translate into daily life in the form of neighborhoods that are self-policing. When problems occur— such as a break-in or an assault—community leaders step in to bring the situation under control.

Log Entry #2
As we started back toward the judge's home, we passed the youth. One had pulled a knife on a masquerade and an argument ensued. Both chiefs quickly intervened. There was pushing and shouting, and angry words were exchanged. By the time our company returned to us, the whole town (it seemed) had converged upon the youth—arrested them and questioned them. They found they weren't even from their village: "we didn't even know their faces." What was really interesting was the conversation that followed. If a yell is heard within a compound, everyone near will respond. They will find out the problem and work out a solution to address the problem right there. The (village) government is such that no decision is ever up to the individual.

Special Needs, Special Measures

Conventional therapeutic assessment techniques presented many challenging dilemmas. Ultimately these approaches were replaced in order to make the intervention relevant to the youths and to produce useable research data. In a setting like the Center for the Homeless, qualitative methods of measuring self-concept are more useful than traditional quantitative methods. The original plan to use the Norwicki and Strickland Locus of Control Scale and other pencil and paper tests was scrapped, it having been found that factors related to ethnicity truly decreased their validity.[15] The pre-post methods to test the impact of the intervention were equally invalid. Transience makes the concept of pre-post testing useless as there is no way of knowing how many, if any, of the original subjects will be participating when it comes time to post-test. Data was collected using unstructured interviews, process logs, and participant observation.

The special psychological needs of these groups require special methods. Lack of cooperation among the youths was a major factor that made conventional methods of intervention ineffective. Youths in the neighborhood YCT coalesced around a few powerful personalities whose wishes tended to sway the entire group. The final plays were strongly imprinted with those personalities. Youths in the homeless center YCT were unable to cooperate with each other. They tended to engage in verbally and physically aggressive behavior, leading finally to five separate projects. Excerpts from field notes illustrate this inability to cooperate:

Log Entry #3
Youths arguing concerning who would be in or out of the group. [Our] regular kids have no sense of sharing or cooperation. The interactions between [resi-

dent] children continue to be negative. Displays of violent problem-solving skills, striking out and hitting, if perceived space is invaded. Threats of violence are most predominant. Lots of perceived threats of losing use of objects in hands, no concept of personal space, boundaries, and responsibilities for actions. This is a very disturbing display, even from kids who were in control and cooperative in previous sessions.

Log Entry #4
We broke up into groups, my group out of control, unable to work together. Everyone talking at once, two groups involved in their own conversations. Constant need to intervene with little success.

Log Entry #5
I felt the evening was a disaster of chaos and had to leave the room. I do not believe that this group will ever have the cohesion to work as one on any project.

Log Entry #6
It was total chaos. We had one last craft session and it was horrible. It was so chaotic that I didn't even have a chance to get a count of kids, moms, or names.

These excerpts illustrate the great difficulty that the children had in cooperating with each other, and how this inability quickly escalated into violent and aggressive behavior.

Strategies for Positive Peacebuilding

It will be remarkably difficult to instill the language of peace—defined as the absence of violence—into youths embedded in U. S. society's most violent neighborhoods. Findings from the SOCACT theater project suggest that teaching youths to understand peace as an ability to find alternatives in the midst of the violence will be most effective. This involves building self-efficacy as well as teaching peacemaking skills.

Cultural Awareness and Self-Efficacy
The link between knowledge about one's cultural heritage and consciousness raising has been clearly established in, for example, the writings of Paolo Freire and bell hooks.[16] Cultural awareness should go beyond making information available to initiate an educational process that incorporates new knowledge into everyday living.

Youths in the SOCACT study were found to be suspicious and distrustful of the unfamiliar. This resistance extended to information the team provided, which was more likely to be rejected out of hand than it was to be explored as an alternative perspective. The youths needed to learn to value education about their heritage, but they needed more than that. Self-efficacy is about the exercise of control. A mechanism to make the facts about African history and culture relevant to their immediate world was sought. In this way the youths could also learn to use their new sense of self to construct nonviolent conflict resolution.

The pen pals activity provided young people in South Bend with personal contacts with Ibo young people in Nigeria. The Nigerian youths had faces, names, and families and provided a human connection to Nigerian culture. Discussions about standards of justice and ethical principles had a personal context for the youths on both sides of the ocean. They exchanged questions and stories about what they did to make a difference in their families and their neighborhoods, sometimes sending pictures (photographs and original artwork) to better explain.

Story #6
My name is ———. I am a boy of 11 years. I am in primary five and my best subject is English. My parents are ———. My father is (*illegible*) and my mother is bright. I have 4 brothers and 2 sisters. We have a happy home. My country Nigeria is a big one. There are 30 states with Ybrahim Babgida as the president. Each state is divided into local governments. Abia state has 17 local governments. We are under the military rule. Our money is *naira* and *kobo*. We have petroleum, cocoa, cotton, groundnuts, oil palm. I would like to know more about you and your country in your next letter. (His letter was accompanied by a drawing of a van, with the caption "Nigerian car.")

Story #7
I am 13 years old. My name is ———. My parents live at ———, Abia State. The name of my father is ———. I am the 4th child of my parents. I am dark in complexion. Please, I want to ask you about your parents. I know that your parents are well. Please reply this letter back to me and I need your own passport [photo] from you. God bless you. Good bye (sic). Thanks.

Story #8
I would like your country. Do you like your country? Everybody like (sic) his/her country. Are you a Christian? Me, I am a Christian. If you don't know it now. And too I am male and 11 years old. Now I am in primary 6 now.

Nonviolent Outlets for Violent Emotions
Working with the children separately at Center for the Homeless was very fruitful and led us to the idea of using interviews. The use of interviews about puppets that the children made proved to be the best

way for children to communicate to us about their views of themselves and their worlds. We noticed that the information in the stories they gave about their puppets seemed to mimic their own lives in many ways, including how central violence is to their day-to-day lives.

The interviews we had with the children were unstructured because the talks were adopted as a research tool only as a result of the children's resistance to standardized assessment tests. The children either treated the tests as if there was a right or wrong answer (and consistently asked team members what the right answer was) or, motivated by their distrust refused to take the test at all.

In future research, the interviews should be much more deliberate with a list of specific questions to be answered. Questions should be asked about the puppet's age, gender, ethnicity, family members, friends, personality, and life history. These questions would enable researchers to ascertain information about the self-concepts of the children with a positive, nonviolent, safe, and creative outlet for thoughts, ideas, and fears.

The puppets could also be used as tools to teach more appropriate problem-solving skills than the violence that comes through in the children's stories. The cloth devices may be used as examples of cooperation and positive problem solving as well as a way to help promote a sense of peaceful community and cooperation in the children and with respect to their interactions. Since the children relate their puppet's lives so closely to their own, learning to alter the behavior and characteristics of the puppet could conceivably help the child make changes in her or his own life.

The puppets were also a tangible possession that the children could keep and take with them when they left the homeless center. This tangible object can in many cases fill the hole from the sense of loss some homeless children experience with the loss of their own possessions. Many times a child's toys and possessions are not the first things grabbed up when leaving a home setting. Parents are more likely to gather clothing and shoes, as they are of more immediate importance than a toy or book.

The idea of possessing something is a need all children have and the puppet can help to fill that need. It also can become of more importance than other objects, for the object is the child's creation, not just a donated toy. This is something that was demonstrated three weeks after the session ended; the children in the Center for the Homeless were still talking to staff about their puppets.

The puppet project allowed the kids to work on their own projects individually to compensate for the lack of privacy they experience living in the environment of the Center for the Homeless. We have found that this kind of one-on-one attention is important, as it seems to help strengthen the children's sense of identity and their need to feel connected to others.

Feelings of being disconnected are common among homeless children. These feelings stem from separation from classmates and friends, family members, and their homes. The environment of the homeless shelter can be cold and unfriendly, a place with many strange faces, odd meal times, and in some cases lack of community. Such circumstances may also make a child feel unsafe and insecure. Both feelings and realities can increase a child's sense of disconnection.

Involvement in the Youth Community Theater project can help increase a child's sense of being connected, being part of, not out of, a group. This sense of belonging can help instill the idea of peacebuilding in the community of the Center, a world of which the child can then feel she or he is a major part.

Regular times set aside for individual theater projects could help defuse some of the violent behavior displayed by the children. It was observed that when the children included their friends and siblings in their stories, it led to more cooperative behavior for the duration of the visit to the setting. Future research will be needed to see if this increased ability to cooperate is incorporated into the child's day-to-day interaction.

Local Lessons From The Global Village

Youths in the United States had many questions about daily life in the Nigerian community. They were surprised to hear that neither crime nor drug use were major social problems. Many young people were even more amazed to hear that their Nigerian counterparts held strong beliefs about social justice and responsibility. For their part, the most frequent comment Nigerian youths made about U.S. life was to marvel that a nation so rich could be so dangerous and lonely. They pointed out that even the existing military dictatorship did not fracture their communities.

Discussion among the youths on separate sides of the world had in common a desire for peace: a sense of community defined as a pursuit of mutual interests, a desire for safety, and a respect for other individuals in the family or surrounding neighborhood.[17] The comparisons between the U.S. youths and their pen pals in Nigeria suggest strategies for setting priorities that meet the needs of individuals and, thereby, empower the communities in which they live.

The questions of cultural differences must be considered as much by advocates in the United States as by those in Nigeria. Peacebuilding, also known as primary prevention in the field of community psychology, can only be done effectively if its strategies are culturally valid. Members of the team directing the Pen Pal project with Nigerian youths did not assume they understood Ibo culture. It would have been an equally grave mistake for members of the Theater team to assume that the homeless and poor in the United States were like the middle class, only with less money.[18]

Cultural differences among economic groups have roots just as deep as those that cross national borders. Social norms transcend consumer opportunities or political regimes to a mindset based on completely different priorities regarding emotional well-being, life skills, support systems, role models, and knowledge of the hidden rules of a group.

Offset the Attractiveness of Violence

The SOCACT was created with the objective to identify action strategies to help people deal with the issues of their lives. For homeless and poor youths, whether in the United States or abroad, this means finding ways to manage violence. The Theater and Pen Pal projects provided youths with opportunities to talk about violence through expression and modeling.

As the U.S. youths wrote stories for plays and puppets, they were able to explore how they handled confrontation and to talk with team members about alternatives. In this way they were able to choose and control emotional responses, particularly to negative situations, without resorting to destructive behavior. This ability was an internal resource that will manifest itself through stamina, perseverance, and ultimately the ability to make better choices in confrontational situations. The letters from Nigerian youths gave U.S. youths a window through which to view a lifestyle by which people handled violence through communal action.

Team members who were part of the Theater project served as role models: adult(s) who were appropriately selecting nonviolent alternatives to conflict resolution, who were nurturing to the child, and who did not engage in self-destructive behavior. Youths in the Theater project had frequent access to these adults, saw these strategies put to work, and had someone to talk with about their outcomes. Each member of the SOCACT team, including those involved with the Theater and

Pen Pals projects makes, as already noted, an eighteen-month commitment. Consequently, they become long-term contacts and consistent voices for YCT participants.

Participants in the Theater and Pen Pals projects were able to help youths identify their own mental abilities and acquired skills (reading, writing, computing). Especially for poor adolescents in the United States, their strengths have rarely been highlighted and they do not see their ability to deal with daily life in positive ways. Teachable moments about the value of their survival skills occurred as the U.S. children were reading letters from their Nigerian correspondents. The stories the U.S. children wrote in response illustrated their ability to see the good in their violent town.

The SOCACT team members modeled nonviolent conflict resolution, compassion, and cultural sensitivity as the youths developed materials for the YCT productions. In this way the team maximized the youths' realizations about their self-efficacy, building strategies for nonviolent alternatives to be transferred to their daily lives.

Although the SOCACT team members were neither a part of the South Bend community nor the Ibo community, they functioned as support systems and as external resources to the youths. In the U.S. they acted as backup support, available in times of need. In Nigeria, they were links to a world beyond the local scope for children in the Ibo community. In both settings, the team members were conduits that allowed information, services, and positive regard to flow between youths in the two communities. Such are the raw materials of peacebuilding.

Building Global Awareness

The structure of power has pancultural dimensions: "out-group," "in-group," and "boundary people" that cross national and socioeconomic lines. Oppression and discrimination work the same no matter what causes a group of people to be an out-group. Privileges provide certain opportunities regardless of the reasons why the in-group dominates in the society. In this context, the SOCACT teams function as the boundary people who can carry information between groups. They contact the "sociometric stars," those who wield social power, real or ascribed. These stars act as change agents in the peacebuilding process by taking their experiences and the things they have learned into their community spheres.[19] In both the Pen Pals and the Theater projects, the youths were the stars.

In their analysis of poor people's movements, Frances Piven and Richard Cloward found that the most viable movements were those whose action moved in concentric circles of influence from the local setting to national initiatives.[20] Dé Bryant's study of the Nestlé Boycott protesting the inhumane marketing of breast milk substitutes concluded that its survival was supported by the connections of local action cells with international counterparts.[21] David Korten came to a similar conclusion about the future of voluntary action as a method of international development.[22]

In her work with homeless unions, Susan Yeich supported the strategy of using interlocking action cells to ultimately eliminate homelessness.[23] Although the process she described is highly politicized, the concept of crossing geographic boundaries to link people with similar problems easily transfers to the work of the Social Action Project. The Youth Community Theater and Pen Pals projects are the mechanisms through which youths from different worlds talk with one another. The plays, puppet shows, and letters that have been written or exchanged have established contacts to allow SOCACT to further develop its local-global structures.

That progression will continue with an eight-week summer program studying issues related to self-esteem, self-efficacy, and relationships, using arts education as the mechanism. The program will include training in drama, storytelling, dance, music, and mural painting. Folklore, rhythms, art, and songs from both cultures will be incorporated into programs wherever appropriate. The program also includes a week of rural camp experience during which the summer's lessons and products may be polished and youth more soundly anchored in new attitudes and behaviors. Upon completion of the camp experience, participants will demonstrate their new skills, creations, and beliefs via community exhibitions and performances. These performances and exhibitions will be a venue for reinforcement from and to families, friends, and significant adults from the communities of the young people.

The program is a two-year effort that also entails follow-up interviews and activities during the regular school year. A second year of the cycle will repeat the training-camp-performance sequence to provide a higher level of experience for participants from the first year. They will act as mentors and counselors for new participants. New programs will utilize the same broad elements (drama, music, dance, and visual art), but will be grounded by insights gained during the first year of operation. The systematic nature of data collection will allow the program to design replicable models for prevention that can be used in other communities.

In keeping with findings from previous research on social movements, the summer program moves the SOCACT program beyond the local scope. With the completion of the two-year pilot program, the SOCACT will move its operations into Redbud Community Retreat. The Redbud will be a year-round rural camp serving communities in a ten-county area of Michigan and Indiana. Links with Nigeria will be maintained and the SOCACT will expand into South Africa to expand the global aspect of its programming. Materials and resources from international connections will continue to be incorporated into the YCT and Pen Pals components. By the year 2000 this peacebuilding effort will potentially benefit thousands of youths and their families in the United States and abroad.

To Bring About Peace
The nonviolent "beloved community" to which so many of us aspire cannot be attained by waiting for nirvana to reveal itself. Primary violence prevention strategies such as the Social Action Project can bring about justice through action research and systematic intervention. There are no magic words, no fiery lights. There is belief, diligence, pragmatism, and endurance. Ultimately, there will be peace.

Notes

1. Susan Yeich (1994) presents an impressive array of statistics about the characteristics and circumstances of the homeless. Her argument about the viability of homeless unions is built on the proposition that the sheer numbers of homeless people will make them a formidable force.

2. The Social Action Project has generated a series of works that have been presented at professional conferences in the United States, Canada, and Nigeria. A number of the papers are unpublished papers given by students at undergraduate research conferences and others that appear in books or professional journals. For example, Bryant (1995, 1997) examines the utility of using the team as social change agents. The challenges of a participant-observer methodology are addressed in Bryant (1996). Bryant and Mettetal (1966) present a model for improving university teaching by combining it with community research.

3. Compelling evidence has been presented documenting the positive effects of an entrepreneurial agent in coordinating effective social interventions. An entrepreneurial agent is an individual or group that facilitates goal attainment during the intervention through problem redefinition, identification of new resources, and the creation of new linkages between groups or individuals. McCarthy and Zald (1973) examined interventions in the United States using an entrepreneurial agent model and reported the effectiveness of these agents. They discuss the dynamics and tactics of movement growth, decline, and change in McCarthy and Zald (1987). Jenkins (1983) reviewed a number of social interventions in which entrepreneurial agents played significant roles. In each case a cadre of individuals helped inspire citizen participation, defined as involvement in any organized activity in which the individual participates without pay in order to achieve a common goal. The entrepreneurs can work within an informal association with representatives from organizations with mutually beneficial goals. The resulting resource network drives the intervention. Sarason and Lorentz (1979) presented a fine discussion of this network and its potential. Steven Buechler (1993) identified ten issues that collectively pose a major theoretical challenge to the dominance of resource mobilization.

4. *American Psychologist* (1991) is a special issue on homelessness that contains sections on research, services, and social policy; homeless persons with alcohol, drug, and mental health disorders; social and physical health issues faced by homeless women, children, and families; and the necessary professional response and appropriate advocacy agenda. Useful discussions about the structural nature of homelessness and its link to aid to dependent children can be found in Bassuk et al. (1997), Bassuk and Galagher (1990), McChesney (1990), McChesney (1995), Salomon et al. (1996), and Bassuk et al. (1996).

5   The Conference on Homelessness was sponsored by the Social Policy and Environmental Administration, Indiana University: South Bend, 1996. The attendees were practitioners and policymakers from across the United States. The objective was to take the initiative in providing research to inform impending policy decisions that will come about as a result of welfare reforms.

6   Barbara Lucas and Lena Hackett, *Street Youths on Their Own in Indianapolis* (1990) was a collaboration between practitioners and policy developers in the Greater Indianapolis Area. The quote is on page 23.

7   The writings of Browne and Bassuk (1997) talk about the role of race and gender in homelessness. They list being a minority and a single female head of household as major risk indicators of becoming homeless and remaining chronically homeless. They also talk about the incidence of substance abuse as contributing to the difficulties homeless people face. Their writings should be compared with those of Perloff and Buckner (1996) that talk about the destructive impact of the absent (or near-absent) father has on the homeless family.

8   The Center for the Homeless provides food, shelter, and comprehensive life-building services for over 200 guests each day through widespread community support, especially volunteerism. The Center offers eighty beds for single men, twenty-one beds for single women, and fifteen apartments for families, all located on-site. The Youth Community Theater was integrated into the Center's services to fill the need for youth programs. The Center gained national attention in 1996 when it was officially designated a training center by the Department of Housing and Urban Development. The Center for the Homeless is located in South Bend, Indiana.

9   E. L. Bassuk and E. M. Galagher, "The Impact of Homelessness on Children" in *Homeless Children: The Watchers and the Waiters*, ed. N. A. Boxill (New York: Haworth Press, 1990).

10 There are many examples of urban theater in the United States.

11 Art therapy has been used most effectively with children who have been victims of sexual or physical abuse. There is a substantial body of literature that can be accessed using PsychLit or a similar computer search program.

12 In observational learning, people who observe a model learn the value of a behavioral performance in terms of what it will achieve. Learning occurs because people are aware of the consequences of their responses. People adopt other people's expectancies of those with whom they share relevant experiences. When an individual possesses self-confidence and self-satisfaction, the presence of such characteristics as assertiveness, optimism, the ability to handle rejection, and adaptive coping strategies are a function of self-perception. Fundamental works in self-esteem and social cognition can be found in G. W. Allport (1961, 1966) and Abraham Maslow (1970). Self-efficacy, the belief that one can achieve what one sets out to do, affects development, mental functioning, and health. Self-efficacy is a powerful self-regulatory process that

influences not only whether a person will attempt a behavior, but also determines the quality of performance once an attempt is made. The best-known proponent of self-efficacy is Bandura (1977, 1997).

13 Citizen participation is most effective when individuals define their own issues and press for social change to address them. P. Florin and A. Wandersman (1990) say that research about individuals who participate as citizens provides valuable insights because their actions emerge from systematic investigations of everyday problems. Zimmerman and Rappaport (1988) and O'Neill et al. (1988) stress the importance of people's perceptions of social reality.

14 Mary Ann Gleason (1996) is President of the National Coalition for the Homeless. Her paper at the Conference on Homelessness cautioned practitioners to remember that social programming for homeless persons is based on an erroneous assumption: the institutionalization of urgent relief. Shelters are an acceptable form of housing for the disadvantaged, but the institutionalization of shelters has made homelessness a problem. We force people to remain in crisis rather than revising policy. We spent more money managing crises than we would if we met the problem in the least expensive fashion with prevention.

15 Paolo Freire, *Pedagogy of the Oppressed* (New York: Continuum, 1989); bell hooks, *Teaching to Transgress: Education as Freedom* (New York: Routledge, 1990).

16 See Freire, *Pedagogy of the Oppressed* and bell hooks, *Teaching to Trangress*.

17 In the community psychology literature, a debate persists about the parameters of sense of community. The SOCACT operates using the definition that encompasses not only the physical environment in the neighborhood, but also intangibles such trust and personal identity (McMillan and Chavis, 1986).

18 Too many times social researchers assume that because neighborhoods are in close proximity to one another neighborhood social norms will be similar. In reality, there can be a world of difference between norms, differences that will interfere with attempts to understand how best to help a neighborhood achieve its goals. Bryant (1996) warned U.S. social scientists not to assume that all live by the same rules and not to indiscriminately apply the same methodologies to all communities.

19 Boundary people become the entrepreneurs that bring about social change. Because they are not truly members of any group, they are not strictly bound by the group's norms. Boundary people can violate those norms and still remain viable in a group because they are not full members anyway. Bryant (1996) discusses network analysis and its utility in creating social change in a U.S. neighborhood and a Nigerian community.

20 Frances Piven and Richard Cloward, *Poor People's Movements: Why They Succeed, How They Fail* (New York: Vintage Books, 1977).

21 Dé C. Bryant, "The Nestlé Boycott Movement: Evolution of a Social Action," (master's thesis, Wilfrid Laurier University, Waterloo, Ontario, 1985).

22 Korten (1990) describes the evolution of voluntary action as a method of international development. He adamantly believes that unless development decentralizes, the rights of individuals will be subsumed under the goals of mega-organizations. The YCT'S evolution into Redbud Community Retreat is driven by the conversations among youths from different parts of the world. The network that will form will be decentralized since its nature and its agenda will be defined by the participants themselves. Yet our expectation is that the conversations will continue to provide strong linkages through which to exchange ideas and information despite the absence of a central administrative hierarchy.

23 Yeich (1994).

Bibliography

Allport, Gordon. W. *Patterns and Growth in Personality.* New York: Holt, Rinehart, and Winston, 1961.

Allport, Gordon. W. "Traits Revisited." *American Psychologist* 21 (1966): 1–10.

Bandura, A. *Self-Efficacy: The Exercise of Control.* New York: W. H. Freeman, 1997.

———. *Social Learning Theory,* Englewood Cliffs, NJ: Prentice-Hall, 1977.

Buechler, Steven. "Beyond Resource Mobilization: Emerging Trends in Social Movement Theory." *The Sociological Quarterly,* 344 (1993): 217–35.

Bassuk, Ellen. "Who Are the Homeless Families: Characteristics of Sheltered Mothers and Children," *Community Mental Health Journal* 26 (1990): 425–34.

Bassuk, Ellen, Angela Browne, and John Buckner. "Single Mothers and Welfare." *Scientific American* 275 (October 1996): 60–67.

Bassuk, E. L., John C. Buckner, Linda Weinreb, Angela Browne, Shari Bassuk, Ree Dawson, and Jennifer Perloff. "Homelessness in Female-Headed Families: Childhood and Adult Risk and Protective Factors." *American Journal of Public Health* 87(1997): 241–48.

Bassuk, E. L., and E. M. Galagher. "The Impact of Homelessness on Children." In *Homeless Children: The Watchers and the Waiters,* ed. N. A. Boxill, New York: Haworth Press, 1990.

Browne, Angela, and Shari Bassuk. "Intimate Violence in the Lives of Homeless and Poor Housed Women: Prevalence and Patterns in an Ethnically Diverse Sample." *American Journal of Orthopsychiatry* 67 (April 1977).

Bryant, D. C. "Network Analysis and Participant Observation: A Network Team Approach," In *Sisterhood, Feminism, and Power,* ed. Obioma Nnaemeka, 55–78. New York: Red Sea Press, 1997.

———. "Survival of the Interventionist: Personal Costs of Community Research." *Odyssey: Interdisciplinary Journal of Study Abroad* 1 (1966): 81–95.

Bryant, Dé C., and Gwynn Mettetal. "Service Learning Projects: Empowerment in Students, Faculty, and Communities." *College Teaching* 44 (1966): 24–28.

Bryant, Dé C., "Lessons for Local-Global Action and Research." *Journal of Community Psychology.* 23 (1995): 250–55.

———. "The Nestlé Boycott Movement: Evolution of a Social Action." Masters thesis, Wilfrid Laurier University, Waterloo, Ontario, 1985.

Florin, P., and A. Wandersman. "An Introduction to Citizen Participation, Voluntary Organizations, and Community Development: Insights for Improvement through Research." *American Journal of Community Psychology* 18 (1990):41–54.

Freire, Paolo. *Pedagogy of the Oppressed*. New York: Continuum, 1989.

Gleason, Mary Ann. "Holes in the Safety Net." Paper presented at the Conference on Homelessness, Indiana University, South Bend, South Bend, IN, September 1966.

hooks, bell. *Teaching to Transgress: Education as Freedom*. New York: Routledge, 1990.

Lucas, Barbara.. *Education for Homeless Students*. Indianapolis, IN: State of Indiana Department of Education, 1990.

Lucas, Barbara, and Lena Hacket. *Street Youths on Their Own in Indianapolis*. Indianapolis, IN.: The Health Foundation of Greater Indianapolis and The Homeless Initiative Program, 1995.

Jenkins, J. C. "Resource Mobilization Theory and the Study of Social Movements." *Annual Review of Sociology* 9 (1983): 327–553.

Korten, David. *Getting to the 21st Century: Voluntary Action and the Global Agenda*. Hartford, CN: Kumarian Press, 1990.

McCarthy, J. and Zald, M. *The Trend of Social Movements in America: Professionalization and Resource Mobilization*. Morristown, NJ: General Learning Press, 1973.

McCarthy, John, and Mayor Zald. "Resource Mobilization and Social Movements: A Partial Theory." In *Social Movements in an Organizational Society*, ed. Mayor Zald and John McCarthy. New York: Transaction Publishers, 1987.

McChesney, Kay. "Family Homelessness: A Systematic Problem." *Journal of Social Issues* 46 (1990): 191–205.

"A Review of the Empirical Literature on Contemporary Urban Homeless Families." *Social Service Review* (September 1995): 429–60.

McMillan, David, and David Chavis. "Sense of Community: A Definition and Theory." *Journal of Community Psychology* 14 (1986):17–23.

Maslow, Abraham. *Motivation and Personality*. New York: Harper & Row, 1970.

Mboya, M. "Development and Construct Validity of a Self-Description Inventory for African-American Adolescents." *Psychological Reports* 72 (1993): 183–91.

Morlock, Beth. Personal Communication, 14 August 1997.

O'Neill, P., C. Duffy, M. Enman, E. Blackmer, and J. Goodwin. "Cognition and Citizen Participation in Social Action." *Journal of Applied Sociology* 18 (1988): 1067–83.

Perloff, Jennifer, and John Buckner. "Fathers of Children on Welfare: Their Impact on Child Well-Being." *American Journal of Orthopsychiatry* 66 (October 1996).

Piven, Frances, and Richard Cloward. *Poor People's Movements: Why They Succeed, How They Fail.* New York: Vintage Books, 1977.

Salomon, Amy, Shari Bassuk, and Margaret Brooks. "Patterns of Welfare Use among Poor and Homeless Women." *American Journal of Orthopsychiatry* 66 (October 1996): 510–25.

Sarason, Seymour, and Elizabeth Lorentz. *The Challenge of Resource Network.* San Francisco: Jossey-Bass, 1979.

Yeich, Susan. *The Politics of Ending Homelessness.* Lanham, MD: University Press of America, 1994.

Zimmerman, M. A., and Julian Rappaport. "Citizen Participation Perceived Control and Empowerment." *American Journal of Community Psychology* 16 (1988): 725–50.

Chapter 15

Community-Based Service: Re-Creating the Beloved Community

Bonnie Winfield

> Service to the community presents real world opportunities to confront problems, consider alternatives and find solutions.[1]

Community-based service (CBS) is a pedagogical tool that provides educators and community leaders with a powerful means to awaken in youth the power of nonviolence. CBS provides activities through which individuals and/or groups of any age explore how they can build or rebuild a sense of community in their neighborhoods. CBS encourages an understanding of this sense of community that, combined with conflict resolution skills, will enable youth to connect with others in the community and reduce the frustrations that lead to violent behavior.

CBS involves needs assessment, action, and, most important, reflection, a vital tool for lifelong learning at any age. This sense of service is not just one of helping but what Mariam Wright Edelman refers to as the "rent we pay for living . . . the very purpose of life and not something you do in your spare time."[2] The grassroots process of CBS provides all members of the community with a renewed sense of place and purpose. As an evaluation specialist for Aguirre International, I witnessed firsthand many fine examples of grassroots involvement in the service of AmeriCorps members. One team in a small urban area in the northeast knocked on every door in their neighborhood during a needs assessment of housing issues. Another team in Michigan visited the home of every schoolchild for the sole purpose of initiating communication with the parents as a beginning to the creation of grassroots involvement.[3] As a professor, I have integrated

CBS into my interdisciplinary courses. During one course the students used the results of a grassroots needs assessment to determine what service projects they would work on. These projects included public service announcements for neighborhood beautification, bike paths on a local bridge reconstruction, and an antiracism group in a local high school.

In this essay, I will provide theoretical foundations for, as well as concrete examples of, CBS learning designed for and by adolescents. Educators and community leaders can apply these grassroots ideas and examples of participatory democracy to their own communities to promote among young people an understanding of the causes of violence and a desire to use nonviolence to create the "beloved community." I will first discuss the potential of community-based service to address problems of youth violence, follow by giving a survey of the theoretical foundations of education for nonviolence, and then show how CBS can integrate these theories into practice for educators and community leaders.

Restructuring the Village

A recent report of the Carnegie Council on Adolescent Development maintains that the learning of basic social skills during adolescence can help teens gain a sense of belonging and personal worth.[4] In his report, "Fighting Back," on a community youth gang services project, William DeJong states: "If we are truly committed to preventing violence, we must do more than rescue individual children from the dysfunctional environments in which they are growing up. We must also work to change those environments . . . including reassertion of community values. The essence of [CBS] is the very act of people coming together in common cause."[5]

Engaging youth in community service is a recent innovation for preventing violence. Research has shown that community service can increase adolescent self-esteem and decrease the likelihood that youth will become either the perpetrators or the victims of violence.[6] Community service and service learning activities such as environmental clean-ups or companionship in local adult homes provide a meaningful role for adolescents, instilling civic responsibility and restructuring the village through partnerships between adults and youth. As the United States embraces the twenty-first century, community service will help to develop an ethic of service and lifelong learning within our youth so that they will be positive, contributing members of society.

The United States is a large, heterogeneous, multiethnic nation with a strong tradition of individualism. These qualities are significant assets that make it difficult for U.S. residents to arrive at a shared understanding of complex social problems or to turn that understanding into solutions involving broad acceptance. Service learning can and does produce a number of desirable outcomes, one of which is a sense of connectedness with other cultures.[7] Furthermore, students who participate in service learning activities that involve political or social action become more open-minded. A student working on an AIDS quilt wrote in her journal, "When I first heard of this project I thought 'oh, that group,' thinking of persons who had AIDS. Now I have experienced a sharing commitment to a community problem. I made new friendships with people I otherwise would not have even said 'hi' to."

An important factor in creating peaceful alternatives is the ability to formulate and evaluate creative options. Research regarding higher-level thinking skills, including problem solving, suggests an increase in students' abstract and hypothetical reasoning skills following CBS learning.[8] This higher-level thinking and ability to solve problems creatively is also vital to the "imagining" needed for win-win outcomes.[9] As one youth, Emma Garcia, a member of Oakland's Teens on Target and a participant in a Reducing Youth Violence Forum, asserts:

> Solutions start with individuals here and, if everyone got involved, we wouldn't have problems in our communities. Respect youth voices; we are losing energy because we are not giving opportunities to youth to speak about programs and budgets. Youth are frustrated by the adult population. What we see are people cutting back on opportunities to youth to speak about programs and budgets. The adult population frustrates youth. What we see is people cutting back on our needs. We feel like we've been written off.[10]

Youth Violence

> There is a new jacket on the market for children and it costs 500 dollars. It is not filled with goose down or emblazoned with a much sought-after brand name. What makes this jacket so expensive is its lining: a flexible sheet of Kevlar capable of stopping a 9 mm slug from a semiautomatic.
> *Violence Prevention for Young Adolescents:*
> *A Survey of the State of the Art*
> Deborah Prothrow-Stith Introduction to *Act against Violence.*

This quotation reminds me of a scene from *There Are No Children Here,* Alex Kotlowitz's account of children in a public housing community in Chicago.[11] Kotlowitz described children hiding low on the floor to avoid the bullets coming through the window of their homes. *There Are No Children Here* chronicled the ways in which violence is stealing childhood away from many of our youth, in both physical and spiritual ways. The number of weapons brought to school by teenagers even in the suburban, more affluent schools in the United States is increasing. One source states that 135,000 children bring weapons to school daily. Educators and community leaders are, of course, not unaware of this problem. The big question is: what can be done about it? How can we teach our children, especially adolescents, to be nonviolent, to use peaceful measures, when our nation seems to glorify violence?

One remarkably successful way is to teach and practice nonviolent conflict resolution skills and peer mediation. Many schools across the United States have incorporated peer mediation programs for conflicts on all levels from kindergarten through high school. These programs work very well to reduce violence on and off the school grounds. Educators also need, however, to address not only the results but also the roots of violence in our communities: widespread hopelessness and despair and feelings of not belonging. For these problems programs integrating community-based learning have been very successful. Such learning gives the participants, both students and community members, a sense of empowerment, of getting things done, and of commitment to their neighborhoods, which can really begin to build what Martin Luther King called the "beloved community."

Theoretical Foundations

Research on Peace Studies and nonviolence emphasizes community, both the community of persons involved in the nonviolent actions and the actual locus of neighborhoods and rural villages. Both of these senses of community help provide individuals with feelings of identity and belonging.[12] Community activists have testified to the importance of belonging to a group for empowering individuals, whether the group is determined by geography or by a commitment to common social visions. Hillary Clinton instructs us as a nation to incorporate the African model of "it takes a village to raise a child."[13]

I remember, as a youth growing up in a small village, being guided by adults in the community other than my parents with admonitions that ranged from being told not to laugh during Sunday morning church service to being queried about why I was riding my bike after dark.

Many youths today grow up in areas where they have no connection to the community; where, more often than not, the elders in the community do not even know their names. How easy it is to spray graffiti, have a fight in the street, or just remain inside watching television if no one in the community recognizes you, reprimands you, or misses you.

This alienation and isolation also has an impact on funding and support for schools and youth activities. The elders of the community are less likely to vote for an increased school budget or volunteer for the local youth dance when they don't know the children and suspect them of the delinquent behavior they read about or see on television. CBS enables community members to know who the youth are, to see them engaged in productive, useful behavior, and even to call them by name.

While evaluating a local AmeriCorps program recently, I interviewed an elderly woman in a small town in the southern tier of New York. She spoke of the work performed by Sharon, Terry, and Jonathan, local AmeriCorps members. How excited she was to see them each day cleaning up after a flood. They, calling her by name, had given real meaning to her life. "I thought of these young people when we had the last school budget vote. Usually I didn't participate in these things. This year I did; actually I called Terry and he gave me a ride to the school the night of the voting. I want to do all I can to support the kids in our community now. We wouldn't have survived the flood without them." CBS thus not only develops a sense of accomplishment for the youth but it also creates an interdependence between the community members and youth and brings increased commitment among community members to schools and other youth programs. In the context of large cutbacks in financial support for and increased criticism of public education today, this can have great importance.

Two words come to my mind when reviewing both the literature and my own experience with CBS learning: empathy and efficacy. According to peace activist and scholar Elise Boulding, empathy is "the ability to feel what another is feeling, [and] can be thought of as the basis of all social interaction."[14] Efficacy is the power to be effective, and in this study, will refer to the power to act on one's sense of empathy. It is the power in a young person to feel effective in changing the conditions in her or his world, which once seemed hopeless. Adolescence, especially early adolescence, is often a time of life when despair and hopelessness is highest, and is often the cause of violent behavior. Betsy Martinez, an eleven-year-old from Washington Heights, stated when interviewed about violence prevention programs that she wanted "to see kids on the street doing positive things instead of shooting each other." To her, community outreach added up to nonviolence. The goal of the Friendly Persuasion program in Worcester, Massachusetts, is "to encourage girls to choose healthy alternatives. To achieve this, girls . . . build peer and community networks." One youth in an elder companion program in Ohio stated in his journal: "This program has really made a difference in my life. It is something really different, I mean it's not like getting 100% on a test or having someone tell you that you look nice today. It's a deeper, more important feeling that I've gained. Maybe it has to do with inspiration and knowing what I can make of my life if I just keep trying like these people have."

Boulding introduced the term "technologically shielded education." She thinks of this kind of education as only "one way of knowing, one way of gaining knowledge, one way of using the mind."[15] Many young people, and adults as well, have come to rely on television, whether through news shows, sitcoms, or talk shows, to learn about the world outside their living rooms. Research on the impact of media on society confirms that many people develop a sense of their world through television's images. Some researchers conclude that the excessive violence on television results in a warped sense of reality as more violent and dangerous than it really is. One such study "supports the conclusion that adolescent aggressiveness and the viewing of violent television programs are statistically associated."[16] With such data in mind, Boulding suggests that a "challenge to educators would be how to insure an adequate firsthand experience on which to build a knowledge structure that corresponds to the real world."[17] She explains that experiences and reflection on such experiences would enable adolescents to gain a better understanding of the reality in which they are situated and would provide a knowledge base from which to choose their responses.

Boulding's ideas in this respect correspond to educational theorist Maxine Greene's "Dialectic of Freedom." As does Boulding, Greene challenges educators "to empower young people to seek out openings in their [life] situations, to tolerate disruptions of the taken-for-granted, to try consciously to become different than they are . . . [By] confronting a void, confronting a nothingness, we may be able to empower the young to create and recreate a common world—and, in cherishing it, in renewing it, discover what it signifies to be free."[18] Mary Pipher's recent work on adolescent girls found that "strong girls manage to hold on to some sense of themselves. Often they have a strong sense of place that gives them roots. They may identify with an ethnic group in a way that gives them pride and focus, or they may see themselves as being an integral part of a community. Their sense of belonging preserves their identity when it is battered by the winds of adolescence."[19] In providing adolescents with a strong sense of belonging, they can develop self-efficacy, that is, the power that enables them to combat the despairing feelings common in communities today. A student participating in the Jones-Village Partnership Program in Upper Arlington, Ohio, describes this transformation: "I don't know exactly how I've changed, but I can feel it inside me. It's like a brand new doorway has been opened. The people here are so wonderful, so beautiful, that they have had a deep impact on me."

Community-based learning is one pedagogical tool to provide adolescents with an opportunity to discover and define their places in the real world that goes beyond any "technologically shielded" way of knowing. In the following section I will demonstrate how specific programs have validated these theories in practice.

Community-Based Service

We cannot live for ourselves alone. Our lives are connected by a thousand invisible threads, and along these sympathetic fibers, our actions run as causes and return to us as results.

Herman Melville

CBS is a pedagogical tool enabling students to discover the invisible threads that Melville sensed. One student, in a Learn 'n Serve program, recognized this in her journal: "These activities made me feel more a part of the community. I now know the struggles and through them have made friendships." CBS not only must be integrated into the classroom curriculum, but also has to have a major reflective component in order to have the desired results. It is not enough to go to the soup kitchen or make placements for a nursing home. One has to learn why there is a soup kitchen and how the residents of the home feel about living away from their families. CBS is an active way of weaving the webs of the community, of building relationships and understanding between students and community members. CBS provides students with what Maxine Greene calls "other ways of knowing." It provides them with an opportunity to see beyond all the different kinds of technologically shielded education, to discover what the community really needs and what resources can be developed to solve community problems.

One good example of all this is the Adopt-A-Park programs of Syracuse, New York. The students of the Frazer School, located in a poor urban neighborhood, took "action to better the surrounding area of their school and [took] ownership of their neighborhood, community and city" by cleaning up the park and all the area streets. Adults in the area pitched in, thus creating a community of all ages at work to solve a local problem. In a similar project, a community staged a celebration at the park, including the sharing of songs, poems, storytelling, food, games, and fun. The fete assuredly gave the students a sense of accomplishment and pride.

Teenagers are rightly known for their abundance of energy and many new, innovative ideas. When challenged to solve community problems, they become a valuable asset. So, how do CBS programs arise? How are they brought to a community?

Many programs have begun with the students. "Community mapping" can start them off. The adolescents discover the community needs by mapping the needs and resources of the neighborhood. A wonderful resource for insights and how-tos for such community mapping is John Kretzmann and John McKnight's *Building Communities from the Inside Out*.[20] The authors describe how mapping can be used to assess needs, identify potential action partners for the youths, and chart plans for community change. The teens can develop an actual map of the community that highlights needs and resources. In some communities, agencies such as the United Way or Citizen Action have already done much of this work. But it is important that the needs be identified by the grassroots community, not by outsiders or exclusively by those with political power. It is especially critical that youth are involved, as their growing grasp of the real issues will help them to gain a sense of worth and value in their community.

Successful CBS programs have several important components: supervision, training, reflection, and recognition.[21] According to Pam Toole, of a Palo Alto, California, Peer Counseling Program, "The single most important factor is who runs the group."[22] The guidance and encouragement of group leaders must be consistent and sensitive to adolescents' needs and development potential. The adult, whether a teacher or volunteer, must be skilled at training, at helping adolescents articulate success and failure, at aiding in finding in teens personal meaning, and must enjoy working with them. According to Kretzmann and McKnight, "Most people do things too easy for kids. When what they are doing is important, [kids] show unexpected responsibility and stability. Program leaders testify that the personal rewards of working in effective programs for these youngsters are immeasurable."[23] Such leaders must have trust in the dignity, intelligence, and goodness of each teen with which she or he is working.

Another important aspect of a successful program is careful training for the young people before they go out into the community. It is extremely important that adequate time and attention are allocated for this. "Adolescents require careful training before they can assume new roles and work with people different from themselves," declares a leading guide to community building.[24] This training can be broken into small increments of time, but it should last a minimum of ten to twenty hours. Training sessions can offer role playing, relevant films, or simulation exercises. Such activities can allow teens to practice new roles and make concrete their fears and expectations. Before taking up an activity at a local nursing home, for example, I had a group of teens watch the film *Peage* in which a teenage boy goes to visit his grandmother at such an institution. The boy's story brought up many of the issues and fears the teens had about being with old people, such as Alzheimer's disease and deaths, what to say, what to do. Discussing these issues both before and after the activity made the teens better able to participate and learn from their experience. This experience taught me that the training must be specific to the roles adolescents will play and the population they will work with. Interpersonal skills such as active listening, assertion, and conflict resolution are a must for anyone who is working in the community. These training sessions can actually be done in the community, allowing the students to join community members in a nonthreatening experience.

Similarly I conducted an interpersonal communication workshop with teens at a women's transitional housing facility. The teens were part of a community service team planning to work at a childcare center. The preceding workshop allowed the teens to share with the mothers of the facility actual parts of their lives. The teens, many from affluent suburban areas, gained valuable insights into the behaviors of the children under pressure and more understanding of women's lives generally. As Mary, a seventeen-year-old volunteer stated, "I worked in a child care center before, I would get angry about how the children would arrive, sometimes dirty, hungry. They seemed to be deprived of attention and nurturing. My mother would have put soap in my mouth if I used the words that came out of them almost naturally. This workshop helped me to understand the bigger picture and not blame only the mother. I began to understand the welfare system, addictions, domestic violence and absent fathers."

Reflection is, as already suggested, vital to real learning. Reflection allows youth to try to make sense of their experiences. If this is a graded experience, it is actually the reflection that is graded and becomes the learning component. One method of reflection that can be adopted comes from Paulo Freire's work with Christian-based communities in Brazil called the Circle of Praxis.[25] Freire's circle consists of movement from action, to social reflection, to planning, and then to more action. Once the young people have spent some time in a community, a session of social reflection might explore its history, or its economic system, or its politics. How, they might ask, did the local park get so run down? Why aren't there public funds to clean the streets? Why are people in that nursing home so lonely? Why do so many people sleep in the streets? Once these questions and, of course, many more, are explored, then the young people can be asked to come up with plans for transformation and nonviolent change. Such reflection can take the form of journals, group discussions, video presentations, poetry and other creative written or visual work, written or oral stories, or artwork. A group in Albany County, New York, for instance, developed a presentation about the voices of the people they had worked with. Each of the teens sat on a stool with a table lamp nearby. The lamps were unlit until the individual youth spoke as the person she or he had been working with. The voices represented elders, children, and persons from a special needs facility. One student spoke as the horse she had been caring for in the recreation center, another as an elderly man of ninety years, and still another as a very young child. The gentle mimicry gave evidence of their commitment of time to the individuals the young people worked with as well as how much they had learned from each.

Finally, the young need recognition for their work. This can take many forms, including such things as baseball caps, T-shirts, or buttons. One AmeriCorps member always wore her T-shirt for the work. "I feel a part of the community, like when I wear my T-shirt, everyone asks me questions. One little boy, around 3 years I think, pointed to my [AmeriCorps] pin and said 'you're one of those people who help.' I felt real fine." Recognition can also be in the form of such public ceremonies as a dinner to honor the students or a day set aside by community leaders in their honor. One community devotes a special column in the local newspaper to news of youth volunteer activities.

Conclusion

As we all know, the world of adolescence is becoming more and more violent. Young people in the United States and in other places in the world are exposed to increasing levels of violence on television, on the streets and in the school community. If we are to teach our children a nonviolent way of life, not only must we expose them to new skills for resolving conflicts and communicating with each other, but we must also help them to recreate a sense of the beloved community in their schools and neighborhoods. Community-based service provides youth with a vehicle to develop both empathy as the youth develop relationships with people different from themselves and efficacy as they are able to get things done in the community that will help relieve them of feelings of hopelessness and despair. "Youth service program operators across the country report that youth service helps build personal character, creates a sense of shared community and shapes our national destiny by bringing youth of all racial, class and cultural backgrounds to work together."[26]

I would like to conclude by using an entry from one teen's journal. This entry was written after a training retreat for a peer service program in Canada.[27] This young man says more about empathy, efficacy, and nonviolent change than my words can ever portray:

> The big, yellow school bus comes to pick me up. When I get in, I see I'm the first passenger. Cool, I can sit anywhere.
>
> I'm not sure why I volunteered for this peer helper training, but it's a weekend away with free food and swimming, and the teacher running this program seems okay. I called my dad to let him know, but he seemed more concerned about this making my grades go even lower than they already are. My mom thought I might learn to get along better with others. Who's she kidding? She's the one that ought to learn how to get along better.
>
> Oh, no. The bus isn't really stopping to pick up these kids. They're geeks. I can't believe they are also going on this trip. Oh, great, and here comes those dorks from ———. Oh, man, this sucks. Why did I agree to do this? At least they are staying at the front of the bus. And that constant chattering.
>
> Holy ———, now look who is getting on. These kids don't even speak English. Uh, oh. Here come the jocks. I'm trapped here.
>
> This was a stupid idea. Maybe I can get the driver to drop me off.

Okay, this was pretty much the way I felt when we started out on this journey. Things have changed. I've changed. I'm not the same person that got on that bus. I got on somewhat skeptical. Then I saw who else was going and I got mad and disgusted. But today I have completely different feelings about all the people on the bus and the others I met at the retreat. And my teachers and parents seem to agree with me more often now.

What changed me? Tears. Yeah, tears probably had the biggest impact on me. I saw people who I thought were worthless cry. I heard other kids talk about pain and hurt. I saw them tell about feeling hated and despised.

At first when I heard the others talk, all I could think of was "what jerks." I felt more like knocking their lites out. But one guy, who I called the nose-ring dude, volunteered with one of the teachers to talk about his anger. What he had to say really surprised me. What was inside him was inside me. How could it be that on the outside we were so different, yet on the inside we were so much the same[?] Other kids started sharing their stories. Eventually my turn came. I told about my life, I talked about my fears. Next thing I knew I had tears. Other kids extended a hand to me, gave me a Kleenex.

What is going on here? The facilitators (I used to call them teachers) for this retreat had us sit in circles. And they asked us to think about certain things. We didn't have to talk; we could pass, if we wanted to. Sometimes we had to pair-up with another person we didn't know and try one of the activities. Mostly we had to learn how to listen to each other. We also had to work out a lot of simple things together like fixing the campfire, preparing meals, doing the dishes; you know, camp stuff. These things actually started to be fun because it gave us a break and gave us a chance to talk to others in ways I didn't know were possible.

Anyway, what I'm trying to say is that I think I can be a better friend to others and I think I know how to actually be a friend now. Things still piss me off when they happen. But I know some other ways to deal with them. I haven't given up on the idea that I might still have to fight someone. After all[,] the grade 10 students are really a bunch of little jerks. And they are too young to learn what I have learned.

DEVELOPING A COMMUNITY-BASED SERVICE (CBS) PROGRAM SUGGESTIONS FOR EDUCATORS AND COMMUNITY LEADERS

CBS PROJECT OUTLINE

THE VISION
With a small group of adults and youth conceptualize your vision of CBS project.
This vision could be written up in a concept paper or proposal for funding.

THE PLANNING

Who: invite participation from adults and youth interested in this project.

> Note: planning committee may be made up of different folk than either the initial conceptualizing group or the implementing group.

Adults
Educators
Community leaders
Grassroots representative
Youth
At least two students who indicate interest in and have had experience in CBS
Remember that youth are major resources in this project-their ideas are vital to success.

Training of planning team:
Be sure all on this planning committee have come to consensus about the vision of the CBS project.
Set aside at least several hours for strategic planning sessions.
There are many resources that offer guides to strategic planning.

THE ACTION PLAN

Five essential elements of an action plan: it is important to identify these elements from the initial planning stages. These elements will be important for future fund-raising if needed.

Community Need is the compelling community problem or issue that the CBS project will address.
A grassroots process should identify the community needs.
The youth volunteers can identify these needs by community mapping and surveys.
One program gave the students throwaway cameras and sent them out into the community to photograph assets and problems. Then the photos were made into a display for the community.
Community needs assessments are sometimes already done by agencies such as the United Way in the area.

Service Activities are what the youth will be doing to address these needs.
Identified by youth participants

Age appropriate
Impact-oriented

Inputs are the resources a project applies to create or sustain the service activity.
Number of volunteers
Hours of service
Financial resources

Accomplishments are what get done.

Impacts are the measurable changes in the community or how the activities had an effect on the community needs identified above.

Vital components
Adult supervision
Training
Action
Reflection
Recognition
Plan for realistic impact, not "saving the world"
Be specific about actions and activities
Be realistic about goals and time objectives

IMPLEMENTING THE ACTION PLAN

Included in this plan is the training necessary for the youth to be successful.
Training includes communication skills, conflict resolution, interviewing, problem solving as well as activity in specific areas.
(See "Training Ideas, Suggestions, and Resources" at the end of this article.)
This action plan must be very specific and include time considerations and supervision.

REFLECTION

This is what especially makes community-based learning different from community service, volunteering, and other activities.
Reflection identifies what learning is taking place.
Examples: journal writing, photography, plays, poetry, public speaking, group discussions, essays, presentations.

RECOGNITION

As in any form of volunteer activities, recognition is vital to the energy and life of the project.

Examples of recognition: T-shirts, buttons, newspaper/television/radio coverage, dinners, awards, "Day of Service" recognition from local government officials.

STRATEGIC PLANNING; THE CYCLE CONTINUES

Strategic planning is based on reflection and the cycle of learning.

Youth and the community grassroots representatives are vital to this process.

Learning from history is critical for the future success of any project.

TRAINING IDEAS, SUGGESTIONS, AND RESOURCES

Training Sessions for Adults and Youth Together

adequate time: 10–20 hours
discovered learning-examples
photography
community mapping
interviews of elders and/or youth in community
neighborhood histories
role-playing exercises
situations the youth might find themselves in
as real as possible
youth can suggest ideas
simulation exercises
power exercise
nonviolent games
case studies
examples of CBS are available from the Corporation for National Service. (202) 606-5000
team-building activities
ropes course
blindfolded walk
building a tower with Popsicle sticks as a team

Topics for Training Sessions
communication skills
feedback techniques
issues facing youth and the community
group management and cooperative learning skills
techniques for improving school success
leadership skills for working with diverse groups
teaching/learning techniques and strategies
peer and intergenerational tutoring techniques
conflict resolution
mentoring skills and approaches
diversity awareness

RESOURCES

Peter L. Bensen, and Eugene C. Roehlkepartain. *Beyond Leaf Raking: Learning to Serve/Serving to Learn.* Nashville: Abingdon Press, 1993.

Carnegie Council on Adolescent Development. *Great Transitions: Preparing Adolescents for a New Century.* New York: Carnegie Corporation, 1996.

Carnegie Council on Adolescent Development. *A Matter of Time: Risk and Opportunity in the Nonschool Hours.* New York: Carnegie Corporation, 1992.

Carnegie Council on Adolescent Development. *Turning Points: Preparing American Youth for the 21st Century.* New York: Carnegie Corporation, 1989.

Robert Coles. *The Call of Service.* New York: Houghton Mifflin, 1993.

Frances Moore Lappe, and Paul Martin Dubois. *The Quickening of America: Rebuilding Our Nation, Remaking Our Lives.* San Francisco: Jossey-Bass, 1994.

Daniel E. Conrad, and Diane Hedin. *Youth Service: A Guide Book for Developing and Operating Effective Programs.* Washington, DC: Independent Sector, 1987.

Jane C. Kendall, and Associates. *Combining Service and Learning: A Resource Book for Community and Public Service, Volumes I and II.* Raleigh: National Society for Internships and Experiential Education, 1990.

Organizations
Campus Compact: The Project for Public and Community Service
(401) 863-1119
Corporation for National Service
(202) 606-5000
http://www.cns.org
National Society for Internships and Experiential Education
(919) 787-3263
nsee@interpath.com

National Service-Learning Cooperative Clearinghouse
(800) 808-7378
http://www.nicsl.coled.umn.edu
National School-To-Work Learning and Information Center
(800) 251-7236
http://www.stw.ed.gov

Notes

1. Diane Harrington and Joan Shine, Connecting: Service Learning in the Middle Grades. New York City: City University of New York. Center for the Advanced Study in Education, 2.

2. Mariam Wright Edelman, *The Measure Of Our Success: A Letter To My Children and Yours* (Boston: Beacon Press, 1992).

3. Reference to programs and quotations by youth are from my work as an evaluator for the Americorp Program, 1996–97, unless otherwise indicated.

4. Carnegie Council on Adolescent Development, *Great Transitions: Preparing Adolescents for a New Century* (New York: Carnegie Corporation, 1996).

5. William DeJong, "Fighting Back: The Community Youth Gang Services Project," in *Act Against Violence: Join the New Peace Movement*. Community Resource Guide (New York: WNET, 1996), 15.

6. P. L. Benson, "Kids Who Care: Meeting the Challenge of Youth Service Involvement," *Search Institute Source* 12 (1993): 1.

7. Ernest Boyer and Fred M. Hechinger, *Higher Education in the Nation's Service* (Washington, DC: Carnegie Foundation for the Advancement of Teaching, 1981).

8. Diane Conrad and Donald Hedin, "The Impact of Experiential Learning on Adolescent Development" in *Children and Youth Services* 4, (1992): 57–76.

9. Roger Fisher and William Ury, *Getting to Yes: Negotiating Agreement Without Giving In* (New York: Penguin Books, 1981).

10. Deborah Prothrow-Stith, Introduction to *Act Against Violence: Join the New Peace Movement.* (New York: WNET 1996), 2.

11. Alex Kotlowitz, *There Are No Children Here* (New York: Doubleday, 1991).

12. Bonnie Winfield, "Creating a Place to Call Home" (Ph.D. diss., Syracuse University 1996).

13. Hillary Rodham Clinton, *It Takes A Village: And Other Lessons Children Teach Us* (New York: Simon & Schuster, 1996).

14. Elise Boulding, *Building a Global Civic Culture: Education for an Independent World* (Syracuse, NY: Syracuse University Press, 1988), 72.

15. Ibid., 83.

16. Steven H. Chaffee, quoted in Lowery and DeFleur, *Milestones in Mass Communication Research* (New York: Longmans Press), 312.

17 Boulding, *Building a Global Civic Culture*, 82.

18 Maxine Greene, "Freedom, Education and Public Spaces," *Cross Currents*, 37 (1987): 442–55.

19 Mary Pipher, *Reviving Ophelia: Saving the Selves of Adolescent Girls* (New York: Ballantine Books, 1994), 265.

20 John P. Kretzmann and John L. McKnight, *Building Communities from the Inside Out: A Path Toward Finding and Mobilizing a Community's Assets* (Evanston, IL, Center for Urban Affairs and Policy Research, Northwestern University, 1993).

21 See "Training Ideas, Suggestions, and Resources" at the end of the article.

22 Kretzmann and McKnight, 43.

23 Ibid.

24 Ibid., 44.

25 Paulo Freire, *Pedagogy of the Oppressed* (New York: Seabury Press, 1970).

26 Catherine Rolzinski, *The Adventure of Adolescence: Middle School Students and Community Service* (Washington, DC: Youth Service America),1990, 4.

27 Journal entry provided by Rey Carr, Peer Resources, Victoria, British Columbia.

Chapter 16

A Summer Institute on Nonviolence

Ian Murray Harris

> Peace is being able to get along with people around you. This doesn't mean that people don't fight. It means that people can use the intellectual and rational way to solve problems. I think that "peace" is a very far goal to reach. It starts with every individual person and their state of mind. We can't just order peace. And we can't just wish for it. We have to work for it and build it up.
>
> Essay written by a fourteen-year-old participant in Summer Institute

Violence is increasingly becoming a problem for young people. Suicides and gun-related homicides are at record high levels.[1] Six percent of adolescents in the United States are estimated to have been the victims of a violent crime.[2] Almost half of teenagers say their schools are getting more violent.[3] Although boys are twice as likely as girls to have direct exposure to violence, adolescent girls are also joining gangs and engaging in criminal behavior.[4] The specters of crime and violence are scaring some of the young people of the United States into carrying weapons, and others into cutting classes and settling for lower grades.[5]

Fears of violence exist more prominently in inner-city at-risk neighborhoods. According to pollster Louis Harris:

> Almost half of all students have changed their behaviors as a result of crime or the threat of crime. One in five have avoided particular parks or playgrounds, one in eight have carried weapons to protect themselves or have gotten lower grades in school than they think they otherwise would have, and one in nine have stayed home from school or cut class. Students in at risk neighborhoods are more than twice as likely to avoid particular parks, three times as likely to have gotten lower grades, and four times as likely to say they have carried weapons or stayed home from school or cut class.[6]

In spite of the evident damaging effects of such violence, many educators have ignored the problems.[7] Rather than responding with compassion to such teenager difficulties, they are implementing so-called get-tough policies designed to frighten youth into conforming.

Young adolescents want respect, power, and love. If they can't find these at home or in school they find them in unhealthy ways on the streets. Because many youth in early adolescence (ages thirteen to fifteen) are engaging in antisocial activities and violence, that age presents a particularly vital opportunity for shaping behavior patterns leading to a successful course for life. Many teenagers that age have not learned how to handle conflict without resorting to violence.

This paper will describe a week-long Summer Institute held on the University of Wisconsin-Milwaukee (UWM) campus that teaches nonviolence to early adolescents, aged thirteen to fifteen, as a way of preparing them to resist peer pressure for violent behaviors. Milwaukee, where this Institute takes place, is the twenty-second largest metropolitan area in the United States. In 1993, 363 children under the age of eighteen were either injured or killed by guns, 105 juveniles were arrested for murder, and 1400 were arrested for battery, 610 for weapons offenses, and 423 for narcotics offenses.

During the summer of 1995, a group of educators created for the first time an innovative program, the UWM Summer Institute on Nonviolence, which was designed to help participants learn alternatives to violent behavior. This initial program, run entirely by volunteers, trained peer leaders in nonviolence in the hopes of reaching a wider population of young people exposed to violence. Second and third programs, in 1996 and 1997, each trained thirty youths.

This paper will present a theoretical framework for this approach to the problems of youth violence, briefly outline its innovative history, discuss its curriculum, and assess its results. As one of the Institute's founders, I worked closely with its development. I am widely experienced in urban education, and became interested in peace education after seeing how many public high school students seemed overwhelmed by problems of violence. As a professor in the School of Education at UWM, I now direct a Peace Studies program and maintain a Peace Resource Institute.

Literature Review

According to the concluding report of a recent Carnegie Council on Adolescent Development, adolescence, a period when young people are making decisions that involve, among other things, education, drugs, weapons, and use of their bodies, is the decisive time to offer training that capitalizes on their emerging cognitive capabilities. The report states:

> Life skills training [which include skills in nonviolent conflict resolution and assertiveness training] should become a vital part of education in all relevant institutions, so that adolescents learn to make informed, deliberate, and constructive decisions. One such life skill that adolescents often lack and that can be taught is the ability to pursue constructive rather than destructive] relations with others.[8]

Adolescents are primarily concerned with their emerging self-identity as juxtaposed to those of their peers. Peer pressure is a phenomenon that occasions tremendous stress for this group. Peers, needless to say, can influence their friends to behave in destructive or constructive ways.

The Carnegie Report calls for youth to be trained with skills in both assertiveness and nonviolent conflict resolution, and it identifies these skills as being of utmost value:

> An aspect of assertiveness is knowing how to resist pressure or intimidation to use drugs or weapons or have sex—without disrupting valued relationships or isolating oneself. Yet another aspect is nonviolent conflict resolution, the ability to achieve personal and social goals in ways that make use of the many nonviolent opportunities that exist in the society.[9]

If sustained over a period of years, the report concludes, such interventions can offset the negative effects of low self-respect, undeveloped social and decision-making skills, indifference to education, low perception of opportunities, and limited incentive for delaying short-term gratification.

Other studies cited by the Carnegie Report show the value of teaching adolescents nonviolence.[10] One of these, calls directly for teaching alternatives to violence:

> Students behave violently to express anger or frustration, to show off, to protect themselves. Throughout their lives, children have learned how to express their feelings by observing their parents and teachers, as well as the Power Rangers, Roseanne, The Simpsons, and Beavis and Butt Head. The more tools students have to choose from to meet their needs and to express their feelings, the greater the likelihood they will use them.[11]

Teaching young adolescents about nonviolence can build in their minds a peace consciousness to help offset some of the destructive methods of dealing with conflict that they learn from media, their family members, neighborhoods, and schools.

Research about young people and violence has shown again and again that teaching youth alternatives not only prevents youth violence, but also has many constructive side effects.[12] Studies have shown that teaching young children peaceful ways to respond to conflict can help lay an important foundation for helping them become more peaceful as adults.[13] Studies on elementary school children, for instance, have shown that peace education can not only reduce aggressive physical acts, but also increase prosocial behavior.[14] Research conducted on middle school children who have been trained in conflict resolution shows that these skills help young adolescents not only to resolve their conflicts, but also to improve their academic achievement.[15]

College students have been shown to experience a change in value orientation as a result of peace education classes.[16] Other studies have demonstrated significant cognitive changes.[17] An article by the author has shown that college students are often more interested in changing their own behavior after such instruction than in trying to work on the external circumstances of violence.[18] Studies of peer mediation programs have shown that young people can learn peacekeeping skills in school and even apply these skills to their own lives.[19]

Projects that have attempted to address the violence among teens have pointed to the need for collaboration between teachers, youth, and the community.[20] A report on one such project, Project STOP, 1991–92 (Schools Teaching Options for Peace), shows that collaboration and cooperation are essential elements needed to support a successful venture. Project STOP provided:

> . . . a comprehensive package of conflict resolution, and information and techniques that helps participants resolve problems constructively rather than destructively. It encouraged ownership of the program, empowering individual students and parents to become competent problem solvers with the ability to choose peaceful alternatives to violence.[21]

Project STOP actually was a rather successful attempt to combine the talents of various established local and national organizations already adept at providing conflict resolution techniques. Its goals were met in part, the report asserts, because it targeted the "right" population, in this case middle school students who were "caught in the struggle between peer group pressure and developing their own identities," but also because of the unique collaboration between project coordinators, educators, schools, and local and national agencies.

Peace educators, concerned about problems of violence faced by their students, do, of course, attempt to educate young people about alternatives to violence.[22] The theory peace educators apply to the various problems of violence faced by teenagers has three levels which can be used to provide youth with strategies for dealing constructively with violence.[23] Most educators rely on peacekeeping strategies that use only the first level, that is, threats to deter young people from violence. The model used at the University of Wisconsin-Milwaukee, however, rests upon not just peacekeeping, but peacemaking and peacebuilding. In the peacemaking category, teenage participants are taught anger management skills, interpersonal conflict management techniques, and such other things as nonviolent dating patterns. Peacebuilding goes further by trying to create in the minds of students a desire to pursue nonviolence.

The University of Wisconsin-Milwaukee Model

The curriculum and pedagogical techniques used in the UWM Summer Institute are based upon current research findings about best practices to deal with the troublesome phenomenon of youth violence. The course gives young adolescents an opportunity to spend constructive time learning to be peacemakers, rather than using their summer vacations for hanging out or getting in trouble. Most young people, studies show, are confused about violence, but they also show a willingness to get involved in seeking a solution:

> Seven in ten (71%) teens say they are willing to participate in youth leadership programs, such as tutoring other kids or being a mentor to a younger student. Six in ten (62%) are willing to participate in anti-violence or anti-drug programs, or programs to teach skills on how to avoid fights, sometimes called "conflict resolution programs."[24]

The Institute helps young adolescents approach problems of youth violence by having each student develop an action plan for the following year. Four times during the first year staff from the Institute meet with the participants to see how their action plans are doing. Such commitments involve the youth in practical peacemaking activities through which they can develop both skills and identities as peacemakers. These new attributes can help them overcome any sense of helplessness they may have while confronting the violence of their worlds. The support students provide each other and receive from the staff reinforces the commitment to build a peaceful world.

The Summer Institute hires trained youth workers so that the participants can learn from peers and other students about perceptions of violence. Studies show that youth often look to each other for guidance on how to deal with difficult problems:

> Some of the most positive and compelling models for young people are older students. Students can be trained to share their wisdom with classrooms of young kids, or to mentor younger kids in one-on-one situations. Older students usually know the plight of younger students better than anyone else.[25]

The didactic format of the Institute thus allows participants to learn from role models about nonviolent behavior, as well as to study alternatives to violence in small groups, to share with their peers concerns about violence, and to brainstorm solutions for their own lives.

Staff of the UWM Summer Institute for Nonviolence

The Institute was created by the Coalition for Nonviolence in Schools (CNS) which was founded in 1991 as an outgrowth of the Southeastern Wisconsin chapter of Wisconsin Educators for Social Responsibility (WESR). To counteract the violence of television programs, movies, and society in general, this multiracial coalition of concerned citizens, parents, educators, community groups, and peace organizations decided to advocate the teaching of nonviolence and conflict resolution in schools in southeastern Wisconsin. Its mission was and is to promote peaceful human relations, to urge adults to teach reverence for life, and to encourage students to seek nonviolent means to resolve conflicts.

CNS's role in the genesis of the Institute began during the summer of 1994, when it raised enough money to send an inner-city high school junior to the Martin Luther King Jr. Center for Nonviolent Change in Atlanta, Georgia, for one week of nonviolence education. During the trip to Atlanta he collaborated with a former patrolman for the Milwaukee Police Department, who would later work as a full-time violence prevention coordinator for the Milwaukee Health Department. The young man, so educated in Atlanta, later returned as staff for the 1995 and 1996 sessions of the Institute. The 1995 Summer Institute on Nonviolence, also through its violence prevention coordinator, recruited two high school students and one college student who became youth workers for the Institute. All of these staff members are African-Americans.

The other adult staff members are Caucasians. They consist of a school psychologist; a substitute teacher; several middle school teachers; a violence prevention coordinator from the Milwaukee Public Schools; the director of Peace Studies at UWM; a graduate student in peace education from the University of Wisconsin-Milwaukee; a middle school teacher from Fort Atkinson, Wisconsin, a rural school district; a staff member from a local recreation center; and a violence prevention expert from the Task Force on Battered Women. All work as volunteers in this community effort to provide an answer for some of the problems of youth violence.

In addition, four students who completed the Institute during the summer of 1995 were hired as youth staff. These peers assisted with some of the activities in 1996 and served as role models for the participants. It was thought that the teenagers attending the Institute would more readily learn to value peace if they heard messages from people their own age. These peer models are an important part of the staff. Their self-expressions provide positive identity models of peaceful teens. Their empathy helps establish strong relationships with teenage participants. They also modeled effective communication skills and demonstrated a strong commitment to nonviolence, which had a powerful impact upon the other teenagers.

Curriculum of the Institute

The Institute curriculum was developed during the summer of 1995 through a collaborative effort of the volunteer staff and the two youth workers. It follows an adult education model wherein the problems of violence are presented, solutions are generated, and participants finally develop action plans.[26] In the latter phase each participant identifies what she or he wants to accomplish, steps necessary to reach such goals, obstacles that might arise, and ideas to overcome such difficulties. This approach to peace education encourages participants to reflect upon problems of violence in their own lives and brainstorm about appropriate solutions. Rather than leaving participants depressed about violence, the course empowers them to seek solutions.

The overall goal of the Institute is to increase the awareness and utilization of nonviolence and encourage leadership in youth. In addition, the Summer Institute provides a fun-filled, inviting place to learn about peace and to appreciate the richness of nonviolence. With the use of cooperative games the Institute creates opportunities for adolescents to communicate concerns about violence with peers and adults. In order to motivate the teenagers to pursue peace, they are told stories about local and international peace heroes, many of them Nobel Peace Prize winners. They receive instruction about alternatives to destructive behaviors, and are urged to become peacemakers themselves. During each week of the summer staff address issues of violence and nonviolence while urging participants to focus on personal nonviolence. Guest speakers often talk about community violence, which helps the young people envisage ways that they could become peacemakers. Many are inspired to pledge publicly to carry out nonviolent behaviors, and to present peace action plans. Students develop a dating contract to help them deal with issues of interpersonal violence.[27] They are also taught anger management techniques and skills in positive communication. In order to manage their own behavior during the week, they actually put together their own peace treaty.[28]

The Institute invites many speakers on such issues as gang violence, drug abuse, family violence, positive interpersonal skills, anger management, environmental sensitivity, violence in popular culture, and, more globally, the military budget. The issues of violence in their lives that students address include bullying, shooting, stabbing, suicide, hitting, stealing, threatening, dating abuse, sexually harassing, using guns, fighting, abusing family members, and brutalizing by police. Students have opportunities to express concerns about these issues in small groups. Twice each day the participants are given quiet time to write in journals. The journals are also collected daily and facilitators use the opportunity to correspond with each student. These journals allow staff to observe and record the impact of the Institute.

During the week the Institute also offers several art activities. The first day the young people choose peace buddies. On the third day each participant uses art materials to construct a panel for a peace flag, which contains their images of peace. On the fourth day they make peace bracelets with their peace buddies. The flag from the third day is hung at a closing ceremony held on the fifth and last day when the students visit a summer camp. At this camp the young people do trust-building and leadership activities.

Since most of the Institute activities take place on the campus of a large university, part of its purpose is to help these youth become comfortable with being on a college campus. The hope is that they may be motivated to pursue higher education themselves.

Participants of the Institute

Youth who attend the Summer Institute are recruited from area middle schools in the metropolitan Milwaukee area by the Pre-College Academy at UWM, which offers a variety of programs to enhance the current and future academic performance of high school and middle school students. Admission requires seventh-, eighth-, or ninth-grade status, good GPAs, teacher recommendations, and such general application information as is required for any precollege program. Beyond the application, a peace essay is required prior to attendance.[29]

In the summer of 1995 a pilot for the Institute was held. Its presurveys of participants' interests indicated that they especially wanted to learn how to manage conflicts in their own lives. A pre-Institute meeting for youth and their parents enhanced the planning, as facilitators had an opportunity to assess the various needs and interests. At a pre-Institute open house, the goals and objectives of the Institute were explained, while parents and participants were given the opportunity to express their desires for the Institute's outcomes. Almost half of these responses wanted interpersonal skill-building in the form of more effective communication strategies, including anger management skills. Among stated goals were wanting to "learn useful ways to solve problems in a nonviolent way" and "help to not become offensive or ready to fight in tense situations." Other suggestions asked for community-based activities that later came to be incorporated into the participants' action plans, such as having each young person provide a written commitment to the principles of nonviolence.

The profile of the seventy-five young people who came together to spend a week of their summer vacation to study nonviolence in 1995, 1996, and 1997 is as varied and enigmatic as the teens themselves often proved to be. The average age was fourteen. Most were still in junior high school. Twenty percent were ninth graders. Sixty-nine percent were female; 31 percent were male; 85 percent were from urban Milwaukee; 12 percent were from the suburbs; and 3 percent were from rural Wisconsin. Seventy-three percent were African-American; 18 percent were Hispanic; 5 percent were Asian; and 4 percent were Caucasian. Twenty participants had, at some time during their lives, witnessed violence with a gun. Thirty-five percent had members of their family who had been shot. Half had family members in prison.

Although the vast majority of these teenagers live in the inner city, they are not for the most part what many call "at-risk" youth. Most indicated involvement in church and after-school activities; some 14 percent in 1997, for example, were involved in scouting. Thirty percent had engaged in peacemaking activities in school, as opposed to 25 percent of a control group.[30] The Institute participants in general have learned more peacemaking skills, describe themselves as more peaceful, and more often help others resolve conflicts than any similar control group of teenagers. They also skipped class less and knew fewer youths with guns. Predictably, however, they felt less safe in their neighborhoods than did those in a control group, evidence that they do live in high-crime areas.

These young people also exhibit considerable leadership abilities. They provide positive role models in their school and do come from families that are highly motivated for them to succeed. At least one can speculate this since the parents chose to enroll their children in this precollege experience. As discussed, many participants had previous exposure to peacemaking skills, with 40 percent taking part in peer mediation programs. A majority came to the Institute interested in becoming peacemakers. Doubtless the skills and understandings they gained during their week reinforced such ambitions.

Impact of Institute

The UWM Summer Institute has had a profound impact upon the young people who have attended it. One girl, for example, said: "This week I realized that there is much more violence out there than I anticipated. I was very surprised to learn that around 80 youths die in Wisconsin per year. I would like to become a peacemaker to help less fortunate kids in violent areas." An analysis of the impact of this Institute derives from three different forms of data: (1) quantitative results from surveys administered to participants, their parents, and a control group of similar teenagers; (2) reports on action plans submitted by students as a result of attending the Institute; and (3) a questionnaire sent to parents prior to and after their children attended the Institute.

The quantitative aspects of this study are divided into three parts: a summary of the Summer Institute evaluations, a comparison of participants' responses to a questionnaire, and the results of a pre- and post-test instrument given to parents of the participants. The participants themselves were given an "Attitudes toward Violence and Nonviolence" questionnaire to fill out on the first day of the Summer Institute and, once again, two months after completing the program. This questionnaire was field tested for readability and reliability during the academic year 1994–95 with a population of youth participating in a Stop the Violence program run by the Milwaukee Urban League which produced an alpha score of eight. Of the twenty stems on this instrument, eight produced statistically significant results in 1995. See appendix C in this volume.

For the 1996 Institute a control group was matched to the experiment group, but the numbers of people participating in the post-test surveys was so small that no significant results were attained. The comparison group consisted of students who returned an identical survey administered before and after the Summer Institute at similar inner-city schools. The comparisons with the control and experimental groups are, nevertheless, descriptive and can contribute to understanding the characteristics of the young people who participate in the Summer Institutes.

On the last day of the Institute, all participants were given an evaluation sheet that contained eight specific and two open-ended questions. Average responses from these evaluations can be found in appendix C. Question 8 of the evaluation asked participants if they would recommend this Institute to a friend. Of the seventy-five who filled out this questionnaire, 87 percent answered "yes." Many of the youngest students from the sixth grade, however, responded "no." Older students, it may be conjectured, appreciated the Institute more. Staff has decided it may be best not to include sixth graders in future institutes. Extensive talking about violence evidently depressed that grade's twelve-year-olds, especially since the topics were complex and at times confusing. Nonviolence in the United States appears to be such a sophisticated concept that only the older, more mature students can comprehend and appreciate it.

The open-ended questions asked students what they liked and what they disliked about the Institute. The aspect most favored was meeting peacemakers from the community. Appreciation was also expressed for new people and learning to value peace. Some of the participants found some of the speakers boring. Others did not like being talked at and asked for more activities. As might be expected among a population of early adolescents, they wanted more games.

Another open-ended question asked participants to list three things they learned about nonviolence. Here are some of the responses from the 1996 Institute:

"walking away from fights; learn how to have self-control"
"It helps reduce deaths. It's more calming."
"relationships, anger management; what to do in violent situations."
"Don't talk to people you can't trust; never listen to no one else; take your own advice."
"not to fight, not to be violent; not to start things."
"to be big and walk away; to be a peacemaker; to control my anger."
"how to stop violence; how violence hurts people."
"to talk it out, be friendly, and have peace."
"Violence hurts everyone. It is everywhere. Violence isn't just hitting."

These young people do seem much concerned about violence and want skills to help them deal with it in their lives.

Table II in appendix C indicates that the staff of the Institute was successful in teaching young people to value peace. Respondents indicated that they had learned valuable peacekeeping behaviors. The decline in scores to "give in" to violence (item B) could mean that they feel stronger in themselves and have a variety of better ways of responding to conflict, rather than traditional "fight-or-flight" responses. Participants also indicated that they had learned to value an outside person, like a mediator, to help them resolve their conflicts. Responses indicate more concern about levels of violence in neighborhoods after the Institute. Responses also indicate that these young people are finding ways other than getting angry or fighting to resolve their conflicts.

The parent questionnaire mailed prior to the 1995 Institute and again six weeks after the Institute was completed by only nine parents for both mailings. Their responses are summarized in table III in appendix C. Although only four items on this twenty-eight-item questionnaire received responses at a statistically significant level, parents did indicate that their children were taking more responsibility for their actions, keeping out of fights more, having fewer emotional outbursts, and applying fairness rules more often.

The data, plus anecdotal comments from parents, do support this model for helping teenagers cope with violence. Several parents commented that the Institute had increased the confidence of their children and made them more interested in current events, especially local news on incidents of violence. Before the Institute those same children had ignored such stories. The parents also felt their children were more mature, often now wondering out loud why certain people behaved so violently. No further parent evaluations have been attempted.

The individual peace pledges developed during the 1997 Institute are interesting. Here are some examples:

As a nonviolent person, I pledge to solve all conflicts verbally instead of physically and not steal or take drugs. I will always display patience and self-control and be open-minded.

As a nonviolent person, I pledge not to hurt anyone for the rest of this month, to show respect to all people, and to help anyone I can at all times.

Never judge another person and treat others like they want to be treated.

As a nonviolent person, I pledge not to insult people and not to kill other humans.

As a nonviolent person, I pledge not to throw balls at other people's windows, not hit a wall and break it, try not to talk about people, and respect my parents.

As a nonviolent person, I pledge not to carry a gun. I will also solve all conflicts verbally instead of physically. I won't use words like nigger, bitch, or whore. I will not sell or have guns or drugs.

As a nonviolent person, I pledge to be as friendly as I can, to respect others, and to respect myself.

As a nonviolent person, I pledge to treat others with respect even if I don't like their opinions or ideals.

As a nonviolent person, I pledge to help others get along with each other, try to mediate myself as well as others, to try to avoid violent situations, say no to drugs, and to teach others what I've learned about being nonviolent.

These pledges made publicly in a full circle with adult and peer witnesses become powerful motivators for the young adolescents to practice nonviolence.

The highlight of the UWM Summer Institutes was the creation of action plans the participants promised to implement during the next school year. As mentioned, for each of these action plans students wrote the steps they needed to reach their goals, the obstacles that might arise, and ideas to overcome the potential obstacles. Some wanted to begin peer mediation programs in their schools, while others wanted to start groups dedicated to supporting and spreading the message of nonviolence in their schools, churches, or neighborhoods. During the first Institute participants pledged to work in their churches and schools to promote peace. One young man, Tom, formed a "men's group" at his high school.[31] This club proved especially helpful to him when one of his friends was shot and killed during the next school year. Another young man became president of the Students Against Violence and Drugs club at his high school.

One girl, Angelina, wrote a grant to the State Department of Public Instruction so that she could run a Nonviolence Institute for her high school the next spring. This Institute, organized by the students themselves, attracted fifty teenagers to a local recreation center. Among other activities, they set up a panel similar to a television talk show, on which the youth talked about violent episodes in their lives. Another young woman, Gail, introduced multicultural activities to a youth group at her church. Two of the girls who attended the 1996 Institute used their artistic talents to promote peace; one in a locally-produced television show, the other in a new gospel group that sang songs with peace themes at churches and schools. Several students who attended the follow-up meetings said they had kept out of trouble, an important accomplishment given the neighborhood odds. Some indicated feeling isolated since there were no peer mediation programs at their schools, or other peacemaking activities.

Students in the 1996 Institute committed themselves to the following action plans:

A. "to bring peace in the community and teach people to be nonviolent"
B. "to promote peace at my school by doing peer mediation"
C. "to organize another peace institute at my high school"
D. "to publish a book on the life of a teenager, written by us, consisting of drawing, poems, and stories"
E. "to start up a Catholic youth organization (CYO) at my church"
F. "community night out"

Action plan A was carried out by five students, who participated in a march for nonviolence during the following fall, one sponsored by a community agency in a high crime neighborhood. Action plan B was accomplished when many graduates of the 1996 Institute became involved in peer mediation programs at those schools that had them. One graduate of the 1995 Institute actually helped start a peer mediation program at his high school. Another teamed up with Angelina (who was mentioned above), to get funding for another Peace Institute serving ninety students at a local recreation center. The new Institute proved to be a success, its peers sharing with each other coping strategies developed earlier. Several of these students submitted drawings and poetry for a book on how teenagers can deal with violence (action plan D). The book remained unpublished. A follow-up meeting was held at the church (mentioned in action plan E), but the three students who attended that church had not been able to get the CYO started again. Several students participated in Safe Nights (action plan F) sponsored by the Milwaukee Health Department at local community-based organizations. At these safe nights teenagers got to dance and party in an environment free of weapons and drugs, but they also had to promise to participate in at least one violence prevention activity.

Discussion

The UWM Summer Institute does provide an innovative solution for the troubling phenomenon of teenage violence. As we have seen, it teaches young people alternative dispute resolution techniques, nonviolent strategies, and anger management skills, allowing them to share their concerns about violence with adults and peers. It commits them to personal behavior as well as to community actions that address problems of violence. Such peace practice helps them overcome very understandable feelings of cynicism about what can be done.

Among the strengths of the program is the way in which it teaches skills participants will be able to use for the rest of their lives. It helps fill their minds with images of peace that they can call upon whenever faced with conflicts. A graduate of the 1996 Institute wrote:

> The meaning of peace is very important to me. It means the power of love, safety, and happiness. This program was very helpful for me and other young people. We need peace in our surroundings and the whole planet. We can help peace and it can help us. We should learn to love one another no matter who we are or where we come from. There should be space for that on this Earth.

Another participant showed similar long-term expectations:

> There are many things that I have learned these couple of days. And I appreciate all the people who made it happen. I was never much concerned with violence. I mean, I thought about it, but not this much. I hope this experience helps me in the future, on the streets, or everywhere I happen to be.

Often departing participants proved quite eloquent. They wanted to share their dreams as did this young person:

> Peace is power. Peace is being able to live with your "brothers and sisters," no matter what their ethnicity, sex, or religion. Peace is being able to recognize the differences we all have and being able to respect them. Peace is within all of us (we may not know it). Peace is love of ourselves, others, and our environment. To achieve peace we need to start realizing how important life is and the fact that we need to respect it. Our world doesn't have to be violent; everyone has a good heart.

The peer teaching model, by which young graduates of the previous summer's Institute became staff, proved particularly effective. The graduates demonstrated sophisticated understandings of peace theory and were adept at in-depth uses of conflict resolution techniques. They were effective communicators with empathic skills.

Several students commented that they enjoyed being on a college campus, where they learned to be independent. The Summer Institute enjoyed a high degree of interagency cooperation, with staff from the university, local schools, peace organizations, teenage recreation centers, women's organizations, and the Milwaukee Health Department all volunteering to help.

The Institute did have, however, several weaknesses. It attracted mostly successful teenagers whose parents had read a newspaper announcement. It did not attract many children who were facing failure in school or the temptation to join gangs. The participants were mostly good students who were active in student affairs. The UWM staff wished the Institute had recruited more at-risk teenagers. Nor was the Institute able to attract enough males to keep its sex ratio near balance. Young women, understandably, were more inclined and able to attend. Since males generally are more vulnerable to all aspects of violence, it would have been better to involve a higher percentage of them.

The UWM Summer Institute has never been able to raise enough money to hire a full-time staff. It relies on teachers for recruiting students. Such individuals have busy schedules and rarely can devote their full energies to the task. The Institute could have used paid staff for recruiting and for conducting follow-up studies. Nor has the Institute yet been able to live up to the goal of creating a nonviolent brigade to help mobilize youth against the violence of an urban area. Most of the Institute graduates remain isolated in their schools. An attempt was made during planning for 1997 to focus on several schools with this in mind but there were not enough students to develop even at one school a solid core of peacemakers to form what Gandhi called a shenti sena, or nonviolent brigade. The effort, nevertheless, left two high schools with three students trained in peacebuilding and a Catholic elementary school with four. Follow-up activities may reveal what success they have had in creating a peaceful climate at their schools.

Conclusion

The Institute does provide a workable model for helping youth deal with violence. It has helped many teachers and youth workers to turn to conflict resolution to teach young people skills that will help them negotiate dangerous situations successfully. The Institute features the peacebuilding that hopes to so fill young people's heads with images of peace that, even in a culture that glamorizes violent behavior, they will lead others to choose nonviolence. This is indeed an "innoculist" model that attempts to educate young people to avoid not only violent behavior but also acquire resilience and real social competence to establish supportive social networks.

The Institute also provides important alternatives to more traditional methods used in schools to address violence. It eschews deterring violence by threatening students with punishment. Instead it stresses the power of nonviolence. Peaceful philosophies taught in tandem with peacemaking strategies can help young people master peaceful behavior. The best way to build peaceful behavior in our youth is to convince young people to value peace.

The Institute promotes a peace consciousness, one that is open-minded, concerned about justice, courageous in the face of violence, empathetic, respectful of others, cooperative, and aware of the alternatives to violence. How well these complex lessons can be mastered in one week is, as we have seen, hard to assess. Preliminary studies, however, do indicate adoptions by many students of alternatives to violence in their own behavior. Few seek to transform the social institutions that cause so much of the violence of current times, but they are ready and able to resolve conflicts in their own lives, the lives of their friends, their school, churches, and communities. Those graduates that have kept in touch have at the very least stayed out of trouble. Several have taken important leadership roles in promoting peace. One can at least hope that youth homicide and crime rates in the city of Milwaukee have gone down in some part because of the activities of the Summer Institute. Certainly the graduates have had a calming influence upon those with whom they have had contact. Though pretty much left on their own to figure out how to follow the path to peace, the complicated journey they started at the Institute will stimulate them throughout their lives to choose peaceful alternatives to conflict.

Graduates of 1998 UWM Summer Institute on Nonviolence

Notes

1. Office of Justice Programs, Bureau of Justice Statistics, *Firearms and Crimes of Violence*, Publication NJC-146844 (Washington, DC: U.S. Department of Justice, February 1994).

2. Federal Bureau of Investigation, *Uniform Crime Reports, 1987* (Washington, DC: U.S. Department of Justice, 1987).

3. Joel Dresang, "Many Teens Say Schools Are Getting More Violent, Poll Finds" *Milwaukee Journal/Sentinel* 12 September 1996, 7a.

4. Christian E. Molidor. "Female Gang Members: A Profile of Aggression and Victimization." *Social Work* 41, no. 3 (May 1996): 251-57.

5. Louis Harris and Associates, *Between Hope and Fear: Teens Speak Out on Crime and the Community* (Washington, DC: National Institute for Citizen Education and the Law, 1995).

6. Ibid., 10.

7. Ian M. Harris, "Peace Education: A Modern Educational Reform," in *Proceedings of the Midwest Philosophy of Education Society*, ed. George W. Stickel and David B. Owen (Chicago, IL: Midwest Philosophy of Education Society, 1995), 253-74.

8. Carnegie Council on Adolescent Development, *Great Transitions: Preparing Adolescents for a New Century* (New York: Carnegie Corporation, 1995), 55.

9. Ibid.

10. Felton Earls, Robert B. Cairns, and James A. Mercy, "The Control of Violence and the Promotion of Nonviolence in Adolescents," in *Promoting the Health of Adolescents: New Directions for the 21st Century*, ed. S. G. Millstein, A. C. Pewterson, and E. O. Nightingale (New York: Oxford University Press, 1993), 285-304.

11. Richard L. Curwin, "A Human Approach to Reducing Violence: A Critical Analysis of Responses to School Violence," *Educational Leadership* 52, no. 5 (February 1996).

12. Pedro Noguera, "Preventing and Producing Violence: A Critical Analysis of Responses to School Violence," *Harvard Educational Review* 65, no. 2 (summer 1995): 189-212.

13. Valerie Bernat, "Teaching Peace," *Young Children* 48, no. 3 (March 1993): 36-39; N. Carlsson-Paige and D. Levin, *Helping Young Children Under-*

stand *Peace, War, and the Nuclear Threat* (Association for Supervision and Curriculum Development: Washington, DC, 1985).

14 David Grossman, Holly Neckerman, Thomas Koepsall, et al., "The Effectiveness of a Violence Prevention Curriculum among Children in Elementary School: A Randomized Controlled Trial," *JAMA* 277 (May 1997): 1605-11.

15 Leslie Stevahn, David Johnson, Robert Johnson, and Don Real, "The Impact of a Cooperative or Individualistic Contest on the Effectiveness of Conflict Resolution Training," *American Educational Research Journal* 33, no. 3 (winter 1996): 801-23.

16 William C. Eckhardt, "Peace Studies and Attitude Change: A Value Theory of Peace Studies," *Peace & Change* 6, no. 1 (spring 1984): 79-85.

17 Robert Feltman, "Change in Peace Attitude: A Controlled Attitude Change Study of Internationalism," *Peace Research* 18, no. 1 (February 1986): 66-71; Philip French, "Preventive Medicine for Nuclear War," *Psychology Today* (September 1984): 70; James K. Lyou, "Studying Nuclear Weapons: The Effect on Students," *Peace Research* 19, no. 1 (February 1987): 11-18.

18 Ian M. Harris, "The Challenge of Peace Education: Do Our Efforts Make a Difference?" *Educational Foundations* 6, no. 4 (1992): 75-98.

19 David Johnson, Robert Johnson, and Bruce Dudley, "Effects of Peer Mediation Training on Elementary School Students," *Mediation Quarterly* 10, no. 1 (fall 1992): 89-97.

20 Irving A. Spergel, *The Youth Gang Problem: A Community Approach* (New York: Oxford University Press, 1995).

21 Project STOP, 1991-92. (New York City Board of Education, Division of Strategic Planning/Research and Development, 1991).

22 Ian M. Harris, *Peace Education* (Jefferson, NC: McFarland & Co., 1988).

23 Ian M. Harris, "From World Peace to Peace in the 'Hood: Peace Education in a Postmodern World," *Journal for a Just and Caring Education* 2, no. 4 (October 1996): 378-95.

24 Louis Harris and Associates, *Between Hope and Fear*, 14.

25 Matthew Leighninger and Mark Niedergang, *Confronting Violence in Our Communities: A Guide for Involving Citizens in Public Dialogue and Problem Solving* (Pomfret, CT: Topsfield Foundation, 1994).

26 Robin Richardson, "The Process of Reflection Workshops and Seminars in Peace Education," *Bulletin of Peace Proposals* 10, no. 4 (1979) 407-13.

27 **Dating Bill of Rights**
    Each individual has . . .
    The right to get out
    The right to be respected

The right to know when something is wrong
The right to honesty
The right to freedom and privacy
The right to your own opinions
The right to say "no" and have it respected.

28   **Peace Treaty**
Raise your hand when you want to talk (except when brainstorming).
Respect one another and everyone's ideas.
Let people speak their minds.
Use put-ups (rather than put-downs).
Act peacefully.
Keep time.
This treaty was designed and signed by all participants prior to leaving the Institute on the first day.

29   Quotes from these essays appear throughout this chapter.

30   These high percentages indicate that most of the children in the experimental group and the control group were selected by teachers involved in peer mediation activities.

31   This and the other names used in this section are fictitious.

Appendix A

Reading List for Adolescents on Nonviolence

General Fiction

Arrick, Fran. *Where'd You Get the Gun, Billy?* Bantam, 1991. It could happen anywhere, and it does. In a small town, a couple fight too hard, too often, and have easy access to a pistol.

Bosse, Malcolm. *79 Squares.* Crowell, 1979. A teenager, on probation, befriends a convicted murderer. In the course of events, he becomes victimized by his friends.

Briggs, Raymond. *When the Wind Blows.* Shocken, 1982. A cartoon book tells the moving story of a British couple preparing for a nuclear holocaust according to government instructions.

Brown, Susan. *You're Dead, David.* Macmillan, 1995. When David is forced to leave his private academy for a public school, he encounters a bullying gang of boys who brutalize and terrorize him without end.

Collier, James. *My Brother Sam is Dead.* Four Winds, 1974. Recounts the tragedy that strikes the Meeker family during the American Revolution when one son joins the rebels while the rest of the family tries to stay neutral in a Tory town.

Cooper, Susan. *Dawn of Fear.* Harcourt, 1976. Boys learn fear when they come face-to-face with the hatred of grown-ups.

Crutcher, Chris. *Running Loose.* Greenwillow, 1983. Louie Banks's senior year takes a downward turn when he stands up to a coach who advocates violence to create a winning football team.

Degens, T. *The Game on Thatcher Island.* Viking, 1977. Harry is flattered when a group of older boys invites him to participate in their game of war, but his elation disappears.

Hinton, S. E. *The Outsiders.* Viking Press, 1967. Fourteen-year-old Ponyboy gives his loyalties only to his brothers and their gang, but that loyalty drags him into a violent chain of events.

Levitin, Sonia. *Adam's War.* Dial, 1994. Adam is a natural-born leader who finds himself at first fearing, then becoming inexplicably drawn to, an inevitable violent altercation.

Lynch, Chris. *Shadow Boxer.* HarperCollins, 1993. After their father dies, George must teach his younger brother Monty how to tell the difference between when to fight and when to walk away.

Mazer, Norma Fox. *Out of Control.* Morrow, 1993. Rollo Wingate and his friends get out of control when they rough up a girl they barely know. The sexual assault goes relatively unpunished, but Rollo has deep regrets that he can't understand.

Miklowitz, Gloria. *Past Forgiving.* Simon & Schuster, 1995. Alex and Cliff seem like a perfect couple, but when Cliff's anger and jealousy turn to violence, Alex needs to decide what she can and cannot forgive.

O'Brien, Robert. *Z for Zacharia.* Atheneum, 1974. Portrays a young girl who was the only human left alive after nuclear doomsday, or so she thought.

O'Dell, Scott. *Sarah Bishop.* Houghton, 1980. A novel about the American Revolution in which the line between the "good guys" and "bad guys" is blurred.

Schlee, Ann. *The Vandal.* Crown, 1981. An orderly society of the future in which citizens are taught that "nothing lost matters." An interesting approach to the importance of history.

Tamar, Erika. *Fair Game.* Harcourt, 1993. A group of popular high school athletes is accused of sexually molesting a mildly retarded teenage girl. Told from three different viewpoints, this hard-hitting novel, based on a true incident, examines the issues behind the story.

Taylor, Mildred D. *The Well: David's Story.* Dial, 1995. Set in the early 1900s, this short novel tells the story of how the Logan family's act of generosity toward a white family erupts into an incident of racial violence.

Thesman, Jean. *Summerspell.* Simon & Schuster, 1995. Jocylen attempts to run away from Gerald, who has been sexually harassing her, only to find that neither she nor her classmate Baily can hide from the fear that haunts them.

Wartseki, Maureen. *Candle in the Wind.* Fawcett, 1995. Drawn from the headlines, this is a shocking story about the murder of a Japanese-American teenager and the climate of racial hate that allowed it to happen.

Autobiographical Accounts

Frank, Anne. *Diary of a Young Girl.* Modern Library, 1952. The diary of a thirteen-year-old Jewish girl in hiding from the Nazis.

Hautzig, Esther. *The Endless Steppe.* Crowell, 1968. Describes the experience of being exiled to Siberia.

Kherdian, David. *The Road from Home.* Greenwillow, 1979. The dislocation of an Armenian family.

Koehn, Ilse. *Mischling, Second Degree.* Greenwillow, 1977. Describes the experiences of a young girl growing up in Nazi Germany.

Osada, Arata, comp. *Children of Hiroshima.* Oelgeschlager, Gunn, & Hain, 1981. Collected in the early 1950s, these essays documenting children's remembrances of the Hiroshima blast create a strong impression.

Reiss, Johann. *The Upstairs Room.* Crowell, 1972. Two sisters in hiding from the Nazis.

Siegel, Aranha. *Upon the Head of the Goat.* Farrar, 1981. A childhood in Hungary, 1939–44.

Books About World War II—Focus on Japan

Coerr, Eleanor. *Isadako and the Thousand Paper Cranes.* Putnam, 1977. Story of a twelve-year-old girl who dies from leukemia after the bombing of Hiroshima.

Davis, Daniel S. *Behind Barbed Wire.* Dutton, 1982. The imprisonment of Japanese-Americans during World War II.

Lifton, Betty. *Return to Hiroshima.* Atheneum, 1970. Photographs indicate the havoc caused by the bomb.

Nakamoto, Hiroko. *My Japan.* McGraw, 1970. A child's view of Japan from 1930 to 1951.

Takashima, Shiziuje. *A Child in Prison Camp.* Morrow, 1974. Life in a Japanese internment camp in Canada.

Uchida, Yoshiko. *Journey Home.* Atheneum, 1978. After Pearl Harbor, a Japanese-American girl and her family are forced to go to an "alien" camp, where they experience suffering and humiliation. *Journey Home* is the sequel in which the family tries to reconstruct their lives after their release.

Books About World War II—Focus on Germany

Davies, Andrew. *Conrad's War.* Crown, 1980. A book of a young boy's fantasies about war, killing, and guns.

Degens, T. *Transport 7-41-R.* Viking, 1974. A powerful statement about the ways in which the devastation of war and misguided patriotism can influence the human spirit.

Greene, Bette. *The Summer of My German Soldier.* Dial, 1973. The unlikely friendship between a Jewish girl and a German soldier.

Haugaard, Eric. *Chase Me, Catch Nobody.* Houghton Mifflin, 1980. A young boy becomes involved in the activities of the anti-Nazi underground.

———. *The Little Fishes.* Houghton Mifflin, 1967. A tale of a war and its effects on the children who must live through it and learn to love mankind in spite of it.

I Never Saw Another Butterfly. McGraw, 1964. Children's drawings and poems from Theresienstadt Concentration Camp, 1942–44.

Levoy, Myron. *Alan and Naomi.* Harper & Row, 1977. A powerful portrait of Naomi, who has been traumatized by having witnessed Nazi brutality to her father in France during the war.

Meltzer, Milton. *Never to Forget.* Harper & Row, 1976. Personal accounts reveal everyday life in the Nazi ghettos and the labor and death camps.

Orgel, Davis. *The Devil in Vienna*. Dial, 1978. A story of individual acts of bravery and love in a world characterized by mass indifference and betrayal.

Richter, Hans. *Frederick*. Holt, 1970. The friendship of two boys in Germany from 1920 to 1942.

Tunis, John. *His Enemy, His Friend*. Morrow, 1967. A story about the brutality of war.

Van Stockum, Hilda. *The Borrowed House*. Farrar, 1975. A German girl, member of the Hitler Youth, goes to live in Amsterdam.

Peace People

Aaseng, Nathan. *The Peace Seekers: The Nobel Peace Prize*. Lerner, 1987.

Blue, Rose. *People of Peace*. Millbrook Press, 1994. The story of a small number of people who have worked for and are working at the same enormous task—creating peace on earth.

Claflin, Edward Beecher. *Sojourner Truth*. Barron's, 1987. A great leader and orator in the fight against slavery and for women's rights. Her strength lay in her firm conviction of her own rights and her knowledge of the law to protect these rights.

Delisle, Jim. *Kids' Stories: Biographies of 20 Young People You'd Like to Know*. Free Spirit Publishing, 1997. Meet twenty young people, ages from eight to eighteen, each of whom has a mission in this life. Each biography begins with a different section called family background, making a difference, lessons learned, personal goals, global concerns.

Jacobs, William Jay. *Great Lives: Human Rights*. Scribner, 1990.

Levine, Ellen. *Freedom's Children: Young Civil Rights Activists Tell Their Own Story*. Putnam's Sons, 1993. Thirty young people tell what it was like to be a black child in the South and talk of their part in the great civil rights struggles of the 1950s and 1960s.

Lewis, Barbara. *Kids With Courage*. Free Spirit Publishing, 1992. True stories of young people who are involved in social action and in saving the environment.

Mitchard, Jacqueline. *Jane Addams: Pioneer in Social Reform and Activist for World Peace.* Gareth Stevens, 1991.

Piatigorsky, Gregor. *Cellist.* Doubleday and Co., 1965. A true story about Pablo Casals.

Sawyer, Kem Knapp. *Lucretia Mott: Friend of Justice.* Discovery Enterprises, Ltd., 1991. This heroine of the women's rights movement was a Quaker who opposed slavery and war. She also believed women were equal to men in all aspects and helped organize the first women's rights convention in Seneca Falls, New York, in 1848.

Sherrow, Victoria. *Mohanda Gandhi: The Power of the Spirit.* Millbrook Press, 1994.

Wade. Linda. *James Carter.* Children's Press, 1989.

Environment

Baker, Jeannie. *Where the Forest Meets the Sea.* Greenwillow Books, 1987. A boy visits the Australian rainforest with his father and wonders if it will still be there if they should travel that way again.

Baylor, Byrd, and Peter Parnall. *The Other Way to Listen.* Charles Scribner's Sons, 1978. Story told from a child's perspective, about being one with creation. If you learn to listen and become at peace with your surroundings, you can hear rocks murmur and hills sing.

Caduto, Michael J., and Joseph Bruchac. *Keepers of the Earth: Native American Stories and Environmental Activities for Children.* Fulcrum, 1988. Stories and activities that teach about the environment.

Carter, Forest. *The Education of Little Tree.* University of New Mexico Press, 1976. The story of a Cherokee boy growing up with his grandparents in Tennessee in the 1930s. Touches on Native American lifestyles and philosophy, with an environmentally sensitive way of looking at the earth.

Giono, Jean. *The Man Who Planted Hope and Grew Happiness.* In *Sharing the Joy of Nature,* by Joseph Cornell. Dawn, 1989. A true and powerful story of a man who spent the last forty years of his life planting trees and reforesting a section of southern France single-handedly. His labors spanned two world wars, restoring the region to life.

General Peace Books for Youth

Carter, Jimmy. *Talking Peace: A Vision for the Next Generation.* Dutton, 1992.

Durrell, Ann. *Big Book for Peace.* Dutton, 1990.

Fry-Miller, Kathleen. *Peace Works: Young Peacemakers Project, Book II.* Brethren Press, 1989.

Lucas, Eileen. *Peace on the Playground: Nonviolent Ways of Problem Solving.* Watts, 1991.

MacDonald, Margaret. *Peace Tables: World Folktales to Talk About.* Shoestring, 1992.

———. *Making Friends: Katya from Moscow and Star from San Francisco.* Holt, 1987.

Meltzer, Milton. *Ain't Gonna Study War No More: The Story of America's Peace Seekers.* Harper & Row, 1985.

Scholes, Katherine. *Peace Begins with You.* Sierra Club, Little, Brown, 1985.

Smith, Samantha. *Samantha Smith: Journey to the Soviet Union.* Little, Brown, 1985.

Vigna, Judith. *Nobody Wants a Nuclear War.* Whitman, 1986.

Social Science

Bode, Janet. *Voices of Rape.* Watts, 1990. Bode documents dramatic first-person accounts of this crime of violence from a variety of viewpoints.

Chalet, Donna. *Staying Safe on Dates.* Rosen, 1995. One of a series of books intended to provide young women with information about avoiding victimization, this title examines violence that occurs in dating relationships, including physical abuse and acquaintance rape.

Hyde, Margaret. *The Violent Mind.* Watts, 1991. Hyde gives a brief introduction to social and physiological causes of violence, with statistics, graphs, and first-person accounts.

Kosof, Anna. *Battered Women.* Watts, 1994. Personal narratives about abusive relationships give readers insight into the problem from the perspective of both the victim and the abuser.

Landau, Elaine. *Sexual Harassment.* Walker, 1993. Drawing on court cases, the Anita Hill-Clarence Thomas hearings, and personal narratives, Landau explores harassment from a variety of viewpoints.

Landau, Elaine. *Teenage Violence.* Silver Burdett, 1990. The many types of violence done by and to teenagers, including gang violence and date rape, are presented in an excellent overview of the problem.

Lang, Susan. *Teenage Violence.* Watts, 1995. First-person accounts, photographs, suggested solutions, and short chapters make this summary of violence and young people easy to read and understand.

Levy, Barrie. *In Love and Danger.* Seal, 1992. Filled with personal narratives and easy-to-read commentary, this self-help book provides solutions to the problem of violence in romantic relationships.

Miller, Maryann. *Coping with Weapons and Violence in School and on Your Streets.* Rosen, 1993. Facts don't lie: More and more teens have access to guns than ever before. Miller explains the reasons, explores the issues, and suggests solutions.

Moe, Barbara. *Coping as a Survivor of Violent Crime.* Rosen, 1995. Using personal narratives and plenty of research, Moe's book is designed to help teens avoid becoming victims, to practice nonviolent conflict resolutions, and to survive violent crime.

Violence in America. Greenhaven, 1990. The roles of the media, broken families, gender roles, the juvenile justice systems, and other factors in creating violence among teenagers are debated.

Voices from the Future. Crown, 1993. In uncensored comments, children and teenagers across the country express their feelings about the effects of growing up in a world of hurt.

Voigt, Cynthia. *When She Hollers.* Scholastic, 1994. Tish decides to put an end to her stepfather's sexual abuse—but at what cost?

Youth Violence. Opposing Viewpoints, Greenhaven, 1992. This collection of essays by various experts and reporters explores the nature and causes of violence among youth, the breadth of the problems, and possible solutions.

Appendix B

Peace!

If the third millennium could begin under the sign of nonviolence
    This is the dream of the Nobel Peace Prize Laureates.
Today, they are inviting you to join them to influence all the governments of the world.

The Dalai Lama
Mother Teresa
Aung San Suu Kyi
Nelson Mandela
Mikhail Gorbachev
Shimon Perez
Elie Wiesel
Mairead Corrigan-Maguire
Norman Borlaug
Betty Williams
Lech Walesa
Desmond Tutu
Oscar Arias Sanchez
Frederik W. de Klerk
Jos, Ramos Horta
Carlos F. X. Belo
Yasser Arafat
UNICEF
Adolfo Perez Esquivel
Joseph Rotblat

The twentieth century which comes to an end has seen the greatest carnage in all of human history. It is urgent that we reverse this trend, that we promote, in the words of the Dalai Lama, an epoch of peace. It is a question of survival!

There is only one way to fight violence with nonviolence: education.

The future of the world hangs on our willingness to really change. Our willingness to be finished with the culture of violence, be it physical, psychological or economic.

Our mentality is archaic. Often we continue to raise our children using ideas developed in times of war and conquest. We need to reject these outmoded principles and teach children that the "other" is not the enemy. We must dare to tell young people, even in history classes, that they will contribute more to the world by living in dignity than by dying heroically, that it is conscience, rather than obedience, which is the basis of human life.

The only real challenge remaining today, the real issue which will define the future, is, for the first time, to live together by respecting ourselves, each other, and the environment. It seems so simple, but nothing could be more complicated.

To make this dream a reality, we want the governments of all of the world countries at the United Nations to adopt a resolution declaring:

1. The year 2000 "Year of Education for Non-Violence"
2. The years 2000 to 2010 "Decade for a Culture of Non-Violence" so that nonviolence will finally be taught

Let's teach our children to help us to be wiser.

Practical measures will develop from this commitment in the areas of culture and, above all, education (an international group of researchers is already developing materials for children). We must learn to seek the nonviolent resolution to our conflicts.

Appendix C

Summer Institute on Nonviolence Evaluations

The youth responded on a four-point scale going from 4=very much to 3=quite a bit to 2=not very much to 1=a little. Data from the first seven questions are presented below in Table I:

Table I Student Evaluations of 1995 and 1996 UWM Summer Institute

Stem	Average	
	1995	1996
a. Was this Institute interesting?	3.26	3.31
b. Do you feel ready to become a peacemaker?	3.64	3.19
c. Was this Institute fun?	3.50	3.23
d. Did you get to know other students?	3.50	3.15
e. Did you learn about the effects of violence?	3.63	3.50
f. Did you learn to value peace?	3.73	3.54
g. Did you enjoy being at UWM?	3.60	3.48

Table II Attitudes Toward Violence and Nonviolence*

When you are faced with conflict, how often do you: Survey Item	Means@	
	Pre-Institute	Post-Institute
A. Turn conflict into a joke	.93	1.00
B. Give in	1.00	.87
C. Get an outside person to decide what is right	1.64	1.93
D. Threaten the other person	1.07	.80
E. Fight it out physically	.80	.73
F. Whine or complain until you get your way	.60	.67
G. Take the problem to peer mediation	1.57	1.86
H. Worry about violence in your neighborhood?	1.62	1.92

*These responses are significant at the p = <.05 level.
@These means come from a 5-point scale:
0=not at all; 1=a little; 2=sometimes; 3=frequently; 4=all the time

Table III Parents' Observations of Children*

Survey Item	Means@	
	Post-Institute	Pre-Institute
Does your child have emotional outbursts?	1.20	1.00
Does your child take responsibility for his or her actions?	3.00	3.20
Does your child apply fairness rules (i.e., sharing)?	2.78	2.89
Does your child keep out of fights?	3.10	3.30

*These responses are significant at the p=<.05 level.
@These means come from a 5-point scale:
0=not at all; 1=a little; 2=sometimes; 3=frequently; 4=all the time

Contributors

Nadja M. Alexander is Assistant Professor in the School of Law, The University of Queensland, Australia. One of her major teaching and research areas is conflict management and within this context, she has been using a range of ABL methods. Her innovative teaching techniques were recognized Australia-wide in 1997, when she was awarded a nation-Wide Teaching Excellence Award.

Rebecca Anderson is Assistant Professor in the Department of Instruction and Curriculum Leadership, The University of Memphis, where she teaches classes in the Reading/Language Arts to undergraduates and graduates. Her main research interests include alternative assessment practices and applications of technology in literacy education.

Dé Bryant 's expertise is in community development and social change. Dr. Bryant is Director of the Social Action Project (SOCACT), which operates in Indiana and Michigan, with international sites in Nigeria and South Africa. In 1994 Indiana University South Bend nominated the Social Action Project for the President's "Thousand Points of Light" award for positive influence in communities. She is Associate Professor of Community Psychology.

Lucille A. Cardella received her master in education in school psychology from Boston College. She served as a school psychologist in both public and private special education schools for more than ten years. She is currently pursuing her doctoral degree in counseling at the State University of New York at Albany.

Teresa B. Carlson is Assistant Professor in the teacher education section of the Human Movement Studies Department at the University of Queensland, Australia. She has been working in the area of ABL for ten years, working with both secondary and college students. Her research interests include the formation of student attitudes, in particular, attitudes toward physical activity. Her research is moving toward working more with alienated or at-risk youth, the wilderness programs, and ABL activities. Her research also includes assessment of sporting involvement on students' behaviors and attitudes.

Robert C. DiGiulio earned his Ph.D. in human development and education from the University of Connecticut. His twenty-seven-year career as educator includes service as a New York City public school teacher, principal, educational researcher, consultant, and writer. Presently Dr. DiGiulio is an Associate Professor of Education at Johnson State College in Vermont. Dr. DiGiulio has written numerous books, including *When You Are a Single Parent, Effective Parenting, Beyond Widowhood* and *After Loss,* and he is coauthor of *Straight Talk about Death and Dying* with Rachel Kranz. In addition, Dr. DiGiulio co-developed "Teen Test," a vocational counseling program for adolescents, and he co-authored educational computer software, *Language Activities Courseware.*

Linda Rennie Forcey, Professor of Human Development and Women's Studies in the School of Education and Human Development at Binghamton University, is a political scientist by training. Her research focuses on the intersection of Peace Studies and feminist theorizing. She has written, edited, or coedited a number of books relating to women and peace, including *Mothers of Sons: Toward An Understanding of Responsibility; Peace: Meanings, Politics, Strategies; Yearning to Breathe Free: Liberation Theologies in the U.S.* with Mar Peter-Raoul and Robert Fredrick Hunter Jr.; and *Mothering: Ideology, Experience, Agency,* with Evelyn Nakano Glenn and Grace Chang.

Matthew W. Greene is an educational consultant, policy analyst, and mediator. He graduated from Dartmouth College in 1990, and received his Ph.D. in political science from the University of Colorado in 1997. He now works in Westport, Connecticut, with Howard Greene Associates, an educational counseling and consulting firm. He has written about institutional learning and problem definition processes, and has researched school violence and educational governance issues as a consultant for the Education Commission of the States. He has worked at both the U.S. Information Agency and the U.S. Department of Education in Washington, DC.

Jennifer Hanis was co-leader of the Theater team for the Social Action Project (SOCACT). During her two-year involvement the Theater wrote and performed a radio play (sent to youths in Nigeria) and created a series of stories for puppets (at the Center for the Homeless). Her interests are in creating community-based interventions in the area of chemical dependency. She is currently pursuing a masters degree in sociology.

Ian Murray Harris directs the Peace Studies program at the University of Wisconsin-Milwaukee, where he is Professor of Educational Policy and Community Studies. He is the author of *Peace Education,* and *Messages Men Hear: Constructing Masculinities.* He is coauthor with Paul Denise of *Exponential Education for Community Development.* He serves as executive secretary of the Peace Education Commission of the International Peace Research Association.

John D. Krumboltz, Professor of Education and Psychology at Stanford University, is a Fellow of the American Psychological Association and the American Association for the Advancement of Science. A former high school counselor, he has been involved in a number of studies with adolescents, including efforts to see how troublesome career beliefs can be identified through counseling interventions. He is coauthor of *Changing Children's Behavior,* and in 1990 the American Psychological Association's Division of Counseling Psychology gave him the Leona Tyler Award.

Alan McCully is a lecturer in Education and Contemporary Society. For twenty years he worked in a high school in a rural, mainly Protestant community teaching history and social studies. During that time he was also involved in a major curriculum project in the field of cultural education, the School's Cultural Studies Project. His publications relate to the teaching of controversial issues, approaches to the teaching of Irish history, and national identity and history teaching. He works for the Speak Your Piece project under the directorship of Dr.

Alan Smith. The project is based at the University of Ulster, Coleraine, Northern Ireland.

Peter Adam Nash is a high school English teacher and writer. His work has been published in *The Minetta Review, Margins, English Journal*, and *The Collegiate Review*. He is currently working on a novel set in turn-of-the-century Rome entitled *Choose a Lonely House*. He lives with his wife and son in Albuquerque, New Mexico.

Linden L. Nelson is Professor of Psychology and Human Development at California Polytechnic State University in San Luis Obispo, California. He and Michael Van Slyck are co-chairs of the Peace and Education Working Group of the Division of Peace Psychology, American Psychological Association. Dr. Nelson's early research studied the development of cooperation and competition in children. Subsequently, his research and publications have addressed the psychology of the nuclear arms race, peace education in the psychology curriculum, assessment of instruction about conflict resolution, and determinants of militaristic attitudes.

Marian O'Doherty was a research officer with the Speak Your Piece project and is currently a lecturer in Education and Contemporary Society at the University of Ulster. She taught at the elementary level before working for several years as an advisory teacher specializing in management issues. Presently, she teaches the special educational needs components of the University of Ulster initial training programs. She is completing her doctoral studies on the political and cultural attitudes of Catholic young people in West Belfast.

Molly K. Pont-Brown became interested in the topic of conflict resolution during her education at Stanford University, where she spent time in local elementary schools, worked on issues of violence during an internship at the Children's Defense Fund in Washington, DC, and wrote a senior honor's thesis on the topic. She received a B.A. from Stanford in 1994 and an M.Ed. from the University of California, Los Angeles in 1995. Ms. Pont Brown currently teaches fifth grade in Palo Alto, California.

Nathan Rousseau is Assistant Professor of Sociology at Muskingum College in New Concord, Ohio. He has organized first Martin Luther

King Jr. celebrations and is working to make Social Justice Studies and service learning prominent components of college curricula.

Sonya Rousseau is a writer and librarian at large and with Nathan Rousseau at Hanover College to make service learning a prominent, stable component of the curriculum.

Paul Smyth is a research officer with the Speak Your Piece project and is now Community Relations Development Officer with the Youth Council for Northern Ireland. He has worked primarily in the Northern Ireland youth service, specializing in community relations work with mixed groups of Protestant and Catholic young people. He has also worked with groups from across Europe and the United States as a speaker and facilitator. His current research interest is peer education, and its wider applications including peer mediation, as a vehicle for resolving conflict and promoting reconciliation in Northern Ireland.

Marilyn Stern is currently Educational Associate Professor in the Department of Counseling Psychology with a joint appointment in the Department of Health Policy, Management, and Behavior, University at Albany. Her primary professional focus is as a counseling health psychologist whose work includes an examination of the issues related to the impact of stereotyping processes on caregiver-child interactions, adolescent coping with stress and conflict. Her work in the area of dispute resolution includes research on parent-child and peer mediation. Her other professional activities include serving on the editorial boards of the *Journal of Counseling Psychology* and the *Counseling Psychologist*. She currently serves the American Psychological Association as Chair of the Health Counseling Psychology Section and as the international Liaison to Israel for the Division of Counseling Psychology.

Charles Stoner has been a member of the Social Action Project (SOCACT) since 1994, working as a co-leader of the Theater team. During his involvement the Theater wrote and performed a play about inner-city life (performed at the neighborhood community center), a radio play (sent to youths in Nigeria), and created a series of stories for puppets at the Center for the Homeless. His interests are in creating community-based interventions for marginalized groups dealing with alcohol and drug addiction. He is currently pursuing a B.A. at Indiana University South Bend with a major in psychology.

Melanie Suriani is a principal in the Memphis City school district, and is an adjunct faculty member in the Department of Instruction and Curriculum Leadership, The University of Memphis. She makes presentations advocating alternatives to the use of corporal punishment in schools at regional and district conferences.

Barbara J. Thayer-Bacon is Associate Professor in the Department of Foundations and Inquiry, Bowling Green State University. Her primary areas of scholarship are the philosophy of education, critical thinking, epistemology, feminist theory, and educational reform.

Michael Van Slyck, Ph.D., is Founder/Principal of the Research Institute for Dispute Resolution, Albany, New York, a consulting organization providing comprehensive dispute resolution services, including research, training, and intervention. He also holds the position of lecturer in the Department of Educational and Counseling Psychology, SUNY Albany. His primary research focus for the last ten years has been on the resolution of conflicts involving adolescents and their peers and parents through mediation. Among his other professional activities, he serves on the editorial board of *Mediation Quarterly* and is currently Co-Chair of the Peace Education Committee of the Division of Peace Psychology, American Psychological Association.

Arjen E. J. Wals is an environmental education researcher and lecturer in the Department of Education of Wageningen Agricultural University, Netherlands. His Ph.D., obtained from the University of Michigan in Ann Arbor, focused on young adolescents' perceptions of nature and environmental issues and their implications for environmental education. He is a member of the North American Committee on Environmental Education Research and currently serves as President of Caretakers of the Environment International, a global network of high school teachers and students active in environmental education.

Rebecca Wasson is Research Associate at the Center for Research in Educational Policy, College of Education, The University of Memphis, and is an adjunct faculty member in the Leadership Department. Her research interests include qualitative methodologies and empowerment models of program evaluations. She has a particular interest in violence intervention strategies that focus on urban youth.

Bonnie Winfield, Assistant Professor in the School of Education and Human Development, Binghamton University, specializes in community-based learning, social policy, institutional ethnography, and feminist qualitative research. She also is an Evaluation and Training Specialist of public policy programs contracted by government and nonprofit organizations for Aguirre International.

Index

A

Ablon, Joan, 205
absenteeism, 5
academic controversy, an approach to teaching conflict resolution, 109
academic performance, improving, 111, 179, 312
accidental violence, 37
action research and community problem solving (AR&CPS), 11, 239, 242-246, 256-258. *See also* Pistons Middle School (Detroit)
active listening, 103, 106
activities, 3, 96, 98, 99, 100, 102, 105, 110, 111
    and adventure-based learning, 167-172
    types of
        minefield activity, 168-169, 171
        raft activity, 169, 171-172
administrators
    and corrective approach, 197, 198-201, 208
    and crime and punishment approach, 196
    participation in conflict resolution programs, 38, 42
    and preventive approach, 197, 201-203
    role of, 207-208
    on school violence, 10
    and supportive approach, 197-198, 203-207
Adopt-A-Park program (Syracuse, NY), 296
adventure-based learning (ABL), 10
    activities and resources, 167-172
    and developing peacemaking skills, 162-167
    philosophy of, 161-162
advertising, 19, 21. *See also* media
African-Americans, 1, 4, 22-23, 31n15
    and sports, 22-23
after-school programs, 198
aggression, 95, 96, 110-111, 139, 140, 294, 312
alcohol use, 2, 4, 62, 77, 140
Alexander, Nadja M., 10
alienation, 23, 202, 293
alternative dispute resolution (ADR) initiatives, 3, 177, 189, 323. *See also* youth-oriented conflict resolution (YOCR)
alternative education programs, 63, 74, 75, 77
alternative public schools, 198
Alternatives to Violence curriculum, 103-104, 107, 108, 111
American Federation of Teachers, 198
American Journal of Preventative Medicine, 46

American Psychological Association
    Violence and Youth report, 202
AmeriCorps, 289, 293, 298
amorphous caring, 154, 157
anger management, 4, 41, 94, 95, 103, 323
antiexpulsion preventionists, 64–65, 77
antisocial behavior, 111, 207, 309
art therapy, 268
assaults, 41, 62, 140
assertiveness training, 9, 95, 106, 311
attitudes toward conflict, 189–190
    changes in, 80–181, 183–185
    correlates and consequences of, 185–187
Austin, Roger, 132–133
authority, adult, 4, 216

B
"the banking concept of education," 215
Bassuck, Ellen, 268
behavior
    altering 180–181, 312
    control of, 49
Belenky, Mary Field, 143
Belk, Richard, 21
"the beloved community" (MLK), 3, 26, 290, 292, 299
Bennett, William, 232
Bodine, Richard, 95
Boulder Valley Study, 9, 58, 59, 60–62, 64, 67, 69–70, 77, 78, 79, 82n18, 83n19
Boulding, Elise, 293–294
Braithwaite, Valerie, 97
Building Communities from the Inside Out (Kretzmann & McKnight), 296
Buka, Stephen, 207
Bryant, Dé C., 11, 279
bullying behavior, 48, 216

C
Cairns, Edward, 119
Cairns, Tara, 119

Cardella, Lucille, 9
caring, 161, 223, 224
    amorphous, 154, 157
    in the community, 10
    defined, 142–144
    and discipline, 79
    examples of lack of, 144–151, 152–157
    false, 147
    mirror, 147–148, 157
    and peacebuilding, 142, 151–152, 153, 156, 158
    in schools, 141, 142
    timid, 149, 157
Carlson, Teresa B., 10
Carnegie Council on Adolescent Development, 290, 311
character building, 11
children, as perpetrators of violence, 37
Children's Creative Response to Conflict (CCRC), 39
Children's Defense Fund (CDF), 36
Circle of Praxis (Brazil), 298
citizenship activity, 5
classism, 7
Clements, Kevin, 8
Clinton, Hillary, 292
closed campuses, 63
Cloward, Richard, 279
Coalition for Nonviolence in Schools (CNS), 314
Cockburn, Alexander, 2
Collins, W. Andrew, 184–185
communication skills, 5, 10, 94, 102, 106, 164
community, 6, 11, 48, 58, 99
community-based environmental education, 239–240
    emphasis on problem solving and action taking, 256–257
    and other emerging educations, 240–242
    project outline, 300–303
    resources, 303–305
community-based service (CBS), 11, 289–290, 295–299
    theoretical foundations of, 292–295

and violence prevention, 290-292
community leaders, 29
  and peacebuilding, 11, 218
  as role models, 24, 27
community mapping, 296
Community Relations Youth Service Support Scheme (CRYSSS), 122, 123
community service. *See* community-based service (CBS)
competitiveness, 18-19, 20, 24, 26, 28
  and grading system, 48-49
confidentiality rules, 70. *See also* rights of adolescents
Conflict Resolution: A Secondary School Curriculum, 104-105, 107, 108
Conflict Resolution curriculum, 101-102, 107, 108
Conflict Resolution Education Network, 92
conflict resolution techniques, 3, 4, 5-6, 9, 63, 65, 73, 80, 133, 182-183, 204, 239, 292, 311, 314, 325. *See also* mediation; problem-solving approach; school-based conflict resolution programs
  administrators, participation in, 38, 42
  Children's Creative Response to Conflict (CCRC), 39
  curricula, 40, 42, 91, 92, 93, 94, 100-105, 111, 203
  developmental approach, 10
  effectiveness of, 43-47
  the "Fourth 'R,'" 46
  incompatible with crime-and-punishment model, 208
  institutionalization of, 46
  multimedia approaches, 41
  and nonviolence, 3, 39, 41, 49, 50, 80, 311
  parents, participation in, 40, 42, 180
  PeaceBuilders, 46
  programs for, 38-42
  The Resolving Conflict Creatively Program (RCCP), 42, 43-45
  students, participation in, 38
  training, 64, 77
consumer role models, 21-23
continuation high school, 202-203
conventionalists, 66-67
cooperative learning, 92, 98-99, 102, 111, 112, 202
cooperativeness, 10, 98-99, 161
coping skills, 10, 181-183, 190
corporal punishment, 195, 196-197, 199, 206, 213, 214
corrective approach, 197, 198-201, 208
Crawford, Donna, 95
Creating the Peaceable School curriculum, 109
Creative Controversy curriculum, 109
crime-and-punishment approach, 10, 195, 196, 208
"crime fear/crime risk" paradox, 81n1
crisis intervention plan, 200
Cross-Community Contact Scheme (CCCS), 122-123
Cultural Heritage, 122, 123, 129
curricula, 7
  and conflict resolution, 40, 42, 91, 92, 93, 94, 100-105, 111, 203
  didactic vs. experiential, 94
  integrating service learning into, 295
  a nature-based alternative. see adventure-based learning (ABL)
  in Northern Ireland, 121-124, 130
  and peacebuilding, 9, 91-112
  peace education, 203-204
  types of
    Alternatives to Violence, 103-104, 107, 108, 111
    Conflict Resolution, 101-102, 107, 108
    Conflict Resolution: A Secondary School Curriculum, 104-105, 107, 108

Creating the Peaceable School, 109
Creative Controversy, 109
Making Choices, 102–103, 107, 108, 111
Managing World Conflict, 100–101, 107, 108
Playing with Fire, 106
Teaching Children To Be Peacemakers, 109
TRIBE, 94–95, 106
Violence Prevention Curriculum of Adolescents, 201
We Can Work It Out!, 106, 109
and violence prevention, 64, 76, 109, 201–202
and youth-oriented conflict resolution (YOCR), 178, 179
Cushman, Philip, 21

D

Dahlberg, Linda, 46
David, James E., 107, 108
Davis, Albie M., 38, 46
defense mechanisms and adolescents, 165
DeJong, William, 290
delinquency, resilience against, 48, 49
DeMorat, Marlene, 45
Department of Education of Northern Ireland (NEMI), 121
detention, 4, 5
deterrence policies, 4
Detroit middle school case study. See Pistons Middle School (Detroit),
developmental approach, and conflict resolution interventions, 10
developmental education, and community-based environmental education, 239, 240–242
Dewey, John, 161–162
dialogue, inclusive, 124–126

Dieringer, Larry, 47, 48
dispute resolution, 41, 177, 178, 179. See also mediation; negotiation; peer mediation
Dittmar, Helga, 20, 25
diversity appreciation, 39, 40, 42. See also multicultural education
domestic violence, prevention of, 4
dropouts, viii, 2, 49
drugs, 2, 4, 41, 62, 140, 163
drum major instinct, 18–19, 21, 25
Durkheim, Emile, 197

E

Earls, Felton, 207
Eckenrod, James S., 107, 108
ecological security, 7
Edelman, Miriam Wright, 289
Education for Mutual Understanding (EMU), 121, 123–124, 129, 130, 133
Educators for Social Responsibility (ESR), 42
empowerment, 11, 98
environment, outdoor, and adventure-based learning, 164–165, 167
environmental education. See community-based environmental education
Espalage, Dorothy, 48
European Americans, 20, 22
experiental learning and training, 163, 183. See also adventure-based learning (ABL)
exploitation, economic, 19–20
expulsion, 2, 4, 5, 57, 58, 63, 65, 66, 74, 75–76, 77, 79, 84n26, 196–200, 213
opposition to, 65, 67, 74–75
expulsion preventionists, 65–66
extracurricular activities, 18

F

false caring, 147

family, 79, 182, 183, 185, 216, 312
  and mediation, 180
  and morality instruction, 140
  versus school responsibility for violence, 72-74
  and violence, 1, 66, 267
fear, 35, 63, 309
feminism, and multicultural reform, 232
fighting, 41, 43, 62, 80, 199, 216
Filner, Judith, 92
firearm violence, youth exposure to, 36. See also guns; handguns; weapons
Fisher, Robert, 95
Fliegel, Sy, 207
Forcey, Linda Rennie, 204
Foucault, Michael, 230
Freire, Paulo, 10, 152, 215, 221, 257-258, 273, 298

G

Galagher, E. M., 268
Galtung, John, 123, 159n2
Galtung, Johan, 227
games, 162
Gandhi, Mohandas K., the Mahatma, 6, 10, 215-216
gangs, 4, 20, 37, 41, 64, 141, 163, 215, 309
Garbarino, James, 36
Gibson, Ann, 38, 39, 47, 50
Gilligan, Carol, 143
Giroux, Henry, 232, 233
Goals 2000: Educate America Act (1994), 47
Goodman, Joan, 206
Gordon, Vivian E., 107, 108
grades
  competitive nature of, 48-49
  as a marker of success, 18
Grant, Carl A., 228
Greene, Matthew, 9
Greene, Maxine, 142, 157, 294, 295
Greig, S., 240, 241
Grimshaw, Jean, 143
Guerra, Nancy, 46

guns, 69, 77, 139, 309. See also firearm violence; handguns; weapons
Guns-Free Schools Act (1994), 198-199

H

Hamburg, David, 201
handguns, 4, 35, 36, 37
Hanis, Jennifer, 11
Harkavy, Ira, 206
Harris, Ian M., 4, 11, 49, 62, 119, 129, 133, 163, 201, 204, 223, 240-241
Harris (Louis Harris) study, 2, 309
Henriquez, Manti, 107, 108
Hirsch, E. D., 232
Hogeland, Lisa Maria, 232
Holmberg, Meg, 107, 108
homelessness, 2, 11, 263, 267-268, 276, 279, 282n7
  and pervasiveness of violence, 269-271
homicide, 1, 35 139, 309
homosexuals, assaults on, 2
hooks, bell, 230, 232, 273
human rights education, and community-based environmental education, 239, 240-242

I

"I" statements, 40, 199
icebreakers, 162, 168, 170, 172
ID badges, 4, 253?
identity, 3, 25
independent schools
  and multiculturalism, 227-230
  and transgressive teaching, 230-231
  and strategies for multicultural reform, 231-234
inequality, socioeconomic, 3, 18, 26-27, 48, 215
inner cities, and exposure to violence, 36, 309
interagency cooperation, 77

inhibitors to, 70–71
interpersonal skills, 65
intervention strategies, 2, 46, 77–78, 80, 110, 180, 183, 187, 196, 213–214. *See also specific types of interventions*
    adult, 10
    corrective approach, 197, 198–201
    and the courts, 5
    nonviolent interventions, 195, 199–200, 207
    preventive approach, 197, 201–203
    supportive approach, 197–198, 203–207
isolation. *See* alientation

J

Jensen, B. B., 257
Jerry Maguire, 23
Johnson, David W., 94, 202, 204
Johnson, Roger T., 94, 202, 204

K

King, Martin Luther, Jr., 21, 23, 24, 91
    "the beloved community," 3, 26, 290, 292, 299
    "giant triplets of racism, materialism and militarism," 9, 17
    and nonviolence, 6, 26, 28–29
    and peace offensive, 25–28
    vision of, 17
Koch, Moses S., 38, 45
Korten, David, 279
Kotlowitz, Alex, 291–292
Kretzmann, John, 296, 297
Krumboltz, John, 9, 48

L

Lam, Julie A., 43, 45
Lantieri, Linda, 6, 8–9, 201
Latess, Dennis, 162
Latinos/Latinas, 4
Laursen, Brett, 184–185
Le Monde, 12

Learn 'n Serve program, 295
learning communities approach, 203, 206
learning for school v. learning for life, 11
Levin, Henry, 206
Lewin, Kurt, 243, 244
Lieber, Carol M., 106, 107, 108
literacy program, 10
    benefits, 219–223
    challenges, 221–222
    components of, 216–219
    implementation, 214–216
    results, 222–224
Looney, John, 106, 107, 108
Lucas, Barbara, 267

M

Making Choices curriculum, 102–103, 107, 108, 111
Managing World Conflict curriculum, 100–101, 107, 108
Martin, Jane Roland, 142, 143
materialism, 17–18, 21–23, 24, 25, 26, 28, 29
Mayeroff, Milton, 143
McCully, Alan, 9
McKnight, John, 296, 297
media, 2, 140, 294, 312
    violence in, 29–30, 36, 46, 77, 138
mediation, 177, 182, 183
    in the community, 38, 39
    and the family, 180
    in schools, 38, 41, 45, 94, 101
metal detectors, 2, 4, 49, 57, 63
Metis study, 43–45
middle-class areas, and exposure to violence, 57
militarism, 3, 6, 18, 24, 26, 28
minefield activity, 168–169, 171
mirror caring, 147–148
Moral Man and Immoral Society (Niebuhr), 229–230
Morton, Catherine, 48
multicultural education, 6, 7–8, 10, 11, 91, 215, 216, 217, 223, 266

defined, 228
and independent school culture, 227-230
and transgressive teaching, 230-231
strategies for reform, 231-234
multimedia approaches to conflict resolution, 41
Murtagh, Brian, 134
music, violence in, 139

N
National Association for Mediation in Education (NAME), 38
National Peace Essay Contest, 100, 115n30
negative peace, 4, 159
negotiation, 94, 95, 101, 102, 106, 164, 177
Nelson, Linden, 9, 178
The New England Journal of Medicine, 36
Niebuhr, Rheinhold, 229
Nigeria, 263, 264, 271-272, 274, 276-278, 280
Nobel Peace Prize, 12
Noddings, Nel, 143, 144
Noguera, Pedro, 202, 208
nonviolence, 30, 79
and community-based service, 289, 290
and conflict resolution, 3, 39, 41, 49, 50, 80, 311
and corrective interventions, 195, 199-200, 207
and Ghandi, 6, 215-216
guiding principles of, 6
and Martin Luther King Jr., 6, 26, 28-29
and Peace Studies, 6-7
and social influence, 93, 94
theoretical foundation of education for, 292-295
and UWM Summer Institute, 11, 313-316, 319-320
Northeastern University's Center for the Study of Sport in Society, 22

Northern Ireland, 9, 119-135
Northern Ireland Council for Educational Development (NICED), 121

O
O'Doherty, Marian, 9
Off the Walls, 124, 129
open enrollment policy, 71
other-preservation, 24, 25
outdoor adventure programs. *See* adventure-based learning (ABL)

P
Pagano, Jo Anne, 147-148
parents, 23, 29, 112, 179, 200, 206, 266
concerns over safety, 58
discipline, 5
participation in conflict resolution programs, 40, 42, 180
and peacebuilding, 11
relationship with child, 41, 185-186
as role models, 24, 27
Patti, Janet, 6, 8-9
peace
defined, 139, 141, 159n2, 268
negative peace, 4, 159
positive, 4-5, 7, 123, 139, 159n2
Peace and Education Working Group of the Division of Peace Psychology of the American Psychological Association, 99
peace consciousness, 11
peace education, 6-7, 59, 76, 80, 223, 256, 258, 315
and community-based environmental education, 239, 240-242
constructive side effects of, 312
and curricula, 203-204
goals and objectives, 91, 92-99, 180, 224
a "holistic philosophy," 129
incompatible with crime-and-punishment model, 208

Peace Studies, 2–3, 6–7, 8, 40, 59, 65, 122, 159n2, 204, 241, 292
PeaceBuilders, 46
peacebuilding, 6, 18, 59, 63, 80, 102, 111, 120, 215, 229, 313, 325
    barriers to, 17
    and caring, 142, 151–152, 153, 156, 158
    in the classroom, 9
    and conflict resolution, 47
    and curricula, 9, 92–112
    defined, 6, 49
    education, cornerstone of, 91
    and expulsion preventionists, 65
    and multicultural reform, 231–234
    and Social Action Project (SOCACT), 273–280
    strategies for, 3–4, 8–12
    and transgressive teaching, 230–231
peaceful people, developing, 91–93, 98, 100, 178, 179
peacekeeping, 91, 208, 312
    and curricula, 94
    defined, 49
    and expulsion preventionists, 65
    strategies for, 3–4, 313
    and traditional educators, 66
peacemaking, 11, 163, 166
    and conflict resolution, 47, 50, 133, 177
    and curricula, 91, 94 ,98, 102
    defined, 49
    and expulsion preventionists, 65
    strategies for, 3–6, 63, 313
peace-through-strength strategies, 4, 196
Pedagogy of the Oppressed (Freire), 152
peer counseling, 76
Peer Counseling Program (Palo Alto, CA), 296
peer education, 133–134
peer leaders, 204, 310, 315, 324

peer mediation, 5–6, 40, 42, 45, 49, 57, 63, 64, 65, 73, 92, 94, 99, 101, 110, 112, 133, 177, 178, 179, 180, 183, 184, 223, 292, 312
peer pressure, 11, 99, 311
"person"-oriented society, 17
Pike, G., 240, 241
Pipher, Mary, 294–295
Pistons Middle School (Detroit), an AP&CPS project, 11, 239
    background/context, 246–248
    implementation, 248–256
    results, 257
Piven, Frances, 279
play, and adventure-based learning, 166, 169
Playing with Fire curriculum, 106
Pollay, Richard, 21
Pont, Molly, 9
popular culture, and violence, 36
positive peace, 4–5, 7, 123, 139, 159n2
posttraumatic stress syndrome, 36
Poussaint, Alvin, 23
poverty, 3, 11, 47, 141
prejudice, 41, 42
preservation of self versus other, 24, 25
preventive approach, 3, 4, 47, 48, 57–58, 64, 66, 76, 77, 79–80, 109, 110, 179, 197, 201–204, 207, 214, 223, 290–292
private schools. *See* independent schools
problem-based learning, 206
problem-solving, 10, 39, 93, 102, 106, 161, 179, 181, 182–183
Project STOP (Schools Teaching Options for Peace), 312
prosocial behavior, 197, 312
Prothrow-Smith, Deborah, 201
Prutzman, Priscilla, 39, 45, 46
punishment, 57, 296

R

racism, 3, 4, 7, 17, 19, 20–21, 24, 26, 28, 41, 71, 141, 215
raft activity, 169, 171–172
Rahim Conflict Management Inventory, 110
rape, 140
Releasing the Imagination (Greene), 157
Research Institute for Dispute Resolution, 10
Resolving Conflict Creatively Program (RCCP), 6, 42, 43–45, 49–50, 201–202
Richardson, Norman, 121
rights of adolescents, 8–9
Riley, Richard W., 42
risk
  and adventure-based learning, 162, 165, 166, 168
  and adolescence, 163–164
risk-taking behavior, 216
Robeson, Paul, Jr., 233
Robinson, Alan, 123–124
role models, 18, 30, 314
  community leaders as, 24, 27
  for consumers, 21–23
  parents as, 24, 27
  in sports, 22–23
  teachers, as, 24, 27
role plays, 40, 98, 100, 101, 102, 103, 105, 111, 167, 218, 219
Rousseau, Nathan, 9
Rousseau, Sonya, 9
Ruddick, Sara, 142

S

Sadella, Gail, 39, 107, 108
Safe Schools Act (1993), 47
Schnack, K., 257
school-as-prison approach, 10, 196
school-based conflict resolution programs, 38–42, 49
  and curriculum, 40, 50
  effectiveness of, 43–47, 58
  future of, 47
  and other violence prevention strategies, 47–49
  and peacebuilding strategies, 49–50, 92
  peer mediation, 40, 45
  teacher mediation, 41
  teacher training, 40
school-based peer mediation programs. *See* peer mediation
school-within-a-school, 206
schools, 11, 247. *See also under* violence
  and caring, 141, 142
  causes of violence in, 77
  concerns for safety in, 239, 251–252
  mediation in, 38, 41, 45, 94, 101
  parental role, 140
  prevalence of violence, 37, 57–59
  and responsibility for violence policy, 76–77
  as a social institution, 140
  versus family responsibility for violence, 72–74
Schrumpf, Frred, 95
searches, 4, 57, 63. *See also* strip searches
security guards, 2, 49, 63
segregation, 19
Selby, D., 240, 241
self-control, 45, 94, 95
self-efficacy, 268, 273, 274, 278, 279, 282n12, 295
self-esteem, 2, 45, 111, 179, 181, 183, 185, 186, 189–190, 266, 268, 279, 290
self-preservation, 24, 25
Selman, Robert, 216
Sergiovanni, Thomas, 205
Serious Habitual Offender Directed Intervention Program (SHODI), 70
service, ethic of, 25, 27, 290
service learning, 290–291. *See* community-based service (CBS)
sexism, 3, 4, 7, 141, 215

sexual harassment, 2, 141, 154
Shanker, Albert, 198
Simon, John, 22-23
Smith, Alan, 123-124
Smith, Caroline, 48, 49
Smyth, Paul, 9
Social Action Project (SOCACT), 11, 263-266, 283n17
    data collection, 272, 274-275
    findings of, 269-272, 273
    Pen Pal Project, 274, 277-278, 279, 280
    Redbud Community Retreat, 280, 284n22
    strategies for positive peacebuilding, 273-280
    theoretical framework, 267-269
    Youth Community Theater (YCT), 11, 264, 266-267, 272, 273, 276, 277-278, 279, 280
social justice, 50, 139, 159n2
social skill development, 290
Socratic approach to learning, 7
Speak Your Piece Project, 9-10, 120, 134-135
    appropriate curriculum provision, 130
    innovative developments, 131-134
    institutional support structures, 129-130
    need for, 124
    philosophy of, 124-127
    resources and methodology, 128-129
    training, 130-131
sports, 18
    and African-Americans, 22-23
Stern, Marilyn, 10
Stone, Charles, 11
strip searches, 195, 196, 197, 199, 206
suburban neighborhoods, and exposure to violence, 57
success
    changing definition of, 25, 28-29

    in school, 18, 48
Summer Institute on Nonviolence (University of Wisconsin-Milwaukee), 11, 310
    curriculum and pedagogical techniques, 313-314, 315-316
    history, 314-315
    participants, 317-318
    results, 318-323, 343-344
    strengths and weaknesses, 323-326
    theoretical framework, 310-313
suicides, 61, 139, 309
summer recreation programs, 198
supportive approach, 197-198, 203-207
suspensions, 5, 43, 45, 74, 75, 83n24, 196, 197, 199, 200, 213
Sutton, Virginia, 206

T

teachers, 29, 203, 312
    and AR&CPS projects, 249, 255
    and community leaders, 24
    concern for students, 37-38
    concerns over safety, 58
    and conflict resolution programs, 38, 41, 44
    example of lack of caring, 145-152
    in independent schools, 229
    and job-related risk, 10
    and mediation, 41
    as role models, 24, 27
    role of in literacy program, 215, 217-218, 219-221, 221-222, 223
    training programs, 40
    and transgression, 230-231
Teaching Children To Be Peacemakers curriculum, 109
Teaching to Transgress (hooks), 230
technologically shielded education, 294, 296
television

and advertising, 21
as a resource, 127, 294
violence on, 36, 69, 77, 139, 294, 299, 314
Thayer-Bacon, Barbara, 10
There Are No Children Here (Kotlowitz), 291–292
"thing"-oriented society, 17
time-out, 197
timid caring, 149, 157
Tolan, Patrick, 46
tolerance, 10, 97, 161
Toole, Pam, 296
transgressive teaching, and independent schools, 230–231
TRIBE curriculum, 94–95, 106
Tronto, Joan, 143, 144
truancy, 43, 62

U
uniforms, in schools, 4
Ury, William, 95

V
values, 7, 8, 18, 26, 28, 29, 67, 95–98, 164, 216, 223
family versus school responsibility for instilling, 72–74
revolution of, 17, 23–25, 26
Van Slyck, Michael, 9, 10
violence
causes of, 3
covert vs. overt, 140, 141, 142
in culture, vii, 1
definition of, 139–140, 143
exposure to, 36, 57, 309
and the family, 1, 46, 267
fear of, as a distraction to learning, 2
and homelessness, 269–271
justifiable, 19
in the media, 29–30, 36, 46, 77, 138
in music, 139
national v. international, 6
in schools, vii, 1–2, 4, 5, 8, 119, 140–141

alternatives to, 9, 11
causes and solutions, 77, 213
definition of, 59, 67–68, 79
family versus school responsibility for, 72–74
increase in intensity, 69–70
nature of, 9
structural, 227–228, 257
on television, 36, 69, 77, 139, 294, 299, 314
Violence Prevention Curriculum of Adolescents, 201
Violence Prevention Initiative, 48
violence prevention strategies. *See* preventive approach
Vriens, L., 257

W
Walker, Pat, 216
Wals, Arjen, 11
wars 19, 20, 36
We Can Work It Out! curriculum, 106, 109
weapons, 41, 61, 62, 69, 270, 309. *See also* firearm violence; guns; handguns
and expulsion policies, 74, 77, 84n26
in schools, 61, 63, 80, 292
Webster, Daniel, 201
Weick, Karl, 255
Wertheim, Eleanor, 95
Whipple, Chris, 48
Williams, Sharon K., 37
Wilson-Brewer, Renee, 201
Winfield, Bonnie, 11

Y
Yaffey, David, 164
Yeh, Christine, 48
Yeich, Susan, 279, 281n1
Youth Community Theater (YCT), 11, 264, 266–267, 272, 273, 276, 277–278, 279, 280
Youth Council of Northern Ireland, 124
youth-oriented conflict resolution (YOCR)

forms and goals, 177–178, 189–190
impact and effectiveness of, 178–180
as a preventive approach to intervention, 187–189
theoretical background, 180–187
Youth Service curriculum, 130

Z

zero tolerance, 84n25, 196, 198
Zhang, 183